# THE QUIZ of the CENTURY

THIS IS A CARLTON BOOK



1 85868 836 1

Senior Art Editor: Tim Brown
Designer: Jessica Hughes
Editorial Assistant: Liam Wickham
Production: Garry Lewis

Questions set by The Puzzle House

Printed and bound in Great Britain

CARLTON

# Contents

# Introduction

The last hundred years has been a fascinating time for the human species. We've made unparalleled technological, social and medical advances. We've invented computers, cars, EastEnders and Global Warming. So it is perfectly natural that *The Quiz of the Century* came into being. Frankly, the human psyche demanded it. We're living in Interesting Times, as the ancient Chinese might have put it. However you judge these things, it's been a monumenally significant century for this planet – maybe the most significant ever. It is also a topic that everyone knows something about, so it's an ideal subject to quiz people on.

Inside *The Quiz of the Century*, you'll find some 7,500 questions covering a stunning range of subjects, themes, topics and areas, divided into easy, medium, and hard sections. The quizzes are divided into themes, but you'll want to allow some slack. To keep things interesting, the different topics are used in a broad sense rather than a narrow one, so as to make sure that even subject-area experts stay on their toes. Similarly, composition varies between difficulty levels... the possible questions to be asked in some areas are just harder than others!

At the back of the book, you'll also find a comprehensive set of guidelines on how to prepare for and run a successful quiz of your own in public (ie. down the local), and some handy answer sheet templates to photocopy and give out to contestants. Running a pub quiz can be a lot of hard work, but it's also very rewarding, even if not usually particularly lucrative! There is one important guideline you should always remember when running a quiz of course, and that is never, ever, under any circumstances, no matter how much you're threatened or cajoled, give out your own pens.

More importantly than that though – seriously for a minute – when you are going to be running a quiz, prepare properly beforehand. Don't just take this book along and read out of it (because apart from anything else, some other wise guy might have bought a copy too, and be checking the answers). Note down all the questions and all the answers, and make sure you've got everything. If an answer makes you think "hang on a moment, is that right?" then double-check it to make sure that it is not only correct, but it is the only correct answer. While every possible effort has been undertaken to make absolutely sure that every answer is accurate, there is a slight possibility that an error may have crept in, and the answer is wrong. Nothing is more humiliating than telling people who are right that they are wrong in front of a lot of witnesses who will remember it and tease you about it mercilessly for the next three years. If you've made sure of your answers, you'll be absolutely 100% safe, not just 99.9% safe.

So there you go. Take your book in hand, put on your 20th Century challenge hat, wade in, and have fun. After all, that's what it's all about.

# The Easy Questions

If you think that Louis Armstrong was the first man on the moon or that Uri Geller was the first man in space then you will no doubt struggle through the next few questions terribly. For the rest of us though these are the EASY questions, so called because if the quizzee falters on these they are either three sheets to the wind or far too young to be in the pub – either state rendering them toddling buffoons whose social graces will equal their breadth of knowledge. So beware their flailing arms as you attempt to collect the answers.

These questions are perfect when used in the first round of an open entry quiz as they lull everyone into a false sense of security although you must beware that contestants don't shout answers out which creates a problematic precedent for the later, harder questions. Another way of placing these questions is to dot them about throughout the quiz thus making sure that on every team everyone should know the answer to at least one question despite their age.

If you are running a league quiz then some of your team members may heap derision on such obvious questions but don't worry even the cleverest quiz team member can come a cropper, as was noted in a championship final. When a contestant was asked to name the continents he deliberated before eventually beaming out the answer, "A, E, I, O, U!".

# Quiz 1 20th C Who's Who

Level 1 

**1** Who thought that everyone would be famous for 15 minutes?
**2** Who led Iraq into the 90s Gulf War?
**3** Which former cabinet minister was jailed for 18 months in 1999?
**4** Who was manager of The Beatles?
**5** Which Russian introduced policies of glasnost?
**6** Who became the first woman to lead a British political party?
**7** Whose dresses raised £2 million for charity in a June 97 auction?
**8** Which British monarch died in 1901?
**9** Which 60s model was known as 'The Shrimp'?
**10** Who became king of Spain in the 70s following General Franco's death?
**11** Which G B wrote the play Pygmalion that was adapted into My Fair Lady?
**12** Whose ancient tomb was discovered in Egypt in 1922?
**13** Who was the ex peanut farmer who became US President?
**14** Who delivered Labour's first budget of the 90s?
**15** Who was awarded a Nobel Peace Prize for her work with the poor in India?
**16** Which Ken was leader of the GLC?
**17** Who was the man who created The Muppets?
**18** Who promised he would bring 'really sexy football' to Newcastle?
**19** Which Screaming Lord stood unsuccessfully in many parliamentary elections?
**20** Which pop star married Linda Eastman in the 60s?
**21** Who declared he had 'a dream' where all Americans would live as equals?
**22** Who teamed up with Benny, Bjorn and Anni-Frid to form Abba?
**23** Which Christian unveiled the New Look of the late 40s?
**24** Mahatma Gandhi led the non-violent struggle for which country to break free from Britain?
**25** Who formulated the theory of relativity early in the century?

## Answers

***20th C Who's Who***

**1** Andy Warhol. **2** Saddam Hussein. **3** Jonathan Aitken. **4** Brian Epstein. **5** Gorbachev. **6** Margaret Thatcher. **7** Princess Diana. **8** Victoria. **9** Jean Shrimpton. **10** Juan Carlos. **11** Shaw. **12** Tutankhamun. **13** Jimmy Carter. **14** Gordon Brown. **15** Mother Theresa. **16** Livingstone. **17** Jim Henson. **18** Ruud Gullit. **19** Sutch. **20** Paul McCartney. **21** Martin Luther King. **22** Agnetha. **23** Dior. **24** India. **25** Albert Einstein.

# Quiz 2 Pot Luck 1

1 Who was the first Spice Girl to leave the group?
2 What or who was Mitch, the bringer of destruction to Honduras?
3 Which Richard scripted Notting Hill?
4 What name do William Hague and Bill Clinton share?
5 Which John was dropped from a series of Sainsbury's ads?
6 What was the occupation of Beirut hostage John McCarthy?
7 What does the letter D stand for in the initials DTP?
8 Which country does soccer star Davor Suker play for?
9 Eric Clapp found fame under which name?
10 Which TV gardener established the garden at Barnsdale?
11 The board game Monopoly produced limited special edition sets linked to which 1998 event?
12 Eva Peron was the subject of which film and musical?
13 On TV, to which Matthew do wannabe stars say, "Tonight, Matthew, I'm going to be...."?
14 Which paper ran the Sophie Topless story about Sophie Rhys-Jones?
15 Where in London was the 80s Live Aid Concert staged?
16 Whose Line Is It Anyway? transferred from radio to which TV channel?
17 Robin Smith represented England at which sport?
18 Which Jack was Agriculture Minister when sale of beef on the bone was banned?
19 What type of music was Ronnie Scott associated with?
20 Which Caroline presented The Mrs Merton Show?
21 In the 90s, Formula 1 racing was controversially exempted from a ban stopping the advertising of what?
22 What two colours are the stripes on the United States of America flag?
23 Whigfield sang about which night of the week?
24 Which country won cricket's 1999 World Cup?
25 Tom Cruise was born in which decade of the century?

**Answers**

***Pot Luck 1***

**1** Ginger Spice - Geri Halliwell. **2** Hurricane. **3** Curtis. **4** Jefferson. **5** Cleese. **6** Journalist. **7** Desk. **8** Croatia. **9** Eric Clapton. **10** Geoff Hamilton. **11** The World Cup. **12** Evita. **13** Kelly. **14** The Sun. **15** Wembley Stadium. **16** Channel 4. **17** Cricket. **18** Cunningham. **19** Jazz. **20** Aherne. **21** Tobacco. **22** Red and white. **23** Saturday. **24** Australia. **25** 60s.

# Quiz 3 Celebs

1 Which Patsy married Liam Gallagher?
2 Jerry Hall hails from which oil state?
3 Where does Dame Edna Everage hail from?
4 Who accompanied Hugh Grant to the premiere of Four Weddings and a Funeral in a dress held together with safety pins?
5 Which blonde Ms Jonsson advertised crisps with Gary Lineker?
6 Which celebrity chef had a TV series called Rhodes Around Britain?
7 Twiggy was the most famous model of which decade?
8 Jane Asher is also famous for baking and selling what?
9 Which Richard did Elizabeth Taylor marry twice?
10 Which Italian actress launched her own perfume Sophia?
11 Which quintet switched on the Oxford Street Christmas lights in 1996?
12 Who was Julia Carling's first husband?
13 Which Prime Minister's son did Emma Noble marry in 1999?
14 Which Spice Girl was the first to marry?
15 Michael Jackson's first wife was the daughter of which 'King'?
16 Which Rolling Stone did Jerry Hall marry?
17 Which supermodel Naomi wrote a novel called Swan?
18 Which Bob who founded Band Aid received an honorary knighthood in 1986?
19 Giorgio Armani is famous in which field?
20 Fashion designer Donatella, sister of the murdered Gianni has which surname?
21 What does the R-J part of the PR agency R-JH stand for?
22 Model Rachel Hunter was married to which veteran rock star?
23 Ivanka Trump has a similar name to her mother; who is she?
24 Brigitte Bardot was awarded the freedom of her capital city; what is it?
25 Which 1980s US president survived an assassination attempt?

## Answers

***Celebs***

**1** Kensit. **2** Texas. **3** Australia. **4** Elizabeth Hurley. **5** Ulrika. **6** Gary Rhodes. **7** 60s. **8** Cakes. **9** Burton. **10** Sophia Loren. **11** The Spice Girls. **12** Will. **13** John Major's. **14** Mel B. **15** Elvis Presley. **16** Mick Jagger. **17** Campbell. **18** Geldof. **19** Fashion design. **20** Versace. **21** Rhys-Jones. **22** Rod Stewart. **23** Ivana Trump. **24** Paris. **25** Ronald Reagan.

# Quiz 4 Pot Luck 2

Level 1

1 What is Cherie Booth's married name?
2 Which animal name was given to the terrorist Carlos who was tried in 1997?
3 In what month did Prince Edward get married?
4 Which MP Mrs Currie landed in hot water about eggs?
5 Who is Griff Rhys Jones' comic TV partner?
6 With which sport is Charles Barkley associated?
7 Which Ford first mass produced the car?
8 Which annual sporting event was hit by sit downs and go slows in 1998?
9 Which song took Rolf Harris back to the charts in the 90s?
10 Which Michael revived his TV chat show of the 70s in the late 90s?
11 In ASCII what does the letter C stand for ?
12 Guides wear what colour of uniform?
13 Who was the first of the Queen's children to marry?
14 Truro is the administrative centre of which English county?
15 Clare Short has represented which party in parliament?
16 What kind of Girls featured in Anna Friel's film set in the Second World War?
17 In banking what does T stand for in TSB?
18 Which comedy show, broadcast around the time of the evening news, launched the career of Rowan Atkinson?
19 Django Reinhardt was associated with which musical instrument?
20 Whose first European ad campaign was for Max Factor in 1999?
21 What did Ceylon change its name to it 1970?
22 Chris Woods represented England at which sport?
23 In which country was comedian Dave Allen born?
24 What colour did the Redcoats adopt at Butlins after a 90s revamp?
25 The deepwater port of Malmo was developed in which country?

**Answers**

***Pot Luck 2***

**1** Blair. **2** The Jackal. **3** June. **4** Edwina. **5** Mel Smith. **6** Basketball. **7** Henry. **8** Tour de France. **9** Stairway To Heaven. **10** Parkinson. **11** Code. **12** Blue. **13** Anne. **14** Cornwall. **15** Labour. **16** Land. **17** Trustee. **18** Not the Nine O'Clock News. **19** Guitar. **20** Madonna. **21** Sri Lanka. **22** Soccer. **23** Ireland. **24** Red. **25** Sweden.

# Quiz 5 TV - On the Box

1 What does E stand for in the medical drama ER?
2 In which series did Dr Frasier Crane first appear?
3 In which country was Ballykissangel set?
4 Which children's show was introduced with, and named after a native North American greeting?
5 Which Colin created Inspector Morse and appeared as an extra in every episode of the series?
6 What type of animal was Basil Brush?
7 Dogtanian and the Three Muskehounds was based on which classic book?
8 In which US TV series did Pamela Anderson shoot to fame?
9 Which long running comedy series about three OAPs was filmed in Holmfirth?
10 Which Sci-Fi freedom fighters were led by a man called Roj Blake?
11 In which show might you see Charlie and Duffy in A & E?
12 In which part of Eastern Britain was Lovejoy set?
Which Andrew wrote the book on which the Sky mini series Diana:
13 Her True Story was based?
14 Who was Tony's flatmate in Men Behaving Badly?
15 On whose show were Gotcha Oscar's presented?
16 Oh Doctor Beeching was a sitcom about the closure of what?
17 Which sport was the subject of the sitcom Outside Edge?
Which drama series told of a Practice called The Beeches in
18 Derbyshire?
19 Rab C. Nesbitt was a native of which Scottish city?
20 80s drama St Elsewhere was set in what type of institution?
21 What was the surname of cartoon characters Homer, Marge and Bart?
22 In which army series did Robson and Jerome find fame?
23 South Park is situated in which US state famous for its ski resorts?
24 What relation was Harold to Albert Steptoe?
25 Which series about twentysomething lawyers starred Daniela Nardini and Jack Davenport?

## Answers

***TV – On the Box***

**1** Emergency. **2** Cheers. **3** Ireland. **4** How. **5** Dexter. **6** Fox. **7** The Three Musketeers. **8** Baywatch. **9** Last of the Summer Wine. **10** Blake's 7. **11** Casualty. **12** East Anglia. **13** Morton. **14** Gary. **15** Noel Edmonds. **16** Railways. **17** Cricket. **18** Peak Practice. **19** Glasgow. **20** Hospital. **21** Simpson. **22** Soldier Soldier. **23** Colorado. **24** Son. **25** This Life.

# Quiz 6 Pot Luck 3

1 What was the name given to the first cloned sheep?
2 Which bear became the mascot of the Children In Need appeals?
3 The Millennium Dome is in which part of London?
4 Doris Kapelhoff found fame by adopting which time related name?
5 Tessa Sanderson is associated with which athletic event?
6 The Cosby Show was set in which American city?
7 In an Evita song what word follows, "Don't cry for me..."?
8 Which Greg was BBC Sports Personality of the Year in 1997?
9 Which Tom married Nicole Kidman?
10 Prince Edward was made Earl of where?
11 Which soccer team does Jarvis Cocker support?
12 Jamie Lee Curtis was born in which decade of the century?
13 Country House was a hit for which band?
14 On a computer keyboard what letter is far left on the top row of letters?
15 Mussolini was dictator in which country?
16 Antonio Carluccio writes about which country's food?
17 Which country does golfer Greg Norman come from?
18 Which Irish presenter introduced the sporting gaffe programme Oddballs?
19 Which RAF pilot Andy broke the sound barrier travelling on land?
20 Which sporting personality was born Shirley Crabtree?
21 In which country were Fiat cars first produced?
22 Which director Mr Berkeley included elaborate choreography in his films?
23 Former athlete Seb Coe became an MP for which party?
24 In which city was Gianni Versace shot?
25 In children's TV how were Anthony McPartlin and Declan Donnelly first known?

**Answers**

***Pot Luck 3***

**1** Dolly. **2** Pudsey. **3** Greenwich. **4** Doris Day. **5** Javelin. **6** New York. **7** Argentina. **8** Rusedski. **9** Hanks. **10** Wessex. **11** Sheff Weds. **12** 50s. **13** Oasis. **14** Q. **15** Italy. **16** Italy. **17** Australia. **18** Eamonn Holmes. **19** Green. **20** Big Daddy. **21** Italy. **22** Busby. **23** Conservative. **24** Miami. **25** Ant & Dec.

# Quiz 7 Soccer

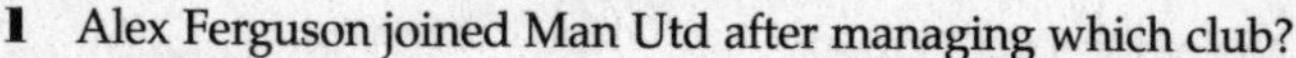

1 Alex Ferguson joined Man Utd after managing which club?
2 Who had the last kick in England's 1998 World Cup campaign?
3 What nickname was Italian superstar Roberto Baggio given?
4 Which country does world record transfer man Christian Vieri play for?
5 Which soccer team moved to the Reebok Stadium in the 90s?
6 Who hit Man Utd's winner in the 1999 European Champions' Cup Final?
7 Who was Blackburn's manager when they won the Premier League?
8 In 1999 Ron Atkinson announced his retirement as a soccer boss while with which club?
9 John Gregory took over from Brian Little as boss of which club?
10 Which Arsenal player was sent to jail for a drink-driving offence in 1990?
11 Carlos Alberto was a World Cup winning skipper of which country?
12 Jonathan Woodgate was with which club when he first played for England?
13 Which 90s star is known as 'The Iceman'?
14 Ronald Coeman was a star international with which country?
15 Alan Shearer and Matt Le Tissier have both been at which club?
16 Manager Jim Smith is known as the Bald what?
17 Which soccer ground did Sunderland leave in 1997?
18 At which soccer club did David O' Leary establish an appearance record?
19 England players Shearer, Sherwood, Sutton have all played for which soccer club?
20 Which British manager put Barcelona back on winning ways in the 1980s?
21 Which English keeper made the "save of the century" against Brazil in a 1970 World Cup game?
22 With which club did John Barnes begin his league soccer career?
23 Which keeper of the 80s and 90s glories in the nickname 'Lurch'?
24 At which British soccer club did an Italian take over from a Dutchman?
25 Dwight Yorke joined Man Utd from which club?

## Answers

**Soccer**

**1** Aberdeen. **2** David Batty. **3** The Divine Ponytail. **4** Italy. **5** Bolton. **6** Solskjaer. **7** Kenny Dalglish. **8** Nottm Forest. **9** Aston Villa. **10** Tony Adams. **11** Brazil. **12** Leeds. **13** Dennis Bergkamp. **14** Holland. **15** Southampton. **16** Eagle. **17** Roker Park. **18** Arsenal. **19** Blackburn. **20** Terry Venables. **21** Gordon Banks. **22** Watford. **23** Dave Beasant. **24** Chelsea. **25** Aston Villa.

# Quiz 8 Pot Luck 4

Level 1 

1. Who set up the Virgin group?
2. Most people know this, but what is Michael Caine's real first name?
3. Who did Ffion Jenkins marry?
4. With which sport is Oliver Bierhoff associated?
5. Which word went with Britannia to describe the supposedly vibrant late 90s?
6. According to the TV theme song what do neighbours become?
7. Which country did Greta Garbo come from?
8. Robbie Coltrane and Whoopi Goldberg have played in films where their characters disguise themselves as what?
9. Which cash-making event was cancelled after revelations about Will Carling's private life in 1998?
10. Which three letters came to describe a farm shop where the buyer gathers in the goods?
11. In which country did Ho Chi Minh come to power?
12. Entertainer Michael Parker changed his last name to what?
13. Which area of West London established a summer holiday carnival?
14. Which Man From Auntie, Ben replaced Terry Wogan temporarily on Wogan while the Irishman went on holiday?
15. The village at Bourneville near Birmingham was set up for workers of which chocolate factory?
16. Which musical instrument did Pablo Casals play?
17. Which English nurse Edith was executed by the Germans in WWI?
18. Catherine and William Booth were founders of which Army?
19. Which country has A as its international vehicle registration letter?
20. Which Kate became the face of L'Oreal in 1998?
21. In 1999, which BBC 1 show was dropped after a rumpus over fake guests?
22. Which Welsh politician Aneurin oversaw the formation of the welfare state?
23. What was the first name of Laurie in A Bit of Fry & Laurie on TV?
24. Everything Changes was a 90s No 1 for which group?
25. What did the U stand for in USSR?

## Answers

***Pot Luck 4***

**1** Richard Branson. **2** Maurice. **3** William Hague. **4** Soccer. **5** Cool. **6** Good friends. **7** Sweden. **8** Nuns. **9** His testimonial. **10** PYO. **11** Vietnam. **12** Barrymore. **13** Notting Hill. **14** Elton. **15** Cadbury's. **16** Cello. **17** Cavell. **18** Salvation Army. **19** Austria. **20** Moss. **21** The Vanessa Show. **22** Bevan. **23** Hugh. **24** Take That. **25** Union.

# Quiz 9 Blockbusters

**1** Who played Jack in Titanic?
**2** Which 1996 musical had Madonna making 85 costume changes?
**3** Which Kevin starred in the spectacularly money-losing Waterworld?
**4** Which Buzz from Toy Story caused a Christmas buying frenzy in 1996?
**5** Which Landings were the subject of Saving Private Ryan?
**6** Which British actor/director Richard was Dr Hammond in Jurassic Park?
**7** Who sang I Will Always Love You in her film, The Bodyguard?
**8** In which Disney classic was Robin Williams first the voice of the Genie?
**9** Whose name appears with Dracula in the title of the 1992 movie?
**10** In which 80s film did Meryl Streep play a Polish holocaust survivor?
**11** Up Where We Belong was the theme music to which 80s film with Richard Gere and Debra Winger?
**12** Which 1982 Spielberg classic was about a little boy and his pet alien?
**13** Which actor Ben played the title role in Gandhi, and also played Ron Jenkins in Coronation Street?
**14** In which 70s film did "Love means never having to say you're sorry."?
**15** Which fruit is named in the title of the controversial Clockwork film directed by Stanley Kubrick?
**16** Which film, the first of a series with Sigourney Weaver, had the line "In Space no one can hear you scream" on the cinema poster?
**17** Which wartime classic, named after a port of North Africa starred Humphrey Bogart and Ingrid Bergman?
**18** In which blockbuster did Anthony Perkins first appear as Norman Bates?
**19** In Some Like It Hot, which gangster city are Jack Lemmon and Tony Curtis forced to leave after witnessing the St Valentine's Day massacre?
**20** In which country did The Sound of Music take place?
**21** Which film about a gorilla was a massive success for RKO in 1933 and has had a cult following ever since?
**22** What was the first full length colour animated film?
**23** If Billy Crystal was Harry who was Meg Ryan?
**24** In which 90s film did Jeremy Irons speak the voice of wicked feline Scar?
**25** Which 30s film about the American Civil War is "the first blockbuster"?

## Answers

***Blockbusters***

**1** Leonardo DiCaprio. **2** Evita. **3** Costner. **4** Lightyear. **5** D Day. **6** Attenborough. **7** Whitney Houston. **8** Aladdin. **9** Bram Stoker's. **10** Sophie's Choice. **11** An Officer and a Gentleman. **12** E.T. **13** Kingsley. **14** Love Story. **15** Orange. **16** Alien. **17** Casablanca. **18** Psycho. **19** Chicago. **20** Austria. **21** King Kong. **22** Snow White and the Seven Dwarfs. **23** Sally. **24** The Lion King. **25** Gone With the Wind.

# Quiz 10 Pot Luck 5

1 In 1990 who got married to Jerry Hall?
2 What does the I stand for in the savings accounts known as ISAS?
3 In which sport did Adrian Moorhouse set world records?
4 Which football song took Baddiel and Skinner to No 1?
5 Bristol is the administrative centre of which English county?
6 Nigel Kennedy is associated with which instrument?
7 In the 90s which Home Secretary had his son named in a drugs case?
8 Which cartoon character says "What's up, Doc?"?
9 Stansted airport was built in which county?
10 In fiction, who was the creator of Jane Marple?
11 Where was comedian Max Boyce born?
12 Which Neville was British Prime Minister at the outbreak of World War II?
13 A J Cronin provided the books - or casebook - that became which TV doctor?
14 Who had a worldwide hit with Strangers In The Night?
15 Which Jo had a TV series called Through The Cakehole?
16 Bill Clinton trained to do which day job?
17 Which Kingsley wrote the novel Lucky Jim?
18 Under what name did Marvin Addy become famous?
19 What was Blackadder's first name as played by Rowan Atkinson?
20 Both father and daughter of the Bhutto family have been Prime Minister of which country?
21 What is the symbol for Comic Relief?
22 In which city was Carla Lane's TV sitcom Bread set?
23 What is the first name of flamboyant chef Floyd?
24 Johnny Depp was born in which decade of the century?
25 Which US state, which joined the Union in 1912, has New and the name of a country in its name?

## Answers

***Pot Luck 5***

**1** Mick Jagger. **2** Individual. **3** Swimming. **4** Three Lions. **5** Avon. **6** Violin. **7** Jack Straw. **8** Bugs Bunny. **9** Essex. **10** Agatha Christie. **11** Wales. **12** Chamberlain. **13** Dr Finlay. **14** Frank Sinatra. **15** Brand. **16** Lawyer. **17** Amis. **18** Meatloaf. **19** Edmund. **20** Pakistan. **21** Red Nose. **22** Liverpool. **23** Keith. **24** 60s. **25** New Mexico.

# Quiz 11 Around The UK

1 The A2 ends up at which Channel port?
2 What colour are road signs which lead to heritage sites and places of interest?
3 What type of Show is held regularly at Farnborough?
4 In 1988 which Norfolk waterways were designated a national park?
5 Aston University was founded in 1966 in which city?
6 What is Britain's second largest airport after Heathrow?
7 On which Devon Moor is there a famous prison?
8 London's Carnaby Street shot to fame in the 60s for what type of shops?
9 In which London Lane is the Dorchester Hotel?
10 In which Scottish city is an annual festival of music and drama held?
11 What sort of thoroughfare is the Grand Union?
12 The Fastnet Race is over what type of surface?
13 In which Yorkshire city is the National Railway Museum?
14 Aintree racecourse is near which UK city?
15 Which industry famously moved to Wapping from Central London in the 1980s?
16 Which leisure park is near Stoke on Trent in Staffordshire?
17 Where in Wales is the Driver and Vehicle Licensing Centre?
18 Which cultural centre, the London base of the RSC, was opened in 1982?
19 In which area of London is the All England Tennis Club?
20 The first Borstal opened in which SE England county in 1902?
21 What type of products does Fortnum & Mason sell?
22 Glamis Castle near Dundee was the home of which royal before her marriage?
23 If you caught the train called The Clansman you would travel from London to which part of the UK?
24 Which Birmingham shopping centre was opened in 1960 on the site of a former cattle market?
25 Holyhead is on which island off Wales?

## Answers

***Around the UK***

**1** Dover. **2** Brown. **3** Air. **4** Broads. **5** Birmingham. **6** Gatwick. **7** Dartmoor. **8** Boutiques. **9** Park Lane. **10** Edinburgh. **11** Canal. **12** Water. **13** York. **14** Liverpool. **15** Newspaper. **16** Alton Towers. **17** Swansea. **18** Barbican. **19** Wimbledon. **20** Kent. **21** Food. **22** The Queen Mother. **23** Scotland. **24** Bull Ring. **25** Anglesey.

# Quiz 12 Pot Luck 6

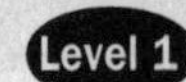

1 The 90s Good Friday agreement sought peace in which country?
2 Elton John was born with which surname?
3 Which Frank formed a comedy writing team with Denis Norden?
4 In which decade did Channel 5 begin broadcasting?
5 Until 1998 what had been banned for 200 years by the MCC?
6 Which actor starred in the TV comedy Father Ted?
7 Who was the outgoing president when Bill Clinton took office?
8 Maurice Cole found fame as which Kenny?
9 The first modern cassette was produced in which decade?
10 Which Justin set the 98 Open alight as an amateur?
11 Which impressionist had a TV series called *Who Else?*
12 What did politician Richard Crossman leave behind that was published in the 70s after his death?
13 What does the letter C stand for in RSPCA?
14 Who had a 90s hit with The Shoop Shoop Song?
15 Which Harold wrote the play The Caretaker?
16 What was the setting for the TV sitcom The Brittas Empire?
17 Which chemist Marie became the first woman to win a Nobel prize?
18 With which sport is Herbie Hide associated?
19 In which city was Charles de Gaulle airport built?
20 Norman Fowler has represented which party in parliament?
21 In 1930 which comic duo made the film Another Fine Mess?
22 PW Botha was Prime Minister of which country?
23 Which Lily was the mistress of Edward VII?
24 What was the occupation of Jacko in TV's Brush Strokes?
25 Andy Gregory represented England at which sport?

**Answers**

***Pot Luck 6***
**1** N Ireland. **2** Dwight. **3** Muir. **4** 90s. **5** Women. **6** Dermot Morgan. **7** George Bush. **8** Everett. **9** 40s. **10** Rose. **11** Rory Bremner. **12** Diaries. **13** Cruelty. **14** Cher. **15** Pinter. **16** Leisure centre. **17** Curie. **18** Boxing. **19** Paris. **20** Conservative. **21** Laurel & Hardy. **22** South Africa. **23** Langtry. **24** House painter. **25** Rugby League.

# Quiz 13 Karaoke

**1** Which song starts, 'It's a little bit funny, This feeling inside'?
**2** Which Shania Twain song includes, "Okay, so you're Brad Pitt"?
**3** What is the first word of She?
**4** In Gina G's Eurovision song what follows "Ooh ahh just a little..."?
**5** Which Cliff Richard hit starts, "Used to think that life was sweet, Used to think we were so complete"?
**6** Which Dire Straits song starts, "These mist covered mountains..."?
**7** Which Swedish Eurovision winner's song said "Take me to your heaven.."?
**8** Which chilly Madonna song begins "You only see what your eyes want to see"?
**9** Which organ of the body is mentioned in the theme song to Titanic?
**10** Judy Garland sang about going somewhere over the what?
**11** Who Get Going When The Going Gets Tough?
**12** Which Queen classic starts, "Is this the real life..."?
**13** In Candle in the Wind 1997 what did Elton John sing instead of Goodbye Norma Jean?
**14** In 1996 which band sang "It's only words and words are all I have....." as The Bee Gees had done in 1968?
**15** What number was Perfect according to The Beautiful South in 1998?
**16** In the Bowie song who was Ground Control trying to make contact with?
**17** How many times did the Spice Girls sing "really" in the first two lines of Wannabe?
**18** What's the response to, "See you later, alligator"?
**19** Which song starts, "Sometimes it's hard to be a woman"?
**20** Which group thought, "It's fun to stay at the YMCA"?
**21** Which Elton John song has the colour yellow in the title?
**22** Which words of encouragement did S Club 7 sing after "Don't stop.." in Bring It All Back?
**23** Who was "the fastest milkman in the West"?
**24** Who made Little Richard sing Good Golly?
**25** Which song begins "I feel it in my fingers"?

## Answers

***Karaoke***

**1** Your Song. **2** That Don't Impress Me Much. **3** She. **4** Bit. **5** We Don't Talk Anymore. **6** Brothers In Arms. **7** Charlotte Nilsson. **8** Frozen. **9** Heart. **10** Rainbow. **11** The Tough. **12** Bohemian Rhapsody. **13** England's rose. **14** Boyzone. **15** 10. **16** Major Tom. **17** 4. **18** In a while, crocodile. **19** Stand By Your Man. **20** Village People. **21** Goodbye Yellow Brick Road. **22** Never give up. **23** Ernie. **24** Miss Molly. **25** Love Is All Around.

# Quiz 14 Pot Luck 7

1 In what type of public building was George Michael arrested and charged with committing a "lewd act"?
2 Which comedian was born as John Cheese?
3 Which Michael led England's cricket team for over 50 games in the 90s?
4 What type of animal was Babe in the film of the same name?
5 In which city was the Barbican Centre built?
6 Who did Tony Blair replace as leader of the Labour Party?
7 Cartoon racer Dick Dastardly exclaims, "Drat and double" what?
8 Which British royal residence was badly damaged by fire in the early 90s?
9 How many colours are there on the Belgian flag?
10 Which car manufacturer introduced the Granada?
11 Steve Redgrave won Olympic gold in which sport?
12 In which country was the ancient tomb of Tutankhamun discovered?
13 Which soccer team does June Whitfield support?
14 Matt Dillon was born in which decade of the century?
15 Which comedienne first introduced herself as a gawky Sheffield housewife when she appeared on New Faces in 1975?
16 Bob Dylan was born in which decade of the century?
17 Which country does cricketer Daryll Cullinan play for?
18 In which sitcom did Wolfie Smith appear?
19 Which Peter was the Yorkshire Ripper?
20 Which John was MP for Huntingdon in the 90s?
21 Which long running TV quiz show had started and finally finished in 1997?
22 Where is comedian Jasper Carrott's home town?
23 Which group recorded the best selling album Stars?
24 Which word connects the FBI and a vacuum cleaner?
25 John Ravenscroft became better known as which DJ?

## Answers

***Pot Luck 7***

**1** Men's lavatory. **2** John Cleese. **3** Atherton. **4** Pig. **5** London. **6** John Smith. **7** Drat. **8** Windsor. **9** Three. **10** Ford. **11** Rowing. **12** Egypt. **13** Wimbledon. **14** 60s. **15** Marti Caine. **16** 40s. **17** South Africa. **18** Citizen Smith. **19** Sutcliffe. **20** Major. **21** Mastermind. **22** Birmingham. **23** Simply Red. **24** Hoover. **25** John Peel.

# Quiz 15 60s Newsround

Level 1 

1 Which Harold became leader of a British political party in the 60s?
2 Who managed England to World Cup triumph?
3 Which Basil was involved in the cancelling of an English tour to South Africa?
4 Mrs Gandhi became Prime Minister in which country?
5 Donald Campbell was killed trying to break which speed record?
6 Which literary Lady had a Lover that resulted in an Old Bailey obscenity trial?
7 Dubcek's reforms were crushed by Soviet tanks in which country?
8 Maria Bueno was a 60s champion in which sport?
9 Which city became Brazil's new capital in 1960?
10 The World Wildlife Fund was set up with which animal as its logo?
11 The LSE, the scene of student unrest, was the London School of what?
12 Which Italian city hosted the 1960 Olympics?
13 Where in America was the world's biggest rock festival staged?
14 Pierre Trudeau became Prime Minister of which country?
15 Who was the only British winner of the British Open in the 60s?
16 Mia Farrow's controversial film concerned whose baby?
17 What type of vehicle was involved in the fatal accident at Chappaquiddick?
18 Which pop star married a Cynthia and later a Yoko?
19 What was Vidal Sassoon creating?
20 What was the name of call girl Miss Keeler involved in a ministerial sex scandal?
21 Which road was linked with the murder trial involving James Hanratty?
22 What type of creature was headline making Goldie who escaped in London?
23 Who was 'the Louisville Lip'?
24 Who was Lee Harvey Oswald charged with murdering?
25 Which Francis completed his solo round the world yacht journey?

## Answers

***60s Newsround***

**1** Wilson. **2** Alf Ramsey. **3** D'Oliveira. **4** India. **5** Water. **6** Lady Chatterley. **7** Czechoslovakia. **8** Tennis. **9** Brasilia. **10** Panda. **11** Economics. **12** Rome. **13** Woodstock. **14** Canada. **15** Tony Jacklin. **16** Rosemary's. **17** Car. **18** John Lennon. **19** Hairstyles. **20** Christine. **21** A6. **22** Eagle. **23** Cassius Clay. **24** President Kennedy. **25** Chichester.

# Quiz 16 Pot Luck 8

1 What was Eileen Drewery's role in England's 1998 World Cup preparations?
2 Which quizmaster said, "I've started so I'll finish"?
3 Who created the three-dimensional cube in the 70s and 80s craze?
4 Whose son was called Prince Michael Jr?
5 Which European country was divided into East and West in 1949?
6 Which Spice Girls hit starts, "I'll tell you what I want"?
7 Which government minister took his dog to work?
8 Which country does Ray Reardon come from?
9 Sophia Scicoloni became famous as which actress?
10 What are the first two words of the much recorded song I Believe?
11 Which Julian once called himself The Joan Collins Fan Club?
12 What does the letter B stand for in RSPB?
13 Chester is the administrative centre of which English county?
14 QWho played James Bond in Doctor No?
15 The legendary cricketer Learie Constantine played for which country?
16 Who did Doctor Crippen poison?
17 What name is given to the charity which was set up by comedians to raise money for those in need?
18 Which high office has been held by Dr George Carey?
19 What was the first name of Rebecca writer du Maurier?
20 If the K stands for Kosovo what do L and A stand for in the KLA?
21 What colour is Mickey Mouse's nose?
22 Which EastEnders landlord found fame as himself on The Comedians?
23 What was The Simpsons 90s No 1 hit?
24 With which sport is Thomas Hearns associated?
25 Madhur Jaffrey chiefly writes about cookery from which country of the world?

## Answers

***Pot Luck 8***
**1** Faith healer. **2** Magnus Magnusson. **3** Rubik. **4** Michael Jackson's. **5** Germany. **6** Wannabe. **7** David Blunkett. **8** Wales. **9** Sophia Loren. **10** I Believe. **11** Clary. **12** Birds. **13** Cheshire. **14** Sean Connery. **15** W Indies. **16** His wife. **17** Comic Relief. **18** Archbishop of Canterbury. **19** Daphne. **20** Liberation Army. **21** Black. **22** Frank Butcher. **23** Do The Bartman. **24** Boxing. **25** India.

# Quiz 17 Famous Names

1 What is novelist Lord Archer's first name?
2 By which first name is Jeremy John Durham Ashdown best known ?
3 What is Zoe Ball's dad called?
4 What is the name of Margaret Thatcher's husband?
5 Which part of him did Ken Dodd insure for £4 million?
6 Betty Boothroyd became the first female Speaker where?
7 How was Elaine Bickerstaff better known on the West End stage?
8 Which chain of environmentally friendly shops did Anita Roddick found?
9 What did Nigel Kennedy change his name to, professionally in the late 90s?
10 Which Gordon was Tony Blair's first Chancellor of the Exchequer?
11 Which musical instrument is Dudley Moore famous for playing?
12 How is Paul O'Grady better known in high heels, blonde wig and Liverpool accent?
13 Martina Navratilova changed nationality from Czech to what?
14 Why would you consult Nicky Clarke professionally?
15 Which two initials is crime novelist Baroness James known by?
16 Henry Cecil is a famous name in which sport?
17 Which Nigel found fame as a writer of a newspaper Diary about celebs?
18 n 1999 Sean Connery campaigned on behalf of which political party?
19 Eddie George became Governor of what in 1993?
20 What is Ffion Jenkins married surname?
21 Michael Flatley was dubbed Lord of the what?
22 Which Spice nickname did Geri Halliwell have?
23 Which actor Stephen walked out of the West End play Cell Mates in 1995?
24 Michael Heseltine's nickname was that of which film hero?
25 Opera star Lesley Garrett hails from which county?

## Answers

***Famous names***

**1** Jeffrey. **2** Paddy. **3** Johnny. **4** Denis. **5** Teeth. **6** House of Commons. **7** Elaine Paige. **8** Body Shop. **9** Kennedy. **10** Brown. **11** Piano. **12** Lily Savage. **13** American. **14** To do your hair. **15** P D. **16** Horse racing. **17** Dempster. **18** Scots Nationalist. **19** Bank of England. **20** Hague. **21** Dance. **22** Ginger. **23** Fry. **24** Tarzan. **25** Yorkshire.

# Quiz 18 Pot Luck 9

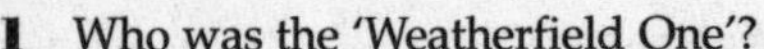

**1** Who was the 'Weatherfield One'?
**2** In which decade was the atomic bomb dropped on Hiroshima?
**3** Which anti-impotence treatment became the 90s fastest selling prescription drug?
**4** Who was C-3PO's robot companion in the original Star Wars movies?
**5** Under what name did sharp-tongued Joan Molinsky become famous?
**6** Which director Stanley made 2001 A Space Odyssey?
**7** Which US Colonel featured in the 'Irangate' court trials?
**8** In fiction and film what is the first name of female FBI agent Starling?
**9** What does the I stand for in the initials IT?
**10** William Hague gave which Peter the push as Tory deputy leader?
**11** Cher was born in which decade of the century?
**12** Which Brian presented the National Lottery Show, promising "it could change your life forever!"?
**13** How did Frances Gumm become known on stage?
**14** A company from which country featured in the 1999 take over of ASDA?
**15** A famous appearance on whose chat show established Billy Connolly's popularity outside his homeland?
**16** Charles Haughey was Prime Minister of which country?
**17** Which Dennis has a dog called Gnasher?
**18** Kenny Sansom represented England at which sport?
**19** Who was Hollywood's first 'Blonde Bombshell'?
**20** At the end of the 20th C how many UK monarchs had been called George?
**21** What was the name of those hazardous good old boys Bo and Luke?
**22** Which year is used as the title of a George Orwell book?
**23** In computer software what goes before XPress?
**24** The deepwater port of Valletta was developed on which island?
**25** In the 80s Roy Jenkins left which political party to launch the SDP?
In which decade was the centenary of the Wimbledon championships?

**Answers**

***Pot Luck 9***
**1** Deirdre Rachid. **2** 40s. **3** Viagra. **4** R2D2. **5** Joan Rivers. **6** Kubrick. **7** North. **8** Clarice. **9** Information. **10** Lillee. **11** Conley. **12** Judy Garland. **13** America. **14** Parkinson. **15** Ireland. **16** The Menace. **17** Soccer. **18** Jean Harlow. **19** Six. **20** Duke. **21** 1984. **22** Quark. **23** Malta. **24** Labour. **25** 70s.

# Quiz 19 TV Classics

1 Which drama series was based on the books of vet James Herriot?
2 Going Straight was the follow up to which classic prison sitcom?
3 In 70s/80s TV how was The Hulk described?
4 Which Croft & Perry sitcom was set in holiday camp?
5 Auf Wiedersehen Pet was chiefly set on a building site where?
6 Which classic game show with a crossbow was called Der Goldener Schuss in Germany?
7 Which show spawned the catchphrase "Here's one I made earlier"?
8 How were Terry Collier and Bob Ferris known collectively?
9 Which children's TV classic asked "Who was that masked man?"?
10 Which satirical series lampooned politicians through latex puppets?
11 Which Citizen's catchphrase was "Power to the People"?
12 What was Dr Who's Time Machine called?
13 Elizabeth R , with Glenda Jackson, was based on the life of whom?
14 The Fall and Rise of which Reginald starred Leonard Rossiter?
15 What was the female follow up to The Man from U.N.C.L.E called?
16 Which green vegetable was the booby prize on Crackerjack?
17 In which comedy classic did John Cleese announce "And now for something completely different."?
18 In Morecambe & Wise shows, Eric's comment "you can't see the join" referred to what?
19 In The Muppet Show what sort of creature was Kermit?
20 Which character's catchphrase was "I don't believe it"?
21 What were Cassandra and Raquel's surnames after they married Del and Rodney?
22 Open All Hours was set in what type of establishment?
23 Which children's character had a famous black and white cat?
24 What was Frank Spencer's wife called in Some Mothers Do 'Ave 'Em?
25 Which silent puppet had friends called Sweep and Soo?

## Answers

***TV Classics***

**1** All Creatures Great and Small. **2** Porridge. **3** Incredible. **4** Hi-De-Hi!. **5** Germany. **6** The Golden Shot. **7** Blue Peter. **8** The Likely Lads. **9** The Lone Ranger. **10** Spitting Image. **11** Smith. **12** Tardis. **13** Elizabeth I. **14** Perrin. **15** The Girl from U.N.C.L.E.. **16** Cabbage. **17** Monty Python's Flying Circus. **18** Ernie's wig. **19** Frog. **20** Victor Meldrew. **21** Trotter. **22** Shop. **23** Postman Pat. **24** Betty. **25** Sooty.

# Quiz 20 Pot Luck 10

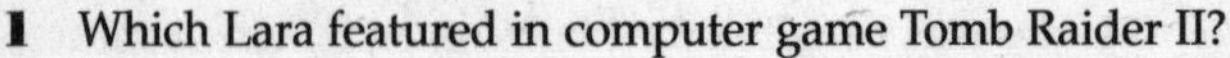

1. Which Lara featured in computer game Tomb Raider II?
2. In what decade did The Sun newspaper launch in Britain?
3. Which Christine featured in a 60s sex scandal involving a cabinet minister?
4. What was Elvis Presley's middle name?
5. Which country has M as its international vehicle registration letter?
6. In Bryan Adams' mega hit which three words come before, "I do it for you"?
7. What were the last names of movie duo Fred and Ginger?
8. In which city was the Three Tenors 1998 World Cup concert?
9. What is the first name of The Queen Mother?
10. Which actor appeared in drag in the movie Tootsie?
11. What does the C stand for in BBC?
12. Jim Moir is better known as which comedian?
13. With which sport is Walter Swinburn associated?
14. Bill Clinton took over from which US President?
15. Who had a 90s No 1 with Ice Ice Baby?
16. Which group of workers staged a year long strike in the 80s over closures?
17. Hull is the administrative centre of which English county?
18. What does P stand for in NSPCC?
19. Which comedian Steve created Portuguese superstar Tony Ferrino?
20. Which Bessie was known as Empress of the Blues?
21. Carlsberg was advertised as "probably the best lager" where?
22. Jim Watt was a world champion in which sport?
23. On TV, what type of goods did Lovejoy deal in?
24. Which classic sitcom was set at Walmington on Sea?
25. On a computer keyboard what letter is far left on the lowest row of letters?

## Answers

***Pot Luck 10***

**1** Croft. **2** 60s. **3** Keeler. **4** Aaron. **5** Malta. **6** Everything I do. **7** Astaire & Rogers. **8** Paris. **9** Elizabeth. **10** Dustin Hoffman. **11** Corporation. **12** Vic Reeves. **13** Horse racing. **14** Bush. **15** Vanilla Ice. **16** Miners. **17** Humberside. **18** Prevention. **19** Coogan. **20** Smith. **21** In the world. **22** Boxing. **23** Antiques. **24** Dad's Army. **25** Z.

# Quiz 21 Sport: 90s Action Replay

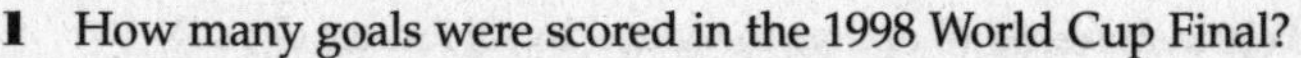

1 How many goals were scored in the 1998 World Cup Final?
2 Rugby's man mountain Jonah Lomu plays for which country?
3 Which country hosted the 1998 Winter Olympics?
4 Who did Man Utd defeat in the 1999 European Champions' Cup Final?
5 In 1998 England won a Test series against which country?
6 Which racing team dropped Damon Hill the season he became world champion?
7 Albertville and Lillehammer were the two 90s venues for which event?
8 Which was the first team not called United to win the Premiership?
9 Which best-on-the-planet trophy did Francois Pienaar collect in 1995?
10 Which team inflicted W Indies' first home Test series defeat in over 20 years?
11 Which team were FA Cup beaten finalists in two consecutive seasons?
12 Where do the Super Bowl winning Cowboys come from?
13 Which England skipper resigned after allegations about taking cocaine?
14 Which man managed victory in all the tennis Grand Slam titles?
15 Teddy Sheringham joined Man Utd from which club?
16 Who does Michael Schumacher drive for?
17 Who advertised Adidas and Brylcreem?
18 What did Miguel Indurain win each year from 1991 to 1995?
19 Which Liverpool star was charged with match fixing?
20 Jonathan Edwards was a world champion in 1995 in which athletic event?
21 Ganguly and Tendulkar have played cricket for which country?
22 Which team bought out the Stewart motor racing team?
23 Defeat by which country prompted the Graham Taylor turnip jibes?
24 Which Rugby League team became known as Rhinos?
25 Which England cricketer was accused of ball tampering in a Test?

## Answers

***Sport: 90s Action Replay***

**1** Three. **2** New Zealand. **3** Japan. **4** Bayern Munich. **5** South Africa. **6** Williams. **7** Winter Olympics. **8** Blackburn Rovers. **9** Rugby World Cup. **10** Australia. **11** Newcastle. **12** Dallas. **13** Lawrence Dallaglio. **14** Andre Agassi. **15** Spurs. **16** Ferrari. **17** David Beckham. **18** Tour de France. **19** Bruce Grobbelaar. **20** Triple Jump. **21** India. **22** Ford. **23** Sweden. **24** Leeds. **25** Mike Atherton.

# Quiz 22 Pot Luck 11

1. Which British soccer club was managed by Christian Gross?
2. Magician David Kotkin managed to change his name to what?
3. What type of animal was 90s Downing Street resident Humphrey?
4. The US declared war on which country after the bombing of Pearl Harbour?
5. Which actor is the dad of Jamie Lee Curtis?
6. With which sport is Chris Cairns associated?
7. Which group backed Bill Haley in the 50s?
8. Who was the last soccer manager to take England to the World Cup semis?
9. Billy Smart produced what type of family entertainment?
10. Which Tory in the 90s became known as the 'Minister For Fun'?
11. What is the main airport in Germany?
12. Which soccer player was married for a time to Sheryl Failes?
13. Which Les performed the famous Cissie and Ada sketch with Roy Barraclough in his TV series?
14. In which country did the McCarthy witch hunts take place?
15. The Last Night of the Proms concert originated in which city?
16. Who wrote about a little helicopter named Budgie?
17. Mike Teague represented England at which sport?
18. Which two numbers go with the Rover car launched in 99?
19. Singer Nat King Cole was also very talented on which musical instrument?
20. Barbara Castle has represented which party in parliament?
21. How did Greta Gustaffson become better known as an actress?
22. Which spectral hound of the moors first appeared in a classic 1902 detective story?
23. Drew Barrymore was born in which decade of the century?
24. Which sport do the Chicago Bears play?
25. The Darling Buds of May was set in which English county?

## Answers

***Pot Luck 11***

**1** Spurs. **2** David Copperfield. **3** Cat. **4** Japan. **5** Tony Curtis. **6** Cricket. **7** The Comets. **8** Bobby Robson. **9** Circus. **10** David Mellor. **11** Frankfurt. **12** Paul Gascoigne. **13** Dawson. **14** USA. **15** London. **16** Sarah Ferguson. **17** Rugby Union. **18** 75. **19** Piano. **20** Labour. **21** Greta Garbo. **22** Hound Of The Baskervilles. **23** 70s. **24** American football. **25** Kent.s.

# Quiz 23 Movies - Who's Who?

**1** Where was Leonardo DiCaprio born?
**2** In which 1998 film did Anderson & Duchovny reprise their TV roles of Mulder & Scully?
**3** Who or what is Gromit?
**4** Who replaced Timothy Dalton as James Bond?
**5** Which star of Home Alone was the highest paid child movie star of the 20th century?
**6** Which star of Grease had a career revival with Pulp Fiction?
**7** Which Tom married Nicole Kidman?
**8** Who met husband Richard Burton on the set of Cleopatra?
**9** Which drummer/singer Phil played the title role in Buster?
**10** Who went to No 1 with Night Fever after writing the music for Saturday Night Fever?
**11** Which film director was involved in a long running custody battle for his children with Mia Farrow?
**12** Which ex Funny Girl starred with Nick Nolte in The Prince of Tides?
**13** Who was the Pretty Woman in the 1990 film with Richard Gere?
**14** Which director of Schindler's List and E.T. was the most commercially successful cinema director of the century?
**15** By which first name is Andrew Blyth Barrymore known in E.T.?
**16** What relation is Jeff to Beau Bridges?
**17** Which star of Rocky said "I built my body to carry my brain around"?
**18** Which ex Brookside actress played Nick Leeson's wife in the film Rogue Trader about the fall of Barings Bank?
**19** Which talk show hostess appeared in The Color Purple?
**20** Which controversial 80s/90s singer/actress married Sean Penn in 1985?
**21** In which country was Arnold Schwarzenegger born?
**22** Which pop star's first film was Purple Rain?
**23** Which Scottish comedian played John Brown in Mrs Brown?
**24** Cate Blanchett won a BAFTA playing which Queen?
**25** Which girl band announced they would make their screen debut in Honest?

## Answers

***Movies – Who's Who***

**1** Hollywood. **2** The X Files. **3** Dog. **4** Pierce Brosnan. **5** Macaulay Culkin. **6** John Travolta. **7** Cruise. **8** Elizabeth Taylor. **9** Collins. **10** The Bee Gees. **11** Woody Allen. **12** Barbra Streisand. **13** Julia Roberts. **14** Steven Spielberg. **15** Drew. **16** Brother. **17** Sylvester Stallone. **18** Anna Friel. **19** Oprah Winfrey. **20** Madonna. **21** Austria. **22** Prince. **23** Billy Connolly. **24** Elizabeth. **25** All Saints.

# Quiz 24 Pot Luck 12

1 In the 60s what was the name of US President Kennedy's wife?
2 With which sport is Michael Jordan associated?
3 What was Georges that left a trail of destruction in Florida in 1998?
4 Which Ted was a 90s Poet Laureate?
5 Which world heavyweight boxing champion was jailed in the 90s?
6 Way Down was a hit for which singer after his death?
7 Which spinach-eating sailor has Robin Williams played on film?
8 In which city were the Shankly Gates built?
9 Under what canine name does rapper Calvin Broadus operate?
10 Sean Fitzpatrick represented New Zealand at which sport?
11 What does the N stand for in NATO?
12 Who was comedian Jack in Jack & Jeremy's Real Lives?
13 Which poet Rupert died on his way to action in World War I?
14 Which royal residence does the Queen use in Norfolk?
15 George Eastman invented what type of equipment?
16 Firestarter was a 90s No 1 for which group?
17 Dick Francis novels revolve around which sport?
18 What's the first name of Frank Sinatra's elder daughter?
19 Which comedian/singer/TV presenter was always the butt of Morecambe & Wise's jokes?
20 Chet Atkins is associated with which musical instrument?
21 Which British city was the Cultural Capital of Europe in 1990?
22 Which Safari Park was set up near to Liverpool?
23 Geoffrey Howe was deputy to which Prime Minister?
24 Which 50s music craze featured a washboard?
25 Which Ken is famous for his vocabulary which includes 'plumpshiousness' and 'tattifilarious'?

**Answers**

***Pot Luck 12*** (see Quiz 3)
**1** Jackie. **2** Basketball. **3** Hurricane. **4** Hughes. **5** Mike Tyson. **6** Elvis Presley. **7** Popeye. **8** Liverpool. **9** Snoopy Doggy Dogg. **10** Rugby Union. **11** North. **12** Dee. **13** Brooke. **14** Sandringham. **15** Photographic. **16** Prodigy. **17** Horse racing. **18** Nancy. **19** Des O'Connor. **20** Guitar. **21** Glasgow. **22** Knowsley. **23** Margaret Thatcher. **24** Skiffle. **25** Dodd.

# Quiz 25 Euro Tour

1 Which southern French town holds an annual international Film Festival?
2 How was Eurotunnel known before its name change in 1998?
3 La Scala is the world's most famous what?
4 Andorra is at the foot of which mountains?
5 Which Arctic country's Finnish name is Lapin Li?
6 Which country is known locally as Osterreich?
7 The Left Bank generally refers to the Left Bank of the Seine in which city?
8 Which Mediterranean island's capital is Valletta?
9 Which country was divided into East and West between the 1940s and 1990s?
10 The Strait of Gibraltar connects the Atlantic Ocean with which Sea?
11 The airline Danair is based where?
12 Which mountainous European country is divided into cantons?
13 Flemish is an official language of which kingdom?
14 Which English location would the French call Douvres?
15 In Greenland a native of the country might be called Inuit or what?
16 Which country is also called the Hellenic Republic?
17 In Norway, a fjord is made up largely of what?
18 Majorca is part of which group of islands?
19 Which German city is known locally as Koln?
20 Tuscany is part of which country?
21 What is Europe's most mountainous country?
22 The province of Calabria is at the southernmost tip of which country?
23 The island of Rhodes belongs to which Mediterranean country?
24 Alsace is a province of which country?
25 What is the currency of Spain?

## Answers

***Euro Tour***

**1** Cannes. **2** Le Shuttle. **3** Opera house. **4** Pyrenees. **5** Lapland. **6** Austria. **7** Paris. **8** Malta. **9** Germany. **10** Mediterranean. **11** Denmark. **12** Switzerland. **13** Belgium. **14** Dover. **15** Eskimo. **16** Greece. **17** Water. **18** Balearics. **19** Cologne. **20** Italy. **21** Switzerland. **22** Italy. **23** Greece. **24** France. **25** Peseta.

# Quiz 26 Pot Luck 13

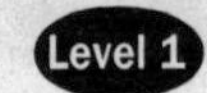


1. Which of the Beatles was first to be widowed?
2. In which country were the 1996 Olympic Games held?
3. In Mask Jim Carrey starred as someone working where?
4. The independent body Oftel regulates which service?
5. In the X Files what is Mulder's first name?
6. Which much repeated comedy series featured ARP Warden Hodges?
7. A UK internet user would use what punctuation mark and letters?
8. In 1998 actor James Brolin married which singer/actress?
9. In which decade did Buckingham Palace first open to the public?
10. Johnny Haynes captained England in which sport?
11. Who played Beattie in a series of telephone ads?
12. Which Terry became a high profile hostage in Lebanon?
13. Which soccer team does Mick Hucknall follow?
14. Woody Allen was born in which decade of the century?
15. Which series with Ellen DeGeneres was originally called These Friends of Mine?
16. Which Spanish Salvador was a surrealist artist?
17. Which country does golfer Ben Crenshaw come from?
18. Which outrageous radio DJ was born Maurice Cole in Liverpool in 1944?
19. Who wrote Charlie and The Chocolate Factory?
20. Bandleader Edward Ellington was known by what nickname?
21. The Dalai Lama fled which country in the 50s?
22. What did Cecil B de Mille make?
23. Which day of the week in Ireland was named Bloody after the shootings of 1972?
24. What was added to Stevie Wonder's name when he was a youngster?
25. Which sitcom with Leonard Rossiter was called Reggie when it was transferred to the USA?

## Answers

***Pot Luck 13***

**1** Paul McCartney. **2** United States. **3** A bank. **4** Telecommunications. **5** Fox. **6** Dad's Army. **7** .uk. **8** Barbra Streisand. **9** 90s. **10** Soccer. **11** Maureen Lipman. **12** Waite. **13** Man Utd. **14** 30s. **15** Ellen. **16** Dali. **17** USA. **18** Kenny Everett. **19** Roald Dahl. **20** Duke. **21** Tibet. **22** Movies. **23** Sunday. **24** Little. **25** The Fall & Rise of Reginald Perrin.

# Quiz 27 Pop Charts

1 What was Billie's first No 1?
2 Which port provided a hit for The Beautiful South?
3 What's the only battle to have been the one-word title of a No 1?
4 What colour was UB40's Wine?
5 Which Bob Dylan song was used as the song for Dunblane?
6 Which magazine shares its name with a Madonna No 1?
7 What went with Tonic for Spacedust?
8 Who had her first No 1 as Mrs Sonny Bono?
9 Which seabird took Fleetwood Mac to No 1?
10 Which chart smashing group featured Adams, Brown and Chisho Elm?
11 50+ Deborah Harry returned to the 99 charts with which group?
12 Which Dad's Army actor had a surprise No 1 with Grandad?
13 Which country does Britney Spears come from?
14 Who did Faith Evans team up with for I'll Be Missing You?
15 Which Starsky and Hutch actor topped the charts?
16 Bitter Sweet Symphony was the first top ten hit for which band?
17 Who is the only Bryan to have had a record at No 1 for 16 weeks?
18 Which Lou wrote A Perfect Day?
19 Who had her first No 1 with Wuthering Heights?
20 Suzanne Vega was in who's Diner?
21 Which song was a No 1 for Nilsson and Mariah Carey?
22 Which film provided a best selling album for Whitney Houston?
23 Who recorded Riders On The Storm?
24 Who did Chrissie Hynde guest with for I Got You Babe?
25 Gazza sang with Lindisfarne about the fog on which river?

## Answers

***Pop Charts***

**1** Because We Want To. **2** Rotterdam. **3** Waterloo. **4** Red. **5** Knockin' On Heaven's Door. **6** Vogue . **7** Gym. **8** Cher. **9** Albatross. **10** Spice Girls. **11** Blondie. **12** Clive Dunn. **13** US. **14** Puff Daddy. **15** David Soul. **16** Verve. **17** Adams. **18** Reed. **19** Kate Bush. **20** Tom's. **21** Without You. **22** The Bodyguard. **23** The Doors. **24** UB40. **25** Tyne.

# Quiz 28 Pot Luck 14

1 A 1997 phenomena, Hale-Bop was a type of what?
2 The charity Oxfam began in which city?
3 The sale of what was prohibited in America during prohibition?
4 Michael Owen scored a wonder World Cup goal against which country?
5 Which former British Prime Minister leader called for clemency for General Pinochet?
6 Which instrument was associated with Stephane Grapelli?
7 What was the name of the scandal that brought down US President Richard Nixon?
8 With which sport is Thierry Henry associated?
9 Who duetted with Kiki Dee on True Love?
10 In which decade was the battle of the Somme?
11 Former MP Neil Hamilton was involved in the cash for what scandal?
12 Which Ian created the character James Bond?
13 In movies, who or what were Lady and The Tramp?
14 What does the M stand for in MCC?
15 Which friend of Carla Lane and fellow campaigning vegetarian appeared in an episode of her sitcom Bread in 1988?
16 Which TV fox went "Boom boom!"?
17 Which trials of 1946 dealt with Nazi war criminals?
18 Archibald Leach became known as which Hollywood actor?
19 The controversial James Pickles hit the headlines while serving as a what?
20 The New York Stock Exchange was established on which street?
21 In fiction, what was the name of Bertie Wooster's manservant?
22 Which American actor refused his Oscar awarded for The Godfather?
23 David Solberg became a famous actor/singer under which name?
24 Which country did Ray Houghton play soccer for?
25 Which series about a group of anarchic priests was set on Craggy Island?

## Answers

***Pot Luck 14***

**1** Comet. **2** Oxford. **3** Alcohol. **4** Argentina. **5** Margaret Thatcher. **6** Violin. **7** Watergate. **8** Soccer. **9** Elton John. **10** Second decade. **11** Questions. **12** Fleming. **13** Dogs. **14** Marylebone. **15** Linda McCartney. **16** Basil Brush. **17** Nuremberg. **18** Cary Grant. **19** Judge. **20** Wall Street. **21** Jeeves. **22** Marlon Brando. **23** David Soul. **24** Republic of Ireland. **25** Father Ted.

# Quiz 29 70s Newsround

1 What did Ceylon change its name to?
2 What was the name of the mansion where Elvis Presley died?
3 Which English soccer team did the only 70s FA Cup and League double?
4 Who had a Christmas special watched by an amazing 28 million people?
5 Who did Captain Mark Phillips marry at Westminster Abbey?
6 Which Brit won the ladies singles at Wimbledon?
7 Queen had their first No 1 with which record?
8 What was introduced in the 70s version of D-Day?
9 What was the nickname of Lord Lucan who vanished in the 70s?
10 Which Spare magazine was founded as part of the feminist movement?
11 Who was Satchmo who passed away in 1971?
12 The monarchy was restored to power in which European country?
13 Who or what was Chia Chia?
14 What type of Fields were linked with Cambodia?
15 The Aswan High Dam was opened in which country?
16 In 1976 which jockey won the Derby for a record seventh time?
17 In 1979 the Shah was forced to flee from which country?
18 Bobby Robson managed which soccer side to their first FA Cup triumph?
19 Sir Anthony Blunt was revealed to have led a secret life as what?
20 Which Czechoslovakian born sportswoman Martina defected to America?
21 What were the sea borne refugees fleeing Vietnam known as?
22 Who won the Eurovision Song Contest for Sweden?
23 In which country was a 2000 year old lifesize terracotta army discovered?
24 Johan Cruyff played in a World Cup Final for which country?
25 What was the name of the fashionable short pants worn by women?

## Answers

***70s Newsround***

**1** Sri Lanka. **2** Graceland. **3** Arsenal. **4** Morecambe & Wise. **5** Princess Anne. **6** Virginia Wade. **7** Bohemian Rhapsody. **8** Decimal coins. **9** Lucky. **10** Spare Rib. **11** Louis Armstrong. **12** Spain. **13** Giant Panda. **14** Killing. **15** Egypt. **16** Lester Piggott. **17** Iran. **18** Ipswich. **19** Spy. **20** Navratilova. **21** Boat People. **22** Abba. **23** China. **24** Netherlands. **25** Hot pants.

# Quiz 30 Pot Luck 15

1 Nick Leeson was involved with the collapse of which bank?
2 In 1998 David Trimble and John Hulme shared The Nobel Prize for what?
3 In which sport did David Moorcroft set world records?
4 Which Ken fronted a TV series about his Hot Wok?
5 What was the film sequel to Jurassic Park?
6 Patrick Swayze teamed up with which Moore in the movie Ghost?
7 Norman Lamont has represented which party in parliament?
8 Kenny Dalglish was born in which city?
9 In pop music what is the surname of teenage chart topper Billie?
10 Which two colours form the background of the Austrian flag?
11 Kevin Costner was born in which decade of the century?
12 Which soap featured the character Beth Jordache?
13 In the 40s Hirohito was Emperor of which country?
14 Who was the first Englishman sent off in a Wembley soccer international?
15 What was the name of the chambermaid in Fawlty Towers?
16 Which was the 50th state to become part of the United States of America?
17 In the Cold War in which country was Checkpoint Charlie?
18 Roy Keane joined Man Utd from which club?
19 Popular entertainer Bing Crosby died after completing a game of what?
20 What is Frasier's surname in the sitcom of the same name?
21 Which Clement was Prime Minister in the 40s?
22 What type of works did W H Auden write?
23 Early in the century which country had a parliament called the Duma?
24 In the title of a J B Priestley play what does An Inspector do?
25 Which soccer club has Jasper Carrot among its supporters?

**Answers**

***Pot Luck 15***

**1** Barings. **2** Peace. **3** Athletics. **4** Hom. **5** Lost World. **6** Demi. **7** Conservative. **8** Glasgow. **9** Piper. **10** Red and white. **11** 50s. **12** Brookside. **13** Japan. **14** Paul Scholes. **15** Polly. **16** Hawaii. **17** West Germany. **18** Nottm Forest. **19** Golf. **20** Crane. **21** Attlee. **22** Poetry. **23** Russia. **24** Calls. **25** Birmingham.

# Quiz 31 Headline Makers

1. Which MP David, was exposed as having an affair in 1992?
2. Which rock legend Mick was David Bailey's best man?
3. Allan Lamb changed nationality from South African to what?
4. Which former actor and US President received an honorary knighthood?
5. Which Foreign Secretary did Gaynor Regan marry in 1998?
6. Which nanny Louise was tried on TV in the US over the death of a baby in her care?
7. What was the first name of Miss Lewinsky whose White House activities almost brought down Bill Clinton?
8. Who stormed off court at the end of the 1999 French Open and had to have her mother coax her back?
9. Who was South Africa's first black president?
10. In 1995 astronaut Michael Foale was the first Briton to walk where?
11. Which US President born in 1946 was called The Comeback Kid?
12. Which leader Boris succeeded Mikhail Gorbachev?
13. Which eastern European country did Pope John Paul II come from?
14. What was the name of Nelson Mandela's wife when he was released from prison?
15. Which Prime Minister was known as The Iron Lady?
16. Which tennis player famously yelled "You cannot be serious!" at an umpire?
17. Lord Lloyd Webber, Jim Davidson and Bob Monkhouse have all famously supported which political party?
18. Which Arthur was the miners' leader in the 1980s?
19. Which soccer star Paul recorded a rap song called Geordie Boys?
20. Which PM's wife of the latter half of the 20th century was made a High Court judge?
21. What is the first name of Dr Mowlam, who was Tony Blair's first Northern Ireland Secretary?
22. Which Julia was the first to present the news on BBC and ITV?
23. What colour suit is Independent MP and former news journalist

## Answers

***Headline Makers***

**1** Mellor. **2** Jagger. **3** British. **4** Ronald Reagan. **5** Robin Cook. **6** Woodward. **7** Monica. **8** Martina Hingis. **9** Nelson Mandela. **10** Space. **11** Bill Clinton. **12** Yeltsin. **13** Poland. **14** Winnie. **15** Margaret Thatcher. **16** John McEnroe. **17** Tory. **18** Scargill. **19** Gascoigne. **20** Cherie Booth. **21** Mo. **22** Somerville. **23** White. **24** Saudi Arabia. **25** Eric Cantona.

# Quiz 32 Pot Luck 16

Level 1

1 Which Sinatra song manages to rhyme a line with "shy way"?
2 Which politician was nicknamed 'Bambi'?
3 Henry Ford claimed that, 'History is...' what?
4 In the cost-a-lot to make movie Waterworld who played Mariner?
5 Rupert Murdoch comes from which country?
6 In 1996, which group of people voted themselves a 26% pay rise?
7 What name is shared by pop star sisters Dannii and Kylie?
8 Black activist Steve Biko died in which country in the 70s?
9 Which John was the star of the film Grease?
10 What colour are the Smurfs?
11 Mark Taylor played cricket for which country?
12 Which group had a 90s hit with These Are The Days of Our Lives?
13 What does the C stand for in LCD?
14 In which TV comedy show was the idea of Absolutely Fabulous launched in a sketch?
15 Churchill, Sherman and Panzer were all developed as types of what?
16 Which motorway forms the Edinburgh to Glasgow route?
17 Who sang in the pop duo with Mel Appleby?
18 With which sport is Fred Couples associated?
19 Which Nigel was an 80s Chancellor?
20 What was the first name of jazz giant Ms Fitzgerald?
21 What is the occupation of Beryl Bainbridge?
22 Robert Menzies was Prime Minister of which country?
23 Which Irving penned the song White Christmas?
24 Who played Rachel Green in Friends?
25 Which country was racing's Niki Lauda born in?

## Answers

***Pot Luck 16***

**1** My Way. **2** Tony Blair. **3** Bunk. **4** Kevin Costner. **5** Australia. **6** MPs. **7** Minogue. **8** South Africa. **9** Travolta. **10** Blue. **11** Australia. **12** Queen. **13** Crystal. **14** French & Saunders. **15** Tank. **16** M8. **17** Kim. **18** Golf. **19** Lawson. **20** Ella. **21** Novelist. **22** Australia. **23** Berlin. **24** Jennifer Aniston. **25**Austria.

# Quiz 33 TV Comedy

1 Absolutely Fabulous started life as a sketch on which comedy duo's show?
2 What was 'dropped' in the comedy about the Globelink newsroom?
3 How was David Jason's Sidney Charles Larkin known in The Darling Buds of May?
4 Which US actress Ellen was the star of Ellen?
5 Which sitcom was based in a French cafe in occupied France?
6 Who hosted Fantasy Football League with David Baddiel?
7 Which laconic comedian Dave first found fame on the Val Doonican show?
8 Which clerical sitcom was set on Craggy Island?
9 Which US series was about a lawyer called Ally?
10 Which Towers provided a comedy series for Torquay?
11 Who completed the trio with Filthy and Rich in the Young Ones styled comedy?
12 Who was Butt-Head's comedy partner?
13 Which female duo first found fame on The Comic Strip Presents?
14 How many friends were there in Friends?
15 Which Ruby was the American in Girls On Top?
16 Which Benny created Fred Scuttle and Professor Marvel in his saucy seaside postcard style show?
17 Goodnight Sweetheart was based in the 90s and which other decade?
18 Which 90s sitcom was about two sisters in Chigwell with a man mad neighbour?
19 Which Tony lived at 23 Railway Cuttings, East Cheam?
20 Who accompanied Hale in the sketches of The Two Rons?
21 Which Mr Atkinson played Blackadder?
22 Which sitcom was based on writer Jimmy Perry's experiences in the Home Guard?
23 Which Harry created Wayne and Waynetta Slob?
24 In which city was Bread set?
25 Which 60s singer Adam played the title role in Budgie?

## Answers

***TV Comedy***

**1** French & Saunders. **2** The Dead Donkey. **3** Pop. **4** Ellen DeGeneres. **5** Allo Allo. **6** Frank Skinner. **7** Allen. **8** Father Ted. **9** Ally McBeal. **10** Fawlty Towers. **11** Catflap. **12** Beavis. **13** French & Saunders. **14** Six. **15** Wax. **16** Hill. **17** 1940s. **18** Birds of a Feather. **19** Hancock. **20** Pace. **21** Rowan. **22** Dad's Army. **23** Enfield. **24** Liverpool. **25** Faith.

# Quiz 34 Pot Luck 17

1 What was the favourite food of the Teenage Mutant Ninja Turtles?
2 Janet Sixsmith has played over a hundred times for England in which sport?
3 Where does Patsy Kensit have a shamrock and the word 'Liam' tattooed?
4 Which Arthur led the miners in the 80s strikes?
5 Who was the first ex-movie actor to become President of the United States?
6 Who was Diana Prince able to change into?
7 Which European city was divided by a wall in the 60s?
8 Who was the Prince of Thieves in a 90s blockbuster movie title?
9 Betamax was a type of what?
10 Which car manufacturer introduced the Hunter, Imp and Minx?
11 Who played Shelley - the only American - in Girls on Top?
12 Who drives a vehicle with the registration PAT 1?
13 The deepwater port of Àlicante was built in which country?
14 David Bailey became famous as a what?
15 What type of films were associated with Ealing in the 40s and 50s?
16 How many lions appear on England's soccer badge?
17 Which country does cricketer Anil Kumble play for?
18 Which detective series was set in Jersey?
19 Thelonious Monk was associated with which musical instrument?
20 In the 90s which political leader said, "Well, who'd have thought it?"?
21 Which stage musical does the song Memory come from?
22 In advertising which animal is linked with Esso?
23 In which country is Barajas airport?
24 Which star of Only Fools and Horses and Goodnight Sweetheart played Ronnie Barker's son in Going Straight?
25 Harrison Ford was born in which decade of the century?

**Answers**

***Pot Luck 17***

**1** Pizza. **2** Hockey. **3** Ankle. **4** Scargill. **5** Ronald Reagan. **6** Wonderwoman. **7** Berlin. **8** Robin Hood. **9** Video. **10** Hillman. **11** Ruby Wax. **12** Postman Pat. **13** Spain. **14** Photographer. **15** Comedies. **16** Three. **17** India. **18** Bergerac. **19** Piano. **20** John Major. **21** Cats. **22** Tiger. **23** Spain. **24** Nicholas Lyndhurst. **25** 40s.

# Quiz 35 Sporting Who's Who

1 Who was the youngest Wimbledon women's champion of the century?
2 In which country was Greg Rusedski born?
3 Which manager was in charge of Nottm Forest for over 18 years?
4 Which boxer took to wearing a monocle?
5 Who was the first member of the Royal family to be BBC Sports Personality Of The Year?
6 Who was Man Utd's captain in the 1999 European Champions' Cup Final?
7 Who was the first rugby union player to reach 50 international tries?
8 Who was England's captain in cricket's 1999 World Cup?
9 Boxer Naseem Hamed was brought up in which English city?
10 Who didn't make England's World Cup squad for France after much publicised kebab consuming sessions?
11 What nickname was given to basketball's Wilt Chamberlain?
12 Who was Edson Arantes do Nascimento?
13 Who is France's most successful motor racing driver of all time?
14 Who resigned as Welsh manager in 1999?
15 Which British runner became the oldest ever Olympic 100m winner?
16 Who was the first person to run a mile in under four minutes?
17 What was Dean's first name in the Torvill & Dean skating partnership?
18 Who was known as 'The Golden Bear'?
19 Who was the Joe who first defeated Muhammad Ali?
20 In the 90s who advertised Umbro, McDonalds and Lucozade?
21 In the 90s who was known as 'Bumble'?
22 Who was the first manager to have taken charge of both Australia and England?
23 In the 96 Olympics which Michael won both 200 and 400m?
24 What name was shared by motor racing's brothers Emerson and Wilson?
25 Which tennis player had a father named Peter who was jailed for tax irregularities?

## Answers

***Sporting Who's Who***

**1** Martina Hingis. **2** Canada. **3** Brian Clough. **4** Chris Eubank. **5** Princess Anne. **6** Schmeichel. **7** David Campese. **8** Alec Stewart. **9** Sheffield. **10** Paul Gascoigne. **11** The Stilt. **12** Pele. **13** Alain Prost. **14** Bobby Gould. **15** Linford Christie. **16** Roger Bannister. **17** Christopher. **18** Jack Nicklaus. **19** Frazier. **20** Alan Shearer. **21** David Lloyd. **22** Terry Venables. **23** Johnson. **24** Fittipaldi. **25** Steffi Graf.

# Quiz 36 Pot Luck 18

1 How was tycoon Robert Maxwell said to have died?
2 In the 90s what was Britain's busiest ferry passenger port?
3 What sort of Bottom did Noel Edmonds introduce to TV?
4 Which soccer side does former PM John Major support?
5 Which royal ship was decommissioned in 1997?
6 Under what name have Barry, Maurice and Robin been operating for over 30 years?
7 Which Kenneth was the independent prosecutor in the Bill Clinton affair?
8 In which country did Marilyn Monroe die?
9 Which team won the 1996 cricket World Cup?
10 Who was the first female presenter of the National Lottery?
11 What colour did guests wear for Mel B's wedding?
12 Nigel Short represented England at which indoor sport?
13 Preston is the administrative centre of which English county?
14 Which Kelvin used to edit The Sun?
15 What does the O stand for in HMSO?
16 What was Gary's surname in Goodnight Sweetheart?
17 In which city was Jan Smuts airport built?
18 With which sport is Vivian Richards associated?
19 Which Aretha has been dubbed the Queen Of Soul?
20 Which family feature in The Darling Buds Of May?
21 In which decade did Sir Cliff Richard receive his knighthood?
22 How many couples made up the main cast of The Good Life?
23 Fictional Grange Hill Comprehensive is set in which real city?
24 Peter Schmeichel played soccer for which country?
25 Which musical features the song As Long As He Needs Me?

## Answers

***Pot Luck 18***

**1** Drowned. **2** Dover. **3** Crinkley. **4** Chelsea. **5** Britannia. **6** The Bee Gees. **7** Starr. **8** United States. **9** Sri Lanka. **10** Anthea Turner. **11** White. **12** Chess. **13** Lancashire. **14** McKenzie. **15** Office. **16** Sparrow. **17** Johannesburg. **18** Cricket. **19** Franklin. **20** Larkins. **21** 90s. **22** Two. **23** London. **24** Denmark. **25** Oliver.

# Quiz 37 Action Movies

1 Which Steven directed Saving Private Ryan?
2 Air Force One deals with the holding to ransom of whom?
3 Which Tom played spy Ethan Hunt in Mission: Impossible?
4 Which 90s James Bond starred in Dante's Peak?
5 Which unlucky Apollo Mission was filmed in 1995 with Tom Hanks?
6 Which Judge from 2000 AD comic appeared on film in 1995?
7 Which Australian actor starred in and directed Braveheart?
8 Which Antarctic creature gives its name to the villain played by Danny De Vito in Batman Returns?
9 What type of creatures were Donatello, Raphael, Michaelangelo and Leonardo?
10 What is the profession of Harrison Ford in the Indiana Jones movies?
11 In which city does the action of Batman take place?
12 Which month is part of the title of the film where Tom Cruise plays war veteran Ron Kovic?
13 Which actor Daniel starred as Hawkeye in The Last of the Mohicans?
14 In which series of films were Danny Glover and Mel Gibson teamed in 1987, 1989, 1992 and 1998?
15 Top Gun is about which of the armed services?
16 The action of The Killing Fields takes place in which country?
17 What was the first Bond movie with Sean Connery?
18 Which actor, famous for spaghetti westerns, got the role in Dirty Harry after Frank Sinatra dropped out?
19 Which Gene played Popeye Doyle in The French Connection?
20 The Poseidon Adventure is about a disaster on what type of transport?
21 Enter the Dragon was the first US kung fu film of which Mr Lee?
22 In which city does Robert de Niro operate as a sinister Taxi Driver?
23 The Shootist was the last film to star which John, famous for his western roles?
24 Which creature was a threat to holidaymakers in Jaws?
25 In which 1999 film did Sean Connery star with Catherine Zeta Jones?

## Answers

***Action Movies***
**1** Spielberg. **2** US President. **3** Cruise. **4** Pierce Brosnan. **5** 13. **6** Dredd. **7** Mel Gibson. **8** Penguin. **9** Turtles. **10** Archaeologist. **11** Gotham. **12** July. **13** Day-Lewis. **14** Lethal Weapon. **15** Air Force. **16** Cambodia. **17** Dr No. **18** Clint Eastwood. **19** Hackman. **20** Ship. **21** Bruce. **22** New York. **23** Wayne. **24** Shark. **25** Entrapment.

# Quiz 38 Pot Luck 19

1 Who described 1992 as an "Annus horribilis"?
2 Which lady replaced David Coleman on TV's A Question Of Sport?
3 Which country kept saying no as Britain tried to join the European Union?
4 Which entertainer Williams wrote the autobiography Just Williams?
5 What's the name of the bird that cartoon cat Sylvester chases in vain?
6 Which country had a president known as LBJ?
7 Which Scottish soccer boss was the first to win the English double twice?
8 Which school did Prince Harry go to when he was 13?
9 Sinead O'Connor comes from which city?
10 Which Julie starred in the film Educating Rita?
11 In athletics, which country topped the medal table at the 1998 European Championship?
12 Which comedian is known as The Big Yin?
13 Which Guy the spy fled to Russia along with Donald Maclean?
14 Iraq invaded which neighbouring state to start the 90s Gulf War?
15 Which American has had most solo No 1 hits in the UK?
16 Stephen Fry was born in which decade of the century?
17 Fred Titmus represented England at which sport?
18 Which actress Brigitte became the leading sex symbol of the 50s?
19 In which year did the Second World War end?
20 What kind of creature was Dylan in the Magic Roundabout?
21 Margaret Beckett has represented which party in parliament?
22 Which John wrote the novel Room at The Top?
23 At the end of the 20th C how many UK monarchs had been called Edward?
24 Which Thomas wrote The Silence Of The Lambs?
25 Which country does motor racing's Jacques Villeneuve come from?

## Answers

***Pot Luck 19***

**1** The Queen. **2** Sue Barker. **3** France. **4** Kenneth. **5** Tweety Pie. **6** United States. **7** Alex Ferguson. **8** Eton. **9** Dublin. **10** Walters. **11** Great Britain. **12** Billy Connolly. **13** Burgess. **14** Kuwait. **15** Elvis Presley. **16** 50s. **17** Cricket. **18** Bardot. **19** 1945. **20** Rabbit. **21** Labour. **22** Braine. **23** Eight. **24** Harris. **25** Canada.

# Quiz 39 On the Road

1 Which city is the southernmost point of the A1?
2 What colour are the lines in a box junction?
3 How frequently must a three year old car have an MOT in Great Britain?
4 What colour Cross Code gives advice on crossing the road?
5 What does a red and amber traffic light mean?
6 On the road, what shape are most warning signs?
7 Which name for a very large truck gets its name from an Indian god?
8 Which London road race is held annually for professionals and those raising money for charity?
9 Which registration letter was the first to be introduced in a month other than August?
10 Which 24 Hour Race in France uses normal roads as part of the race track?
11 What is the minimum number of L plates a learner driver must have?
12 What is the type of driving license a learner driver must have called?
13 Which government publication for all road users was first published in 1931?
14 Which Garages near Oxford originally produced the MG sports car?
15 The Milk Race is an annual race around Britain's roads on what form of transport?
16 How is the London Orbital Motorway also known?
17 An orange badge displayed in a car's windscreen means the driver is what?
18 Which Way begins West of Sheffield and stretches to Southern Scotland?
19 A memorial to which Queen stands in front of Buckingham Palace?
20 Which motoring association has an actual club in London, as its name implies?
21 Which national BBC Radio news and sport station broadcasts travel updates, usually every 15 minutes?
22 What colour card allows a motorist to travel abroad?
23 The letter H on a road sign means?
24 What does G stand for in HGV?
25 What colour is the background of motorway signs?

## Answers

***On the Road***

**1** London. **2** Yellow. **3** Once a year. **4** Green. **5** Stop. **6** Triangular. **7** Juggernaut. **8** Marathon. **9** T. **10** Le Mans. **11** Two. **12** Provisional. **13** Highway Code. **14** Morris. **15** Cycles. **16** M25. **17** Disabled. **18** Pennine Way. **19** Victoria. **20** RAC - Royal Automobile Club. **21** Radio 5 Live. **22** Green. **23** Hospital. **24** Goods. **25** Blue.

# Quiz 40 Pot Luck 20

1 In which Scottish town did Thomas Hamilton carry out a shooting atrocity?
2 Which Spice Girl wore a Union Jack dress?
3 What type of creature was the star of the film Jaws?
4 What colour goes with white and red on the Bulgarian flag?
5 Soccer's Peter Nicholas won 73 international caps for which country?
6 Princess Grace of Monaco died after an accident in which form of transport?
7 In books and pop music, who tidied up on Wimbledon Common?
8 Who produced the car known as The Silver Ghost ?
9 Which TV Michael is linked with underestimating the 1987 hurricanes?
10 Which musical does Cabaret come from?
11 The driving test introduced a written section in which decade?
12 Derek Wilton appeared in which TV soap?
13 With which sport is Helena Sukova associated?
14 Which country has B as its international vehicle registration letter?
15 The description situation comedy is usually shortened to what?
16 What does the S stand for in GCSE?
17 Matlock is the administrative centre of which English county?
18 How many Goodies were there?
19 Who was the British monarch at the start of the 20th century?
20 Which folksinger Joan featured in the civil rights and anti-Vietnam movements?
21 What does the letter S stand for in AIDS?
22 Grace and Favour was the sequel to which sitcom about Grace Brothers?
23 What instrument did 50s and 60s star Russ Conway play?
24 Which country did Bjorn Borg come from?
25 On TV, what colour was Inspector Morse's jag?

## Answers

***Pot Luck 20***

**1** Dunblane. **1** Geri Halliwell - Ginger Spice. **3** Shark. **4** Green. **5** Wales. **6** Car. **7** The Wombles. **8** Rolls Royce. **9** Fish. **10** Cabaret. **11** 90s. **12** Coronation Street. **13** Tennis. **14** Belgium. **15** Sitcom. **16** Secondary. **17** Derbyshire. **18** Three. **19** Victoria. **20** Baez. **21** Syndrome. **22**Are You Being Served?. **23** Piano. **24** Sweden. **25** Red.

# Quiz 41 Music - Who's Who

1 Who wrote the lyrics for the 90s Candle In The Wind?
2 Who is the Sid of Nancy and Sid notoriety?
3 Who is Blur's lead singer?
4 Who led the Blonde Ambition world tour of 1990?
5 Who wrote, sang and played the guitar on The Streets of London?
6 Which group's music featured in the frock horror film Priscilla Queen Of The Desert ?
7 Who had his first No 1 in the 70s with Maggie May?
8 Who first hit the top ten with Cornflake Girl?
9 Who said Go West in 1993?
10 Who was the Gary who sang with the Union Gap?
11 Who created the character Ziggy Stardust?
12 Who was 'The Boss'?
13 Under what name had the late Mary O'Brien been famous?
14 Who did Louise Nurding leave in 1995?
15 Who charted by saying Eh-Oh!?
16 Who had a singer Roger Daltrey and a drummer Keith Moon?
17 Which country does Bjork come from?
18 Who has been both Bad and Dangerous?
19 Who linked up with Aitken and Waterman?
20 Who was backed by Blockheads?
21 Who first charted back in the 70s with Seven Seas Of Rhye?
22 Who was Addicted to Love in the 80s?
23 Who had a hit with Orinoco Flow?
24 Who was backed by the Wailers?
25 Who was the big O?

## Answers

***Music – Who's Who***

**1** Bernie Taupin. **2** Sid Vicious. **3** Damon Albarn. **4** Madonna. **5** Ralph McTell. **6** Abba. **7** Rod Stewart. **8** Tori Amos. **9** Pet Shop Boys. **10** Puckett. **11** David Bowie. **12** Bruce Springsteen. **13** Dusty Springfield. **14** Eternal. **15** Teletubbies. **16** The Who. **17** Iceland. **18** Michael Jackson. **19** Stock. **20** Ian Dury. **21** Queen. **22** Robert Palmer. **23** Enya. **24** Bob Marley. **25** Roy Orbison.

# Quiz 42 Pot Luck 21

1 Which city became the capital of Serbia?
2 Who is Gromit's partner?
3 In which decade did Great Britain go into Europe?
4 Which Pamela married Billy Connolly?
5 Which revolutionary's face appeared on countless 60s posters with the words Viva Che?
6 Which comedian's catchphrases included "Shut That Door"?
7 Which Orson directed the film classic Citizen Kane?
8 Which country does soccer star Christian Vieri play for?
9 Who recorded the album Dark Side Of The Moon?
10 In telecommunications, what does the second D stand for in IDD?
11 Goldie Hawn was born in which decade of the century?
12 Which comic duo has the first names Gareth & Norman?
13 Which Graham wrote the novel Brighton Rock?
14 Which country does Wayne Gretzky come from?
15 Berry Gordy became famous as a producer of what?
16 Which company took over Rover in 1994?
17 Which late great comedian created the character whose first names were Anthony Aloysius St John?
18 Which was the most heavily blitzed UK city in World War II?
19 At the end of the 20th C how many UK monarchs had been called Anne?
20 On a computer keyboard what letter is between Q and E?
21 Angela Mortimer represented Britain at which sport?
22 Disney World is situated in which US State?
23 Which Alan Partridge show has the name of an Abba hit?
24 The character Norma Desmond appears in which musical?
25 Which soccer team does Danny Baker follow?

## Answers

***Pot Luck 21***

**1** Belgrade. **2** Wallace. **3** 70s. **4** Stephenson. **5** Che Guevara. **6** Larry Grayson. **7** Welles. **8** Italy. **9** Pink Floyd. **10** Dialling. **11** 40s. 12 Hale & Pace. **13** Greene. **14** Canada. **15** Records. **16** BMW. **17** Tony Hancock. **18** London. **19** One. **20** W. **21** Tennis. **22** Florida. **23** Knowing Me, Knowing You. **24** Sunset Boulevard. **25** Millwall.

# Quiz 43 80s Newsround

1 Which Scottish border town was the scene of a jumbo jet disaster?
2 Who or what was Mary Rose, making an appearance after 500 years?
3 Which soap had Britain asking, "Who shot JR?"?
4 Which US President was linked with the 'Star Wars' policy?
5 An IRA car bomb was detonated outside which major London store?
6 Which Neil was elected leader of the Labour Party?
7 Who won the ladies singles most times at Wimbledon in the 80s?
8 Which John portrayed The Elephant Man on film?
9 Solidarity was the mass movement of the people in which country?
10 Sarah Ferguson became Duchess of where?
11 What kind of disaster claimed some 100,000 lives in Armenia in 1988?
12 Which golfer Sandy triumphed at the US Masters?
13 In 1980 the SAS spectacularly freed hostages in which embassy in London?
14 Don't Die Of Ignorance was the message put out to combat which disease?
15 Which tennis ace completed his fifth successive Wimbledon singles triumph?
16 What did the L stand for in GLC?
17 Who became the world's youngest ever boxing heavyweight champion?
18 Which Jeffrey resigned as deputy chairman of the Tory party?
19 Which city was devastated by an earthquake in 1985 and then hosted the World Cup in 1986?
20 What was the so-called Black day for the City in the late 80s?
21 There was fighting around Port Stanley on which Islands?
22 Tiananmen Square was a scene of conflict in which country?
23 In which English city were Liverpool supporters crushed by crowds at an FA Cup semi final?
24 Which organisation had their ship the Rainbow Warrior sunk?
25 What type of disaster happened at Bradford City's stadium?

## Answers

***80s Newsround***
**1** Lockerbie. **2** Ship. **3** Dallas. **4** Reagan. **5** Harrods. **6** Kinnock. **7** Martina Navratilova. **8** Hurt. **9** Poland. **10** York. **11** Earthquake. **12** Lyle. **13** Iranian. **14** AIDS. **15** Bjorn Borg. **16** London. **17** Mike Tyson. **18** Archer. **19** Mexico. **20** Monday. **21** Falkland Islands. **22** China. **23** Sheffield. **24** Greenpeace. **25** Fire.

# Quiz 44 Pot Luck 22

1 Which 90s British political leader gave his marriage vows in Welsh?
2 With which sport is Shaquille O'Neal associated?
3 What type of skirt was the main fashion style of the 60s?
4 In Notting Hill what does the Hugh Grant character deal in?
5 In the 90s certain Newcastle Utd directors described the women of the area as being like which creatures?
6 Chancellor Helmut Kohl led which country in the 80s and 90s?
7 What does the G mean in GBH?
8 Which comedian Mike called himself The Rochdale Cowboy?
9 The William Tell Overture provided the title music to which TV western?
10 In finance what does the E in ERM stand for?
11 Which motorway links Carlisle to the Midlands?
12 What is the first name of sci-fi writer Asimov?
13 Which Hank played lead guitar with The Shadows?
14 Who did Jelena Dokic beat in the first round of Wimbledon 1999?
15 Who had a 90s No 1 with Don't Look Back In Anger?
16 In 1970 Germaine Greer produced the feminist book The Female what?
17 Keir Hardie was the first leader of which 20th C political party?
18 In which country is Archangel airport?
19 Quincy Jones was associated with which brass instrument?
20 Buster Mottram represented Britain at which sport?
21 What type of tragedy blighted Omagh in 1998?
22 What was the surname of Harry Enfield's creations Wayne and Waynetta?
23 Which Simon sang with Duran Duran?
24 Which Raymond wrote the detective novel Farewell My Lovely?
25 Relating to the TV show Auntie's Bloomers, who is Auntie?

## Answers

***Pot Luck 22***

**1** William Hague. **2** Basketball. **3** Mini. **4** Books. **5** Dogs. **6** Germany. **7** Grievous. **8** Harding. **9** The Lone Ranger. **10** Exchange. **11** M6. **12** Isaac. **13** Marvin. **14** Martina Hingis. **15** Oasis. **16** Eunuch. **17** Labour. **18** Russia. **19** Trumpet. **20** Tennis. **21** Bomb. **22** Slob. **23** Le Bon. **24** Chandler. **25** The BBC.

# Quiz 45 Heroes & Villains

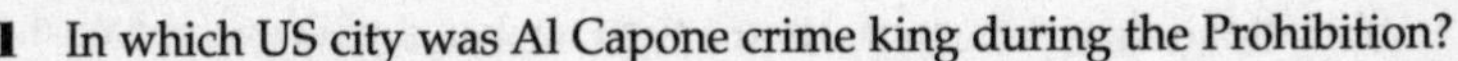

1 In which US city was Al Capone crime king during the Prohibition?
2 Which US President George was the US's youngest ever pilot in WWII?
3 Which American leader did Lee Harvey Oswald assassinate?
4 What was the first name of Mr Waite held hostage in Beirut in the 1980s?
5 In 1987 Lester Piggott was jailed for not paying what?
6 In 1995 O.J. Simpson was cleared of murdering which of his relatives?
7 Pol Pot led the Khmer Rouge on which continent?
8 Archbishop Desmond Tutu fought for civil rights in which country?
9 Which ex Minister Aitken was jailed in 1999 over a failed libel case?
10 Simon Weston became famous for his courage following horrific injuries in which war?
11 What nationality was Brian Keenan, held hostage with John McCarthy?
12 Which nickname was given to Boston murderer Albert de Salvo?
13 Which Lord vanished after his children's nanny was found murdered?
14 Which media magnate mysteriously disappeared off his yacht in 1991?
15 John Glenn became the oldest man to travel where when he boarded the Discovery in 1998?
16 Richard Bacon resigned from which TV show after drug allegations?
17 Which part of Evander Holyfield did Mike Tyson bite off during a fight?
18 Prosecutor Kenneth Starr was involved in impeachment proceedings against which US President?
19 Which French footballer David was chosen to publicise the dangers of landmines after the death of Diana Princess of Wales?
20 Which controversial politician Ann became Shadow Home Secretary in William Hague's 1999 Shadow Cabinet reshuffle?
21 Which colour precedes the name of Mr Adair, the firefighter who fought the Piper Alpha blaze in the 1980s?
22 What was the occupation of Nick Leeson when he brought down Barings?
23 Which disgraced Duchess had a satellite TV show called Surviving Life?
24 What was the nationality of the driver of the car in which Princess Diana died?
25 Who left his job on Radio 1 because he didn't want to work on Fridays?

## Answers

***Heoroes & Villains***

**1** Chicago. **2** Bush. **3** John F Kennedy. **4** Terry. **5** Taxes. **6** His wife. **7** Asia. **8** South Africa. **9** Jonathan. **10** Falklands. **11** Irish. **12** Strangler. **13** Lucan. **14** Robert Maxwell. **15** Space. **16** Blue Peter. **17** Ear. **18** Clinton. **19** Ginola. **20** Widdecombe. **21** Red. **22** Banker. **23** York. **24** French. **25** Chris Evans.

# Quiz 46 Pot Luck 23

1 Which Madeline became the first US Secretary of State?
2 Which former England soccer coach was banned from holding company directorships?
3 On TV, Baldrick was attracted to what type of vegetable?
4 Sir Alan Ayckbourn became famous for writing what?
5 Politician Enoch Powell graphically spoke of rivers of what?
6 On TV, what was Worzel Gummidge?
7 Which Tim co-wrote the musical Chess?
8 What type of cargo was carried by the stricken vessel the Torrey Canyon?
9 In 1983 which Tony became MP for Sedgefield?
10 Francis Lee represented England at which sport?
11 Which member of TV's Tiswas team impersonated Trevor McDonald as Trevor McDoughnut?
12 Writer Arnold Bennett gave his name to what type of food dish?
13 Which British Prime Minister resigned over the Suez Crisis?
14 Which Kara acted ignobly by flogging a saucy shot of Sophie Rhys-Jones?
15 Which tennis player had an acrimonious split with coach Tony Pickard in 1998?
16 In fiction, which bear was found at a London station?
17 Which country does golfer Ernie Els come from?
18 Which host of The Generation Game starred in the sitcom Home James?
19 In which country did The Flying Doctor usually do his rounds?
20 Diane Abbott has represented which party in parliament?
21 David Bowie was born in which decade of the century?
22 Dramatist Brendan Behan came from which country?
23 Who or what were Gropius and Le Corbusier?
24 Archbishop Makarios was president of which Mediterranean island?
25 Which Roy's comedy radio series about items in the news began in 1975?

## Answers

***Pot Luck 23***

**1** Albright. **2** Terry Venables. **3** Turnip. **4** Plays. **5** Blood. **6** A scarecrow. **7** Rice. **8** Oil. **9** Blair. **10** Soccer. **11** Lenny Henry. **12** Omelette. **13** Eden. **14** Noble. **15** Greg Rusedski. **16** Paddington. **17** South Africa. **18** Jim Davidson. **19** Australia. **20** Labour. **21** 40s. **22** Ireland. **23** Architects. **24** Cyprus. **25** Hudd.

# Quiz 47 TV Cops & Robbers

1 Which US cop show was set in Hill Street Station?
2 PC Rowan upheld law and order in Aidensfield in which series?
3 Which Inspector was famous for his red Jag, Crosswords and Wagner?
4 Which 80s hit was set on the island of Jersey?
5 Which John starred as Kavanagh QC?
6 Which crime series with Telly Savalas was known as The Lion Without a Mane in Germany?
7 Which 90s series was dubbed Between the Sheets because of its main character's personal affairs?
8 What was the profession of medieval sleuth Cadfael?
9 Where was the Vice tackled by Sonny Crockett and Ricardo Tubbs?
10 Which 80s/90s show once held a 30 minute slot three times a week?
11 Which unmarried female detective was created by Agatha Christie?
12 Which Lynda La Plante series featured DCI Jane Tennison?
13 In which country was Prisoner: Cell Block H set?
14 Which show featured private eye Jim Rockford?
15 Which Geordie actor Jimmy starred as Spender?
16 How was Ken Hutchinson known in the 70s series with David Soul and Paul Michael Glaser?
17 In which series did Robbie Coltrane play Fitz?
18 Which Hamish operated in Lochdubh?
19 On which channel was LA Law first broadcast in the UK?
20 Who was Dalziel's detective partner, from the novels by Reginald Hill?
21 Which series with Dennis Waterman and John Thaw got its name for the rhyming slang for Flying Squad?
22 What sort of Line was a police sitcom with Rowan Atkinson?
23 In which Dutch city did Van der Valk take place?
24 Which Cars provided police transport in the classic crime series of the 60s and 70s?
25 Which thriller series had a team of crime fighters with lots of electronic devices to help with their investigations?

## Answers

***TV Cops & Robbers***

**1** Hill Street Blues. **2** Heartbeat. **3** Morse. **4** Bergerac. **5** Thaw. **6** Kojak. **7** Between the Lines. **8** Monk. **9** Miami. **10** The Bill. **11** Miss Marple. **12** Prime Suspect. **13** Australia. **14** The Rockford Files. **15** Nail. **16** Hutch. **17** Cracker. **18** Macbeth. **19** ITV. **20** Pascoe. **21** The Sweeney. **22** Thin Blue. **23** Amsterdam. **24** Z Cars. **25** Bugs.

# Quiz 48 Pot Luck 24

1 Which ex Yorkshire cricketer was involved in a French assault case?
2 Who played Emma Peel in the 90s film version of The Avengers?
3 The Beeching report led to drastic reductions in which service?
4 Which veteran pop singer has the first names Roderick David?
5 Which TV 'Dame' has a friend called Madge Allsop?
6 After ruling as a monarch who became The Duke of Windsor?
7 Who liked Richard Burton so much that she married him twice?
8 In which decade did people last get the chance to see Haley's Comet?
9 With which sport is Colin Hendry associated?
10 Taggart was set in which city?
11 Which heroic nickname was given to statesman Harold Macmillan?
12 Dialling 100 on a BT telephone will put you through to which service?
13 The novel Airport was a best seller for which author?
14 Which female sang the Bond theme to Goldeneye?
15 Which Denis presents ITV's show of outtakes It'll be Alright On the Night?
16 The D Day landings took place in which country?
17 Who was the first man to fly in space?
18 What did teenager Anne Frank leave behind that was published after her death?
19 Which country did soccer keeper Jack Kelsey play for?
20 In her first TV appearances Ulrika Jonsson presented information about what?
21 Who was Bill Clinton's first vice president?
22 What does N stand for in NIMBY?
23 Which character is the most famous creation of Edgar Rice Burroughs?
24 Which Bruce declared he was Born In The USA?
25 Who was Kate's friend in the 80s sitcom with Susan Saint James and Jane Curtin?

## Answers

***Pot Luck 24***

**1** Geoff Boycott. **2** Uma Thurman. **3** Railway. **4** Rod Stewart. **5** Edna Everage. **6** Edward VIII. **7** Elizabeth Taylor. **8** 1980s. **9** Soccer. **10** Glasgow. **11** Supermac. **12** Operator. **13** Arthur Hailey. **14** Tina Turner. **15** Norden. **16** France. **17** Yuri Gagarin. **18** Diary. **19** Wales. **20** Weather. **21** Al Gore. **22** Not. **23** Tarzan. **24** Springsteen. **25** Allie.

# Quiz 49 Summer Sports

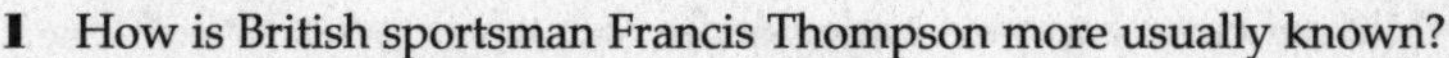

1 How is British sportsman Francis Thompson more usually known?
2 Which county did Brian Lara first play for in England?
3 Which 30 plus player won his first golf Major at the 1998 US Masters?
4 Which country does tennis player Pat Rafter come from?
5 Which team play cricket at home at Grace Road?
6 Which golfer was Europe's leading moneywinner of 1998?
7 Who started his breakaway cricket 'Circus' in the 70s?
8 How many times did Ivan Lendl win Wimbledon singles?
9 Which cricketing County added Lightning to their name?
10 What is Denise Lewis's main athletic event?
11 Which British golfer regained the US Masters in 1996?
12 Who won Wimbledon in 1998 after twice losing in the final?
13 How many teams reached the second round of cricket's 1999 World Cup?
14 Which country does Goran Ivanisevic come from?
15 In which month is The Derby run?
16 What sport is the winner of the Harry Vardon trophy playing?
17 What is the specialist fielding position of India's Moin Khan?
18 Which Mark was captain of the European 1999 Ryder Cup team?
19 Which British Fred was a Wimbledon singles winner in the 1930s?
20 Athlete Zola Budd was born in which country?
21 Who captained the West Indies in the 1999 World Cup?
22 What sport is staged at the Roland Garros?
23 Which golfer split from his coach David Leadbetter in 1998?
24 How many Brits were in the top ten seeds for Wimbledon 1999?
25 Which phone company has sponsored the Derby?

## Answers

***Summer Sports***

**1** Daley Thompson. **2** Warwickshire. **3** Mark O'Meara. **4** Australia. **5** Leicestershire. **6** Colin Montgomerie. **7** Kerry Packer. **8** Never. **9** Lancashire. **10** Heptathlon. **11** Nick Faldo. **12** Jana Novotna. **13** Six. **14** Croatia. **15** June. **16** Golf. **17** Wicket keeper. **18** James. **19** Perry. **20** South Africa. **21** Brian Lara. **22** Tennis. **23** Nick Faldo. **24** Two. **25** Vodafone.

# Quiz 50 Pot Luck 25

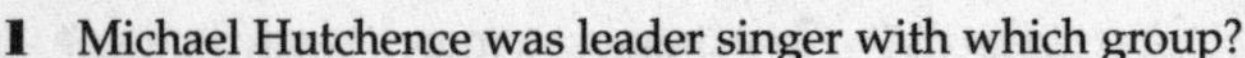

1 Michael Hutchence was leader singer with which group?
2 Foyle's in London sells what product?
3 In which film did Madonna play Breathless Mahoney?
4 In which sport did Phil Taylor become a world champion?
5 Which DJ became known as 'Fluff'?
6 Which caped crusader operated in Gotham City?
7 Aylesbury is the administrative centre of which English county?
8 Which controversial American sportsman had the first names Orenthal James?
9 Which Twins were involved in an incident in East End's Blind Beggar pub?
10 Which Ferry helped launch Roxy Music?
11 Which Yorkshire batsman played cricket for England from 1964 to 1981?
12 Demi Moore married which Bruce?
13 Marlon Brando was born in which decade of the century?
14 Ms Bhutto became Prime Minister in which state?
15 QWhich actress did John McEnroe marry?
16 Which decade received A Kick Up it in the form of a TV comedy sketch show?
17 Which bandleader Benny was 'The King of Swing'?
18 Which author JM wrote Peter Pan?
19 In 1987 Madonna filed for divorce from which husband?
20 Sean Kerley represented Britain at which sport?
21 In which decade did people last get the chance to see Haley's Comet?
22 Who was Kit's comedy partner in the 90s TV show?
23 What does the F stand for in FBI?
24 Who was Sue Cook's replacement on Crimewatch UK?
25 What type of sport is played at Gay Meadow?

## Answers

***Pot Luck 25***

**1** INXS. **2** Books. **3** Dick Tracy. **4** Darts. **5** Alan Freeman. **6** Batman. **7** Buckinghamshire. **8** O J Simpson. **9** Kray. **10** Bryan. **11** Geoff Boycott. **12** Willis. **13** 20s. **14** Pakistan. **15** Tatum O'Neal. **16** Eighties. **17** Goodman. **18** Barrie. **19** Sean Penn. **20** Hockey. **21** 1980s. **22** The Widow. **23** Federal. **24** Jill Dando. **25** Soccer.

# Quiz 51 90s Movies

Level 1 

1. Where are the Sliding Doors in the movie with Gwyneth Paltrow?
2. The action of Saving Private Ryan takes place during which war?
3. In which movie is Truman Burbank a popular character?
4. Which ex 007 played the Scottish villain in The Avengers?
5. In Doctor Dolittle Eddie Murphy has the ability to talk to whom?
6. Which Zorro film was released in 1998?
7. Which giant lizard was the star of the 1998 movie with Matthew Broderick?
8. Which star of ER played Batman in the 1997 Batman & Robin?
9. What was the first Spice Girls' film called?
10. Which part does Matt Damon play in Good Will Hunting?
11. Which 1996 remake replaced animated dogs with real ones and starred Glenn Close?
12. Which Fiennes starred in The English Patient?
13. Which 90s film of a Shakespeare play starred Leonardo DiCaprio and Claire Daines?
14. In which country of the UK was Trainspotting set?
15. In Batman Forever which villain was played by Jim Carrey?
16. What sort of animal was Babe?
17. Which Disney movie was based on the life of a native North American?
18. What was the occupation of Susan Sarandon in Dead Man Walking?
19. Which Story was the first ever completely computer animated movie?
20. Which knighted British pop star wrote the music for The Lion King?
21. Philadelphia became the first mainstream Hollywood film to tackle which disease?
22. Which blonde famously crossed her legs in Basic Instinct?
23. Who shared the title with Thelma in the 1991 film directed by Ridley Scott?
24. What sort of shop does Hugh Grant own in Notting Hill?
25. Val Kilmer played Jim Morrison in the 1991 movie about which rock band?

## Answers

***90s Movies***

**1** Tube Train. **2** WWII. **3** The Truman Show. **4** Sean Connery. **5** Animals. **6** The Mask of Zorro. **7** Godzilla. **8** George Clooney. **9** Spiceworld: The Movie. **10** Will Hunting **11** 101 Dalmatians. **12** Ralph. **13** Romeo & Juliet. **14** Scotland. **15** The Riddler. **16** Pig . **17** Pocahontas. **18** Nun. **19** Toy Story. **20** Elton John. **21** AIDS. **22** Sharon Stone. **23** Louise. **24** Bookshop. **25** The Doors.

# Quiz 52 Pot Luck 26

1 Which MP John got a soaking at the Brit Awards?
2 Which cookery writer produced a Summer and a Winter Collection which rocketed to the top of the bestseller list?
3 Dock Of The Bay was a hit for which singer after his death?
4 Which Welshman Colin became a world record holder in hurdling?
5 The movie Platoon was about war in which country?
6 What was the nickname of US President Dwight Eisenhower?
7 White and what other colour feature on the Canadian flag?
8 An accident in which sporting activity claimed Sonny Bono's life?
9 Which sitcom has had elderly characters called Foggy Dewhurst, Seymour Utterthwaite and Wally Batty?
10 In which sport did John Lloyd represented Britain?
11 What does the D stand for in a DIY store?
12 In the 90s Paul Keating was Prime Minister of which country?
13 Which Melvyn is a TV arts presenter and a novelist?
14 The deepwater port of Alicante was built in which country?
15 Darren Gough plays cricket for which county?
16 How many Likely Lads were there?
17 What are the international vehicle registration letters of Australia?
18 With which sport is Corey Pavin associated?
19 First World War flying ace Manfred von Richtofen was what coloured Baron?
20 Quick Draw McGraw was what kind of cartoon creature?
21 Which of the Marx Brothers never spoke on film?
22 Tom Thumb and Little Gem were developed as types of what?
23 Virginia Bottomley has represented which party in parliament?
24 Which British boxer successfully defended his WBC heavyweight title in 1997?
25 Ray Charles was associated with which musical instrument?

**Answers**

***Pot Luck 26***

**1** Prescott. **2** Delia Smith. **3** Otis Redding. **4** Jackson. **5** Vietnam. **6** Ike. **7** Red. **8** Skiing. **9** Last of the Summer Wine. **10** Tennis. **11** Do. **12** Australia. **13** Bragg. **14** Spain. **15** Yorkshire. **16** Two. **17** AUS. **18** Golf. **19** Red. **20** Horse. **21** Harpo. **22** Lettuce. **23** Conservative. **24** Lennox Lewis. **25** Piano.

# Quiz 53 World Tour

1 Which city is called Kapstad in Afrikaans?
2 Which language apart from English is an official language of Canada?
3 Okinawa is a volcano in which country?
4 In which country is an Afghani a unit of currency?
5 Lesotho is a southern African kingdom surrounded by which country?
6 Madagascar is off which coast of Africa?
7 Antigua and Barbuda lie in which Sea?
8 Ottawa is which country's capital?
9 The Chinese city of Beijing was previously known as what?
10 Argentina's east coast lies on which ocean?
11 Which South American Canal joins the Atlantic to the Pacific oceans?
12 What is the largest country in South America?
13 Which two letters follow the name of the US capital Washington?
14 What is the Great Barrier Reef made from?
15 Which Chinese landmark was viewed from space?
16 For most of the 20th Century St Petersburg has been named after which Soviet hero?
17 Which US holiday state has the Everglades National Park?
18 How was the Cote d'Ivoire previously known?
19 Which northerly US state, one of four beginning with A, joined the Union in 1959?
20 In the USA what is a zip code?
21 The Victoria Falls are shared between Zimbabwe and which other country beginning with the same letter?
22 Which US state is famous for Disneyland and the film industry?
23 Manhattan is a part of which US city?
24 What are the Islas Canarias in English?
25 Which Australian province has New at the beginning of its name?

## Answers

***World Tour***

**1** Cape Town. **2** French. **3** Japan. **4** Afghanistan. **5** South Africa. **6** East. **7** Caribbean. **8** Canada. **9** Peking. **10** Atlantic. **11** Panama. **12** Brazil. **13** DC. **14** Coral. **15** Great Wall of China. **16** Lenin. **17** Florida. **18** Ivory Coast. **19** Alaska. **20** Post code. **21** Zambia. **22** California. **23** New York. **24** Canary Islands. **25** South Wales.

# Quiz 54 Pot Luck 27

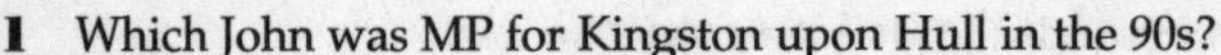

1. Which John was MP for Kingston upon Hull in the 90s?
2. Who wrote the children's classic The Wind In The Willows?
3. Scene of an 80s soccer crowd disaster, Heysel Stadium is in which country?
4. James Baumgarner changed his name slightly to become which actor?
5. The majority of London buses are what colour?
6. What does the D stand for in CND?
7. Nicholas Cage was born in which decade of the century?
8. Which TV sleuth was played by Jeremy Brett?
9. Eamon de Valera was Prime Minister of which country?
10. Which car manufacturer introduced the Eclat, Elan and Elite models?
11. A crash in what type of vehicle claimed John Denver's life?
12. Which soccer team does Zoe Ball follow?
13. In the 90s most Bank Holidays fall on which day?
14. How were contrasting comedy duo Syd and Eddie better known?
15. In which decade did Star Wars hit the movie screens?
16. Which British leader famously said, "This was their finest hour"?
17. Which country does cricketer Stuart MacGill play for?
18. In which country was Karl Marx born?
19. Who was the male lead in the 30s song and dance film Top Hat?
20. Malcolm Little replaced his surname with which letter of the alphabet?
21. Which Birds were Beryl and Sandra on TV?
22. Which motorway links London to Winchester?
23. Danny McGrain represented Scotland at which sport?
24. In the 60s, in which Asian country did a Cultural Revolution take place?
25. In which branch of the arts did Dame Alicia Markova find fame?

## Answers

***Pot Luck 27***

**1** Prescott. **2** Kenneth Grahame. **3** Belgium. **4** James Garner. **5** Red. **6** Disarmament. **7** 60s. **8** Sherlock Holmes. **9** Ireland. **10** Lotus. **11** Plane. **12** Man Utd. **13** Monday. **14** Little & Large. **15** 70s. **16** Winston Churchill. **17** Australia. **18** Germany. **19** Fred Astaire. **20** X. **21** Liver Birds. **22** M3. **23** Soccer. **24** China. **25** Ballet.

# Quiz 55 Bands

1 Which band included Phil Collins and Peter Gabriel?
2 Which band recorded the album The Joshua Tree?
3 Marti Pellow was the lead singer with which group?
4 In the 70s who put A Message In A Bottle?
5 Who fronted the Boomtown Rats?
6 Which boy band had No 1s with Babe and Sure?
7 Dave Gilmore and Roger Waters were in which long lasting group?
8 Which group became the first to have the word Pumpkins in their name?
9 Which group flew into the Hotel California?
10 Which Paul was in Style Council and Jam?
11 Who did Vic Reeves sing with?
12 Which US Boys band featured three members of the Wilson family?
13 Which band recorded the album Parallel Lines?
14 How many members were there in the Eurythmics?
15 Which movement did The Sex Pistols begin?
16 What word was replaced by the letter T in T. Rex?
17 How many brothers were in the original Jackson family line up?
18 How many boys were there in the Pet Shop Boys?
19 What was Adam backed by?
20 Which band actually had Noddy as lead singer?
21 What did the letter O stand for in ELO?
22 Pictures of Matchstick Men was the first hit for which veteran rockers?
23 Teeny boppers The Bay City Rollers were from which country?
24 Which band featured Paul McGuigan on bass?
25 Which all time great band featured Harrison and Starkey?

## Answers

***Bands***

**1** Genesis. **2** U2. **3** Wet Wet Wet. **4** Police. **5** Bob Geldof. **6** Take That. **7** Pink Floyd. **8** Smashing Pumpkins. **9** The Eagles. **10** Weller. **11** The Wonder Stuff. **12** The Beach Boys. **13** Blondie. **14** Two. **15** Punk. **16** Tyrannnosaurus. **17** Five. **18** Two. **19** The Ants. **20** Slade. **21** Orchestra. **22** Status Quo. **23** Teeny boppers. **24** Oasis. **25** The Beatles.

# Quiz 56 Pot Luck 28

Level 1 

1 In 1998 Freddie Shepherd resigned as club chairman of which soccer club?
2 Which parenting guru Doctor wrote Baby and Child Care?
3 Who was in charge of the Merry Men in the role reversal children's sitcom about Robin Hood?
4 At the end of the 20th C how many UK monarchs had been called Charles?
5 In which decade did Eric Morecambe die?
6 In pop music, what did the Police find In A Bottle?
7 In book and film what was St Trinian's?
8 Paul McGrath played soccer for which international team?
9 Dutch born spy Mata Hari was a dancer in which European city?
10 Which film was about the Olympic Games of 1924?
11 President Kennedy international airport is in which US city?
12 Which country does opera diva Lesley Garrett come from?
13 Whose name was part of a TV Experience where she would have certainly disapproved of the show's content?
14 Norwich is the administrative centre of which English county?
15 Louis B Mayer had which job in the film industry?
16 Australian singer Nellie Melba had a dish named after her containing which fruit?
17 Who was Speaker of the House of Commons for the greater part of the 90s?
18 With which sport is Nick Price associated?
19 In which city was the Marco Polo airport built?
20 Which entertainer said, "Nice to see you, to see you - nice"?
21 Which Raymond wrote the novel The Big Sleep?
22 In 1990 Lithuania declared its independence from what?
23 At the end of the 20th C how many UK monarchs had been called George?
24 Who teamed up with Hanna to form a studio producing cartoon films?
25 What is the last word of the James Herriot book It Shouldn't Happen To A ______?

## Answers

***Pot Luck 28***

**1** Newcastle. **2** Spock. **3** Maid Marian. **4** Two. **5** 80s. **6** Message. **7** School. **8** Republic Of Ireland. **9** Paris. **10** Chariots of Fire. **11** New York. **12** England. **13** Mary Whitehouse. **14** Norfolk. **15** Producer. **16** Peach. **17** Betty Boothroyd. **18** Golf. **19** Venice. **20** Bruce Forsyth. **21** Chandler. **22** USSR. **23** Six. **24** Barbera. **25** Vet.

# Quiz 57 Leaders

1 Bob Hawke and Paul Keating were Prime Ministers of which country?
2 In which country did Gadaffi seize power in the 60s?
3 Who was British Prime Minister at the time of the Gulf War?
4 What was the last name of Ferdinand and Imelda, leaders of the Philippines?
5 Who was Prime Minister of the UK throughout the 80s?
6 Who seized power in Cuba in the late 50s?
7 Which words did Winston Churchill use to describe the East and West divide in Europe?
8 Diana, Princess of Wales led the campaign against the use of which explosive devices?
9 Haile Selassie ruled in which country?
10 How many general elections did Mrs Thatcher win?
11 Which 90s leader said, "I did not have sexual relations with that woman"?
12 Who was the leader of the brutal Khmer Rouge government?
13 In which decade was Nelson Mandela sent to prison in South Africa?
14 What did the letter A stand for in Mandela's ANC?
15 Who became Britain's youngest Prime Minister of the century?
16 The death of which General led to the restoration of the monarchy in Spain?
17 In the 90s Silvio Berlusconi won the general election in which country?
18 David Ben-Gurion was the first Prime Minister of which new state?
19 In which country did Lech Walesa lead the conflict against the communist government?
20 Which Chris was the last British governor of Hong Kong?
21 Who was known as Il Duce ?
22 Ayatollah Khomeini ordered a death threat on which UK based writer?
23 Which US President had a daughter named Chelsea?
24 Nicholas II was the last person to hold which title in Russia?
25 Idi Amin became president of which country?

## Answers

***Leaders***

**1** Australia. **2** Libya. **3** John Major. **4** Marcos. **5** Margaret Thatcher. **6** Castro. **7** Iron Curtain. **8** Land mines. **9** Ethiopia. **10** Three. **11** Bill Clinton. **12** Pol Pot. **13** 60s. **14** African. **15** Tony Blair. **16** Franco. **17** Italy. **18** Israel. **19** Poland. **20** Patten. **21** Mussolini. **22** Salman Rushdie. **23** Clinton. **24** Tsar. **25** Uganda.

# Quiz 58 Pot Luck 29

1 Rik Mayall suffered a serious accident in the 90s involving what type of vehicle?
2 In which decade was Prince Charles born?
3 Which chef has a restaurant called City Rhodes?
4 In which British city was Dyce airport built?
5 Who set out his political views in Mein Kampf?
6 In the 70s Arab countries reduced exports of what to the West?
7 Which American city is the site of an annual 500 mile motor race?
8 Which sitcom about an army hospital in Korea was transmitted in the UK without the canned laughter of the US version ?
9 Who wrote the controversial book The Satanic Verses?
10 Which fictional bear thought he had "very little brain"?
11 Phil DeFreitas played for England at which sport?
12 Which Tory minister Parkinson resigned in an 80s scandal?
13 What does the E stand for in the NEC established at Birmingham?
14 Michael Caine was born in which decade of the century?
15 In the 80s what type of environmentally damaging rain was causing concern?
16 Playwright Arthur Miller was married to which famous blonde actress?
17 US bandleader Glenn Miller disappeared after setting off on a journey in what type of transport?
18 Which member of The Goons wrote Adolf Hitler, My Part in his Downfall?
19 John Betjeman was famous for writing what type of works?
20 In the 90s Alan Beith has represented which party in parliament?
21 Which A road in Britain used to be known as the Great North Road?
22 Which famous father had daughters called Beatrice and Eugenie?
23 Jacqueline Du Pre was associated with which musical instrument?
24 In the sitcom if Zoe Angell was May what month was Alec Callender?
25 Which country does motor racing's Jarno Trulli come from?

## Answers

***Pot Luck 29***

**1** Quad bike. **2** 40s. **3** Gary Rhodes. **4** Aberdeen. **5** Hitler. **6** Oil. **7** Indianapolis. **8** M*A*S*H. **9** Salman Rushdie. **10** Winnie-The-Pooh. **11** Cricket. **12** Cecil. **13** Exhibition. **14** 30s. **15** Acid rain. **16** Marilyn Monroe. **17** Plane. **18** Spike Milligan. **19** Poems. **20** Lib/Dem. **21** A6. **22** Prince Andrew. **23** Cello. **24** December. **25** Italy.

# Quiz 59 Personalities

1 What is David Bailey famous for?
2 What colour is Barbara Cartland's most seen in?
3 Which Max is famous as a PR man?
4 Dr Stefan Buczacki is an expert in what?
5 Which large opera star launched a perfume for men named after him?
6 What is the name of Joan Collins novelist sister?
7 Which part of his body did goalkeeper David Seaman insure for £1 million?
8 Which actor Kenneth was Emma Thompson's first husband?
9 Who is Gloria Hunniford's TV presenter daughter?
10 Brooklyn Beckham is the son of which Spice Girl ?
11 What is Hillary Clinton's daughter called?
12 What type of dance was Rudolf Nureyev famous for?
13 How did US Ambassador Shirley Temple Black earn fame as a child?
14 Which singer Cleo is married to Johnny Dankworth?
15 What is the name of Wendy Turner's older TV presenter sister?
16 What is the name of the MEP who is Neil Kinnock's wife?
17 Unlike his name suggests, who is the oldest daily presenter on BBC Radio 2?
18 Which Yorkshire cricketer Geoffrey was born the same day as Manfred Mann?
19 What is the birthday of Mario Andretti, who only has a real birthday every four years?
20 Which musical was based on Wild West star Annie Oakley?
21 Whose has a catchphrase "You'll like this - not a lot!"?
22 Which comedy duo were 'the one with the glasses and the one with the short fat hairy legs'?
23 Which cricket commentator was known as Johnners?
24 Which Prime Minister's wife became a Dame in the 1999 Queen's birthday honours?
25 Eileen Drewery was a spiritual healer who helped which England football manager?

## Answers

***Personalities***

**1** Photography. **2** Pink. **3** Clifford. **4** Gardening. **5** Luciano Pavarotti. **6** Jackie. **7** Hands. **8** Branagh. **9** Caron Keating. **10** Victoria. **11** Chelsea. **12** Ballet. **13** Film star. **14** Laine. **15** Anthea. **16** Glenys. **17** Jimmy Young. **18** Boycott. **19** 29th February. **20** Annie Get Your Gun. **21** Paul Daniels. **22** Morecambe & Wise. **23** Bryan Johnston. **24** Norma Major. **25** Glenn Hoddle.

# Quiz 60 Pot Luck 30

**1** Dana International won the Eurovision Song Contest for which country?
**2** The disastrous poison gas leak at Bhopal took place in which country?
**3** In the US what became known as a 'greenback'?
**4** In advertising PAL was said to prolong active what?
**5** In which country is Ciampino airport?
**6** In Julie Andrews first film she played which nanny?
**7** Who or what was Piper Alpha?
**8** What is the main colour on the Chinese flag?
**9** The UK's Summer Bank Holiday falls in which month?
**10** Sir Anthony Hopkins was born in which part of the UK?
**11** The TV special Men Behaving Very Badly Indeed concentrated on the lads' fixation with which Australian singer/actress?
**12** Which stage musical was set in the Paris Opera House?
**13** With which sport is Cedric Pioline associated?
**14** Carlisle is the administrative centre of which English county?
**15** Which two words did Churchill use to dub the Battle of Britain pilots?
**16** What is the first name of Zimbabwean statesman Mugabe?
**17** On what type of vehicle did Rupert Murdoch remarry in 1999?
**18** Claude Oscar Monet was famous for what ?
**19** Lord Mountbatten was murdered off the coast of which country?
**20** In the 80s Shirley Williams left which political party to launch the
**21** SDP?
Freddie Laker set up low cost travel in what type of transport?
**22** In which decade did Elvis Presley die?
**23** Mike Denness captained England in which sport?
**24** The deepwater port of Gdansk was developed in which country?
**25** Which veteran stand up comic Bob had his own show On the Spot in the mid 90s?

## Answers

***Pot Luck 30***
**1** Israel. **2** India. **3** Dollar. **4** Life. **5** Italy. **6** Mary Poppins. **7** An oil rig. **8** Red. **9** August. **10** Wales. **11** Kylie Minogue. **12** The Phantom Of The Opera. **13** Tennis. **14** Cumbria. **15** The Few. **16** Robert. **17** Yacht. **18** Paintings. **19** Ireland. **20** Labour. **21** Aeroplanes. **22** 70s. **23** Cricket. **24** Poland. **25** Monkhouse.

# Quiz 61 TV Famous Faces

1 Which comedian Paul shares his surname with campaigner Mary?
2 Which Royal read one of his own stories on Jackanory in 1983?
3 Which Kenny's shows were "in the best possible taste"?
4 Which June was married to Terry in a series of classic sitcoms?
5 Which Alan was a character created by Steve Coogan?
6 Which New Faces winner created the characters PC Ganga and
Theophilus P Wildebeeste?
7 Which female Radio DJ succeeded Emma Forbes on Live & Kicking?
8 Which actress Alex played Moll Flanders then moved to the US for ER?
Which former tennis player and sports presenter hosted the BBC
9 coverage of the last Royal Wedding of the century?
Which Pamela was the female comedian on Not the Nine O'Clock News?
10 Which Sean starred as Sharpe in the series about the Napoleonic Wars?
11 Which pop drummer narrated Thomas the Tank Engine on TV?
12 Dawn French played the Vicar of which English village in the sitcom of
13 the same name?
14 Which comedienne and writer Victoria had a series As Seen on TV?
In which Files would Mulder and Scully appear?
15 Which knighted Cabinet Secretary was played by Nigel Hawthorne in
16 Yes Minister?
17 Colin Firth played Darcy in which classic Jane Austen adaptation in 1995?
18 Which four brothers, Joe, Mark, Paul and Stephen, starred in the
drama set in Ireland, The Hanging Gale?
19 Which Attenborough brother presented The Private Life of Plants?
20 What was the occupation of Jemma Redgrave in the Victorian drama
21 Bramwell?
22 Which Paula featured on Cue Paula on The Big Breakfast?
23 Which Jonathan replaced Barry Norman on BBC's Film programme in
1999?
24 Which newsreader Trevor received a knighthood in the last Queen's
Birthday Honours of the century?
25 Which Nick was the first presenter of Crimewatch UK?

## Answers

***TV Famous Faces***

**1** Whitehouse. **2** Prince Charles. **3** Everett. **4** Whitfield. **5** Partridge. **6** Lenny Henry. **7** Zoe Ball. **8** Kingston. **9** Sue Barker. **10** Stephenson. **11** Bean. **12** Ringo Starr. **13** Dibley. **14** Wood. **15** The X Files. **16** Sir Humphrey. **17** Pride & Prejudice . **18** McGann. **19** David. **20** Doctor. **21** Yates. **22** Ross. **23** McDonald. **24** Ross. **25** Jack.

# Quiz 62 Pot Luck 31

1. Which newspaper was involved in the Jonathan Aitken perjury affair?
2. Who did Kevin Lloyd play in The Bill?
3. Robert Carlyle was born in which decade of the century?
4. Which cult comedy team first performed the Dead Parrot Sketch?
5. Shimon Peres was Prime Minister of which country?
6. In police matters what does the D stand for in CID?
7. Which actor played Forrest Gump?
8. Which country does soccer star Tore Andre Flo play for?
9. Which Douglas wrote The Hitch Hiker's Guide To The Galaxy?
10. What is the Queen's favourite breed of dog?
11. What kind of creature is Muppet Fozzie?
12. In which decade was the General Strike in Britain?
13. Who wrote the novels Sons And Lovers and Women In Love?
14. Pavarotti singing Nessun Dorma was used in 1990 alongside broadcasts of which sport?
15. Anna Pavlova found fame in what field?
16. In which film did Gary Oldman get to act Vicious?
17. Which country has D as its international vehicle registration letter?
18. What is the occupation of Maeve Binchy?
19. Who had a 90s No 1 with Forever Love?
20. Wade Dooley represented England at which sport?
21. In which country was Prince Philip born?
22. What is the first name of the chef who opened Mosimann's in London in 1988?
23. Glenda Jackson, Andre Previn and Shirley Bassey were famous guests on which comedy duo's famous shows?
24. What did John Paul Getty make his fortune from?
25. On a computer keyboard what letter is far left on the second row of letters?

## Answers

***Pot Luck 31***

**1** The Guardian. **2** Tosh Lines. **3** 60s. **4** Monty Python. **5** Israel. **6** Department. **7** Tom Hanks. **8** Denmark. **9** Adams. **10** Corgi. **11** Bear. **12** 20s. **13** D H Lawrence. **14** Football. **15** Ballet. **16** Sid and Nancy. **17** Germany. **18** Novelist. **19** Gary Barlow. **20** Rugby Union. **21** Greece. **22** Anton. **23** Morecambe & Wise. **24** Oil. **25** A.

# Quiz 63 Darts & Snooker

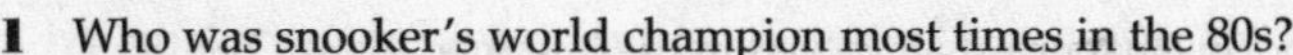

**1** Who was snooker's world champion most times in the 80s?
**2** What does the letter O stand for in BDO?
**3** Cliff Thorburn - 'The Grinder' - came from which country?
**4** Which ball is worth one point less than a black?
**5** Which John scored the first nine-dart 501 in a major tournament?
**6** Moving anti clockwise on a dartboard which number is after 1?
**7** Which snooker player was nicknamed 'Whirlwind'?
**8** Which Sunday paper ran a darts competition from the 40s to the early 90s?
**9** In which decade was snooker's World Championship first staged at The Crucible?
**10** Which Leighton became darts' first World Professional Championship?
**11** Who took over No 1 ranking from Stephen Hendry?
**12** Which English darts player was awarded an MBE in 1989?
**13** Which London soccer team is Barry Hearne connected with?
**14** Dennis Priestley plays for which country?
**15** Which snooker player was known as 'Hurricane'?
**16** On a dartboard which number is directly opposite the 6?
**17** Which 'veteran' sensationally beat Stephen Hendry in the first round of the 1998 World Championship?
**18** What's the smallest three-dart score made with three trebles all in different even numbers?
**19** Which player broke up Hendry's World Championship monopoly of the early 90s?
**20** What does the B stand for in the WPBSA?
**21** Which darts player is known as 'Barney Rubble'?
**22** Who is Gary Lineker's big mate in the snooker world?
**23** Can you raise a glass and name the sponsor of the WDC Darts Championship?
**24** Which ball is worth one point more than a blue?
**25** Who is the first Ken to win snooker's World Championship?

## Answers

***Darts & Snooker***

**1** Steve Davis. **2** Organisation. **3** Canada. **4** Pink. **5** Lowe. **6** 20. **7** Jimmy White. **8** News Of The World. **9** 70s. **10** Rees. **11** John Higgins. **12** Eric Bristow. **13** Leyton Orient. **14** England. **15** Alex Higgins. **16** 1. **17** Jimmy White. **18** 36. **19** John Parrott. **20** Billiards. **21** Raymond Van Barneveld. **22** Willie Thorne. **23** Skol. **24** Pink. **25** Docherty.

# Quiz 64 Pot Luck 32

1 The Louise Woodward affair was tried in which country?
2 In its early days what was offered for sale "in any colour as long as it's black"?
3 Which Russian leader had a pronounced birthmark on his forehead?
4 Which Joe wrote the play Entertaining Mr Sloane?
5 Which country was readmitted into international rugby fixtures in 1993?
6 Which future superstar Robin played Mork in Mork and Mindy?
7 Which Private magazine led the 60s satire boom?
8 David Owen, now Lord Owen, was trained in what profession before becoming a politician ?
9 In the world of plants and gardening what type of Royal Society is the RHS?
10 Tony Doyle represented Britain at which sport?
11 What do players try to collect in the board game Trivial Pursuit?
12 What is the name of Neil Kinnock's wife?
13 The influential Russian figure Rasputin followed which profession?
14 Mary Robinson became the first president of which country in 1990?
15 Which nickname did fighter Ray Robinson have?
16 Geoff Boycott has had which kind of plant named after him?
17 Paul Boateng has represented which party in parliament?
18 Which royal married Lord Snowdon?
19 In the cookery world, what relation is Albert to Michel Roux?
20 Mrs Merton took her chat show - and her pensioner audience - to which US entertainment venue for a series of her shows?
21 Warren Beatty was born in which decade of the century?
22 With which sport is Grant Hill associated?
23 Maud Grimes is a character from which soap?
24 Brian Mulrooney was Prime Minister of which country in the 80s and 90s?
25 Early in the century who wrote the novels Lord Jim and Heart of Darkness?

**Answers**

***Pot Luck 32***

**1** United States. **2** Motor car. **3** Gorbachev. **4** Orton. **5** South Africa. **6** Williams. **7** Eye. **8** Doctor. **9** Horticultural. **10** Cycling. **11** Wedges. **12** Glenys. **13** Monk. **14** Ireland. **15** Sugar. **16** Rose. **17** Labour. **18** Princess Margaret. **19** Brother. **20** Las Vegas. **21** 30s. **22** Basketball. **23** Coronation Street. **24** Canada. **25** Joseph Conrad.

# Quiz 65 Actresses

1 Who cried during her Oscar winning speech for Shakespeare in Love?
2 Who starred in Mermaids and went to No 1 with The Shoop Shoop Song?
3 Which pop star Lisa made her movie debut in Swing?
4 Sigourney Weaver in Alien II and Demi Moore in G.I. Jane shaved what?
5 Who won an Oscar for her first film role in Mary Poppins?
6 Which actress and fitness guru Jane married CNN mogul Ted Turner?
7 Which actress appeared on the cinema poster for Titanic?
8 In The Seven Year Itch whose white skirt is billowing around because of hot air blowing up from a grating?
9 Which superstar was nicknamed 'The Swedish Sphinx'?
10 What is Goldie Hawn's real name?
11 How is Mary Elizabeth Spacek known in the film world?
12 Who was cast as Princess Leia in Star Wars after her film debut in Shampoo with Warren Beatty?
13 Melanie Griffith married which star of Evita and The Mask of Zorro?
14 Which Oscar winning black actress played the medium Oda Mae Brown in Ghost?
15 For which role did Michelle Pfeiffer wear 63 catsuits in Batman returns?
16 Which plant was Uma Thurman named after in Batman & Robin?
17 Which actress has children called Scout and Rumer from her marriage to Bruce Willis?
18 In which 1979 film with Bo Derek was the title simply a number?
19 Which actress who starred in Fatal Attraction won a Tony for her role in Sunset Boulevard on Broadway?
20 Which star of Sliding Doors split with fiance Brad Pitt in 1997?
21 Which wife of Paul Newman played Tom Hanks mother in Philadelphia?
22 Which Ms Smith played the Mother Superior opposite Whoopi Goldberg in Sister Act?
23 Which Redgrave was Oscar nominated for Gods and Monsters?
24 Janet Leigh played one of the most horrific scenes where in a motel?
25 Which French sex symbol became an animal rights campaigner later in her life?

**Answers**

***Actresses***

**1** Gwyneth Paltrow. **2** Cher. **3** Stansfield. **4** Heads. **5** Julie Andrews. **6** Fonda. **7** Kate Winslet. **8** Marilyn Monroe. **9** Greta Garbo. **10** Goldie Hawn. **11** Sissy. **12** Carrie Fisher. **13** Antonio Banderas. **14** Whoopi Goldberg. **15** Catwoman. **16** Ivy. **17** Demi Moore. **18** 10. **19** Glenn Close. **20** Gwyneth Paltrow. **21** Joanne Woodward. **22** Maggie. **23** Lynn. **24** Shower. **25** Brigitte Bardot.

# Quiz 66 Pot Luck 33

1 Which soccer player David became part of the campaign against landmines?
2 Who played Steed in the 90s film version of The Avengers?
3 In the 80s Afghanistan was occupied by troops from which country?
4 What does the A stand for in BAFTA?
5 In the 60s in which American city were you supposed to wear flowers in your hair?
6 The song Bright Eyes is about what kind of animals?
7 The Aga Khan is renowned as a breeder of which animals?
8 What is the trade of Martin Amis?
9 Which company launched the first personal stereo system?
10 Peter Elliott represented Britain at which sport?
11 Which character did Peter Adamson play in Coronation Street?
12 Dennis Bergkamp has a fear of travelling in what?
13 What was the first name of Franklin D Roosevelt's wife and US First Lady?
14 What letter does a car driver display until gaining a full licence?
15 A worldwide ban on what was introduced in 1990 to try and save the elephant population?
16 Helena Bonham-Carter was born in which decade of the century?
17 Which country does cricketer Jacques Kallis play for?
18 Which comedy actress and wife of Lenny Henry played the sinister lead roles in Murder Most Horrid?
19 Which motorway links London and Leeds?
20 Sitar player Ravi Shankar came from which country?
21 What was the profession of sportsman Sir Gordon Richards?
22 Where was Dame Kiri Te Kanawa born?
23 Which soccer club did Alf Garnett support?
24 In the 80s sitcom what was the occupation of Alan B'Stard as played by Rik Mayall?
25 Jesus To A Child was a 90s No 1 for which solo singer?

## Answers

***Pot Luck 33***

**1** Ginola. **2** Ralph Fiennes. **3** USSR. **4** Arts. **5** San Francisco. **6** Rabbits. **7** Racehorses. **8** Novelist. **9** Sony. **10** Athletics. **11** Len Fairclough. **12** Aeroplanes. **13** Eleanor. **14** L. **15** Ivory trading. **16** 60s. **17** South Africa. **18** Dawn French. **19** M1. **20** India. **21** Jockey. **22** New Zealand. **23** West Ham. **24** MP. **25** George Michael.

# Quiz 67 Books

1 Which Book of Records was first published in 1955?
2 Which book by Peter Benchley made into a film by Spielberg, was originally called The Summer of the Shark?
3 Which tennis player Martina wrote a novel called Total Zone?
4 Which MP Tony wrote lengthy diaries of his years in office?
5 James Alfred Wright was better known as James who when writing about his experiences as a Yorkshire vet?
6 In Peter Pan what sort of animal was Nana?
7 What was Thomas Harris's sequel to Silence of the Lambs called?
8 Cornish restaurateur Rick Stein's books are about what type of food?
9 Which novelist Barbara was Princess Diana's step grandmother?
10 Which King's novels such as Carrie and The Shining have been made into successful films?
11 Who is Dalziel's detective partner as created by Reginald Hill?
12 Which offbeat fictional detective was created by R.D. Wingfield and was played on TV by David Jason?
13 Which crime writing Dame is the best selling fiction author in the world?
14 What was the name of Martin Amis's famous author father?
15 What is the name of Joan Collins novelist sister?
16 Novelist Jeffrey Archer was once Chairman of which political party?
17 Which Jaguar driving, crossword fanatic detective was created by Colin Dexter?
18 Whose autobiography, written with the help of Andrew Morton was written about the Clinton White House Scandal?
19 Jamie Oliver wrote a book about his work called The Naked what?
20 Which tycoon and entrepreneur in the fields of music, airlines and cola wrote Losing My Virginity?
21 Which Bill wrote Notes From a Small Island?
22 Pongo was one of 101 what in the novel by Dodie Smith?
23 The novel The Sheep Pig was turned into a movie called what?
24 Which Cooper followed Polo and Riders with Score!?
25 One of the Famous Five was what type of pet animal?

## Answers

***Books***

**1** Guinness. **2** Jaws. **3** Navratilova. **4** Benn. **5** Herriot. **6** Dog. **7** Hannibal. **8** Fish. **9** Cartland. **10** Stephen. **11** Pascoe. **12** Frost. **13** Agatha Christie. **14** Kingsley. **15** Jackie. **16** Tory. **17** Morse. **18** Monica Lewinsky. **19** Chef. **20** Richard Branson. **21** Bryson. **22** Dalmatians. **23** Babe. **24** Jilly. **25** Dog.

# Quiz 68 Pot Luck 34

1 Which Derek was finally cleared of murder 45 years after he was hanged?
2 Which Godfrey was an England wicket keeper?
3 In a Spice Girls hit what follows "swing it, shake it, move it..."?
4 What is the main colour featured on the flag of Denmark?
5 What did Britain stage in 1908 and 1948?
6 What does the letter S stand for in SAE?
7 Who appeared with Peter Cook in Not Only... But Also?
8 Which Tory became Deputy Prime Minister in 1995?
9 The world's longest tunnel the Seikan tunnel was built in which country?
10 Rachel Heyhoe Flint played for England at which sport?
11 Garrett Fitzgerald was Prime Minister of which country?
12 Who wrote the thriller novel The Day Of The Jackal?
13 With which sport is Marcelo Salas associated?
14 Albert and Michael are which brothers in the world of food?
15 Magician Paul Daniels was born in which decade?
16 Michael Dukakis missed out in his attempts to become President of where?
17 The American Not Necessarily the News was based on which UK show with Pamela Stephenson, Mel Smith and others?
18 In the 80s which country was responsible for ethnic attacks on the Kurds?
19 Despite owning an airline and a railway, Richard Branson makes headlines travelling by what means?
20 What was Stalin's first name?
21 Which Shroud was declared a fake in the 80s?
22 Which West Indian cricketer had the first names Garfield St Auburn?
23 What was the Sopwith Camel?
24 Which Rugby League side became Warriors in the late 90s?
25 Remembrance Day is in which month?

## Answers

***Pot Luck 34***

**1** Bentley. **2** Evans. **3** Make it. **4** Red. **5** Olympic Games. **6** Stamped. **7** Dudley Moore. **8** Michael Heseltine. **9** Japan. **10** Cricket. **11** Ireland. **12** Frederick Forsyth. **13** Soccer. **14** Roux. **15** 20s. **16** USA. **17** Not the Nine O'Clock News. **18** Iraq. **19** Hot-air balloon. **20** Joseph. **21** Turin. **22** Sobers. **23** Plane. **24** Wigan. **25** November.

# Quiz 69 Musical Superstars

1 Who recorded the Immaculate Collection?
2 What was certainly the debut album by Oasis?
3 Which Lionel sang with The Commodores?
4 In which US state was Elvis Presley's mansion?
5 What was the title of the first album from The Spice Girls?
6 I Will Always Love You was an early 90s hit for which superstar?
7 Alan, Jay and Donny were part of which 70s group?
8 Who first charted as a solo performer with Careless Whisper?
9 Which group is made up of Gibbs?
10 What instrument does Charlie Watts play in the Rolling Stones?
11 Who was the first to leave Take That?
12 Who teamed up with Barbra Streisand for Tell Him?
13 Who was the original lead singer with The Supremes?
14 How many people were in the original Queen?
15 Who became the most famous group formed in Colchester?
16 In which decade was Elton John's original Candle In The Wind a hit?
17 Baker, Bruce and Clapton formed which 60s supergroup?
18 In 1996 Robert Hoskins was convicted of stalking which star?
19 Which supergroup contains The Edge?
20 Who has recorded with Elton John, Queen, Lisa Stansfield and Toby Bourke?
21 Which band produced the mega selling album Rumours?
22 What was the first All Saints record to sell a million?
23 Visions Of Love was the first British top ten hit for which female superstar?
24 Which Hotel gave Elvis his first British chart hit?
25 Which group wrote the songs for the movie Saturday Night Fever?

## Answers

***Musical Superstars***

**1** Madonna. **2** Definitely Maybe. **3** Richie. **4** Tennessee. **5** Spice. **6** Whitney Houston. **7** The Osmonds. **8** George Michael. **9** The Bee Gees. **10** Drums. **11** Robbie Williams. **12** Celine Dion. **13** Diana Ross. **14** Four. **15** Blur. **16** 70s. **17** Cream. **18** Madonna. **19** U2. **20** George Michael. **21** Fleetwood Mac. **22** Never Ever. **23** Mariah Carey. **24** Heartbreak. **25** The Bee Gees.

# Quiz 70 Pot Luck 35

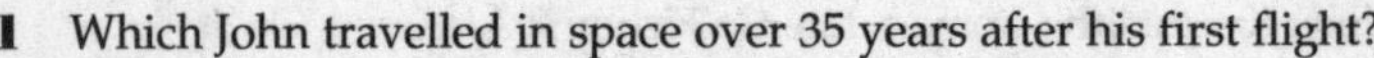

1 Which John travelled in space over 35 years after his first flight?
2 Which Chris appeared in a beach snap with Sophie Rhys-Jones?
3 In which sport was Willie Wood a world champion?
4 What is the first name of Mr Sumner aka Sting?
5 Which cartoon character says "Dagnabit"?
6 Maidstone is the administrative centre of which English county?
7 Who played James Bond in Tomorrow Never Dies?
8 What does the C stand for in BBC?
9 Brad Pitt was born in which decade of the century?
10 Which country does Enya come from?
11 What type of elm disease swept through Britain in the 70s?
12 On a BT phone what number is dialled to find the number of your last caller?
13 Which soccer star was known as the 'Preston Plumber'?
14 Which surname is shared by comics Des and Tom, one from London the other from Liverpool?
15 Who had a 90s No 1 with Fairground?
16 Which Stanley was a British Prime Minister in the 20s and 30s?
17 In which branch of the arts was John Barbirolli connected?
18 In which European country is Klagenfurt airport?
19 Which horror movie actor was quite literally a Pratt from birth?
20 Suzanne Lenglen was a champion in which sport?
21 Margarete Steiff made what kind of toy creature?
22 Which group backed Buddy Holly?
23 Which Prince was a helicopter pilot during the Falklands War?
24 Which A road links Oxford and London?
25 Patrick and Pippa lived next door to which Margaret and Victor?

**Answers**

***Pot Luck 35***

**1** Glenn. **2** Tarrant. **3** Bowls. **4** Gordon. **5** Deputy Dawg. **6** Kent. **7** Pierce Brosnan. **8** Corporation. **9** 60s. **10** Ireland. **11** Dutch. **12** 1471. **13** Tom Finney. **14** O 'Connor. **15** Simply Red. **16** Baldwin. **17** Music. **18** Austria. **19** Boris Karloff. **20** Tennis. **21** Bears. **22** The Crickets. **23** Andrew. **24** A40. **25** Meldrew.

# Quiz 71 Rich & Famous

1. Which Knightsbridge store did Mohammed Al-Fayed buy by outwitting rival Tiny Rowland?
2. Who was the first Beatle to be knighted?
3. Habitat was founded by which Terence?
4. What was the profession of Margaret Thatcher's father?
5. Which Princess was the youngest daughter of Mrs Frances Shand Kydd?
6. Which Rupert launched the satellite TV station which became Sky?
7. To the nearest five years, how old would Marilyn Monroe have been in 2000?
8. Which Swedish tennis player was John McEnroe's best man?
9. How many Beatles were not known by their real names?
10. Which opera singer gave her name to a kind of peach dessert?
11. Which tennis player was nicknamed Pistol Pete?
12. The ship Queen Elizabeth was named after who?
13. Which MP was immortalised in Madame Tussaud's in 1995 shortly after becoming leader of his party?
14. Dame Shirley Porter is heiress to which major supermarket chain?
15. Which Spice Girl sang Happy Birthday to Prince Charles at his 50th birthday party?
16. Whose head was due to be lost on banknotes when Britain joined the single European currency?
17. Who was enganged to Michael Hutchence of INXS when he died?
18. What was Camilla Shand's surname after her first marriage?
19. In which country did Princess Anne marry for the second time?
20. Which skinny Sixties model married actor Leigh Lawson?
21. Carol Vorderman agreed a multi million pound contract to do sums on which TV show?
22. William Henry Gates III amassed his fortune from which source?
23. Which British PM's father was a trapeze artist?
24. Which Duchess had a weeping Jana Novotna on her shoulder after the Czech player lost her Wimbledon final?
25. Which 90s Wimbledon champion married actress Brooke Shields?

## Answers

***Rich & Famous***

**1** Harrods. **2** Paul McCartney. **3** Conran. **4** Grocer. **5** Diana. **6** Murdoch. **7** 74. **8** Bjorn Borg. **9** One. **10** Melba. **11** Pete Sampras. **12** Queen Mother. **13** Tony Blair. **14** Tesco. **15** Geri. **16** The Queen. **17** Paula Yates. **18** Parker-Bowles. **19** Scotland. **20** Twiggy. **21** Countdown. **22** Computer software. **23** John Major. **24** Kent. **25** Andre Agassi.

# Quiz 72 Pot Luck 36

1 Which Eddie was a 90s governor of the Bank of England?
2 In the game Monopoly what colour are both Mayfair and Park Lane?
3 What type of mask was issued to all people in Britain in 1939?
4 Which Charles appears on the back of a £10 note?
5 Imagine was a hit for which singer after his death?
6 Whose business vehicle has New York, Paris, Peckham written on the side?
7 Albert Schweitzer is best remembered for his work on which continent?
8 What does the H stand for in the world organization WHO?
9 Where was the action of Please Sir! set?
10 Keith Fletcher captained England at which sport?
11 In which country did the Bolsheviks seize power?
12 Which actress Mirren was the star of TV's Prime Suspect?
13 What letter is used for numbers relating to food additives?
14 John Lee Hooker is associated with which type of music?
15 Who or what was the Flying Scotsman?
16 Who wrote Animal Farm?
17 The deepwater port of Faro was developed in which country?
18 With which sport is Ronan Rafferty associated?
19 Chrissie Hynde first had a No 1 as lead singer with which group?
20 How was Arkwright's shop described in the title of the sitcom with Ronnie Barker and David Jason?
21 Which car manufacturer introduced the Robin?
22 Who wrote the play The Importance of Being Earnest?
23 The Tamil Tigers were fighting for a separate state within which country?
24 In which decade was Radio 1 launched?
25 The Pompidou centre was built in which European city?

## Answers

***Pot Luck 36***

**1** George. **2** Dark blue. **3** Gas mask. **4** Dickens. **5** John Lennon. **6** The Trotters. **7** Africa. **8** Health. **9** School. **10** Cricket. **11** Russia. **12** Helen. **13** E. **14** Blues. **15** Steam train. **16** George Orwell. **17** Portugal. **18** Golf. **19** The Pretenders. **20** Open All Hours. **21** Reliant. **22** Oscar Wilde. **23** Sri Lanka. **24** 60s. **25** Paris.

# Quiz 73 TV Quiz & Game Shows

1 Wolf, Amazon and Saracen competed in which show?
2 Which satirical show hosted by Angus Deayton was derived from Radio 4's The News Quiz?
3 Which knockabout game show spawned a version with The Duke & Duchess of York, Princess Anne and Prince Edward as contestants?
4 Which show first hosted by Terry Wogan gave losers a model of a cheque book and pen?
5 Which show named after Superman's home planet tried to find the 'Super being of Great Britain'?
6 Which show introduced the phrase "I've started so I'll finish."?
7 Which Cilla Black show was called The Dating Game in the USA?
8 What is reduced from fifteen to one in Fifteen to One?
9 On Blockbusters who was often asked "Can I Have a P please Bob"?
10 Who presented the first series of The Generation Game on UK TV?
11 Which Marti hosted New Faces?
12 Which Stars programme featured the catchphrase 'Ulrika-ka-ka-ka-ka'?
13 How was Michael Barrymore's show Strike It Lucky renamed?
14 Which afternoon programme was based on the French show Les Chiffres et les Lettres - Numbers and Letters?
15 Which Ms Rice led contestants in Treasure Hunt?
16 Which student quiz had a starter for ten?
17 In which show did one contestant throw darts and one answer questions?
18 Which Ian has edited Private Eye and was a regular on Have I Got News For You?
19 What was the name of the National Lottery show which included a quiz?
20 Who first hosted Who Wants to be A Millionaire?
21 In which show hosted by Roy Walker did contestants try to guess well known phrases from computerised images?
22 Which group of people make up the audience of Man O Man?
23 What is Masterchef for young contestants called?
24 In the title of the cookery challenge show what follows Can't Cook?
25 Which Sue was the first regular female presenter of A Question of Sport?

## Answers

***TV Quiz & Games Shows***

**1** Gladiators. **2** Have I Got News For You. **3** It's A Knockout. **4** Blankety Blank. **5** The Krypton Factor. **6** Mastermind. **7** Blind Date. **8** Number of contestants. **9** Bob Holness. **10** Bruce Forsyth. **11** Caine. **12** Shooting Stars. **13** Strike It Rich. **14** Countdown. **15** Anneka. **16** University Challenge. **17** Bullseye. **18** Hislop. **19** Winning Lines. **20** Chris Tarrant. **21** Catchphrase. **22** Women. **23** Junior Masterchef. **24** Won't Cook. **25** Barker.

# Quiz 74 Pot Luck 37

1 Which Ron resigned from the government after a "moment of madness" on Clapham Common?
2 In medicine, what does the A stand for in BMA?
3 Viktor Chernomyrdin was Prime Minister of which country?
4 Who had a 90s solo No 1 with Earth Song?
5 What was the Luftwaffe in World War II?
6 In which decade did The Big Issue go on sale in London?
7 Which monarch launched HMS Sheffield and HMS Invincible?
8 In advertising which bank was described as the listening bank?
9 Which Coe was a world record breaking middle distance runner?
10 The game Scrabble uses tiles of what colour?
11 What was Gulf War general Norman Schwarzkopf's nickname?
12 Which soccer team does Michael Parkinson support?
13 Which colour follows Porterhouse in the comedy series with David Jason?
14 In the movie title, where was Macauley Culkin left Alone?
15 What does the M mean in GMT?
16 At which sporting arena did Cliff Richard lead a sing-a-long when rain stopped play in 1996?
17 Which country does cricketer Carl Hooper play for?
18 Gillian Shepherd has represented which party in parliament?
19 Which company developed Sonic the Hedgehog?
20 Which country developed the TGV high speed train?
21 Madonna was born in which decade of the century?
22 Which comedy series about life behind bars was called On the Rocks in the USA?
23 The 20s crash on which Street triggered America's 'Great Depression'?
24 Allison Fisher was a world champion in which sport?
25 The character Lofty Holloway appeared in which TV soap?

## Answers

***Pot Luck 37***

**1** Davies. **2** Association. **3** Russia. **4** Michael Jackson. **5** German airforce. **6** 90s. **7** Elizabeth II. **8** Midland. **9** Sebastian. **10** White. **11** Stormin' Norman. **12** Barnsley. **13** Blue. **14** Home. **15** Mean. **16** Wimbledon. **17** West Indies. **18** Conservative. **19** Sega. **20** France. **21** 50s. **22** Porridge. **23** Wall. **24** Snooker. **25** EastEnders.

# Quiz 75 Sporting Chance

1 Wentworth Golf Club is in which English county?
2 Susan Brown was the first woman to take part in which race?
3 Which country was captained by Dunga?
4 Which sporting ground has a Nursery End and a Pavilion End?
5 In which sport does the Fastnet Race take place?
6 What is the colour of the stage leader's jersey in the Tour de France?
7 Who did England have to beat to stay in cricket's 1999 World Cup - and didn't?
8 In what year was soccer's World Cup last held in the 80s?
9 Rugby is played at Ellis Park in which city?
10 Mark Spitz landed how many golds in the 1972 Olympics?
11 Yapping Deng was a world champion in which sport?
12 Who captained South Africa in cricket's 1999 World Cup?
13 In which sport were Lonsdale Belts awarded?
14 Who was England's first Italian Footballer Of The Year?
15 Andy Caddick played for England at which sport?
16 In which decade did Man Utd players die in the Munich Air Disaster?
17 Which baseball team are Giants?
18 In a nickname, what rank of the peerage was given to Ted Dexter?
19 The Australian Dawn Fraser was famous for which sport?
20 Which soccer team used to play at Ayresome Park?
21 Who or what became known as The Crafty Cockney?
22 The final of which tennis Grand Slam tournament is played in a Meadow?
23 At which circuit does the San Marino Grand Prix take place?
24 The Fosbury Flop was developed in which sport?
25 In which country in mainland Europe did Ian Rush play club soccer?

## Answers

***Sporting Chance***

**1** Surrey. **2** The Boat Race. **3** Brazil. **4** Lord's. **5** Yachting. **6** Yellow. **7** India. **8** 1986. **9** Johannesburg. **10** Seven. **11** Table tennis. **12** Hanse Cronje. **13** Boxing. **14** Gianfranco Zola. **15** Cricket. **16** 50s. **17** San Francisco. **18** Lord. **19** Swimming. **20** Middlesbrough. **21** Eric Bristow. **22** US Open. **23** Imola. **24** High jump. **25** Italy.

# Quiz 76 Pot Luck 38

1. Who sang Happy Birthday to Prince Charles on his 50th bash?
2. What colour are the stars on the United States of America flag?
3. What did mime artist Marcel Marceau do in the film Silent Movie for the first and only time in his career as an entertainer?
4. Which politician Paddy was a former Marine?
5. Which musical instrument is associated with Vladimir Ashkenazy?
6. In which decade was Britain's worst storm of the century?
7. Which Mr Reeves' real name is Jim Moir?
8. What does the C stand for in TUC?
9. What colour were Frank Sinatra's eyes?
10. Which 1987 the Russians and the Americans signed the Washington summit agreement to limit what?
11. In 1993 which pop artist changed his name to a symbol?
12. Who did F W de Klerk share the Nobel Peace prize with?
13. Identified in the 80s, global warming is known as what 'Effect'?
14. Euro Disney is on the outskirts of which city?
15. In what year was the 50th anniversary of VE Day?
16. Which Al had a starring role in the epic movie The Godfather?
17. Neil Fox represented Great Britain at which sport?
18. Ipswich is the administrative centre of which English county?
19. What was Rab Nesbitt's middle initial?
20. At the end of the 20th C how many UK monarchs had been called Victoria?
21. Which entertainment industry Dame sang the praise of the gladiola?
22. What was the name of flight pioneers Orville and Wilbur?
23. What's Love Got To Do With It? was a film about which female singer?
24. With which sport is Steve Cauthen associated?
25. John Travolta was born in which decade of the century?

## Answers

***Pot Luck 38***

**1** Geri Halliwell. **2** White. **3** Speak. **4** Ashdown. **5** Piano. **6** 80s. **7** Vic. **8** Congress. **9** Blue. **10** Nuclear missiles. **11** Prince. **12** Nelson Mandela. **13** Greenhouse. **14** Paris. **15** 1995. **16** Pacino. **17** Rugby League. **18** Suffolk. **19** C. **20** One. **21** Edna Everage. **22** Wright. **23** Tina Turner. **24** Horse racing. **25** 50s.

# Quiz 77 Comedies

1 Which Jim played Truman in The Truman Show?
2 Who was the near silent subject of The Ultimate Disaster Movie in 1997?
3 Which 90s movie told of a group of stripping Sheffield steel workers?
4 In the 1994 movie what did Jim Carrey find that turned him from a bank clerk into a comic book character, in the film of the same name?
5 Which Blackadder star played the vicar in Four Weddings and a Funeral?
6 Which 1994 movie was based on a TV cartoon and was set in Bedrock?
7 In Forrest Gump, his mum says Life is like a box of what?
8 What was A Fish called in the movie with Michael Palin and John Cleese?
9 Which blonde country star had a cameo role in The Beverly Hillbillies?
10 What is the name of the nanny Robin Williams becomes to look after his estranged children in the 1993 film?
11 Where did Deloris, played by Whoopi Goldberg, find refuge in Sister Act?
12 Whose World was a 1992 film with Mike Myers and Dana Carvey?
13 Which Carry On film was released in the 500th anniversary year of Columbus' arrival in the Americas?
14 Postcards From the Edge was based on the life of which actress Carrie?
15 In which movie did Macaulay Culkin first play abandoned child Kevin McCallister?
16 Which Bruce is the voice of Mikey in Look Who's Talking?
17 Why was Mick Dundee nicknamed Crocodile?
18 Which Michael played teenager Marty in Back to the Future?
19 In which 80s comedy did Dustin Hoffman play an actor who pretends to be a woman to get a part in a soap?
20 Which member of Arthur's staff was played by John Gielgud in the 80s film with Dudley Moore?
21 There's Something About whom in the politically incorrect comedy with Cameron Diaz?
22 Which crawling insects are the major stars of A Bug's Life?
23 Which spinach eating cartoon character was played by Robin Williams?
24 Which silent movie star created the comic character The Little Tramp?
25 Which brothers starred in Monkey Business and A Night at the Opera?

## Answers

***Comedies***

**1** Carrey. **2** Bean. **3** The Full Monty. **4** The Mask. **5** Rowan Atkinson. **6** The Flintstones. **7** Chocolates. **8** Wanda. **9** Dolly Parton. **10** Mrs Doubtfire. **11** Convent. **12** Wayne's. **13** Carry on Columbus. **14** Fisher. **15** Home Alone. **16** Willis. **17** He survived a crocodile attack. **18** J Fox. **19** Tootsie. **20** Valet. **21** Mary. **22** Ants. **23** Popeye. **24** Charlie Chaplin. **25** Marx Brothers.

# Quiz 78 Pot Luck 39

1 Assassinated Prime Minister Rabin led which country?
2 Who were beaten finalists in cricket's 1999 World Cup?
3 Julia Roberts was born in which decade of the century?
4 Which Yarns were a series of comedy films with stars such as Michael Palin?
5 Remembrance Sunday is linked with which flower?
6 Dame Peggy Ashcroft became famous as what?
7 The Wellington aircraft was built to carry what?
8 Mia Farrow was once married to which Andre?
9 Which country has I as its international vehicle registration letter?
10 Bernard Gallagher played for Scotland at which sport?
11 Killing Me Softly was a 90s No 1 for which group?
12 Meeting disaster in the 80s, what was the Herald of Free Enterprise?
13 In which British city was Turnhouse airport built?
14 Desiree and Pentland Javelin have been developed as varieties of what?
15 Iran was at war with which neighbour for most of the 80s?
16 Which Rugby League team added Dragons to their name in the 90s?
17 Which Mr Kipling wrote The Jungle Book and the Just So Stories?
18 Naturalist Sir Peter Scott's father perished exploring which continent?
19 In which area of the entertainment industry did Mack Sennett find fame?
20 Which motorway links Liverpool and Humberside?
21 Muddy Waters was associated with which musical instrument?
22 Which former child movie star Shirley became a US ambassador?
23 In Rising Damp what was the occupation of Rigsby?
24 What was the surname of brother and sister pop duo Richard and Karen?
25 Which country does motor racing's Eddie Irvine come from?

**Answers**

***Pot Luck 39***

**1** Israel. **2** Pakistan. **3** 60s. **4** Ripping. **5** Poppy. **6** Actress. **7** Bombs. **8** Previn. **9** Italy. **10** Golf. **11** Fugees. **12** Ferry. **13** Edinburgh. **14** Potato. **15** Iraq. **16** Doncaster. **17** Rudyard. **18** Antarctic. **19** Films. **20** M62. **21** Guitar. **22** Temple. **23** Landlord. **24** Carpenter. **25** United Kingdom.

# Quiz 79 Media

1 In which city is Anglia TV based?
2 In 1991 which BBC World Service was added to the radio service?
3 Which flagship BBC TV programme for children began in 1958?
4 GMTV broadcasts on which TV channel?
5 Which major independent radio station opened in 1973 to broadcast to London?
6 Which classical radio station has its own magazine?
7 Granada TV is based in which city?
8 Grandstand is chiefly broadcast on which day of the week?
9 Which city name did The Guardian have in its name until 1961?
10 Which magazine is an English version of the Spanish celebrity mag Hola!?
11 Which sister paper to the Independent is not published Monday to Friday?
12 What did J stand for in the music station JFM?
13 What did W stand for in LWT?
14 Which UK soccer club was the first to have its own TV station?
15 In spring 1999 which late evening news programme disappeared from our TV screens?
16 What does E stand for in the music paper NME?
17 In which newspaper were 'Page 3' girls first seen?
18 What name is given to papers like The Sun and The Mirror as opposed to broadsheets?
19 What is the subject of The Nigel Dempster pages in The Daily Mail?
20 Which major TV listings magazine does not have TV or television in its title?
21 Which radio programme comes from Borsetshire?
22 What does the second B stand for in BSkyB?
23 Where is Channel TV based?
24 Border TV is based on the borders of which two countries?
25 In which decade of the 20th century was GQ magazine founded?

## Answers

***Media***

**1** Norwich. **2** TV. **3** Blue Peter. **4** ITV. **5** Capital Radio. **6** Classic FM. **7** Manchester. **8** Saturday. **9** Manchester. **10** Hello. **11** Independent on Sunday. **12** Jazz. **13** Weekend. **14** Manchester Utd. **15** News At Ten. **16** Express. **17** The Sun. **18** Tabloids. **19** Celebrity gossip. **20** Radio Times. **21** The Archers. **22** Broadcasting. **23** Channel Islands. **24** England & Scotland. **25** 80s.

# Quiz 80 Pot Luck 40

1 Who declared, "The lady's not for turning"?
2 In the 90s film, who played G I Jane?
3 Who won the Eurovision Song Contest along with the Waves?
4 In February 1996 the Princess of Wales agreed to Prince Charles' request for what?
5 Who won a Grammy for Kiss From A Rose?
6 Who stepped down as Lib Dem leader in 1999?
7 What does the I stand for in CBI?
8 Rowan Atkinson was born in which decade of the century?
9 In which country was John Lennon murdered?
10 Johnny Giles represented the Republic of Ireland at which sport?
11 Which singer David starred in The River in the 80s sitcom?
12 Chernobyl witnessed a disaster at what type of power station?
13 With which sport is Peter Ebdon associated?
14 Winchester is the administrative centre of which English county?
15 Dennis Skinner has represented which party in parliament?
16 Which item of clothing introduced by Mary Quant symbolised the Swinging Sixties ?
17 Robert Carlyle was born in which part of the UK?
18 In which decade did the sitcom Roseanne begin?
19 Who had a 90s No 1 with A Different Beat?
20 At which seaside town was an 80s Tory party conference victim of an IRA bomb?
21 Which sport did Fred Perry take up after becoming world champion at table tennis?
22 Double agent Harold Philby was known by which first name?
23 In which country was Pablo Picasso born?
24 In which decade of the 20th century did Elvis Presley shoot to fame?
25 What followed the names of Rowan and Martin in the classic 60s comedy series?

## Answers

***Pot Luck 40***

**1** Margaret Thatcher. **2** Demi Moore. **3** Katrina. **4** Divorce. **5** Seal. **6** Paddy Ashdown. **7** Industry. **8** 50s. **9** United States. **10** Soccer. **11** Essex. **12** Nuclear power. **13** Snooker. **14** Hampshire. **15** Labour. **16** Miniskirt. **17** Scotland. **18** 1980s. **19** Boyzone. **20** Brighton. **21** Tennis. **22** Kim. **23** Spain. **24** 50s. **25** Laugh In.

# Quiz 81 80s

Level 1 

1 Duran Duran were part of which New movement?
2 What Purple thing topped the US album charts for 20 weeks?
3 What was the second name of the group starting Spandau?
4 Which pop singer starred in the movie The Jazz Singer?
5 Who was Shaky?
6 Who had the best selling album Diva?
7 What number featured in the name of the Fun Boy band?
8 Which Belinda sang that Heaven Is A Place On Earth?
9 Who sang - in Australian - Je Ne Sais Pas Pourquoi?
10 Which King was back in the charts with the re-issued When I Fall In Love?
11 What colour of Box recorded Ride On Time?
12 Who teamed up with Barbara Dickson for I Know Him So Well?
13 Which Bunny had a string of dance successes?
14 What was Diana Ross' only 80s No 1?
15 Who duetted with David Bowie on the No 1 hit Dancing In The Street?
16 Which female solo singer had most chart weeks in 1985,1986 and 1987?
17 How many hits did Rolf Harris have in the 80s?
18 According to Michael Ball, Love Changes what?
19 Who charted with the old Supremes hit You Can't Hurry Love?
20 Who duetted with Kylie Minogue for a No 1?
21 Which Jennifer sang about The Power of Love?
22 Which charity song was a hit for Band Aid?
23 Every Loser Wins was a winner for which soap actor?
24 Which Sledge had a hit with Frankie?
25 Who was Saving All My Love For You?

**Answers**

***80s***

**1** Romantics. **2** Rain. **3** Ballet. **4** Neil Diamond. **5** Shakin' Stevens. **6** Annie Lennox. **7** Three. **8** Carlisle. **9** Kylie Minogue. **10** Nat King Cole. **11** Black. **12** Elaine Paige. **13** Jive Bunny. **14** Chain Reaction. **15** Mick Jagger. **16** Madonna. **17** None. **18** Everything. **19** Phil Collins. **20** Jason Donovan. **21** Rush. **22** Do They Know It's Christmas?. **23** Nick Berry. **24** Sister Sledge. **25** Whitney Houston.

# Quiz 82 Pot Luck 41

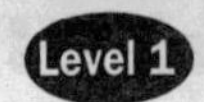

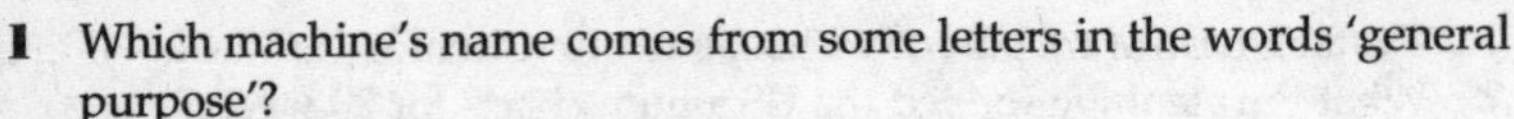

1. Which machine's name comes from some letters in the words 'general purpose'?
2. Who did writer Laurie Lee take Cider with?
3. Ursula Andrews was the Bond girl in which movie?
4. In the 90s which European country had a King Albert?
5. In the 70s who formed a singing duo with Peters?
6. In Are You Being Served, what was John Inman's catchphrase?
7. In the mid 90s what were the Newbury protesters protesting about?
8. Which country does soccer star Pierre Van Hooijdonk play for?
9. Lynda Bellingham who appeared in Second Thoughts was famous for advertising which cooking ingredient?
10. Who did Liam Gallagher marry in April 1997?
11. On a computer keyboard what letter is immediately to the right of the R?
12. The Home Guard was popularly known as whose Army?
13. Piccadilly Radio broadcasts to which major city?
14. In what decade was the FA Cup game known as the Matthews' Final?
15. Which thriller writer uses the initials PD?
16. The BSE crisis related to what type of meat?
17. Which Goon was Welsh?
18. Who played the movie role of Mrs Doubtfire?
19. Mark Knopfler is associated with which musical instrument?
20. Gillian Gilks played for England at which sport?
21. On which Common could you discover The Wombles?
22. Andy Cole joined Man Utd from which club?
23. What did Tony Bennett leave in San Francisco?
24. On TV what is the name of Jason and Bunty Savage's mum?
25. Which Midlands soccer team does Frank Skinner follow?

## Answers

***Pot Luck***

**1** Jeep. **2** Rosie. **3** Dr No. **4** Belgium. **5** Lee. **6** I'm free. **7** Bypass. **8** Holland. **9** Oxo cubes. **10** Patsy Kensit. **11** T. **12** Dad's. **13** Manchester. **14** 50s. **15** James. **16** Beef. **17** Harry Secombe. **18** Robin Williams. **19** Guitar. **20** Badminton. **21** Wimbledon. **22** Newcastle. **23** His heart. **24** Lily. **25** WBA.

# Quiz 83 Famous Firsts

1 Which type of transport was designed by Christopher Cockerell in the 50s?
2 C-Curity was the name of the first type of what?
3 Who was the first man to set foot on the moon?
4 Ruud Gullit became the Premiership's first black manager at which club?
5 Golda Meir was the first female Prime Minister of which country?
6 In which country did the Grunge movement first begin?
7 Helen Sharman was the first British woman to go where?
8 The Bates Motel first appeared in which film?
9 Christiaan Barnard carried out which medical first?
10 Who was the first Spanish golfer to win the British Open?
11 In which decade did the first wheel clamps arrive in Britain?
12 Which Charles first flew non-stop across the Atlantic?
13 Who was the first of Tony Blair's MPs to have won a film Oscar?
14 In 1975, which Arthur became the first black champion in the Men's Singles at Wimbledon?
15 Who starred in the first talkie movie?
16 The first successful cloning of an adult took place with what type of animal?
17 Which major sporting contest first took place in 1930?
18 Which Alexander discovered the first antibiotic?
19 Who was the leader of the first successful expedition to the South Pole?
20 Who were the first group seen on Channel 5?
21 In Jan 1974 professional football in Britain was played for the first time on which day?
22 Which brothers made the first powered plane flight?
23 Which famous first is claimed by Hillary and Tenzing?
24 Who was the first British monarch to abdicate in this century?
25 Which country was the first to send a woman into space?

## Answers

***Famous Firsts***

**1** Hovercraft. **2** Zip fastener. **3** Neil Armstrong. **4** Chelsea. **5** Israel. **6** United States. **7** Space. **8** Psycho. **9** Heart transplant. **10** Severiano Ballesteros. **11** 80s. **12** Lindbergh. **13** Glenda Jackson. **14** Ashe. **15** Al Jolson. **16** Sheep. **17** Soccer World Cup. **18** Fleming. **19** Roald Amundsen. **20** Spice Girls. **21** Sunday. **22** Wright. **23** Climbing Everest. **24** Edward VIII. **25** USSR.

# Quiz 84 Pot Luck 42

1 Don't Tell Sid was used in adverts to promote sales of shares in what?
2 In a toy store, who became Ken's girlfriend?
3 If I stands for Intelligence what does Q stand for in IQ?
4 In 1991, which Boris became president of the Russian Federation?
5 Frederick Austerlitz became better known as which entertainer?
6 What colour is the background of the Turkish flag?
7 What is Seinfeld's first name?
8 Which Attenborough made the Life On Earth TV series?
9 Which fruit along with an apple gave its name to a computer range?
10 Which cartoon family who first appeared in the US in the 80s were created by Matt Groening?
11 In the 80s David Owen left which political party to launch the SDP?
12 With which sport is Gabriel Batistu associated?
13 The deepwater port of Fray Bentos was built in which country?
14 Who had a 90s No 1 with Never Forget?
15 Implementation of the National Curriculum concerns which establishments?
16 English soccer clubs were banned from Europe in the mid 80s after a final involving which English club?
17 Who wrote the play Blithe Spirit?
18 In which city was teenager Stephen Lawrence stabbed to death?
19 In which decade did Croatia appoint their first president?
20 Who created Noddy?
21 Duncan Goodhew represented Britain at which sport?
22 Francois Mitterand was born during which 20th century war?
23 Who wrote the poetic study of Welsh life Under Milk Wood?
24 What was the surname of Steve Coogan's brother and sister creations Paul & Paula?
25 Which country does motor racing's Mika Hakkinen come from?

## Answers

***Pot Luck 42***

**1** British Gas. **2** Barbie. **3** Quotient. **4** Yeltsin. **5** Fred Astaire. **6** Red. **7** Jerry. **8** David. **9** Apricot. **10** The Simpson. **11** Labour. **12** Soccer. **13** Uruguay. **14** Take That. **15** Schools. **16** Liverpool. **17** Noel Coward. **18** London. **19** 90s. **20** Enid Blyton. **21** Swimming. **22** WWI. **23** Dylan Thomas. **24** Calf. **25** Finland.

# Quiz 85 The Royals

1. John Bryan was reputedly what type of adviser to the Duchess of York?
2. Which prince is the Queen's youngest son?
3. What is Prince Harry's real first name?
4. How is Prince Michael of Kent's wife known?
5. Which princess has a holiday villa on Mustique?
6. What is Prince Charles' Gloucestershire home called?
7. Who was Princess Diana referring to when she said her marriage was 'a bit crowded'?
8. Which Prince was born on the Greek island of Corfu?
9. Which Scottish school did Princes Charles, Andrew and Edward all attend?
10. Which Princess is the mother of Peter Phillips?
11. How many daughters does the Queen Mother have?
12. In which cathedral did Prince Charles marry Lady Diana Spencer?
13. Which Royal was once the BBC Sports Personality of the Year?
14. Anthony Armstrong Jones took an Earldom named after which mountain after his marriage to Princess Margaret?
15. Which hair colour is shared by Earl Spencer and his nephew Prince Harry?
16. What is the name of the Spencer ancestral home in Northamptonshire?
17. With which royal's name was Koo Stark's linked in the early 80s?
18. Which name of a castle does Prince Edward use as a professional surname when working in the media?
19. At which English university did Prince Charles study?
20. Which school did Princess William and Harry attend in the late 90s?
21. In which 80s war did Prince Andrew serve?
22. Major Ronald Ferguson is the father of which Duchess?
23. Which Royal wrote The Old Man of Lochnagar?
24. Which branch of the construction industry is Viscount Linley involved in?
25. Which Royal has had a collection of his paintings exhibited?

## Answers

***The Royals***

**1** Financial. **2** Edward. **3** Henry. **4** Princess Michael of Kent. **5** Margaret. **6** Highgrove. **7** Camilla Parker Bowles. **8** Philip. **9** Gordonstoun. **10** Anne. **11** Two. **12** St Paul's. **13** Princess Anne. **14** Snowdon. **15** Red. **16** Althorp. **17** Prince Andrew. **18** Windsor. **19** Cambridge. **20** Eton. **21** Falklands. **22** York. **23** Prince Charles. **24** Carpentry. **25** Prince Charles.

# Quiz 86 Pot Luck 43

1 Which TV tech was played by Mark McManus?
2 Which car manufacturer introduced the Ventura, Victor and Viscount?
3 In 1990 there was serious rioting in Strangeways prison in which city?
4 Chubby Checker was linked with which dance craze?
5 In 80s politics which Michael resigned over the Westland affair?
6 In which city did Prince Andrew marry Fergie?
7 Singer Anne Mae Bullock found fame under which name?
8 In World War II people were urged to Dig For what?
9 Winona Ryder was born in which decade of the century?
10 Ronnie Clayton played for England at which sport?
11 In fiction, what kind of factory was Roald Dahls Charlie connected with?
12 Nylon gets its name from London and which other city?
13 Who played Frank Spencer before achieving huge success as The Phantom of the Opera?
14 Which volatile tennis player asked Steffi Graf to partner him in WimbledonÕs 1999 Mixed Doubles?
15 In the 90s Macedonia has declared its independence from which country?
16 Andrew Ridgeley was the less famous half of which 80s pop duo?
17 Which country does cricketer Paul Reiffel play for?
18 What does the letter A stand for in AIDS?
19 Stay Another Day was a 90s No 1 which group?
20 Trainspotting was set in which country?
21 John McGregor has represented which party in parliament?
22 Which film star Paul promotes his own salad dressing?
23 Which Italian film star with the same first name as himself did Rudolf Nureyev play in a film in 1977?
24 What was the first name of Baron Olivier of Brighton?
25 What are the first names of Smith & Jones?

## Answers

***Pot Luck 43***

**1** Taggart. **2** Vauxhall. **3** Manchester. **4** Twist. **5** Heseltine. **6** London. **7** Tina Turner. **8** Victory. **9** 70s. **10** Soccer. **11** Chocolate. **12** New York. **13** Michael Crawford. **14** John McEnroe. **15** Yugoslavia. **16** Wham. **17** Australia. **18** Acquired. **19** East 17. **20** Scotland. **21** Conservative. **22** Newman. **23** Valentino. **24** Laurence. **25** Mel & Griff.

# Quiz 87 TV Trivia

1. Who with Greg Dyke was credited with saving TV am?
2. Which model advertised Pizza Hut with Jonathan Ross?
3. Who found fame in the docu soap about a driving school?
4. Which TV personality appeared on The Archers - as himself - for their 10,000th episode?
5. From which part of her house did Delia Smith present her 90s TV series?
6. Which duo began as stand up comics called The Menopause Sisters?
7. Which airline did Jeremy Spake from Airport work for?
8. In which supermarket ad did Jane Horrocks play Prunella Scales' daughter?
9. Fred Housego shot to fame as a winner on which TV show?
10. Who replaced Danny Baker on Pets Win Prizes?
11. Who provided the music for The Wombles?
12. Who or what did Barbara Woodhouse train?
13. Which Ready Steady Cook regular was also a regular presenter on Breakfast Time?
14. What is the subject of the Quentin Wilson show All the Right Moves?
15. What was Keith Floyd's TV show based on Far East cooking called?
16. Who interviewed Prince Edward and Sophie Rhys Jones in a pre wedding programme?
17. Who wrote and sang the theme music to Spender?
18. Which early presenter of the Big Breakfast wore glasses?
19. Who was the original presenter of Gladiators with Ulrika Jonsson?
20. Which drama series was based on the Constable novels by Nicholas Rhea?
21. Which series had the tag line "The truth is out there...."?
22. Who worked together on The Frost Report and went on to have their own successful series together?
23. Which quiz began with "Your starter for ten.."?
24. Which work of reference do the celebrity and the expert possess in Countdown?
25. Which soap powder did Robbie Coltrane advertise?

## Answers

***TV Trivia***

**1** Roland Rat **2** Caprice **3** Maureen Rees **4** Terry Wogan **5** Conservatory **6** French & Saunders **7** Aeroflot **8** Tesco **9** Mastermind **10** Dale Winton **11** Mike Batt **12** Dogs **13** Fern Britton **14** Property **15** Far Flung Floyd **16** Sue Barker **17** Jimmy Nail **18** Chris Evans **19** John Fashanu **20** Heartbeat **21** The X Files **22** The Two Ronnies **23** University Challenge **24** Dictionary **25** Persil

# Quiz 88 Pot Luck 44

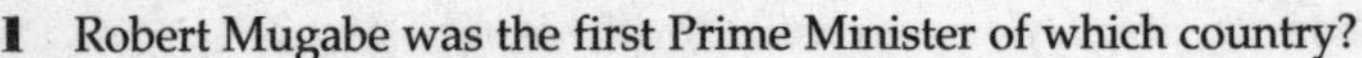

1 Robert Mugabe was the first Prime Minister of which country?
2 Boy George fronted which Club?
3 QWhich Nazi died in jail after being imprisoned for 46 years?
4 In fiction what is the last name of Dr Hannibal - the Cannibal?
5 Who sang Little Donkey with Nina?
6 How did Allen Stewart Konigsberg become better known?
7 Brown-Eyed Handsome Man was a hit for which singer after his death?
8 Chelmsford is the administrative centre of which English county?
9 Which Jeremy was a 90s University Challenge presenter?
10 What was developed in the 40s Manhattan Project?
11 Which character did Johnny Briggs play in Coronation Street?
12 Which group sacked drummer Pete Best before they hit the big time?
13 In medicine, what does the D stand for in CJD?
14 Fluck & Law were famous for their puppets on which show?
15 Which William wrote the novel Lord Of The Flies?
16 Which sitcom with Rowan Atkinson was set in Gasforth Police station?
17 Who had a 90s No 1 with Back For Good?
18 What was the surname of the father and son rag and bone men who lived at Mews Cottage, Oil Drum Lane?
19 What is the first name of best selling sci fi writer Pratchett?
20 Cookery writer and TV presenter Loyd Grossman hails from which country?
21 Which late comedian had "short, fat, hairy legs"?
22 Which motorway links London to Cambridge?
23 Timothy Dalton and Pierce Brosnan have both played which character?
24 Which sport in the Olympics includes pikes, tucks and twists?
25 Which Freddie, born Freddie Fowell, earned a reputation as one of Britain's most outrageous comedians?

**Answers**

***Pot Luck 44***

**1** Zimbabwe. **2** Culture. **3** Rudolf Hess. **4** Lecter. **5** Frederick . **6** Woody Allen. **7** Buddy Holly. **8** Essex. **9** Paxman. **10** Atomic Bomb. **11** Mike Baldwin. **12** The Beatles. **13** Disease. **14** Spitting Image. **15** Golding. **16** The Thin Blue Line. **17** Take That. **18** Steptoe. **19** Terry. **20** USA. **21** Ernie Wise. **22** M11. **23** James Bond. **24** Diving. **25** Starr.

# Quiz 89 TV Soaps

1. Which Grove was a popular teen soap?
2. In which soap was Blake married to Alexis then Krystle?
3. Which member of the Mitchell family was killed on New Year's Eve 1998?
4. Which soap community has the postcode E20?
5. In which soap was the body of a wife beater famously buried under the patio?
6. Which day of the week is the EastEnders omnibus edition?
7. Which chocolate makers first sponsored Coronation Street in 1996?
8. Which doomed BBC soap was set in Spain?
9. The Colbys was a spin off from which US soap?
10. What was Emmerdale called when it was first screened in the afternoon?
11. Knots Landing was a spin off from which oil based soap?
12. As opposed to oil, Falcon Crest was about which commodity California is famous for?
13. Which Ken is the only original member of the Coronation Street cast?
14. In which Ward was the Emergency in TV's first medical soap?
15. In 1993 Emmerdale suffered an air disaster similar to which real life tragedy?
16. Which late comedian Larry was Meg Richardson's wedding chauffeur in Crossroads?
17. Which soap launched the pop careers of Kylie Minogue and Jason Donovan?
18. Which soap ran the classic cliff hanger 'Who shot J.R.?'?
19. How did Take The High Road change its name form 1995 onwards?
20. Which blonde replaced Vera behind the bar at the Rovers Return?
21. In Coronation Street what does Mike Baldwin's factory make?
22. In EastEnders, who did Peggy marry in 1999?
23. In which Cheshire location was Hollyoaks set?
24. Which soap from Down Under was created to rival Neighbours?
25. Which soap for children was set in a London comprehensive?

## Answers

***TV Soaps***

**1** Byker. **2** Dynasty. **3** Tiffany. **4** Walford. **5** Brookside. **6** Sunday. **7** Cadbury's. **8** ElDorado. **9** Dynasty. **10** Emmerdale Farm. **11** Dallas. **12** Wine. **13** Barlow. **14** 10. **15** Lockerbie. **16** Grayson. **17** Neighbours. **18** Dallas. **19** High Road. **20** Natalie. **21** Underwear. **22** Frank. **23** Chester. **24** Home & Away. **25** Grange Hill.

# Quiz 90 Pot Luck 45

1 Which Earl was the brother of Diana, Princess of Wales?
2 In music who "just called to say I love you"?
3 A Swedish car displays which international vehicle registration mark?
4 Which of the Barrymore family featured in the film Batman Forever?
5 What type of beer is served in Coronation Street's Rovers' Return?
6 Derek Underwood played which sport for England?
7 The MRLP is what kind of Raving Loony Party?
8 Marion Morrison become famous under which name?
9 Who wrote the novel The Shining?
10 What does the B stand for in SCUBA diving?
11 On which day was the midweek Lottery first drawn?
12 Which Welsh city had a millennium sports stadium built?
13 The deepwater port of Kagoshima was built in which country?
14 In advertising, Fry's Turkish Delight was described as being "Full of Eastern" what?
15 Which soccer team does Jo Brand follow?
16 Which Joseph was Hitler's minister of propaganda?
17 On which Isle was Ronaldsway airport built?
18 With which sport is Curtis Strange associated?
19 Cheery entertainer Jim Davidson was born is which decade?
20 General Pinochet was a former ruler of which country?
21 Who lost part of his ear to the teeth of Mike Tyson in 1997?
22 Which Liverpool comedian Jimmy went to the same school as John Lennon?
23 BB King is associated with which musical instrument?
24 Lord Mountbatten was the last viceroy of which country?
25 In which chapel did Edward and Sophie Rhys-Jones get married?

## Answers

***Pot Luck 45***

**1** Spencer. **2** Stevie Wonder. **3** S. **4** Drew. **5** Newton and Ridley. **6** Cricket. **7** Monster. **8** John Wayne. **9** Stephen King. **10** Breathing. **11** Wednesday. **12** Cardiff. **13** Japan. **14** Promise. **15** Crystal Palace. **16** Goebbels. **17** Isle of Man. **18** Golf. **19** 50s. **20** Chile. **21** Evander Holyfield. **22** Tarbuck. **23** Guitar. **24** India. **25** St George's.

# Quiz 91 Horse Racing

**1** Who returned to racing in 1990 when he was over 50?
**2** Which horse was first to win the Grand National three times?
**3** Where is the William Hill Lincoln Handicap held?
**4** Trainers Lynda and John Ramsden won a libel case against which paper?
**5** In which country was Shergar captured?
**6** In which month is the Melbourne Cup held?
**7** Who was National Hunt champion jockey from 1986 to 1992?
**8** Which horse Benny won the 1997 Derby?
**9** Which English classic is held at Doncaster?
**10** What is a £500 bet known as?
**11** Which horse race was abandoned in 1997 after a bomb scare?
**12** The Prix du Jockey-Club is held at which race course?
**13** Which horse had the nickname Corky?
**14** Which Gordon a trainer of over 2000 winners died in September 1998?
**15** Which country hosts the Belmont and Preakness Stakes?
**16** Who chartered a train from Victoria to Epsom to watch the 1997 Derby at a cost of over £11,000?
**17** Which race meeting is described as Glorious?
**18** The 12th Earl of where gave his name to a famous race?
**19** Which horsewoman was the first Mrs Mark Phillips?
**20** After a Saturday bomb threat in 1997 on which day was the National run?
**21** The Curragh is in which Irish County?
**22** Which horse was the first to win Horse of the Year four times?
**23** Where did Frankie Dettori have his record breaking seven wins?
**24** Which horse won the Derby by a record distance in 1981?
**25** In which country is Flemington Park race course?

## Answers

***Horse Racing***
**1** Lester Piggott. **2** Red Rum. **3** Doncaster. **4** The Sporting Life. **5** Ireland. **6** November. **7** Peter Scudamore. **8** The Dip. **9** St Leger. **10** Monkey. **11** National. **12** Chantilly. **13** Corbiere. **14** Richards. **15** United States. **16** The Queen. **17** Goodwood. **18** Derby. **19** Princess Anne. **20** Monday. **21** Kildare. **22** Desert Orchid. **23** Ascot. **24** Shergar. **25** Australia.

# Quiz 92 The Oscars

1 Which veteran actress Katharine was the first actress to win four Oscars?
2 Which 1997 movie equalled Ben Hur's record 11 Oscars?
3 Which Emma won an Oscar for her screenplay of Sense and Sensibility?
4 Who won his second Oscar in successive years for Forrest Gump?
5 Judi Dench won an Oscar as which Queen in Shakespeare in Love?
6 Who won Best Actor and Best Director Oscar for Dances With Wolves?
7 Who won his second Oscar for the autistic Raymond in Rain Man?
8 In the 70s which gangster film won an Oscar as did its sequel?
9 In 1997 James Cameron won an Oscar for which blockbuster?
10 Geoffrey Rush won an Oscar for Shine, as what type of musician?
11 For which film about a Scottish hero did Mel Gibson win his first Oscars for Best Picture and Best Director?
12 Which Nick won an Oscar for The Wrong Trousers?
13 Which lyricist who has worked with Elton John and Andrew Lloyd Webber won an award for A Whole New World from Aladdin?
14 In which film did Jodie Foster play FBI agent Clarice Starling?
15 Who won an Oscar wearing an eye patch in True Grit?
16 Which film with Ralph Fiennes won Anthony Minghella an Oscar?
17 Which Jessica was the then oldest Oscar winner for Driving Miss Daisy?
18 Nigel Hawthorne was Oscar nominated for The Madness of which King?
19 Which Oscar nominated film had You Sexy Thing as its theme song?
20 The multi Oscar winning The Deer Hunter was about steelworkers who went to fight where?
21 Which Julie won an Oscar for Darling in 1965 and was Oscar nominated in 1998 for Afterglow?
22 For which 80s film was Pauline Collins nominated for playing a bored Liverpool housewife?
23 Which Oscar winner from The Silence of the Lambs campaigned to save Snowdonia in 1998?
24 Which musical based on Romeo & Juliet was a 60s Oscar winner?
25 Raindrops Keep Falling On My Head was an Oscar winner from which movie with Robert Redford & Paul Newman?

## Answers

***The Oscars***

**1** Hepburn. **2** Titanic. **3** Thompson. **4** Tom Hanks. **5** Elizabeth I. **6** Kevin Costner. **7** Dustin Hoffman. **8** The Godfather. **9** Titanic. **10** Pianist. **11** Braveheart. **12** Park. **13** Tim Rice. **14** The Silence of the Lambs. **15** John Wayne. **16** The English Patient. **17** Tandy. **18** George. **19** The Full Monty. **20** Vietnam. **21** Christie. **22** Shirley Valentine. **23** Anthony Hopkins. **24** West Side Story. **25** Butch Cassidy & The Sundance Kid.

# Quiz 93 On Line

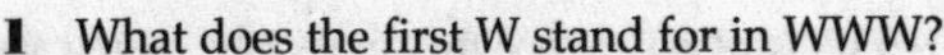

1 What does the first W stand for in WWW?
2 If you surf the Internet what do you do?
3 Which page of a Web site is called a Home Page?
4 In addition to the computer what else must a modem be plugged into?
5 What does Q mean in FAQ?
6 What does S mean in ISP?
7 In which country did the Internet start?
8 A small a in a circle (@) is pronounced how?
9 What name is given to the software program needed to access the Web?
10 What goes after Netscape in the name of a popular Internet browser?
11 If you have an active Internet connection you are said to be on what?
12 What is the opposite of downloading?
13 What is freeware?
14 If you log off what do you do?
15 What is netiquette?
16 What is the minimum number of computers which can be networked?
17 What letter appears on the computer screen when you are using Microsoft Internet Explorer?
18 Which name of something used by avid readers is the Netscape Navigator name for Favorites?
19 Where does bounced e mail return to?
20 Which 'space' refers to the Internet and all that goes with it?
21 What does offline mean?
22 A newbie is a new what?
23 In an e mail address how is a symbol like a full stop said out loud?
24 What name is given to a program designed to cause damage by attaching itself to other programs?
25 What is Microsoft's browser software called?

**Answers**

***On Line***
**1** World. **2** Look around. **3** First. **4** Phone. **5** Question. **6** Service. **7** USA. **8** At. **9** Browser. **10** Navigator. **11** Line. **12** Uploading. **13** Free software. **14** Disconnect. **15** Good behaviour on the net. **16** Two. **17** E. **18** Bookmarks. **19** Sender. **20** Cyberspace. **21** Not connected. **22** Internet user. **23** Dot. **24** Virus. **25** Internet Explorer.

# Quiz 94 Pop 90s

1 What was finally a top ten hit for Ce Ce Peniston on its 1992 re-release?
2 Who recorded the album Nevermind?
3 Who had a Christmas No 1 in 1996, 1997 and 1998?
4 Who had a hit with the old song I Believe?
5 What kind of Doll did Aqua sing about?
6 Whose debut album was called Doggystyle?
7 Which girl group led the 1995 Party In The Park for the Prince's Trust?
8 Edele and Keavy Lynch were together in which group?
9 What is Billie's surname?
10 Which film revived the 70s song You Sexy Thing?
11 How did Kurt Kobain end his life?
12 Which team do the Gallagher brothers support?
13 What was the first single of The Spice Girls?
14 Which soccer team sang Come On You Reds?
15 Whose debut album was Talk On Corners?
16 Norman Cook is better known as which club DJ?
17 Which group's first No 1 was Some Might Say?
18 Richie Edwards vanished in 1995 leaving behind which group?
19 Who had success with Abba-esque?
20 Who was Mrs Bob Geldof when the 90s started?
21 Which alternative dance group first charted with Charly?
22 Which Heather sang with M People?
23 Which chart topper was pink, tall, spotted and very destructive?
24 Whose Nothing Compares 2 U made No 1 in both the UK and the US?
25 An advert for which drink led to Perez Prado back in the charts?

## Answers

***Pop 90s***

**1** Finally. **2** Nirvana. **3** Spice Girls. **4** Robson & Jerome. **5** Barbie. **6** Snoop Doggy Dog. **7** All Saints. **8** B*Witched. **9** Piper. **10** The Full Monty. **11** He shot himself. **12** Man City,. **13** Wannabe. **14** Man Utd. **15** The Corrs. **16** Fatboy Slim. **17** Oasis. **18** Manic Street Preachers. **19** Erasure. **20** Paula Yates. **21** Prodigy. **22** Small. **23** Mr Blobby. **24** Sinead O'Connor. **25** Guinness.

# Quiz 95 Technology

1 What does the G stand for in WYSIWYG?
2 In which decade was the Sony Walkman stereo launched?
3 Oftel regulates which industry?
4 Which phone company adopted a colour name before going into the red?
5 Which UK motor company produced the Prefect?
6 What kind of codes did American supermarkets introduce in the mid 70s?
7 What does the B stand for in IBM?
8 The Three Mile Island nuclear leak in the 70s was in which country?
9 What did pirate radio stations broadcast?
10 Which Bill formed Microsoft?
11 Which 'unsinkable' craft sank in 1912?
12 Which Clarence pioneered quick freezing in the food industry?
13 The tallest tower of the 70s, the Sears Tower, was built in which country?
14 Foods will not brown in what type of oven?
15 What used to go round at thirty three and a third r.p.m.?
16 In which decade was the Channel Tunnel first opened?
17 What did Lazlo Biro invent in the 30s?
18 The wide-bodied passenger carrying Boeing 747 became known as what type of jet?
19 Which popular small car was introduced by Austin Morris at the end of the 50s?
20 Which country combined with Britain in building Concorde?
21 What touches the surface of a CD when playing?
22 What does the F stand for in FM?
23 The Sony company originated in which country?
24 Modulator-Demodulator is usually shortened to what?
25 What was the middle name of TV pioneer John Baird?

**Answers**

***Technology***
**1** Get. **2** 70s. **3** Telecommunications. **4** Orange. **5** Ford. **6** Bar codes. **7** Business. **8** United States. **9** Pop music. **10** Gates. **11** Titanic. **12** Birdseye. **13** United States. **14** Microwave. **15** Long playing records. **16** 90s. **17** Ballpoint pen. **18** Jumbo. **19** Mini. **20** France. **21** Nothing. **22** Frequency. **23** Japan. **24** Modem. **25** Logie.

# Quiz 96 Unforgettables

**1** Which member of T Rex died exactly the same day as Maria Callas?
**2** Which part of the brilliant Albert Einstein was preserved after his death?
**3** Which Princess and former film star died in a car crash near Monte Carlo in 1982?
**4** How many times did Greta (I want to be alone) Garbo marry?
**5** Linda McCartney launched a range of what type of food?
**6** Which opera singer's real name was Maria Kalogeropoulos?
**7** Yitzhak Rabin was Prime Minister of which country when he was assassinated in 1995?
**8** Which Yuri made the first human journey into space?
**9** Which fuel made millions for J. Paul Getty?
**10** How was Argentinian revolutionary Ernesto Guevara de la Serna better known?
**11** Charles de Gaulle was President of which European country?
**12** Who was the youngest US President to die in office?
**13** T.E.Lawrence's name is mostly associated with which country?
**14** Yehudi Menuhin was famous for playing which musical instrument?
**15** Glenn Miller's plane disappeared during which war?
**16** QWhich blonde icon made her name in Gentlemen Prefer Blondes?
**17** Fans visit Graceland in the USA to pay tribute to which rock legend?
**18** In which country did Mother Theresa found her mission to help the destitute?
**19** Who was the first Queen of England in the 20th century?
**20** What was the name of the musical about rock legend Buddy Holly?
**21** Who killed Cleopatra?
**22** To the nearest five years, how old would John Lennon have been in 2000?
**23** Which knighted Man Utd manager switched on the Blackpool illuminations in 1968?
**24** John Wayne had an airport named after him in his home country. Where is it?
**25** Which British born veteran American comedian Bob received a knighthood in 1998?

## Answers

***Unforgettables***

**1** Marc Bolan. **2** Brain. **3** Grace. **4** Never. **5** Vegetarian. **6** Maria Callas. **7** Israel. **8** Gagarin. **9** Oil. **10** Che Guevara. **11** France. **12** Kennedy. **13** Arabia. **14** Violin. **15** World War II. **16** Marilyn Monroe. **17** Elvis Presley. **18** India. **19** Victoria. **20** Buddy. **21** Cleopatra. **22** 60. **23** Matt Busby. **24** USA. **25** Hope.

# Quiz 97 TV Times

1 In which country was Due South set?
2 Which George played Doug Ross in ER?
3 Which show was set in a Boston bar "Where everybody know your name"?
4 In which decade was the first Eurovision Song Contest?
5 In which Yorkshire location was Band of Gold set?
6 Which ex Bond Girl Jane played Dr Quinn: Medicine Woman?
7 Which animated series was originally to have been called The Flagstones?
8 Which other Kelly presented the first series of Game For A Laugh with Henry?
9 Henry Winkler's Arthur Fonzarelli was better known as what?
10 How many sisters established The House of Elliot?
11 Which Jim might have fixed it for you?
12 What was the first name of arch snob Mrs Bucket - pronounced Bouquet?
13 The Larry Sanders Show was a spoof of what type of show?
14 In Last of the Summer Wine what wrinkled part of Nora Batty was a source of fascination for Compo?
15 Which action drama centred on Blue Watch B25, Blackwall?
16 The Mary Whitehouse Experience came to TV from which radio station?
17 I Could Be So Good for You was a Dennis Waterman hit from which show he starred in with George Cole?
18 Caroline Aherne was the alter ego of which pensioner chat show hostess?
19 Which cult sci fi series was originally to have been called Wagon Train to the Stars?
20 Which show featured Noo Noo the vacuum cleaner?
21 Which so called yuppie drama series was set in Philadelphia and was first shown in the UK on Channel 4?
22 Which East London football team did Alf Garnett support?
23 In the 70s series what followed Tinker, Tailor, Soldier in the title?
24 Which line followed "It's goodnight from me..." on The Two Ronnies?
25 What was the job of Hudson in Upstairs Downstairs?

## Answers

***TV Times***

**1** Canada. **2** Clooney. **3** Cheers. **4** 50s. **5** Bradford. **6** Seymour. **7** The Flintstones. **8** Matthew. **9** The Fonz. **10** Two. **11** Saville. **12** Hyacinth. **13** Chat show. **14** Stockings. **15** London's Burning. **16** Radio 1. **17** Minder. **18** Mrs Merton. **19** Star Trek. **20** Teletubbies. **21** Thirtysomething. **22** West Ham. **23** Spy. **24** And it's goodnight from him. **25**Butler.

# Quiz 98 Sports Bag

1. What is 'Magic' Johnson's first name?
2. How many attempts at the target does a player get in curling?
3. In which Spanish city were the 1992 Olympics held?
4. Eric Cantona joined Man Utd from which club?
5. The Vince Lombardi trophy is awarded in which sport?
6. Gabriela Sabatini comes from which country?
7. In which event did Bob Beaman hold an Olympic record for over 20 years?
8. Graeme Le Saux was born in which group of islands?
9. What did Dionico Ceron win three years in a row in England's capital city?
10. In which month of the year is the Super Bowl held?
11. In 1999 Ian McGeechan became coach of which international rugby team?
12. What word can follow American, Association or Gaelic to name a sport?
13. Which sport has a team that plays at a Cottage?
14. Which country won cricket's 1996 World Cup?
15. In which sport is the Cowdray Park Cup awarded?
16. In American Football where do the Colts come from?
17. What was athlete Florence Griffith-Joyner usually known as?
18. Rugby's William Henry Hare was better known by what nickname?
19. In athletics, what does the first A stand for in the initials IAAF?
20. Which team did Jock Stein lead to European Cup success?
21. Micky Mantle played which sport?
22. Which Nigel was BBC Sports Personality in 1992?
23. In which city does the Tour de France finish?
24. Norman Whiteside became the youngest soccer player of the century for which international side?
25. Who played Australia in cricket's drawn 1999 World Cup semi-final?

## Answers

***Sports Bag***

**1** Earvin. **2** Two. **3** Barcelona. **4** Leeds. **5** American Football. **6** Argentina. **7** Long jump. **8** Channel. **9** Marathon. **10** January. **11** Scotland. **12** Football. **13** Soccer - Fulham. **14** Sri Lanka. **15** Polo. **16** Baltimore. **17** Flo-Jo. **18** Dusty. **19** Amateur. **20** Celtic. **21** Baseball. **22** Mansell. **23** Paris. **24** N Ireland. **25** S Africa.

# Quiz 99 Screen Greats

1 Boris Karloff starred as which monster in one of the first horror movies?
2 Which actor is the father of actress Jamie Lee Curtis?
3 Arnold Schwarzenegger married the niece of which US president?
4 Which TV soap was Rock Hudson a star of shortly before his death?
5 Which actress born Ruth Elizabeth Davis was the first female president of the Academy of Motion Picture Arts & Sciences?
6 Which Ford of Star Wars was voted Film Star of the century by a panel of critics in 1994?
7 In which city did Steve McQueen take part in the car chase in Bullitt?
8 Richard Gere is a follower of which eastern religion?
9 Which screen great was Lauren Bacall married to at the time of his death?
10 In which country was Marlene Dietrich born?
11 Who found fame as Alfie?
12 Which Oscar winner for From Here To Eternity, more famous as Ol' Blue Eyes the singer, died in 1998?
13 In which country was Cary Grant born as Archie Leach?
14 Which star of The Godfather in the 70s played opposite Vivien Leigh in A Streetcar Named Desire in the 50s?
15 Which dancing duo's first film together was called Flying Down to Rio?
16 Which dancer, the star of Singing in the Rain, never won an Oscar?
17 Rebel Without A Cause made a star of which actor whose life was cut short in a car accident?
18 Grace Kelly became Princess of which principality where her film To Catch a Thief was set?
19 In which movie did Alec Guinness first appear as Ben Obi Wan Kenobi?
20 Which comedian starred with Bing Crosby in the Road films?
21 What was the name of Michael Douglas's father?
22 Which star Joan was the subject of the movie Mommie Dearest?
23 Which Jack won an Oscar for One Flew Over the Cuckoo's Nest?
24 Which Russian Doctor was played in the 60s by Omar Sharif?
25 Who found fame trying to resist the charms of Mrs Robinson in The Graduate?

## Answers

***Screen Greats***

**1** Frankenstein. **2** Tony. **3** John F Kennedy. **4** Dynasty. **5** Bette Davis. **6** Harrison. **7** San Francisco. **8** Buddhism. **9** Humphrey Bogart. **10** Germany. **11** Michael Caine. **12** Frank Sinatra. **13** England. **14** Marlon Brando. **15** Fred Astaire/Ginger Rogers. **16** Gene Kelly. **17** James Dean. **18** Monaco. **19** Star Wars. **20** Bob Hope. **21** Kirk. **22** Crawford. **23** Nicholson. **24** Zhivago. **25** Dustin Hoffman.

# Quiz 100 Entertainment

1 Which association for magicians was founded in 1905?
2 The Lord's Taverners raise money by entertaining with what activity?
3 The Aldeburgh Festival takes place in which east of England county?
4 What type of shooting season begins on 12th August?
5 Which London theatre takes its name form the Mermaid Tavern where writers met in Shakespeare's time?
6 Which playwright Sir Alan founded a theatre in Scarborough?
7 Pinewood Studios provide material for which industry?
8 If you watched a point to point what would you be watching?
9 If a film has a PG classification whose Guidance is needed to watch it?
10 In which London Hall does the Last Night of the Proms take place?
11 Who are G & S?
12 What type of entertainer is Wayne Sleep?
13 What did the King do during the Hallelujah Chorus of Handel's Messiah which means now everyone has to do it?
14 Which playwright Noel whose centenary is celebrated in 1999 wrote Hay Fever and Private Lives which were revived in London that year?
15 What would you be most likely to be watching if the audience shouted "He's behind you" to someone on the stage?
16 Which peer who writes musicals attended the wedding of Prince Edward and Sophie Rhys-Jones?
17 Which musical instrument does Vanessa Mae play?
18 What entertainment consists of people singing to a backing tape?
19 If you were watching the Red Arrows what type of display would you be watching?
20 What was the New Philharmonia Orchestra called after it had been established 32 years?
21 What does O stand for in NYO, the leading group of young musicians?
22 Which town in Sussex has hosted a drama festival annually since 1962?
23 What type of Derby was first held at the White City in 1927?
24 In 1990 the Sadler's Wells Ballet moved to which Midlands city?
25 The NFT is a National Theatre which shows what?

## Answers

***Entertainment***

**1** Magic Circle. **2** Cricket. **3** Suffolk. **4** Grouse. **5** Mermaid. **6** Ayckbourn. **7** Film. **8** Horse race. **9** Parental. **10** Albert Hall. **11** Gilbert & Sullivan. **12** Dancer. **13** Stand up. **14** Coward. **15** Pantomime. **16** Andrew Lloyd Webber. **17** Violin. **18** Karaoke. **19** Air Display. **20** The Philharmonia Orchestra. **21** Orchestra. **22** Chichester. **23** Greyhound. **24** Birmingham. **25** Films.

# The Medium Questions

This next selection of questions is getting a little more like it. For an open entry quiz then you should have a high percentage of medium level questions – don't try to break people's spirits with the hard ones just make sure that they play to their ability.

Like all questions these can be classed as either easy or impossible depending on whether you know the answer or not and although common knowledge is used as the basis for these questions, there is a sting in the tail of quite a few. Also, if you have a serious drinking squad playing then they can more or less say goodbye to the prize, but that isn't to say they will feel any worse about it.

Specialists are the people to watch out as those with a good knowledge of a particular subject will doubtless do well in these rounds so a liberal sprinkling of pot-luck questions are needed to flummox them.

# Quiz 1 Pot Luck 1

**1** Most of The Three Tenors come from which country?
**2** Who remarked that, "every Prime Minister needs a Willie"?
**3** In which decade was the World Wildlife Fund set up?
**4** Which soccer player's 1998 book was titled Addicted?
**5** On which date was the movie Independence Day screened in America?
**6** Who had an 80s No 1 with I Want To Wake Up With You?
**7** In cricket which English team became Sptifires in the 90s?
**8** What was 'Pie in the Sky' in the name of the series with Richard Griffiths?
**9** What were ladies asked not to wear at Prince Edward and Sophie's wedding?
**10** What did Dr Howard Carter discover?
**11** Which Sir Christopher was a 90s chairman of the BBC?
**12** In which decade of this century was the Cullinan diamond discovered?
**13** Which Bond girl was played by Diana Rigg?
**14** Whose last words were reputedly, "Either this wallpaper goes or I do"?
**15** At which sport did Neil Adams win international success?
**16** Post WWII tanks all begin with which letter of the alphabet?
**17** Who wrote the song Mad Dogs And Englishmen?
**18** In which year did the UK join the European Union?
**19** How many years does it take to paint the Forth Railway Bridge from end to end?
**20** Which England soccer player has the middle names Emerson Carlyle?
In which decade was Kim Basinger born?
**21** Who wrote the children's classic The Lion, The Witch And The
**22** Wardrobe?
**23** Amarillo airport was built in which US state?
**24** Bones of which Man were supposedly discovered in Sussex in 1912?
**25** What's the link between boxing champion James Corbett and country singer Jim Reeves?

## Answers

***Pot Luck 1***

**1** Spain. **2** Margaret Thatcher. **3** 60s. **4** Tony Adams. **5** 4th July. **6** Boris Gardiner. **7** Kent. **8** A restaurant. **9** Hats. **10** Tutankhamen's tomb. **11** Bland. **12** First decade. **13** Tracy Vincenzo. **14** Oscar Wilde. **15** Judo. **16** C. **17** Noel Coward. **18** 1973. **19** Four. **20** Paul Ince. **21** 50s. **22** C S Lewis. **23** Texas. **24** Piltdown Man. **25** Both known as Gentleman Jim.

# Quiz 2 20th C Who's Who

Level 2

1 Who did Pope John Paul II succeed as Pope?
2 What did the letter F stand for in the name of President J F Kennedy?
3 Gitta Sereny courted controversy for writing a book about which convicted killer?
4 Who became the first woman prime minister of an Islamic nation?
5 Who said, "The Trent is lovely too. I've walked on it for 18 years"?
6 Tom Whittaker was the first man to climb Everest in what circumstances?
7 Who was posthumously pardoned in 1998 after being hanged for the murder of a policeman in 1953?
8 Who replaced Mary Robinson as president of Ireland in 1997?
9 Which American president had the middle name Baines?
10 Which Russian dictator imposed a reign of terror throughout the 30s and 40s?
11 On TV who originally asked contestants to Take Their Pick?
12 Who was the only female MP in The Gang of Four?
13 Who made the official speech opening the Scottish Parliament?
14 Who once described his paintings as "hand-painted dream photographs"?
15 Donald Woods escaped which country in 1979, a story later made into a film Cry Freedom?
16 What was the name of the Chinese leader whose widow was arrested for trying to overthrow the government in the 1970s?
17 Where was Ronnie Biggs arrested in 1974 after over eight years on the run?
18 Which manager signed the first Catholic player for Glasgow Rangers?
19 In 1968 The Oscars were postponed for 48 hours because of whose death?
20 Who succeeded Lal Bahadur Shastri as Prime Minister of India?
21 In the 1960s the Queen dedicated an acre of ground in the UK to the memory of whom?
22 Who created Fantasyland, Adventureland and Frontierland?
23 Who led so called witch hunts against communists in the USA after WWII?
24 Which kidnap victim was involved in a bank raid, brandishing a gun, even after a ransom had been paid?
25 Who was Master of the Rolls from 1962 to 1982?

## Answers

***20th C Who's Who***

**1** John Paul I. **2** Fitzgerald. **3** Mary Bell. **4** Benazir Bhutto. **5** Brian Clough. **6** He only has one leg. **7** Derek Bentley. **8** Mary McAleese. **9** Lyndon Johnson. **10** Stalin. **11** Michael Miles. **12** Shirley Williams. **13** The Queen. **14** Salvador Dali. **15** South Africa. **16** Mao Tse Tung. **17** Brazil. **18** Graeme Souness. **19** Martin Luther King. **20** Indira Gandhi. **21** President Kennedy. **22** Walt Disney. **23** McCarthy. **24** Patty Hearst. **25** Lord Denning.

# Quiz 3 Pot Luck 2

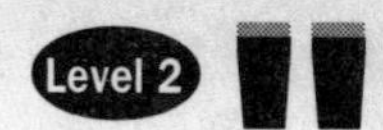

1. After a tennis match with Amelia Mauresmo who said "...I thought I was playing a guy"?
2. Which spoof crime series was a spin off from Canned Carrott?
3. What post did Edward Shevardnadze hold in the USSR from 1985 to 1990?
4. Who wrote the 90s novel Gridlock?
5. What was Wet Wet Wet's first No 1?
6. In baseball where do the Braves come from?
7. Which musical featured the song Wouldn't It Be Luvverly?
8. In which decade of the 20th century was HMS Ark Royal withdrawn from service?
9. Which country did the composer Frederick Delius come from?
10. Which lady was the BBC Sports Personality of 1977?
11. In 70s car seat belt ads, what should you do every trip?
12. Who did Clement Attlee replace as Prime Minister?
13. Who left EastEnders and starred in a series set in a Derby telephone exchange?
14. Who made No 1 with Ready Or Not?
15. De Efteling Theme Park is in which country?
16. Erik Thorstvedt won the FA Cup as a keeper at which club?
17. According to the Monty Python team what does a lumberjack do all night?
18. Agno international airport is in which country?
19. Who said, "There will be no whitewash in the White House"?
20. At which sport did Paul Ackford represent England?
21. How did William Cody become better known?
22. Early in the century who wrote the novel Nostromo?
23. What did the letter C stand for in ACAS?
24. What part of Betty Grable was insured for over a million dollars?
25. In which decade was Top Of The Pops first broadcast?

## Answers

***Pot Luck 2***

**1** Lindsay Davenport. **2** The Detectives. **3** Minister of Foreign Affairs. **4** Ben Elton. **5** With A Little Help From My Friends. **6** Atlanta. **7** My Fair Lady. **8** 70s. **9** England. **10** Virginia Wade. **11** Clunk, click. **12** Winston Churchill. **13** Letitia Dean. **14** Fugees. **15** The Netherlands. **16** Spurs. **17** Sleep. **18** Switzerland. **19** Richard Nixon. **20** Rugby Union. **21** Buffalo Bill. **22** Joseph Conrad. **23** Conciliation. **24** Legs. **25** 60s.

# Quiz 4 Diana, Princess of Wales

**1** Who designed Diana's wedding dress?
**2** Who coined the phrase The People's Princess about Diana?
**3** What was the name of the kindergarten where Diana worked before her marriage?
**4** What colour suit did Diana wear in her engagement photograph?
**5** Which film star did Diana famously dance with at The White House?
**6** Diana became an ambassador for which charity's campaign to ban land mines?
**7** Which auctioneers auctioned Diana's dresses in 1997?
**8** Which Palace was Diana's home in the last year of her life?
**9** Who interviewed Diana during her famous Panorama interview?
**10** With which ballet dancer did Diana dance to Uptown Girl at a charity gala in 1985?
**11** In 1996 Diana visited the Shaukat Kanum cancer hospital in Pakistan which was built in the memory of whose mother?
**12** What was the name of Diana's mother at the time of Diana's marriage?
**13** In which hospital was Diana photographed watching a heart operation?
**14** Which official title did Diana have after her divorce?
**15** To the nearest £3 million what was Diana's divorce settlement?
**16** In which city did the auction of Diana's dresses take place?
**17** What was the name of the driver of the car in which Diana met her death?
**18** Who wrote the 1992 biography, written with Diana's knowledge, which revealed personal details of Charles and Diana's married life?
**19** In early July 1997 Diana and her sons were on holiday on whose yacht?
**20** What are Diana's two sister called?
**21** In 1987 what special ward, the first in Britain, was opened by Diana?
**22** At which theme park was Diana photographed, soaking wet, with William and Harry in 1994?
**23** On which Royal estate was Diana born?
**24** In what capacity was Paul Burrel employed by Diana?
**25** Whose book in 1998 criticised Diana and was itself disapproved of by Prince Charles and Camilla Parker-Bowles?

## Answers

***20th C Diana, Princess of Wales***

**1** The Emanuels. **2** Tony Blair. **3** Young England. **4** Blue. **5** John Travolta. **6** Red Cross. **7** Christie's. **8** Kensington. **9** Martin Bashir. **10** Wayne Sleep. **11** Imran Khan. **12** Frances Shand Kydd. **13** Harefield. **14** Diana, Princess of Wales. **15** £15 Million. **16** New York. **17** Henri Paul. **18** Andrew Morton. **19** Mohammed Al Fayed's. **20** Sarah & Jane. **21** Aids. **22** Thorpe Park. **23** Sandringham. **24** Butler. **25** Penny Junor.

# Quiz 5 Pot Luck 3

**1** Opened in June 1999, the Matthew Street Gallery in Liverpool was dedicated to the works of who?
**2** Neil Armstrong was a pilot in which war?
**3** Which international soccer keeper of the 90s also played cricket for Scotland?
**4** Who wrote the Scarlet Pimpernel?
**5** In 1997 which long running TV quiz had started so it finished?
**6** Who had an 80s No 1 with Frankie?
**7** Which snooker star has a son called Blain?
**8** Which series was based on the 'Constable' novels by Nicholas Rhea?
**9** Which item of clothing cost Isadora Duncan her life?
**10** Which soccer country beat the Republic of Ireland in the play off for France 98?
**11** In which country was Ursula Andress born?
**12** Zoe Redhead was headmistress of which school in the news in the 90s?
**13** Who had the novels Spy Hook and Spy Line published in the 80s?
**14** What was the first UK Top Ten hit for 911?
**15** At which sport did Gary Armstrong represent Scotland?
**16** Which motorway goes from London to Winchester?
**17** In the summer of 1999 Anna Kournikova signed a lucrative contract to model what?
**18** In which decade did Belgium join the European Union?
**19** In which series did Neil Pearson play Tony Clark?
**20** In which city did Man Utd win the 1999 European Champions' Cup Final?
**21** Louis Armstrong sang the title song for which Bond film?
**22** What did Clarice Cliff create?
**23** To the nearest million what is the population of London?
**24** In Rugby League what did Wigan add to their name in the 90s?
**25** Which city is the home of Yorkshire TV?

## Answers

***Pot Luck 3***

**1** John Lennon. **2** Korean. **3** Andy Goram. **4** Baroness Orczy. **5** Mastermind. **6** Sister Sledge. **7** Stephen Hendry. **8** Heartbeat. **9** Scarf - it was caught in a moving car wheel. **10** Belgium. **11** Switzerland. **12** Summerhill. **13** Len Deighton. **14** Don't Make Me Wait. **15** Rugby Union. **16** M3. **17** Bras. **18** 50s. **19** Between The Lines. **20** Barcelona. **21** On Her Majesty's Secret Service. **22** Pottery. **23** 7 million. **24** Warriors. **25** Leeds.

# Quiz 6 20th C TV Soaps

**1** Which character did Paul Nicholls play in EastEnders?
**2** Lorraine Brownlow was what relation to Natalie in Coronation Street?
**3** What was the name of Deirdre's blonde cellmate played by Margi Clarke?
**4** Which future EastEnders actor played runaway Graham Lodsworth in Emmerdale?
**5** Which Queen Vic landlady won The Rear of the Year award in 1987?
**6** Which country did Kathy go to when she left Albert Square?
**7** By the beginning of 1999 how many wives had Ken Barlow had?
**8** Onslow from Keeping Up Appearances was a regular in which soap for eight years?
**9** Which Jacob was buried in the very first episode of Emmerdale?
**10** Which soap had a supermarket called Bettabuys?
**11** What is Betty Williams' speciality in the Rovers Return?
**12** Which ex Vic landlady was in a pop group called Milan?
**13** What was the name of Alec Gilroy's granddaughter who married Steve McDonald?
**14** Which Neighbours' star's sister appeared in rival soap Home & Away?
**15** Who wrote the theme to Crossroads and Neighbours?
**16** The video Naked Truths is about which soap family?
**17** Who was the hairdresser Ms Middleton played by Angela Griffin in Coronation Street?
**18** Civvy Street was a one hour special spin off from which soap?
**19** How many times a week was Coronation Street broadcast when it began?
**20** At which Farm did Kim and Frank Tate live in Emmerdale?
**21** Which soap was the first to have an Afro Caribbean character as a regular cast member?
**22** In which decade did the magazine soap Compact begin?
**23** Which soap was headed in its early days by the Lockhead family?
**24** What was the name of Anna Friel's character when she was in Brookside?
**25** In Coronation Street what was Deirdre's first married name?

## Answers

***20th C TV Soaps***

**1** Joe Wicks. **2** Niece. **3** Jackie. **4** Ross Kemp. **5** Angie. **6** South Africa. **7** Three. **8** Coronation Street. **9** Sugden. **10** Coronation Street. **11** Hotpot. **12** Tiffany. **13** Vicky. **14** Kylie Minogue's - Dannii. **15** Tony Hatch. **16** The Mitchells. **17** Fiona. **18** EastEnders. **19** Twice. **20** Home Farm. **21** Crossroads. **22** 60s. **23** Eldorado. **24** Beth Jordache. **25** Langton.

# Quiz 7 Pot Luck 4

1 Nick Leeson hid his debts in a secret account with which number?
2 Louis Washkansky was the first recipient of what?
3 Which musical featured the song Hello Young Lovers?
4 In cricket what did Yorkshire add to their name in the 90s?
5 In which country was Mel Gibson born?
6 Which Spice Girl teamed with Bryan Adams on When You're Gone?
7 Where is the Glasgow terminus of the M8?
8 Canaan Banana was the first president of which country?
9 What was Britain's first breakfast TV programme called?
10 Which athlete was the BBC Sports Personality the year after Steve Ovett won the award?
11 What did the W H stand for in the name of the poet W H Auden?
12 In TV ads, who shared a glass of Cinzano with Joan Collins?
13 Who made No 1 with Breakfast At Tiffany's?
14 In which sport could the Trailblazers take on the Warriors?
15 1999 is the Chinese year of which creature?
16 What was the name of Natalie's drug dealer son in Coronation Street?
17 Which sporting event was featured in the first outside TV broadcast?
18 Who wrote the novel Brave New World?
19 Asturias international airport is in which country?
20 In which decade was Jenny Agutter born?
21 Goalkeeper Bernard Lama has played for which country?
22 What did the Q originally stand for in the magazine GQ?
23 East Pakistan has become known as what?
24 Who married Mickey Rooney, Artie Shaw and Frank Sinatra?
25 Which dog clocked up an amazing 550 plus hours of air time on BBC TV?

## Answers

***Pot Luck 4***

**1** 88888. **2** Heart transplant. **3** The King And I. **4** Phoenix. **5** USA. **6** Mel C. **7** Airport. **8** Zimbabwe. **9** Breakfast Time. **10** Sebastian Coe. **11** Wystan Hugh. **12** Leonard Rossiter. **13** Deep Blue Something. **14** Basketball. **15** Hare. **16** Tony. **17** The Derby. **18** Aldous Huxley. **19** Spain. **20** 50s. **21** France. **22** Quarterly. **23** Bangladesh. **24** Ava Gardner. **25** Petra.

# Quiz 8 Soccer

Level 2 

1 Peter Schmeichel joined Man Utd from which club?
2 Which side finished fourth in the 1998 World Cup?
3 In 1999's European Champions' Cup Final which player scored the first goal?
4 Which soccer club began the century known as Newton Heath?
5 What was the half-time Argentina v England score in the 1998 World Cup?
6 Pierluigi Casiraghi joined Chelsea in 1998 from which club?
7 At which club did Ron Atkinson replace Dr Josef Venglos as manager?
8 Which club became Britains first to have an all-seater stadium?
9 Who was the first England manager to be born in Worksop?
10 In the 60s and 70s Ron Harris set an appearance record at which soccer club?
11 Who scored Scotland's only goal from outfield play in France 98?
12 Darren Anderton first played league soccer with which club?
13 Which British club in the 1980s became the first to install an artificial pitch?
14 Who was the first 50 plus player to turn out in a top flight league game in England?
15 Who became the first Croatian international to play for an English club?
16 Which German team were first to win the European Cup?
17 Who was the first World Cup winning skipper to play in the Premiership?
18 Which manager took Peter Beardsley to Newcastle?
19 With 96 caps Jan Ceulemans set an appearance record for which country?
20 In the 90s, which British manager won successive titles with PSV Eindhoven?
21 Which Scottish international played for Barcelona in the 80s?
22 Who were England's first opponents in the 1998 World Cup in France?
23 Who was the first keeper to captain an FA Cup winning team at Wembley?
24 Who followed Bob Shankly as Liverpool manager?
25 Coventry first won the FA Cup in which decade?

## Answers

***Soccer***

**1** Brondby. **2** Holland. **3** Basler. **4** Man Utd. **5** 2-2. **6** Lazio. **7** Aston Villa. **8** Aberdeen. **9** Graham Taylor. **10** Chelsea. **11** Craig Burley. **12** Portsmouth. **13** QPR. **14** Stanley Matthews. **15** Igor Stimac. **16** Bayern Munich. **17** Deschamps. **18** Kevin Keegan. **19** Belgium. **20** Bobby Robson. **21** Steve Archibald. **22** Tunisia. **23** Dave Beasant. **24** Bob Paisley. **25** 80s.

# Quiz 9 Pot Luck 5

1. Which company replaced Thames TV in the early 1990s?
2. How did Jean Batten achieve fame?
3. In which country was Menachem Begin, a Prime Minister of Israel born?
4. With which sport is Bernard Hinault associated?
5. Which character from Albert Square played DI Mick Raynor in a 90s crime series?
6. Who had an 80s No 1 with China In Your Hand?
7. Who did Gottlieb Daimler team up with to form a motor company?
8. Who penned Alexander's Ragtime Band?
9. Which Jane married Gerald Scarfe?
10. What was the first UK Top Ten hit for Sleeper?
11. Copeland has been the 90s seat of which prominent Labour politician?
12. What are the international registration letters of a vehicle from Bulgaria?
13. Who released the single Secret Agent Man - James Bond Is Back in '87?
14. Which co founder of TV am was once married to Tony Blair's Leader of the House of Lords?
15. What was the first name of Dr Barnardo founder of Barnardo's Homes?
16. On which river was the Aswan High Dam built?
17. Which famous magazine was started by Alexander Graham Bell?
18. In which city was Jimmy's set?
19. In American Football where do the Redskins come from?
20. In African politics, what does the letter C stand for in ANC?
21. In which country was Kenneth Branagh born?
22. Who played the tough cop character Jack Regan?
23. Which soccer team did Ian Botham play for?
24. In which country is the deepwater port of Agadir?
25. Which writer created Bilbo Baggins?

## Answers

***Pot Luck 5***

**1** Carlton. **2** Aviator. **3** Poland. **4** Cycling. **5** Den Watts. **6** T'Pau. **7** Karl Benz. **8** Irving Berlin. **9** Asher. **10** Sale Of The Century. **11** Jack Cunningham. **12** BG. **13** Bruce Willis. **14** Peter Jay. **15** Thomas. **16** Nile. **17** National Geographic. **18** Leeds. **19** Washington. **20** Congress. **21** N Ireland. **22** John Thaw. **23** Scunthorpe. **24** Morocco. **25** J R R Tolkein.

# Quiz 10 20th C Blockbusters

Level 2 

1 What was Anna Chancellor's nickname in Four Weddings and a Funeral?
2 Which member of the Corleone family did Al Pacino play in The Godfather?
3 In which film did Michael Douglas and Glenn Close play Dan Gallagher and Alex Forrest?
4 Who played Amon Goeth in Schindler's List?
5 Which of his characters did Robin Williams say was a cross between Bill Forsyth, Alastair Sim and the Queen Mother?
6 The Third Man was set in which European city?
7 The action of which 70s movie revolves around the Kit Kat Club in Berlin?
8 In which part of New York did Shaft take place?
9 Which trilogy of films with Michael J Fox featured a De Lorean sports car?
10 Who played the role on film in Shadowlands which Nigel Hawthorne had made his own on the stage?
11 What was the first name of Private Ryan?
12 Which Orson Welles movie was voted top US movie of all time by the US Film Institute in 1998?
13 The action of Trainspotting takes place in Edinburgh, but where was the movie filmed?
14 Which Scottish hero was released on video to coincide with the opening of the 90s Scottish Parliament?
15 Who played the villainous Sir August de Wynter in The Avengers?
16 What was the sequel to Jurassic Park called?
17 Which actor was the narrator in Evita?
18 Dante's Peak featured which type of natural disaster?
19 In which country does the action in The Piano take place?
20 In which blockbusting 60s musical did the Sharks meet the Jets?
21 How many tunnels were built in The Great Escape?
22 Who was Julius Caesar in Cleopatra with Elizabeth Taylor in the title role?
23 What was the second Bond movie with Sean Connery?
24 Who played the architect of the skyscraper in The Towering Inferno?
25 Who played Dr Zhivago's wife in Dr Zhivago?

## Answers

***20th C The Movies Blockbusters***

**1** Duckface. **2** Michael. **3** Fatal Attraction. **4** Ralph Fiennes. **5** Mrs Doubtfire. **6** Vienna. **7** Cabaret. **8** Harlem. **9** Back To The Future. **10** Anthony Hopkins. **11** James. **12** Citizen Kane. **13** Glasgow. **14** Braveheart. **15** Sean Connery. **16** The Lost World: Jurassic Park. **17** Antonio Banderas. **18** Volcano. **19** New Zealand. **20** West Side Story. **21** Three. **22** Rex Harrison. **23** From Russia With Love. **24** Paul Newman. **25** Geraldine Chaplin.

# Quiz 11 Pot Luck 6

1 Who lived under the pseudonym of Harriet Brown in New York from the 40s to the 90s?
2 In baseball where do the Red Sox come from?
3 What was Wham's first No 1?
4 In which year was Bloody Sunday in Londonderry?
5 What was the main colour of a Stormtrooper in Star Wars?
6 Which club did Stan Collymore join when he left Nottm Forest?
7 Which country did Albert Einstein move to as the Nazis rose to power?
8 Which lawyer made Raymond Burr famous?
9 Who joined The Wonder Stuff on the UK No 1 Dizzy?
10 Who was Prime Minister when England won the World Cup?
11 If I Were A Rich Man was a big hit from which stage show?
12 Sir Leslie Porter is a former chairman of which supermarket chain?
13 Which TV reporter's stories of the famine in 1984 inspired Bob Geldof to set up Band Aid?
14 Who made No 1 with Boom Boom Boom?
15 At which sport did Nigel Aspinall win international success?
16 Which musical featured the song You'll Never Walk Alone?
17 Which EastEnders actress directed Barbara Windsor in her harrowing cancer scare scenes in the soap?
18 Who wrote the novels on which BBC's classic series The Forsythe Saga was based?
19 Luxor international airport is in which country?
20 In the 90s how many points have been awarded for finishing first in a Grand Prix?
21 Which footballer was the BBC Sports Personality of 1990?
22 Which? is the magazine of which Association?
23 Who played Private Godfrey in Dad's Army?
24 David Seaman first played for England when he was with which club?
25 What was the name of Gene Autry's horse?

## Answers

***Pot Luck 6***

**1** Greta Garbo. **2** Boston. **3** Wake Me Up Before You Go Go. **4** 1972. **5** White. **6** Liverpool. **7** America. **8** Perry Mason. **9** Vic Reeves. **10** Harold Wilson. **11** Fiddler on the Roof. **12** Tesco. **13** Michael Buerk. **14** Outhere Brothers. **15** Croquet. **16** Carousel. **17** Susan Tully. **18** John Galsworthy. **19** Egypt. **20** 10. **21** Paul Gascoigne. **22** Consumers. **23** Arnold Ridley. **24** QPR. **25** Champion.

# Quiz 12 Around The UK

Level 2

1 The research laboratories at Porton Down ar near which cathedral town?
2 To the nearest 100ft how tall is the Canary Wharf Tower?
3 Where did the Royal Mint move to from Tower Hill London in 1968?
4 According to a University of East Anglia report which year of the 90s was the hottest ever recorded in the UK?
5 Where did the National Horseracing Museum open in 1983?
6 Where was the site of the Millennium Exhibition and the Millennium Dome chosen to be?
7 Which Cheshire village was the home of nanny Louise Woodward?
8 Which castle was restored by the end of 1997 at a cost of £37 million?
9 Which English county has the place with the longest name - Sutton-Under-Whitestonecliffe ?
10 Where is the annual music festival founded by Benjamin Britten held?
11 The first of a chain of which holiday centres opened in Skegness in 1936?
12 Which branch of the armed services is trained at Cranwell in Lincolnshire?
13 Where is the Government Communications Headquarters?
14 In the 1990s which theatre was rebuilt on the site of an Elizabethan theatre?
15 Which military museum was founded in London in 1917?
16 Which airport in the English capital was built in 1987?
17 Which social organisation's name is the Latin word for table?
18 Metrolink operates a train service around which city?
19 Which city has a railway station called Temple Meades?
20 Beaulieu in Hampshire has a famous museum of what?
21 In 1991 the Sainsbury Wing was built as an extension to which Gallery?
22 The Burrell Gallery is in which Scottish city?
23 In which inner city was the first National Garden Festival held in 1984?
24 Which company merged with Stena to face the cross Channel competition for services through the Channel Tunnel?
25 Where is the Open University based?

## Answers

***Around the UK***

**1** Salisbury. **2** 800ft. **3** Cardiff. **4** 1995. **5** Newmarket. **6** Greenwich. **7** Elton. **8** Windsor. **9** North Yorkshire. **10** Aldeburgh. **11** Butlin's. **12** RAF. **13** Cheltenham. **14** Globe. **15** Imperial War Museum. **16** London City Airport. **17** Mensa. **18** Manchester. **19** Bristol. **20** Cars. **21** National Gallery. **22** Glasgow. **23** Liverpool. **24** P & O. **25** Milton Keynes.

# Quiz 13 Pot Luck 7

1 In which decade did Alexander Fleming discover penicillin?
2 Which Dutch graphic artist - initials M C - was a creator of optical illusions?
3 In which city is O'Hare International airport?
4 Who played Claire Maitland in Cardiac Arrest?
5 Which US President was backed by the "I like Ike" campaign?
6 Who had an 80s No 1 with Freedom?
7 Which Wimbledon champion once had soccer trials with Bayern Munich?
8 Which movement was founded by Mary Baker Eddy?
9 In which decade was Dennis Potter's Lipstick on Your Collar set?
10 What was the speciality of jewellery maker Peter Faberge?
11 Which city with 3 million inhabitants is Australia's largest by population?
12 In decimal currency how much did the first TV licence cost?
13 Which Rugby League team became Rhinos in the 90s?
14 Which musical featured the song All I Ask Of You?
15 Which was the second city to be hit by an atomic bomb in World War II?
16 Who famously said, "Well he would say that, wouldn't he?"?
17 In the movie of the same name, what is The Lion King's name?
18 Under what name did Peggy Hookham entertain audiences?
19 In TV ads what should you do with Brut according to Henry Cooper?
20 Paul McCartney and Wings provided the title song for which Bond film?
21 As a child who called herself 'Lilibet'?
22 What was the first UK Top Ten hit for the Run-DMC?
23 Who wrote the novel Gone With The Wind?
24 In which decade did Greece join the European Union?
25 Who played the first TV Doctor Who?

**Answers**

***Pot Luck 7***

**1** 20s. **2** Escher. **3** Chicago. **4** Helen Baxendale. **5** Dwight Eisenhower. **6** Wham!. **7** Boris Becker. **8** Christian Science Church. **9** 50s. **10** Jewelled eggs. **11** Sydney. **12** 50p. **13** Leeds. **14** Phantom Of The Opera. **15** Nagasaki. **16** Mandy Rice Davies. **17** Simba. **18** Margot Fonteyn. **19** Splash it all over. **20** Live And Let Die. **21** Queen Elizabeth II. **22** Walk This Way. **23** Margaret Mitchell. **24** 80s. **25** William Hartnell.

# Quiz 14 Music - Girl Power

1 How many of The Corrs are female?
2 In which decade was vocalist Karen Carpenter born?
3 Whose real name is Gaynor Hopkins?
4 Which soap star had a 1990 hit with Just This Side of Love?
5 Shout was the first hit for which solo female star?
6 Which comedienne featured on the B side of the Comic Relief hit The Stonk?
7 In 1995 the album Daydream topped the charts for which female vocalist?
8 How many girls were in the group Ace of Base?
9 In which decade was vocalist Lisa Stansfield born?
10 Who released an album called Jagged Little Pill?
11 Who asked Unbreak My Heart in 1997?
12 Which Spice Girls hit was No 1 at the beginning of 1997?
13 In 1995 which soapstar was Happy Just to Be with You?
14 Who was a Professional Widow according to her 1997 hit?
15 What was Madonna's third UK No 1?
16 In which country was Neneh Cherry born?
17 What was Whitney Houston's first UK top ten hit?
18 Who released a UK No 1 album in 1992 called Shepherd Moons?
19 Which country was represented by Celine Dion at the Eurovision Song Contest?
20 Which female vocalist said All I Want for Christmas is You in 1994?
21 Who duetted with Peter Gabriel on Don't Give Up?
22 Who got to No 1 in 1994 in her first-ever week in the UK charts?
23 Who released the top selling album Guilty in 1980?
24 Which female artist had huge success with the album The Kick Inside?
25 Who won a US Song of the Year Award in 1995 for Breathe Again ?

## Answers

***Music - Girl Power***

**1** Three. **2** 1950s. **3** Bonnie Tyler. **4** Malandra Burrows. **5** Lulu. **6** Victoria Wood. **7** Mariah Carey. **8** Two. **9** 60s. **10** Alanis Morisette. **11** Toni Braxton. **12** 2 Become 1. **13** Michelle Gayle. **14** Tori Amos. **15** La Isla Bonita. **16** Sweden. **17** Saving All My Love For You. **18** Enya. **19** Switzerland. **20** Mariah Carey. **21** Kate Bush. **22** Whigfield. **23** Barbra Streisand. **24** Kate Bush. **25** Toni Braxton.

# Quiz 15 Pot Luck 8

1 In which country did the notorious security force the Tontons Macoutes operate?
2 Which producer of Kavanagh QC has been a regular on Food & Drink?
3 In cricket which English team became Royals in the 90s?
4 What was the first UK Top Ten hit for the Smashing Pumpkins?
5 What became the capital of Australia during the 20th century?
6 On which Caribbean island did Princess Diana spend her first Christmas after her divorce was announced?
7 Which musical featured the song Thank Heaven For Little Girls?
8 What breed of dog did Columbo own?
9 In basketball where do the Mavericks come from?
10 British Honduras has become known as what?
11 Which song was released to raise funds for Children in Need in 1997?
12 For many years Fred Basset has been a regular of which Daily paper?
13 To the nearest million what is the population of Australia?
14 Who made No 1 with Deeply Dippy?
15 Who wrote The Good Companions?
16 Which Prime Minister replaced Anthony Eden?
17 Who did Liz leave Coronation Street with?
18 The Queen Elizabeth liner was destroyed by fire in the 70s in which harbour?
19 Gracie Fields sang about the Biggest what In The World?
20 Who took over as President of the European Commission in January 1985?
21 Malpensa international airport is in which country?
22 Which were the initials of Doctor Finlay creator Cronin?
23 Who was Cohen's fullback partner in England's World Cup winning team?
24 1998 is the Chinese year of which creature?
25 Which country does musician Alfred Brendel come from?

**Answers**

***Pot Luck 8***

**1** Haiti. **2** Chris Kelly. **3** Worcestershire. **4** Tonight Tonight. **5** Canberra. **6** Barbuda. **7** Gigi. **8** Basset hound. **9** Dallas. **10** Belize. **11** Perfect Day. **12** Mail. **13** 18 million. **14** Right Said Fred. **15** J B Priestley. **16** Harold Macmillan. **17** Michael. **18** Hong Kong. **19** Aspidistra. **20** Jacques Delors. **21** Italy. **22** A J. **23** Wilson. **24** Tiger. **25** Austria.

# Quiz 16 War Zones

1 Which US General along with Schwarzkopf was leader in the Gulf War?
2 The Taliban were a guerrilla group in which country?
3 How long did the Arab Israeli War of 1967 last?
4 Who, during the Vietnam war was known as Hanoi Jane?
5 Which breakaway Russian republic had Grozny as its capital?
6 Which country's 'Spring' was halted by the arrival of Soviet tanks in 1968?
7 Where was the Bay of Pigs whose invasion sparked a world crisis in the 60s?
8 Which country pulled out of Vietnam in the 1950s?
9 Where did the Enola Gay drop a devastating bomb in WWII?
10 In which country is Passchendaele, scene of battle in WWI?
11 Whose forces were defeated at the Battle of Midway in 1942?
12 Who were defeated along with the Germans at El Alamein?
13 During World War 1 what kind of gas was used in the trenches?
14 What Operation was the codename for the D Day landings?
15 Which major weapon of war was used for the first time in 1916?
16 The Tamil Tigers were fighting for a separate state on which island?
17 Muhammad Ali refused to fight in which war?
18 War broke out in Biafra in the 60s when it broke away from which country?
19 Where did Nazi leader Rudolf Hess crashland in 1941?
20 Which 'Lord' was executed for treason in 1946 for broadcasting Nazi propaganda?
21 During which war was OXFAM set up?
22 In WWII who was in charge of the Afrika Korps?
23 The EOKA were a terrorist group operating on which island?
24 What was the number of the British Armoured Division known as The Desert Rats?
25 Which city was besieged by German troops for over 900 days in WWII?

## Answers

***War Zones***

**1** Powell. **2** Afghanistan. **3** Six Days. **4** Jane Fonda. **5** Chechenia. **6** Czechoslovakia. **7** Cuba. **8** France. **9** Hiroshima. **10** Belgium. **11** Japan. **12** Italians. **13** Mustard gas. **14** Overlord. **15** Tank. **16** Sri Lanka. **17** Vietnam. **18** Nigeria. **19** Scotland. **20** Lord Haw-Haw. **21** WWII. **22** Rommel. **23** Cyprus. **24** 7th. **25** Leningrad.

# Quiz 17 Pot Luck 9

1 In which decade was the last execution at the Tower of London?
2 Which element along with polonium did the Curies discover?
3 Which Wine Bar did Rumpole frequent?
4 Who had an 80s No 1 with A Good Heart?
5 What does Blitz mean?
6 Nigel Winterburn joined Arsenal from which soccer club?
7 On a computer keyboard which letter is between A and D?
8 Which musical featured the song Flash Bang, Wallop?
9 What is the Japanese share index called?
10 In which TV series sequel did Bob marry Thelma?
11 Hamilton has been the 90s seat of which prominent Labour politician?
12 What are the international registration letters of a vehicle from Turkey?
13 Who hosted the Proms on TV when Richard Baker retired?
14 Who wrote the Turn of The Screw in the 19th C and The Ambassadors in the 20th?
15 At which sport did Phil Barber win international success?
16 Who were the first act to have three singles enter at the UK No. 1?
17 Which branch of medicine is concerned with disorders of the blood?
18 What is the surname of William in Richal Crompton's William books?
19 In which year did Muhammad Ali announce his retirement?
20 Whose 80s recording of Vivaldi's Four Seasons sold a million?
21 What was the 60s equivalent of the 90s series The Verdict called?
22 What is the correct name of laughing gas?
23 Jak and Trog were examples of what?
24 In which decade was Kirstie Alley born?
25 In American Football where do the Vikings come from?

**Answers**

***Pot Luck 9***

**1** 40s. **2** Radium. **3** Pomeroy's. **4** Fergal Sharkey. **5** Lightning. **6** Wimbledon. **7** S. **8** Half A Sixpence. **9** Nikkei. **10** Whatever Happened To The Likely Lads. **11** George Robertson. **12** TR. **13** James Naughtie. **14** Henry James. **15** Hockey. **16** Slade. **17** Haematology. **18** Brown. **19** 1979. **20** Nigel Kennedy. **21** Crown Court. **22** Nitrous oxide. **23** Newspaper cartoonists. **24** 50s. **25** Minnesota.

# Quiz 18 20th C Famous Names

1 Which British Dame became the first woman to win two Olivier awards for best actress in the same year - in 1996?
2 Israel Moses Sieff was head of which British chain of stores?
3 Who was Deep Blue, Gary Kasparov's famous chess opponent?
4 Which comic became the BBC's youngest scriptwriter in 1980, aged 21?
5 Which chef opened a restaurant called Woz?
6 Which MP announced in 1996 that she had been reunited with the son she gave up for adoption 31 years before?
7 What relation was the Queen's Private Secretary Robert Fellowes to the late Diana Princess of Wales?
8 Who is the great grand daughter of Prime Minister Herbert Asquith?
9 What is the name of gourmet Egon Ronay's designer daughter?
10 In 1991 who was voted 'the most successful Australian to get to the top with least ability' by students in Adelaide?
11 What was the first name of the baby in the Louise Woodward case?
12 Which Rugby player did Julia Smith marry in 1994?
13 What is Tony Blair's daughter called?
14 Which musical instrument does astronomer Patrick Moore play?
15 Gerald Scarfe is famous as what?
16 What was the name of Mrs Neil Hamilton who forcefully defended her husband over sleaze allegation?
17 Ulrich Salchow was the first Olympic medallist in his sport and gave his name to one of its jumps; what sport is it?
18 Which veteran DJ's autobiography was called As It Happens?
19 Which photographer have Catherine Deneuve and Marie Helvin married?
20 Which cartoon strip was Charles Schulz most famous creation?
21 Who was the sole survivor of the car crash in which Princess Diana died?
22 Who sold the story of David Mellor & Antonia de Sancha to the papers?
23 In which area of London did Ronnie Scott open his jazz club in 1959?
24 Which singer and comedian published a volume of autobiography in 1989 called Arias and Raspberries?
25 David Sheppard, the Bishop of Liverpool, was famous for what sport?

## Answers

***20th C Famous Names***

**1** Judi Dench. **2** Marks & Spencer. **3** Computer. **4** Ben Elton. **5** Anthony Worrall-Thompson. **6** Claire Short. **7** Brother in Law. **8** Helena Bonham Carter. **9** Edina. **10** Kylie Minogue. **11** Matthew. **12** Will Carling. **13** Kathryn. **14** Xylophone. **15** Cartoonist. **16** Christine. **17** Skating. **18** Jimmy Savile. **19** David Bailey. **20** Peanuts. **21** Trevor Rees-Jones. **22** Max Clifford. **23** Soho. **24** Harry Secombe. **25** Cricketer.

# Quiz 19 Pot Luck 10

1. Which university is at Milton Keynes?
2. In Cluedo what is the colour of the vicar?
3. Which singer "ain't gonna work on Maggie's farm no more"?
4. Middlesex play most of their home cricket fixtures at which ground?
5. Which Princess's husband was killed in 1990 when his powerboat went out of control?
6. In baseball where do the White Sox come from?
7. On which docu soap did Emma Boundy find fame?
8. What was the first UK Top Ten hit for Sash!?
9. Which race course is at Esher?
10. Which creature is seen when Coronation Street starts?
11. Which Peter was artistic director of London's National Theatre?
12. Where is the wine growing Barossa Valley?
13. Which monarch reigned in Britain at the start of the First World War?
14. Who made No 1 with Sleeping Satellite?
15. Crick, Watson and Wilkins determined the structure of what?
16. Which star of Men Behaving Badly once presented The Tube?
17. In which decade did writer Thomas Hardy die?
18. Who wrote the novels A Judgement In Stone and The Killing Doll?
19. In which country is the deepwater port of Ashdod?
20. What was Michael Jackson's first solo No 1 in the UK?
21. In which country was Julie Christie born?
22. Who wrote that "the female of the species is deadlier than the male"?
23. Key West airport was built in which US state?
24. Which BBC periodical first came out in 1929?
25. Lots of Hughes's have played soccer for Wales, but who is England's most capped Hughes?

## Answers

***Pot Luck 10***

**1** Open. **2** Green. **3** Bob Dylan. **4** Lord's. **5** Caroline. **6** Chicago. **7** Lakesiders. **8** Encore Une Fois. **9** Sandown. **10** Cat. **11** Hall. **12** Australia. **13** George V. **14** Tasmin Archer. **15** DNA. **16** Leslie Ash. **17** 20s. **18** Ruth Rendell. **19** Israel. **20** One Day In Your Life. **21** India. **22** Rudyard Kipling. **23** Florida. **24** Radio Times. **25** Emlyn.

# Quiz 20 20th C Famous Faces

1 Scott Chisholm found fame promoting what type of TV programmes?
2 Who left News At Ten to help launch the BBC's Breakfast Time?
3 Who was the antiques expert on the 1999 series of Going For a Song?
4 Trude Mostue found fame in a docu soap about which profession?
5 Which Dingle from Emmerdale presented You've Been Framed?
6 Which They Think It's All Over regular had a beard?
7 Which extrovert TV chef was a member of the Calypso Twins?
8 How is Meg Lake better known?
9 On which show did Jane McDonald shoot to fame?
10 Who was the Six O'Clock News anchorman when the programme was revamped in 1999?
11 Who was The Naked Chef?
12 Who replaced Peter Sissons as host of Question Time?
13 Who presented the BBC's daytime Wimbledon coverage in the late 1990s?
14 My Kind of People was LWT talent spotting show fronted by whom?
15 Who played gamekeeper Mellors opposite Joely Richardson in the D H Lawrence TV adaptation?
16 In 1997 who played Max de Winter in a TV adaptation of Daphne DuMaurier's Rebecca?
17 Who moved from Whose Line Is It Anyway to Call My Bluff?
18 Who was the sole regular male team member in Victoria Wood - As Seen on TV?
19 Which ex Blue Peter presenter introduced Mad About Pets?
20 Who was the team captain opposing Jack Dee in the first series of It's Only TV but I Like It?
21 Which character had a hit single with a song of the theme music from EastEnders?
22 Who presented the very first edition of Top of the Pops?
23 David Jason's first long running serious TV role was as which character?
24 Who was behind the yoof series DEF II?
25 Who became Gardener's World's regular presenter after the death of Geoff Hamilton?

## Answers

***20th C Famous Faces***

**1** Children's. **2** Selina Scott. **3** Eric Knowles. **4** Vets. **5** Mandy. **6** Rory McGrath. **7** Ainsley Harriott. **8** Mystic Meg. **9** The Cruise. **10** Huw Edwards. **11** Jamie Oliver. **12** David Dimbleby. **13** Desmond Lynam. **14** Michael Barrymore. **15** Sean Bean. **16** Charles Dance. **17** Sandi Toksvig. **18** Duncan Preston. **19** John Noakes. **20** Julian Clary. **21** Angie. **22** Jimmy Savile. **23** Jack Frost. **24** Janet Street Porter. **25**Alan Titchmarsh.

# Quiz 21 Pot Luck 11

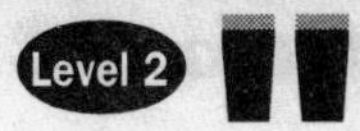

1 In which decade was the last hanging of a woman in the UK?
2 Inspector Slack was always on the case with which amateur sleuth?
3 Robert Gallo was one of the pioneers in the identification of which virus?
4 In cricket what did Derbyshire add to their name in the 90s?
5 What is the home state of ex US President Jimmy Carter?
6 Who had an 80s No 1 with Respectable?
7 In Only Fools and Horses what does Trigger call Del Boy?
8 Where is the HQ of the multinational Samsung?
9 Until his death in 1969, Brian Jones was in which pop band?
10 Which speed star was the BBC Sports Personality of the Year in 1986 and 1992?
11 Who wrote the Father Brown novels?
12 Where in the UK was Tom Conti born?
13 Which Bond girl was played by Maud Adams?
14 Which mountain range to the west of Sydney, was badly damaged by bush fires in 1993?
15 Which flowers gave the title to a No 8 UK hit in 1982 for Patrice Rushen?
16 Which Irish presenter works on Animal Hospital?
17 In which decade did Austria join the European Union?
18 Which Raymond created The Snowman?
19 Which US President was inaugurated in 1969?
20 In the patriotic World War I song what should we Keep the Home Fires doing?
21 Translated as The People's Daily, in which country is this a major seller?
22 Vehicles from which country use the international registration letter Z?
23 In finance what does the letter P stand for in APR?
24 In which decade was comic actor Frank Thornton born?
25 In TV ads which breakfast cereal did Jackie Charlton and his grandson tuck into?

**Answers**

***Pot Luck 11***

**1** 50s. **2** Miss Marple. **3** HIV. **4** Scorpions. **5** Georgia. **6** Mel and Kim. **7** Dave. **8** South Korea. **9** The Rolling Stones. **10** Nigel Mansell. **11** J K Chesterton. **12** Paisley. **13** Octopussy. **14** The Blue Mountains. **15** Forget Me Nots. **16** Shauna Lowry. **17** 90s. **18** Briggs. **19** Richard Nixon. **20** Burning. **21** China. **22** Zambia. **23** Percentage. **24** 20s. **25** Shredded Wheat.

# Quiz 22 Sport - 90s Action Replay

Level 2

1 Which English bowler took a 90s hat trick against the West Indies?
2 In which US state were the last summer Olympics of the century held?
3 Who were the opponents in Schmeichel's last league game for Man Utd?
4 Who beat Tim Henman in his first Wimbledon singles semi-final?
5 Who missed England's last penalty in the Euro 96 shoot out v Germany?
6 In 1995, which England captain was sacked and then reinstated within a few days?
7 Who inflicted Nigel Benn's first defeat as a professional?
8 Who was the last team to be relegated from the Premiership in the 20th century?
9 Which team won cricket's county championship in 1990 and 1991?
10 Yuan Yuan was caught carrying drugs for which Chinese team?
11 Which Grand Slam did Pete Sampras not win in the century?
12 Man Utd bought Gary Pallister from and sold him back to which club?
13 In baseball who set a record with 70 home runs?
14 In 1998 Tegla Loroupe set a new world record in the women's section of which event?
15 Which soccer team moved to Pride Park in the 90s?
16 How long was swimmer Michelle de Bruin banned for attempting to manipulate a drugs test?
17 Who did Mike Atherton replace as England's cricket captain?
18 In which sport did Andy Thomson become a world champion?
19 Which legendary American golfer played his last British Open in 1995?
20 The scorer of Romania's last minute winner v England in the 98 World Cup played with which English club?
21 Which cricketing county won a sideboard full of trophies with Dermot Reeve as skipper?
22 Which jockey rode over 200 winners in both 1997 and 1998?
23 Who won a record ninth Wimbledon singles title in 1991?
24 In 1995 Man Utd set a record Premier score by beating which team 9-0 ?
25 Which English wicket keeper set a new record of 11 dismissals in a test in 1995?

## Answers

***Sport - 90s Action Replay***

**1** Dominic Cork. **2** Georgia. **3** Spurs. **4** Pete Sampras. **5** Gareth Southgate. **6** Will Carling. **7** Chris Eubank. **8** Charlton Athletic. **9** Essex. **10** Swimming. **11** French. **12** Nottm Forest. **13** Mark McGwire. **14** Marathon. **15** Derby. **16** 4 years. **17** Graham Gooch. **18** Bowls. **19** Arnold Palmer. **20** Chelsea - it was Dan Petrescu. **21** Warwickshire. **22** Kieren Fallon. **23** Martina Navratilova. **24** Ipswich. **25** Jack Russell.

# Quiz 23 Pot Luck 12

1 In 1999 Pepsi-Cola launched a series of collectable cans linked with what?
2 What was the profession of Philip Lawrence who was tragically killed in the 90s?
3 Which sport did aristocratic sleuth Lord Peter Wimsey play?
4 When The Sound of Music was first shown in Korea what was not included?
5 What kind of ride was taken by Roxette in a No 4 UK hit from 1991?
6 What was Kojak's pet name for people?
7 How many trombones featured in a title of a song from The Music Man?
8 With which sport is Marc Giradelli associated?
9 Whose name features in the title of the Book Of Practical Cats?
10 1997 was the Chinese year of which creature?
11 Which satellite channel used the slogan 'You can't help getting involved'?
12 The DPP is the director of public what?
13 What is wine writer Ms Robinson's first name?
14 Who made No 1 with The Power?
15 At which sport did Stuart Barnes win international success?
16 Publishing magnate Lord Gnome is connected with which publication?
17 Which consumer programme was a follow up to Braden's Week?
18 In which royal residence did Queen Victoria die?
19 Pamplona international airport is in which country?
20 In which sport could the Jazz take on the Grizzlies?
21 Who sang the title song for the Bond film For Your Eyes Only?
22 Who wrote the detective novel The Maltese Falcon?
23 In which decade was comedian Benny Hill born?
24 Gary Lineker played his last ever England game under which manager?
25 Which Francis was the first regular weatherman on BBC's Breakfast Time?

## Answers

***Pot Luck 12***

**1** Star Wars. **2** Teacher. **3** Cricket. **4** The music. **5** Joy. **6** Pussycat. **7** Seventy Six. **8** Skiing. **9** Old Possum. **10** Ox. **11** UK Living. **12** Prosecution. **13** Jancis. **14** Snap. **15** Rugby Union. **16** Private Eye. **17** That's Life. **18** Osborne House. **19** Spain. **20** Basketball. **21** Sheena Easton. **22** Dashiell Hammett. **23** 20s. **24** Graham Taylor. **25** Wilson.

# Quiz 24 Movies Who's Who

Level 2

1 Who has the nickname Sly?
2 Which Richard found fame in Withnail and I?
3 Who won best actress at the 1997 Cannes Film festival for her role in Nil By Mouth?
4 Which activist did Denzel Washington play in Cry Freedom?
5 Which actress's official title is Lady Haden-Guest?
6 Which actor shot to fame in 1980 with American Gigolo?
7 Who briefly changed his name to Lenny Williams but returned to his Italian sounding name?
8 Who could not accept the offer to play 007 first time round as he was committed to playing Remington Steele?
9 What is the name of John Travolta's son - so called because of the actor's passion for aeroplanes?
10 How was Joanne Whalley known after her marriage to her husband?
11 Actress Glenda Jackson became MP for which constituency?
12 Who dubbed Kenneth Branagh's voice for the French version of Henry V?
13 Who reputedly was in discussion with Diana, Princess of Wales about making a sequel to The Bodyguard shortly before her death?
14 How did Christopher Reeve suffer the appalling injuries which brought about his paralysis in 1995?
15 Which Oscar winning actor was the voice of John Smith in Pocahontas?
16 Who is Jason Gould's mum who starred with him in Prince of Tides?
17 Which James Bond appeared in Spiceworld: The Movie?
18 Who did Antonio Banderas marry after they met on the set of Two Much?
19 Who wrote the novel on which Trainspotting was based?
20 Which actress won an Oscar for her screenplay adaptation of Jane Austen's Sense & Sensibility?
21 In which city was Hugh Grant arrested with Divine Brown?
22 Which English actor was the voice of Scar in The Lion King?
23 Which child star appeared in Richie Rich?
24 Who or what was Clyde in Clint Eastwood in Any Which Way You Can?
25 Who played the doctor who cared for John Merrick in The Elephant Man?

## Answers

***20th C The Movies Who's Who***

**1** Sylvester Stallone. **2** E. Grant. **3** Kathy Burke. **4** Steve Biko. **5** Jamie Lee Curtis. **6** Richard Gere. **7** Leonardo DiCaprio. **8** Pierce Brosnan. **9** Jett. **10** Joanne Whalley Kilmer. **11** Hampstead & Highgate. **12** Gerard Depardieu. **13** Kevin Costner. **14** Fell from a horse. **15** Mel Gibson. **16** Barbra Streisand. **17** Roger Moore. **18** Melanie Griffith. **19** Irvine Welsh. **20** Emma Thompson. **21** Los Angeles. **22** Jeremy Irons. **23** Macaulay Culkin. **24** Orang Utan. **25** Anthony Hopkins.

# Quiz 25 Pot Luck 13

1 Who moved up to No 1 ranking for snooker's 1998-99 season?
2 Whose clothes shop Bazaar was a trendsetter in the 60s?
3 Which detective lived on a boat called St Vitus Dance?
4 NUPE was the National Union of what?
5 In WWII where did the Bevin Boys work?
6 Who had an 80s No 1 with Like A Prayer?
7 In which eastern country were the Moonies founded in 1954?
8 In Coronation Street what was the surname of Colin and the late Des?
9 Truman Capote wrote about Breakfast at which place?
10 Abyssinia has become known as what?
11 Which US singer said, "You're not drunk if you can lie on the floor without holding on"?
12 What are the international registration letters of a vehicle from India?
13 What is the name of the USA's main space exploration centre in Florida?
14 How long is Indianapolis's most famous motor race?
15 Who was the first female to have three consecutive US No 1 albums?
16 On which river was the Grand Coulee built?
17 Which star of Are You Being Served? became a regular panellist on radio's Just A Minute?
18 In the Arab world what does the letter E stand for in UAE?
19 In which decade was Ewan McGregor born?
20 What kind of orchard did Chekhov write a play about?
21 In Rugby League what did Widnes add to their name in the 90s?
22 On a computer keyboard which letter on the same line is immediately right of the O?
23 To the nearest million what is the population of New York?
24 In TV advertising which beer was said to "work wonders"?
25 In American Football where do the Saints come from?

## Answers

***Pot Luck 13***

**1** John Higgins. **2** Mary Quant. **3** Crockett. **4** Public Employees. **5** Mines. **6** Madonna. **7** Korea. **8** Barnes. **9** Tiffany's. **10** Ethiopia. **11** Dean Martin. **12** IND. **13** Cape Canaveral. **14** 500 miles. **15** Donna Summer. **16** Columbia. **17** Wendy Richard. **18** Emirates. **19** 70s. **20** Cherry. **21** Vikings. **22** P. **23** 7 million. **24** Double Diamond. **25** New Orleans.

# Quiz 26 Euro Tour

1 What colour did Air France repaint some Concorde jets to advertise Pepsi?
2 How was Eurotunnel known before its name change in 1998?
3 Where is the French terminus for the Hoverspeed service?
4 Which European town gave its name to a Treaty which symbolises closer economic links between European countries?
5 In which European country did Victoria Adams marry David Beckham?
6 What is the oldest university in Northern Ireland called - founded in 1908?
7 Sullom Voe is famous for exporting which commodity?
8 How are Belgian World Airlines also known?
9 Which country lies to the north of Austria and to the south of Poland?
10 How many independent 'Baltic states' are there?
11 On which date in 1999 did Duty Free Shopping dramatically change?
12 Where is the Belgian terminus for Eurostar trains?
13 When did Euro Disney - now Disneyland Paris - open?
14 In 1998 a new breed of mosquito was discovered on which underground system?
15 Where is the Donana National Park?
16 In which country was the Angel of the North erected in 1998?
17 Which home of champagne in France was also where the German High Command surrendered in WWII?
18 What name is given to the popular holiday area between Marseille and La Spezia?
19 Which British architect was responsible with Renzo Piano for the famous Pompidou Centre in Paris?
20 In which European city is The Atomium?
21 Which tourist islands include the lesser known Cabrera and Formentera?
22 Which winter sports venue, home of the Cresta Run, has hosted two Olympic Games in the 20th century?
23 What is Ireland's longest river and greatest source of electric power?
24 The Simplon Tunnel links Italy with which country?
25 On which Sea does Croatia stand?

## Answers

***Euro Tour***

**1** Blue. **2** Le Shuttle. **3** Boulogne. **4** Maastricht. **5** Ireland. **6** Queen's University. **7** Oil. **8** SABENA. **9** Czech Republic. **10** Three. **11** 30th June. **12** Brussels Midi. **13** 1992. **14** London. **15** Spain. **16** England. **17** Reims. **18** Riviera. **19** Richard Rogers. **20** Brussels. **21** Balearics. **22** St Moritz. **23** Shannon. **24** Switzerland. **25** Adriatic.

# Quiz 27 Pot Luck 14

1 Which company took over Rover in 1994?
2 "Honey, I just forgot to duck" were the words of which sportsman?
3 On TV which character painted The Fallen Madonna with the Big Boobies?
4 What was Celine Dion's first UK No 1?
5 How many individual bets make up a Yankee?
6 Which comedian said, "Marriage is a wonderful invention - but so is the bicycle repair kit"?
7 Which colour appears with blue on the U N flag?
8 Which musical featured the song Too Darn Hot?
9 In basketball where do the Supersonics come from?
10 Who wrote The Loneliness Of The Long Distance Runner?
11 Which late rock star said, "When you're dead you're made for life"?
12 Which toy was the brainchild of Ole Kirk Christiansen of Denmark?
13 In which country is Chernobyl, scene of a nuclear leak when it was still part of the USSR?
14 Who made No 1 with Inside?
15 In which US state was the J Paul Getty Museum founded?
16 In 1928 what became the minimum age at which a woman could vote?
17 Advertising which product caused Carol Vorderman to be dropped from hosting Tomorrow's World?
18 Osaka international airport is in which country?
19 What were Suede in their No 9 UK hit from 1997?
20 Which soccer player was the BBC Sports Personality of 1966?
21 Which US town became known as the home of jazz?
22 Which James Bond appeared in The Persuaders?
23 What were marketed as Celluwipes when they were first developed?
24 Roger Osborne's goal sealed the first FA Cup Final triumph for which club?
25 In fiction, what was the name of Charlie the Chocolate Factory owner?

## Answers

***Pot Luck 14***

**1** BMW. **2** Jack Dempsey. **3** Van Clomp. **4** Think Twice. **5** Eleven. **6** Billy Connolly. **7** White. **8** Kismet. **9** Seattle. **10** Alan Sillitoe. **11** Jimi Hendrix. **12** Lego. **13** Ukraine. **14** Stiltskin. **15** California. **16** 21. **17** Ariel. **18** Japan. **19** Lazy. **20** Bobby Moore. **21** New Orleans. **22** Roger Moore. **23** Paper handkerchiefs. **24** Ipswich. **25** Buckett.

# Quiz 28 Charts

1. Which all boy group's first No 1 in 1989 was You Got It (The Right Stuff)?
2. Denis was the first UK hit for which group?
3. Who had an album in the 90s called Said and Done?
4. Which film featured the No 1 UK hit Take My Breath Away?
5. What was the Osmonds' only UK No 1 hit?
6. Who had an 80s hit with Good Tradition?
7. Which decade saw the introduction of the Grammy award?
8. Which group's first hit was Labour of Love?
9. What was Simply Red's first top ten single?
10. How many centimetres did an LP measure across?
11. In which decade did Imagine by John Lennon reach No 1 in the UK?
12. Who wrote the UK chart topper I Will Always Love You?
13. Which artist has had the most chart album hits in the US?
14. Who spent most weeks in the UK singles charts in 1996?
15. Who topped the album charts in 1990 with But Seriously?
16. Which American's first Top Ten album was 52nd Street?
17. Which game was in the title of a Pet Shop Boys hit from 1988?
18. During which decade did CDs officially go on sale in Europe?
19. Which group topped the album charts with Turtle Power?
20. Whose first hit in the 90s was End of the Road?
21. Who released an album in 1996 called Travelling Without Meaning?
22. Which country singer from the 80s sang Thank God I'm a Country Boy?
23. Who had an album called Take Two released in 1996?
24. Roxy Music had their first UK hit in which decade?
25. Which group topped the album charts in 1995 with Nobody Else?

## Answers

***Charts***

**1** New Kids On The Block. **2** Blondie. **3** Boyzone. **4** Top Gun. **5** Love Me For A Reason. **6** Tanita Tikaram. **7** 50s. **8** Hue and Cry. **9** Holding Back The Years. **10** 30. **11** 80s. **12** Dolly Parton. **13** Elvis Presley. **14** Oasis. **15** Phil Collins. **16** Billy Joel. **17** Dominoes. **18** 80s. **19** Partners In Kryme. **20** Boyz II Men. **21** Jamiroquai. **22** John Denver. **23** Robson and Jerome. **24** 1970s. **25** Take That.

# Quiz 29 Pot Luck 15

1 Who is the Queen's eldest grandson?
2 Which soccer star hosted a Friday Night TV chat show?
3 In which country was power seized in the 70s by the Gang Of Four?
4 What was the nationality of composer Aaron Copland?
5 What was the occupation of Edith Cavell who was shot by the Germans in WWI?
6 Who had an 80s No 1 with West End Girls?
7 In cricket which English team became Foxes in the 90s?
8 How many Nobel prizes did Marie Curie win?
9 Who was the youngest of the Jackson family when they left Albert Square for their own protection?
10 Livingstone has been the 90s seat of which prominent politician?
11 The Suez Canal connects the Mediterranean Sea to which other Sea?
12 Which summer month is the title of an album by Eric Clapton?
13 What are Ena Sharples and Elizabeth of Glamis?
14 What is Terry Wogan's first name?
15 At which sport did Jonah Barrington win international success?
16 How are PJ and Duncan also known?
17 How did Satyajit Ray achieve fame?
18 In which decade did France join the European Union?
19 In TV advertising who promoted Barclaycard by the fact that he didn't possess one?
20 In which country is the deepwater port of Belem?
21 In computer language what does the letter C stand for in ASCII?
22 Which Russian writer wrote Cancer Ward?
23 Vehicles from which country use the international registration letter E?
24 In baseball where do the Blue Jays come from?
25 In which country was Danny De Vito born?

## Answers

***Pot Luck 15***

**1** Peter Phillips. **2** Ian Wright. **3** China. **4** American. **5** Nurse. **6** Pet Shop Boys. **7** Leicestershire. **8** Two. **9** Billy. **10** Robin Cook. **11** Red. **12** August. **13** Roses. **14** Michael. **15** Squash. **16** Ant and Dec. **17** Film director. **18** 50s. **19** Rowan Atkinson. **20** Brazil. **21** Code. **22** Alexander Solzhenitzyn. **23** Spain. **24** Toronto. **25** USA.

# Quiz 30 80s Newsround

1 The world was first aware of the Chernobyl disaster after detectors were triggered at a nuclear plant in which country?
2 Christa McAuliffe died in an accident in what type of vehicle in 1986?
3 Where was John Paul II when an attempt was made on his life in 1981?
4 Which form of death penalty was abolished by Francois Mitterand?
5 Who succeeded Brezhnev as Soviet premier?
6 Which drink did the Cocoa Cola Company launch in 1982?
7 Which film actor became mayor of Carmel, California in 1986?
8 How did James F Fixx, promoter of jogging for good health, die in 1984?
9 Where did teenager Mathias Rust land his plane in 1987 much to the surprise of the country's authorities?
10 What colour wedding gown, veil and train did Paula Yates wear for her wedding to Bob Geldof?
11 Where did Torvill and Dean win Olympic gold with their Bolero routine?
12 Where did the US side of the Band Aid concert tale place?
13 Natan Sharansky was released from prison in the USSR to begin a new life where?
14 Which country was the first to make catalytic convertors compulsory?
15 Which organ was transplanted with heart and lungs in the first triple transplant operation in the UK?
16 How were the balls at Wimbledon different in 1986 from previous years?
17 In which country was the first permanent bungee jumping site situated?
18 Which capital city was the scene of a major summit between Reagan and Gorbachev in 1986?
19 Proceedings in which House were first on TV in January 1985?
20 Who co-wrote the Band Aid song with Bob Geldof?
21 Virgin Atlantic flights first went to New York from which UK airport?
22 Which keeper was beaten by Maradona's "hand of God" 1986 World Cup goal?
23 Which oil tanker disastrously ran aground off Brittany in 1987?
24 In which year did the £1 note cease to be legal tender in England?
25 Which country celebrated its bicentenary in 1988?

## Answers

***80s Newsround***

**1** Sweden. **2** Space Shuttle. **3** Rome. **4** Guillotine. **5** Andropov. **6** Diet Coke. **7** Clint Eastwood. **8** Heart attack while jogging. **9** Red Square. **10** Scarlet. **11** Yugoslavia. **12** Philadelphia. **13** Israel. **14** Switzerland. **15** Liver. **16** Yellow. **17** New Zealand. **18** Reykjavik. **19** House of Lords. **20** Midge Ure. **21** Gatwick. **22** Peter Shilton. **23** Amoco Cadiz. **24** 1988. **25** Australia.

# Quiz 31 Pot Luck 16

1 Andy Warhol's 60s exhibition featured cans of which product?
2 Which doubles partner of Martina Navratilova commentated for the BBC at Wimbledon during the 1990s?
3 Who became US vice president when Spiro Agnew resigned?
4 What claimed the life of the singer Kathleen Ferrier?
5 Which George invented the Kodak roll-film camera?
6 In TV ads which coffee did Gareth Hunt and Diane Keen drink?
7 What type of pens did Pentel create?
8 Which children's show had a pink hippo called George?
9 Which writer created the series Prime Suspect which starred Helen Mirren?
10 Ezzard Charles was a world champion in which sport?
11 Who was the first woman to make a solo flight across the Atlantic?
12 Harold Larwood's bowling for England v Australia ensured the series was known as what ?
13 Who or what was Schnorbitz?
14 Who made No 1 with Ebeneezer Goode?
15 Who along with Philips developed the CD in the late 70s?
16 San Giusto international airport is in which country?
17 Where is the multinational Nestl based?
18 Who was in goal for Man Utd in the 1990 FA Cup Final replay but not in the original Final?
19 1996 is the Chinese year of which creature?
20 In the 90s how many points have been awarded for finishing second in a Grand Prix?
21 Rita Coolidge sang the title song for which Bond film?
22 Who hosted a TV Madhouse and played Fagin on stage in the 1990s?
23 In which decade of the century was Sir John Hall born?
24 Who wrote the novel Brideshead Revisited?
25 Which country became the first in the world to issue the dreaded parking ticket?

## Answers

***Pot Luck 16***

**1** Soup. **2** Pam Shriver. **3** Gerald Ford. **4** Cancer. **5** Eastman. **6** Nescafe. **7** Felt tips. **8** Rainbow. **9** Lynda La Plante. **10** Boxing. **11** Amelia Earhart. **12** Bodyline. **13** St Bernard dog. **14** Shamen. **15** Sony. **16** Italy. **17** Switzerland. **18** Les Sealey. **19** Rat. **20** 6. **21** Octopussy. **22** Russ Abbot. **23** 30s. **24** Evelyn Waugh. **25** France.

# Quiz 32 20th C Celebs

Level 2 

1 Who did Myte Garcia marry in 1996 by pointing to his symbol?
2 What did Bob Geldof and Paula Yates agree to swap as part of their divorce settlement?
3 In 1992 whose name was linked with then Tory minister David Mellor?
4 What is the name of Prince Edward's TV production company?
5 Who in 1994 put an ad in The Times with Richard Gere to say their marriage was still strong?
6 Which perfume house did Madonna advertise in the late 1990s?
7 Who accused Bill Clinton of sexual harassment after an incident in a hotel in 1991?
8 Model Ms Bourret is usually known by her first name alone; what is it?
9 Which royal spouse designed the Aviary at London Zoo?
10 Sir Richard Attenborough was a director of which London soccer side from 1969-1982?
11 Who did Anthea Turner say she was leaving husband Pete Powell for in 1998?
12 Which film producer is the father in law of Loyd Grossman?
13 Which gourmet and wit described Margaret Thatcher as Attila the Hen?
14 In 1998 Cristina Sanchez became the first woman to become what?
15 Which celebrity restaurants do Stallone, Willis and Schwarzenegger own?
16 Derrick Evans is better known as which Mr?
17 How many brothers and sisters does Dale Winton have?
18 Who protested about Michael Jackson during the Brit Awards in 1996?
19 Which British redhead did Paris Match sign as a regular writer in 1996?
20 Who has Patsy tattooed on his arm?
21 Which racing driver has a wife called Georgie?
22 Sir Magdi Yacoub became famous in which medical field?
23 In 1997 who did Kelly Fisher claim she was engaged to when photos of him with someone else appeared in the papers?
24 Where in London was the house Peter Mandelson bought with the help of a loan from Geoffrey Robinson?
25 Where was Nick Leeson released from jail in July 1999?

## Answers

***20th C Celebs***

**1** Prince. **2** Houses. **3** Antonia de Sancha. **4** Ardent. **5** Cindy Crawford. **6** Max Factor. **7** Paula Jones. **8** Caprice. **9** Lord Snowdon. **10** Chelsea. **11** Grant Bovey. **12** David Puttnam. **13** Clement Freud. **14** Matador. **15** Planet Hollywood. **16** Motivator. **17** None. **18** Jarvis Cocker. **19** The Duchess of York. **20** Liam Gallagher. **21** Damon Hill. **22** Heart transplants. **23** Dodi Fayed. **25** Notting Hill. **26** Singapore.

# Quiz 33 Pot Luck 17

1 Which Stones' song title did Mandy Smith use for her book following her marriage to Bill Wyman?
2 The treaty signed to establish the EEC was the Treaty Of where?
3 Mrs Stubbs and Mrs Theodopolopoudos were the stars of which TV series?
4 Who wrote Spycatcher in 1987?
5 With which sport is Matt Biondi associated?
6 Who had an 80s No 1 with Hand On Your Heart?
7 On a computer keyboard which letter is between T and U?
8 In which year was Germany unified towards the end of the 20th century?
9 What is Del Boy's local in Only Fools and Horses?
10 Which Rugby League team became Cougars in the 90s?
11 For what was Frederick Ashton famous?
12 What is the international registration letter of a vehicle from Hungary?
13 Which comedian was Rockin' Around the Christmas Tree in a 1987 hit?
14 At the end of his life Indian chief Geronimo had taken to what kind of work?
15 In American Football where do the Seahawks come from?
16 Who was the first director of the National Theatre Company in Great Britain?
17 Who was famous for his impersonations of Harold Wilson and Edward Heath?
18 In language teaching what does the letter F stand for in TEFL?
19 Who wrote The Lives And Loves Of A She Devil?
20 Arnold Sidebottom a Man Utd player of the 70s played first class cricket for which county?
21 In which decade was Demi Moore born?
22 Which TV playwright wrote the controversial Casanova?
23 Which gas shares its name with Superman's home?
24 "They're grrrreat!" describes which product in advertising?
25 In horse racing what is Dick Hern's real first name?

## Answers

***Pot Luck 17***

**1** It's All Over Now. **2** Rome. **3** Birds of a Feather. **4** Peter Wright. **5** Swimming. **6** Kylie Minogue. **7** Y. **8** 1990. **9** The Nag's Head. **10** Keighley. **11** Choreography. **12** H. **13** Mel Smith. **14** Farming. **15** Seattle. **16** Laurence Olivier. **17** Mike Yarwood. **18** Foreign. **19** Fay Weldon. **20** Yorkshire. **21** 60s. **22** Dennis Potter. **23** Krypton. **24** Frosties. **25** William.

# Quiz 34 20th C TV Presenters

Level 2 

1 Who first presented The Good Sex Guide?
2 Who interviewed Tony Blair at the launch of 5 News on Channel 5?
3 Who went on from being a researcher on Kilroy to co presenting Watchdog with Anne Robinson?
4 Who replaced Gaby Roslin on The Big Breakfast?
5 Carol Vorderman was dropped from the BBC's Tomorrow's World for advertising what commodity?
6 Which GMTV presenter is the wife of its chief reporter Martin Frizell?
7 Which duo, who were successful on TV am, provided BBC opposition to Richard & Judy on the morning sofa?
8 Which sport is Chris Tarrant's main hobby?
9 Who presented Blue Peter and The Money Programme?
10 Which news presenter went to school with Paul McCartney?
11 Which regular stand in for Wogan had her own - unsuccessful - show Saturday Matters?
12 Which 90s news presenter bemoaned the fact that there was too little good news on TV?
13 Who was the first regular presenter of Nine O'Clock Live on GMTV?
14 Paradise Gardens was the last series made by which TV favourite?
15 Who was the first presenter of Don't Forget Your Toothbrush?
16 Who was dubbed TV's Mr Sex?
17 Whose third wife is a former Puerto Rican beauty queen Wilnelia Merced?
18 Who was the presenter of The Cook Report?
19 Who moved on from Newsround to The Travel Show?
20 Which lady presented Sunday Sunday for LWT for eight years in the 80s?
21 On Breakfast Time what feature did The Green Goddess always present?
22 Who presented LWT's long time Saturday night celebrity show from 1984-1993?
23 Which knight presents Through the Keyhole?
24 Which former Blue Peter presenter took over form Sean Maguire as Marty in Dangerfield?
25 Which TV and radio journalist wrote and broadcast the Letter to Daniel?

## Answers

***20th C TV Presenters***

**1** Margi Clarke. **2** Kirsty Young. **3** Alice Beer. **4** Zoe Ball. **5** Soap powder. **6** Fiona Phillips. **7** Anne & Nick. **8** Fishing. **9** Valerie Singleton. **10** Peter Sissons. **11** Sue Lawley. **12** Martyn Lewis. **13** Lorraine Kelly. **14** Geoff Hamilton. **15** Chris Evans. **16** Angus Deayton. **17** Bruce Forsyth. **18** Roger Cook. **19** Juliet Morris. **20** Gloria Hunniford. **21** Keep fit. **22** Michael Aspel. **23** David Frost. **24** Tim Vincent. **25** Fergal Keane.

# Quiz 35 Pot Luck 18

1. Who won an Oscar in 1994 for best animation for The Wrong Trousers?
2. Which New York thoroughfare is famous for its fashionable stores?
3. Who had a 90s hit with Elephant Stone?
4. In cricket what did Surrey add to their name in the 90s?
5. Why were British soldiers in WWI called Tommies (short for Tommy Atkins)?
6. Before his resignation in 1996 which Royal did Patrick Jephson work for?
7. What does E stand for in OPEC?
8. Who was the father of Lady Antonia Fraser?
9. In addition to Denmark and the Faeroe Islands where is the Danish krone a unit of currency?
10. Which John was the BBC Sports Personality of the Year in 1976?
11. Who was the last Briton of the 20th century to win the men's singles at Wimbledon?
12. UNICEF is responsible for which specific group of people?
13. To the nearest million what is the population of Canada?
14. What was the first name of Le Carre's spy Smiley?
15. With which sport was David Bedford associated?
16. Who did a cover of the Carpenters' Santa Claus is Comin' To Town in 1985?
17. In To The Manor Born what was the butler called?
18. In which sport could the Lakers play the Clippers in a derby game?
19. The Gold Coast has become known as what?
20. Who made No 1 with Show Me Heaven?
21. Which soap back in the 60s was about a soccer club?
22. Gazza injured himself in an FA Cup Final for Spurs against which team?
23. Who wrote The Prime Of Miss Jean Brodie?
24. Agno international airport is in which country?
25. What notable thing did tough guy Humphrey Bogart do throughout his wedding to Lauren Bacall?

## Answers

***Pot Luck 18***

**1** Nick Park. **2** Fifth Avenue. **3** Stone Roses. **4** Lions. **5** Sample name on a recruitment form. **6** Princess of Wales. **7** Exporting. **8** Lord Longford. **9** Greenland. **10** John Curry. **11** Fred Perry. **12** Children. **13** 30 million. **14** George. **15** Athletics. **16** Bruce Springsteen. **17** Brabinger. **18** Basketball. **19** Ghana. **20** Marua McKee. **21** United. **22** Nottm Forest. **23** Muriel Spark. **24** Switzerland. **25** Cry.

# Quiz 36 Sporting Legends

Level 2

1. Which jockey was born on Bonfire Night?
2. Michael Jordan was a super scorer for which team?
3. Who was the Louiseville Lip?
4. Cricket's Alfred Freeman was known by which nickname?
5. In which decade was Daley Thompson born?
6. Who won swimming gold in the 100m freestyle at the 56, 60 and 64 Olympics?
7. Sergey Bubka has broken the world record on over 30 occasions in which event?
8. Ian Botham made his England debut while playing for which county?
9. How old was Nadia Comaneci when she won Olympic Gold in as a gymnast?
10. Joe diMaggio was known as what kind of Joe?
11. Apart from sprinting in which event did Carl Lewis twice take Olympic gold?
12. Who was the first Brit to be British and US Open champion at the same time?
13. Gary Sobers hit six sixes in an over against which county?
14. Walter Swinburne won his first Derby on which legendary horse?
15. Who was the first British soccer player to be transferred to a foreign club?
16. Racing's Juan Manuel Fangio came from which country?
17. What did the G stand for in W G Grace's name?
18. Who was the first Scottish soccer player to gain 100 caps?
19. What position did Bill Beaumont play?
20. Who is Pakistan's all time leading Test wicket taker?
21. Which England soccer World Cup winner was knighted in 1998?
22. Which country did long distance runner Emil Zatopek come from?
23. Who was the first batsman to hit over 500 in a first class cricket game?
24. Who did Pete Sampras beat in the final to take his sixth Wimbledon singles title?
25. Who has been champion jockey on the flat most times this century?

## Answers

***Sporting legends***

**1** Lester Piggott. **2** Chicago Bulls. **3** Muhammad Ali - born as Casius Clay. **4** Titch. **5** 50s. **6** Dawn Fraser. **7** Pole vault. **8** Somerset. **9** 14. **10** Jolltin'. **11** Long jump. **12** Tony Jacklin. **13** Glamorgan. **14** Shergar. **15** John Charles. **16** Argentina. **17** Gilbert. **18** Kenny Dalglish. **19** Lock. **20** Wasim Akram. **21** Geoff Hurst. **22** Czechoslovakia. **23** Brian Lara. **24** Andre Agassi. **25** Gordon Richards.

# Quiz 37 Pot Luck 19

Level 2 

1 Who had sidekicks called Eric and Tinker?
2 Which physicist was involved in the development of nuclear weapons in the USSR but became a dissident under Communist rule?
3 What type of plays did Georges Feydeau specialise in writing?
4 Which French brothers invented the first films?
5 What does A stand for in GATT?
6 Who had an 80s No 1 with Rock Me Amadeus?
7 Who was boxing's heavyweight champion throughout the 40s?
8 Who presented News Swap on Multi Coloured Swap Shop?
9 Which musical featured the song When I Marry Mr Snow?
10 In TV ads Shane Ritchie knocked at doors holding a packet of what?
11 What did the W C stand for in W C Fields' names?
12 Field Marshal Montgomery became Viscount Montgomery of where?
13 Who first sang the theme music to Heartbeat?
14 Who was Queen Elizabeth II's paternal grandfather?
15 In which city was Sean Connery born?
16 Where would you see the Dow Jones index?
17 Vehicles from which country use the international registration letter N?
18 Early in the century who wrote the novel The Lost World?
19 Who was the first person to interview George Michael about his arrest?
20 Which member of the Gibb family made a cameo appearance on Only Fools and Horses?
21 What does the letter F stand for in ASLEF?
22 In which decade did Denmark join the European Union?
23 Which group used a Bond film title for a 1996 top ten hit?
24 In American Football where do the Falcons come from?
25 Which language does the word ombudsman derive from?

**Answers**

***Pot Luck 19***

**1** Lovejoy. **2** Andrei Sakharov. **3** Farce. **4** Lumiere Brothers. **5** Agreement. **6** Falco. **7** Joe Louis. **8** John Craven. **9** Carousel. **10** Daz. **11** William Claude. **12** Alamein. **13** Nick Berry. **14** George V. **15** Edinburgh. **16** Wall Street. **17** Norway. **18** Arthur Conan Doyle. **19** Michael Parkinson. **20** Barry. **21** Firemen. **22** 70s. **23** Ash - it was Goldfinger. **24** Atlanta. **25** Swedish.

# Quiz 38 Sci Fi& Fantasy Movies

Level 2

1 Who played Dr Who in the 90s movie made for TV?
2 Who starred in the lead role in the The Fly opposite Geena Davis?
3 What was the fourth Alien film called?
4 Who received $3 million to recreate her five year TV role on film with her male partner?
5 Who tries to save the world from virtual reality in The Matrix?
6 Which spin off from a 60s sitcom was a 1999 movie with Jeff Daniels and Christopher Lloyd?
7 Who played Batman immediately before George Clooney?
8 In which 1998 film did Bruce Willis lead a team to confront a deadly threat from outer space?
9 Which tough guy played Mr Freeze in Batman & Robin?
10 Which 1996 film has its climax on 4th July?
11 In which sci fi classic did the space ship Nostromo first appear?
12 Which important US building has its roof ripped off in Superman II?
13 What was the first sequel to Star Wars?
14 What was the name of Drew Barrymore's character in E.T.?
15 Who played Rick Deckard in Blade Runner?
16 What number Star Trek movie was called The Wrath of Khan?
17 Which UK pop singer and environmental campaigner appeared in Dune?
18 Which decade does Michael J Fox go back to in Back to the Future?
19 Which Star Trek star directed Three Men and a Baby?
20 Who played the young Obi-Wan Kenobi in the Star Wars prequel?
21 Which 1968 sci fi classic was based on The Sentinel by Arthur C Clarke?
22 What was the subtitle of Terminator 2?
23 In which city does the action of the 1998 movie Godzilla take place?
24 What is the name of the Darth Vader to be in Episode 1 _ The Phantom Menace?
25 Who did Jane Fonda play in the 60s movie of the same name where she constantly lost her clothes?

**Answers**

***20th C The Movies Sci Fi & Fantasy***

**1** Paul McGann. **2** Jeff Goldblum. **3** Alien Resurrection. **4** Gillian Anderson - in The X Files. **5** Keanu Reeves. **6** My Favourite Martian. **7** Val Kilmer. **8** Armageddon. **9** Arnold Schwarzenegger. **10** Independence Day. **11** Alien. **12** The White House. **13** The Empire Strikes Back. **14** Gertie. **15** Harrison Ford. **16** II. **17** Sting. **18** 50s. **19** Leonard Nimoy. **20** Ewan McGregor. **21** 2001: A Space Odyssey. **22** Judgment Day. **23** New York. **24** Anakin Skywalker. **25** Barbarella.

# Quiz 39 Pot Luck 20

1 In which decade this century did Ronnie Scott's Soho jazz club open?
2 How was Oflag IVC prison camp better known?
3 Which Dad's Army character was married in real life to Hattie Jacques?
4 Which film theme did the BBC use for the 1984 Olympics?
5 Who wrote the line, "Come friendly bombs fall on Slough"?
6 Who advertised Pizza Hut along with Stuart Pearce and Chris Waddle?
7 Who recorded the When Harry Met Sally soundtrack?
8 Who presented The Price is Right in the UK before Bruce Forsyth?
9 Who was the last inmate of Spandau jail in Berlin?
10 Del Ballard Jnr was a world champion in which sport?
11 Who sang the title song for the Bond film You Only Live Twice?
12 Which national park, famous for aboriginal rock paintings is near Darwin?
13 Who was British Prime Minister when World War II broke out?
14 To whom did the Bee Gees pay tribute to in Tapestry Revisited?
15 Which cricket county decided they had become Dynamos in the 90s?
16 In which country is the deepwater port of Brindisi?
17 Where did Dr Baz Samuels work?
18 Which group starts a meeting by singing the words, "And did those feet....."?
19 In basketball where do the Hawks come from?
20 In which country was Omar Sharif born?
21 Who wrote The Picture Of Dorian Gray?
22 Peter Shilton completed his 1000th league game with which London club?
23 Spokane airport was built in which US state?
24 Who presented On The Ball in 1999 with Barry Venison?
25 Who sang with Crosby, Stills and Young?

## Answers

***Pot Luck 20***

**1** 50s. **2** Colditz. **3** Wilson. **4** Chariots of Fire. **5** John Betjeman. **6** Gareth Southgate. **7** Harry Connick Jnr. **8** Leslie Crowther. **9** Rudolf Hess. **10** Bowls. **11** Nancy Sinatra. **12** Kakadu National Park. **13** Neville Chamberlain. **14** Carole King. **15** Durham. **16** Italy. **17** Holby City Hospital. **18** Women's Institute - it's Jerusalem. **19** Atlanta. **20** Egypt. **21** Oscar Wilde. **22** Orient. **23** Washington. **24** Gabby Yorath. **25** Nash.

# Quiz 40 On the Road

1 Which rules of the road for children was first published in 1971?
2 GT after a car's name means what?
3 Which margarine company sponsored the 1997 London Marathon?
4 How is a pedestrian light controlled crossing more commonly known?
5 How many National Parks does the Pennine Way pass through?
6 Which illegal act is committed most frequently in cars?
7 What is London's Middlesex Street called on Sundays?
8 In 1974 roads in Rutland became roads in which county?
9 How was Sellafield known before 1981?
10 Which motorway crosses the estuary of the river Severn?
11 Which county saw the protests about the building of the Newbury bypass in the mid 90s?
12 What was the car toll for the new Severn Bridge when it opened in 1996?
13 What name is given to low bumps in the road which slow down traffic?
14 In which Road is the headquarters of the Labour Party?
15 How is a Denver boot also known?
16 How many yellow lines show that you can never park or unload in that location?
17 What letter or letters make up the sign for a Tourist Information office?
18 The Scilly Isles come under the authority of which English county?
19 What is the maximum speed limit in kilometres on a motorway?
20 What name is given to a short narrow road which links an A road to a motorway?
21 Which two counties do the North Downs run through?
22 What is the maximum custodial penalty for causing death by dangerous driving?
23 30 inside a blue circle with no red border means what when on the road?
24 What is the administrative centre of Cornwall?
25 What colour is a sign indicating an English Heritage site?

## Answers

***On the Road***

**1** Green Cross Code. **2** Gran turismo. **3** Flora. **4** Pelican crossing. **5** Three. **6** Speeding. **7** Petticoat Lane. **8** Leicestershire. **9** Windscale. **10** M4. **11** Berkshire. **12** £3.80. **13** Sleeping policeman. **14** Walworth. **15** Wheel clamp. **16** Two. **17** I. **18** Cornwall. **19** 113. **20** Slip road. **21** Kent & Surrey. **22** 10 years. **23** Minimum speed 30. **24** Truro. **25** Brown.

# Quiz 41 Pot Luck 21

1. Which colour were David Beckham and Posh's going away outfits?
2. Sean O'Feeney worked under what name as a movie director?
3. The hole in the ozone layer formed over which continent?
4. Who had an 80s No 1 with First Time?
5. In WWII what was called Operation Dynamo?
6. In baseball where do the Expos come from?
7. What was Wilhelm Rontgen's most important discovery?
8. Which US state gave its name to a musical by Rodgers & Hammerstein?
9. Who said, "I never had any problems with drugs only with policemen"?
10. What are the international registration letters of a vehicle from Gibraltar?
11. What is the magazine of the Consumer's Association called?
12. Susan Devoy has been a 90s world champion in which sport?
13. Which Bond girl was played by Lois Chiles?
14. What replaced purchase tax in 1973?
15. At which sport did Diane Bell win international success?
16. People loved the ads, but which make of car did Papa promote?
17. Which tropical island was a UK top ten hit for David Essex in 1983?
18. In which English city were Walkers crisps first manufactured?
19. Who won the 1998 Benson & Hedges cricket final by 192 runs?
20. What does the letter R stand for in SERPS?
21. Which ex MP wrote the novel A Parliamentary Affair?
22. In which London Street was the first Virgin record shop?
23. Which singer compered the 1998 Miss World contest for TV in the UK?
24. What was Tim Henman seeded at for Wimbledon 1999?
25. In the movie Junior what was different about the Schwarzenegger character?

## Answers

***Pot Luck 21***

**1** Purple. **2** John Ford. **3** Antarctica. **4** Robin Beck. **5** Evacuation of Dunkirk. **6** Montreal. **7** X-rays. **8** Oklahoma. **9** Keith Richard. **10** GBZ. **11** Which?. **12** Squash. **13** Holly Goodhead. **14** VAT. **15** Judo. **16** Renault. **17** Tahiti. **18** Leicester. **19** Essex. **20** Related. **21** Edwina Currie. **22** Oxford Street. **23** Ronan Keating. **24** 6. **25** He was pregnant.

# Quiz 42 Who's Who

Level 2 

1 Which female vocalist was a member of the Eurythmics?
2 Which vocalist's real name is Michael Barratt?
3 Paul Weller was the lead singer of which group in the early 80s?
4 Which Gibb brother is the eldest?
5 Who played Aiden Brosnan in Eastenders?
6 Who duetted with Peabo Bryson on Beauty and the Beast?
7 What is Paul McCartney's real first name?
8 Who sang on If You Ever with East 17 in 1996?
9 Which country does Eddy Grant originate from?
10 Sting's Englishman in New York was used to advertise which make of car?
11 The Kemp brother were in which 80s group?
12 Who was the lead singer of Yazoo?
13 William Broad became better known under which name?
14 Morten Harket was part of which 80s group?
15 Who accompanied Boyz II Men on the hit One Sweet Day?
16 Which liquid refreshment was advertised by Bob Geldof in 1987?
17 Who duetted on the '93 hit I've Got You Under My Skin with Frank Sinatra?
18 Who said drug taking was as normal as having a cup of tea in 1997?
19 Who Lost her Heart to a StarShip Trooper?
20 Which popular singer duetted with Elton John on Slow Rivers?
21 Vincent Furnier became better known as whom?
22 Who sang with Phil Collins on the 1985 hit Separate Lives?
23 In which decade was female vocalist Annie Lennox born?
24 Who sang with Kenny Rogers on We've Got Tonight?
25 Whose debut single in 1996 was called Anything?

## Answers

***Who's Who***

**1** Annie Lennox. **2** Shakin' Stevens. **3** The Jam. **4** Barry. **5** Sean Maguire. **6** Celine Dion. **7** James. **8** Gabrielle. **9** Guyana. **10** Rover. **11** Spandau Ballet. **12** Alison Moyet. **13** Billy Idol. **14** A-ha. **15** Mariah Carey. **16** Milk. **17** Bono. **18** Noel Gallagher. **19** Sarah Brightman. **20** Cliff Richard. **21** Alice Cooper. **22** Marilyn Martin. **23** 50s. **24** Sheena Easton. **25** 3T.

# Quiz 43 Pot Luck 22

1 Mark O'Meara first won the British Open at which course?
2 Which country designated Chachoengsao as its new capital?
3 Who had an 80s hit with Golden Brown?
4 Which village is the home of Agatha Christie sleuth Miss Marple?
5 The Duke of Wellington appeared on the back of which British banknote?
6 What was Mahatma Gandhi's profession outside politics?
7 In cricket which English team turned into Eagles in the 90s?
8 What rose from the Solent in 1982?
9 Which musical featured the song Sunrise Sunset?
10 Sergey Golubitsky has been a world champion in which sport?
11 What was Take That's first UK No 1?
12 In which sport could the Bucks take on the Raptors?
13 Who presented Football Focus before moving to ITV in the mid 90s?
14 What is the second of Prince William's four names?
15 In which decade did Germany join the European Union?
16 In which city was Michael Jackson a Stranger in 1996?
17 Which actress wrote the novel Prime Time in the 1980s?
18 Vigo international airport is in which country?
19 Who said, "When you are as great as I am, it's hard to be humble"?
20 Which jazz trumpeter hosted radio's I'm Sorry I Haven't A Clue?
21 On which river was the Hoover dam built?
22 If you lose on Ready Steady Cook what do you receive?
23 1995 was the Chinese year of which creature?
24 Shearer and who else scored when England beat Scotland in Euro 96?
25 The train in the Great Train Robbery was making which journey?

## Answers

***Pot Luck 22***

**1** Birkdale. **2** Thailand. **3** Stranglers. **4** St. Mary Mead. **5** £5. **6** Law. **7** Essex. **8** Mary Rose. **9** Fiddler On The Roof. **10** Fencing. **11** Pray. **12** Basketball. **13** Bob Wilson. **14** Arthur. **15** 50s. **16** Moscow. **16** Joan Collins. **18** Spain. **19** Muhammad Ali. **20** Humphrey Lyttleton. **21** Colorado. **22** Food Hamper. **23** Bear. **24** Paul Gascoigne. **25** Glasgow to London.

# Quiz 44 90s Newsround

Level 2 

1 Which hotel had Princess Diana and Dodi Fayed just left when they were involved in their fatal car crash?
2 Who ran against Bill Clinton in the 1996 US election?
3 Ian Botham and Allan Lamb lost a libel case against which other cricketer?
4 Who in 1997 met an old school friend in The Big Issue office?
5 13 year old Sarah Cook hit the headlines after marrying a waiter while on holiday where?
6 Sandra Gregory was given a 25 year sentence for drug smuggling where?
7 In 1999 what sort of savings plan replaced Tessa?
8 In which city was Mother Teresa buried?
9 Which English city was blasted by an IRA bomb in June 1996?
10 Which Club finally voted in 1998 to admit women members?
11 In which city did Louise Woodward's US trial take place?
12 Which toy was the panic buy of Christmas 1997 due to a shortage in supply?
13 Who recorded Monica Lewinsky's conversations about her affair with Bill Clinton?
14 In '98 the US Embassy was bombed in which country with many fatalities?
15 Legal proceedings began against Scotsman Jim Sutherland for flouting a ban on what?
16 The Duchess of York's mother was killed near her home in which country?
17 How was eco warrior Daniel Hooper better known?
18 Which American was the first US pop star to perform in a sanction free South Africa?
19 What was the name of the low fat burger launched by McDonalds?
20 Neil & Jamie Acourt were involved in the court case about which victim?
21 Which politician said her boss, "had something of the night about him"?
22 Which Building Society was floated in 1997 with members each receiving a windfall?
23 Which former MP did William Hague make Party Chairman in 1997?
24 In which town was Gianni Versace shot?
25 In 1991 which country mourned the loss of King Olaf?

## Answers

***90s Newsround***

**1** Ritz. **2** Bob Dole. **3** Imran Khan. **4** Prince Charles. **5** Turkey. **6** Thailand. **7** Isa. **8** Calcutta. **9** Manchester. **10** MCC. **11** Boston. **12** Teletubbies. **13** Linda Tripp. **14** Kenya. **15** Selling beef on the bone. **16** Argentina. **17** Swampy. **18** Paul Simon. **19** McLean. **20** Stephen Lawrence. **21** Ann Widdecombe. **22** Halifax. **23** Lord Parkinson. **24** Miami. **25** Norway.

# Quiz 45 Pot Luck 23

1 Bill Rodgers and Roy Jenkins were founder members of which party?
2 Athina Roussel is the daughter of which multi millionairess?
3 Who won the first Rugby Union World Cup, held in 1987?
4 What was the name of the family that led the suffragette movement?
5 Which Michigan town is well known as a manufacturer of motor vehicles?
6 Who had an 80s No 1 with The Edge Of Heaven?
7 What nickname was given to the group of performers which included Sammy Davis Jr and Frank Sinatra?
8 Which country has the greatest number of Roman Catholics?
9 Who first sponsored the cricket trophy now known as the NatWest Trophy?
10 Which writer was married to archaeologist Sir Max Mallowan?
11 What is Paul McCartney's first Christian name?
12 In which year did Britain's lease on Hong Kong officially expire?
13 Who made No 1 with End Of The Road?
14 In Rugby League what did Warrington add to their name in the 90s?
15 Which museum has been established at Beaulieu?
16 On a computer keyboard which letter is immediately right of the Z?
17 What was advertised by Rod Stewart and Tina Turner's version of It Takes Two?
18 Who won the first Celebrity Stars in their Eyes?
19 Where was the soap Albion Market set?
20 In American Football where do the Oilers come from?
21 Who wrote Dirk Gently's Holistic Detective Agency?
22 Vehicles from which country use the international registration letter L?
23 What did the letter B stand for in BSE?
24 To the nearest million what is the population of Tokyo?
25 In advertising who said, "Hello boys"?

## Answers

***Pot Luck 23***

**1** The Social Democratic Party. **2** Christina Onassis. **3** New Zealand. **4** Pankhurst. **5** Detroit. **6** Wham!. **7** The Rat Pack. **8** Brazil. **9** Gillette. **10** Agatha Christie. **11** James. **12** 1997. **13** Boyz II Men. **14** Wolves. **15** National Motor. **16** X. **17** Pepsi. **18** Carol Vorderman. **19** Manchester. **20** Houston. **21** Douglas Adams. **22** Luxembourg. **23** Bovine. **24** 8 million. **25** Eva Herzigova.

# Quiz 46 20th C Brat Pack

**1** Nigel Short was the youngest champion in which game in 1984?
**2** What did Woody Allen call his son as a tribute to Louis 'Satchmo' Armstrong?
**3** Which comedian is the father of Lucy David who plays Hayley in The Archers?
**4** Linus Roache's father plays which character in a TV soap?
**5** Which 80s Wimbledon Men's Singles champion is the father of twins?
**6** Which soul singer is Whitney Houston's godmother?
**7** Who was the most famous Head Girl at Kesteven and Grantham Girls' School?
**8** What did Mel B call her baby with Jimmy Gulzar?
**9** Where did Princess Anne's daughter Zara famously sport a stud in 1998?
**10** What type of car did Prince William receive for his 17th birthday?
**11** What is the name of Paul and Linda McCartney's only son?
**12** Which son of Camilla Parker Bowles was exposed in a drugs scandal in the summer of 1999?
**13** Which pop star has a son called Prince Michael?
**14** Which politician was writer Vera Brittain's daughter?
**15** What relation is Joely Richardson to Vanessa Redgrave?
**16** What are the surnames of the Sawalha sisters of AbFab and EastEnders fame?
**17** Melanie Molitor is the mum of which former tennis world No 1?
**18** How is John Major's celebrity brother known?
**19** Finty Williams is the daughter of which film and theatre Dame?
**20** Which Biblical name does Boris Becker's older son have?
**21** Princess Anne's son Peter Phillips was Head Boy at which famous school?
**22** Who is Julian Lennon's step mother?
**23** Which university did Tony Blair and Bill Clinton both attend in their younger days?
**24** How many sisters and half sisters combined does Cherie Booth have?
**25** Which footballer had his baby's name printed on his football socks?

## Answers

***20th C Brat Pack***

**1** Chess. **2** Satchel. **3** Jasper Carrott. **4** Ken Barlow. **5** Pat Cash. **6** Aretha Franklin. **7** Margaret Thatcher. **8** Phoenix Chi. **9** Tongue. **10** Golf. **11** James. **12** Tom. **13** Michael Jackson. **14** Shirley Williams. **15** Daughter. **16** Julia & Nadia. **17** Martina Hingis. **18** Terry Major-Ball. **19** Judi Dench. **20** Noah. **21** Gordonstoun. **22** Yoko Ono. **23** Oxford. **24** Six. **25** David Beckham.

# Quiz 47 Pot Luck 24

1 In July 1999 it was announced Kim Wilde would host a TV show about what?
2 Which tanker was the cause of a massive oil spill in Alaska in 1989?
3 Released in 1998, in which country had Deborah Parry been imprisoned?
4 Who flew in The Spirit Of St Louis?
5 In which decade did Levi's first use a classic hit to advertise?
6 In baseball where do the Twins come from?
7 What made John D Rockefeller seriously rich?
8 What does H stand for in the video system VHS as launched by JVC in 1976?
9 Which 70s group's members were Les, Eric, Woody, Alan and Derek?
10 Which country took the name Myanmar officially in 1989?
11 Which sport takes place at Hurlingham?
12 Who wrote Bitter Sweet and Private Lives?
13 Who succeeded Nixon as President of the USA in 1974?
14 Lulu sang the title song for which Bond film?
15 Terry Biddlecombe was connected with which sport?
16 Which canal was the work of Ferdinand de Lesseps?
17 Which product used the advertising slogan, "Gives a meal man appeal"?
18 Who wrote the novels Humboldt's Gift and Herzog?
19 Which English international soccer player was nicknamed 'Mighty Mouse'?
20 The Dutch East Indies have become known as what?
21 Which London theatre used to claim that, "we never closed"?
22 US students used aluminium flan cases to 'invent' what?
23 Who made No 1 with Sadness Part 1?
24 Punto Arenas International airport is in which country?
25 Who rode a hat-trick of Prix de l'Arc de Triomphe victories in the mid 80s?

## Answers

***Pot Luck 24***

**1** Gardening. **2** Exxon Valdez. **3** Saudi Arabia. **4** Charles Lindbergh. **5** 80s. **6** Minnesota. **7** Oil. **8** Home. **9** The Bay City Rollers. **10** Burma. **11** Polo. **12** Noel Coward. **13** Ford. **14** The Man With The Golden Gun. **15** Horse racing. **16** Suez. **17** Oxo. **18** Saul Bellow. **19** Kevin Keegan. **20** Indonesia. **21** Windmill. **22** Frisbees. **23** Enigma. **24** Chile. **25** Pat Eddery.

# Quiz 48 20th C TV Classics

1 Who was News At Ten's first woman presenter?
2 What was Kojak's first name?
3 In which English county was Lovejoy filmed?
4 Which Olympic Games were the first to be televised?
5 Who was Edina's PA in AbFab?
6 Who was the astrologer on the BBC's Breakfast Time?
7 How much were the 'cheapest' questions worth in the first series of Sale of the century?
8 What was the name of the 70s comedy series based on the Carry On films?
9 Which game was Celebrity Squares based on?
10 Which ship featured in Sailor?
11 When the Boat Comes In was set in which part of the UK?
12 Which classic 80s drama series shot Anthony Andrews and Jeremy Irons to fame?
13 Which actor was The Bounder?
14 What was the name of the David Attenborough series set in the south Atlantic?
15 Which character in The X Files is the name of a mystery person implicated in the Watergate affair?
16 Which cult series asked, "Who killed Laura Palmer?"?
17 Which classic British sitcom spawned the catchphrase "you dirty old man!"?
18 Which show was blamed by a British police chief for making police officers "drive like maniacs"?
19 Who plays the nurse in Hancock's classic The Blood Donor?
20 In the early 80s if David McCallum was Steel who was Sapphire?
21 What was Rumpole's first name?
22 Which drama series featured a ship called The Charlotte Rhodes?
23 Which actress played the scatty mum in Not In Front of the Children?
24 Which future husband of Demi Moore found fame in the TV series Moonlighting?
25 How many Monkees were there?

## Answers

***20th C TV CLassics***

**1** Anna Ford. **2** Theo. **3** Suffolk. **4** 1948. **5** Bubbles. **6** Russell Grant. **7** £1. **8** Carry on Laughing. **9** Noughts & Crosses. **10** Ark Royal. **11** North East England. **12** Brideshead Revisited. **13** Peter Bowles. **14** Life in the Freezer. **15** Deep Throat. **16** Twin Peaks. **17** Steptoe and Son. **18** Starsky & Hutch. **19** June Whitfield. **20** Joanna Lumley. **21** Horace. **22** The Onedin Line. **23** Wendy Craig. **24** Bruce Willis. **25** Four.

# Quiz 49 Pot Luck 25

1 Which month in 1914 did WWI begin?
2 Who was Princes William and Harry's nanny after their parents separation?
3 Who had an 80s No 1 with Beat Surrender?
4 In cricket what did Glamorgan add to their name in the 90s?
5 What was Crockett's pet in Miami Vice?
6 What stopped Suzanne Lenglen playing at Wimbledon after 1926?
7 What was the nickname of Klaus Barbie the Nazi war criminal?
8 Which veteran DJ used to advertise Brentford Nylons?
9 Who wrote The Inspector Alleyn Mysteries?
10 Which Australian city hosted its final Formula 1 race in 1995?
11 Which actress gave birth to twins at the age of 44 in 1995?
12 What are the international registration letters of a vehicle from Peru?
13 On TV who interviewed Earl Spencer at length several months after Princess Diana's death?
14 With which sport is Said Aouita associated?
15 In which city was Robbie Coltrane born?
16 Which company used the Hollies hit I'm Alive to advertise in 1997?
17 In which decade did Portugal join the European Union?
18 In which country was Jean Claude van Damme born?
19 Who wrote the novel Eating People Is Wrong?
20 Who presented You've Been Framed before Lisa Riley?
21 The name Stanley Gibbons has become associated with what?
22 In which country is the deepwater port of Dampier?
23 Which city has a team of Reds and a team of Bengals?
24 In which decade was Andie MacDowell born?
25 How did the German V-1 flying bomb become known?

**Answers**

***Pot Luck 25***

**1** August. **2** Tiggy Legge Bourke. **3** Jam. **4** Dragons. **5** Alligator. **6** She became a professional. **7** Butcher Of Lyons. **8** Alan Freeman. **9** Ngaio Marsh. **10** Melbourne. **11** Jane Seymour. **12** PE. **13** Sally Magnusson. **14** Athletics. **15** Glasgow. **16** Boots. **17** 80s. **18** Belgium. **19** Malcolm Bradbury. **20** Jeremy Beadle. **21** Stamps. **22** Australia. **23** Cincinnati. **24** 50s. **25** Doodlebug.

# Quiz 50 Cricket

1 Who followed Viv Richards as West Indian captain?
2 Who along with Mark Waugh accepted money from an Indian bookmaker for "weather forecasts"?
3 Who was the last man out in the Australia v S Africa semi final tie in 1999?
4 Who were England playing in the Atherton 'ball tampering' incident?
5 What was the nickname of England pace bowler David Lawrence?
6 Who were the opponents in Mike Atherton's last series as England skipper?
7 Who was man of the match in the 1999 World Cup final?
8 Administrator Lord MacLaurin was a former chairman of which supermarket group?
9 Who was the first bowler since Laker to take all ten wickets in the same Test innings?
10 Which country were the last to be admitted to the County circuit in the century?
11 Which team won the 1992 World Cup?
12 Which visiting bowler took nine wickets in a Test in England in the 90s?
13 At which ground did Atherton and Donald have their famous 'battle' of 1998?
14 Who preceded Ray Illingworth as chairman of the Test selectors?
15 England batsman Aftab Habib managed only one first class game for which county?
16 Who was England's leading wicket taker on the 97-98 W Indies tour?
17 What was Clive Lloyd's middle name?
18 Where are the Eden Gardens?
19 In what year did Graham Gooch first play for England?
20 Which Minor County did England keeper Chris Read play for?
21 Steve James was playing for which county when first capped for England?
22 Which team have won the county championship most in the century?
23 What colour were the Australian trousers in the 1999 World Cup final?
24 Who was the first player to score 100 and take eight wickets in an innings in the same Test?
25 Which English keeper had the middle names Philip Eric?

## Answers

***Cricket***

**1** Richie Richardson. **2** Shane Warne. **3** Allan Donald. **4** South Africa. **5** Syd. **6** W Indies. **7** Shane Warne. **8** Tesco. **9** Anil Kumble. **10** Durham. **11** Pakistan. **12** Muttiah Muralitharan. **13** Trent Bridge. **14** Ted Dexter. **15** Middlesex. **16** Angus Fraser. **17** Hubert. **18** Calcutta. **19** 1975. **20** Devon. **21** Glamorgan. **22** Yorkshire. **23** Yellow. **24** Ian Botham. **25** Alan Knott.

# Quiz 51 Pot Luck 26

1 The Queen's first corgi was bought for her by whom?
2 What was George Michael's first solo No 1?
3 Who created the flying ace Biggles?
4 Which part of New York borough is most famous for its skyline of high rise buildings?
5 In which decade of the century did Yorkshire last win cricket's County Championship?
6 Which one time wife of Frank Sinatra starred in Peyton Place?
7 What did the 'S' stand for in Harry S Truman's name?
8 Which musical featured the song Sit Down You're Rockin' The Boat?
9 In basketball where do the Wizards come from?
10 Who was the first regular female presenter of TV's Points of View?
11 Who did Neil Kinnock succeed as Labour Party leader?
12 Which Enid Blyton spoof was made by the Comic Strip?
13 Which country did USSR invade in 1979?
14 Who made No 1 with Mr Vain?
15 In the 90s how many points have been awarded for finishing fourth in a Grand Prix?
16 Quintin Hogg became which Lord?
17 Who wrote The Great Gatsby?
18 Adona international airport is in which country?
19 In which Bond film did Jane Seymour appear?
20 Who did Real Madrid beat in the famous 7-3 European Cup Final?
21 Which William was in the title of an opera by Benjamin Britten?
22 Which singer led the dance troupe Hot Gossip on The Kenny Everett Video Show?
23 What did the letter A stand for in SAS?
24 Wood and Walters trolleyed into the country to advertise which supermarket?
25 What was Muhammad Ali said to float like?

**Answers**

***Pot Luck 26***

**1** Her father. **2** Careless Whisper. **3** Capt W E Johns. **4** Manhattan. **5** 60s. **6** Mia Farrow. **7** Nothing. **8** Guys And Dolls. **9** Washington. **10** Anne Robinson. **11** Michael Foot. **12** Five Go Mad in Dorset. **13** Afghanistan. **14** Culture Beat. **15** 3. **16** Hailsham. **17** F Scott Fitzgerald. **18** Turkey. **19** Live And Let Die. **20** Eintracht Frankfurt. **21** Budd - Billy Budd. **22** Sarah Brightman. **23** Air. **24** Asda. **25** A butterfly.

# Quiz 52 20th C 90s Movies

1 Which ER star played opposite Jenny Seagrove in Don't Go Breaking My Heart?
2 Beloved in 1999 was whose first movie since The Color Purple in 1985?
3 In Stepmom who played Susan Sarandon's daughter?
4 Who played the colliery band leader in Brassed Off?
5 In which 90s movie did Al Pacino play retired Colonel Frank Slade?
6 Which sitcom star appeared on the big screen in The Object of My Affection?
7 Who played Drew Barrymore's stepmother in Ever After?
8 Which US president did Anthony Hopkins play in a film whose title was simply his name?
9 Which Schwarzenegger movie about a man who gets pregnant was originally titled Oh Baby?
10 In which movie did Jane Horrocks play a girl who can sing like the great musical stars?
11 Which star of Cheers co starred with Whoopi Goldberg in Made in America?
12 Which The Bridges of Madison County star became a father again aged 65?
13 Who was the star of the dark thriller 8mm?
14 Where was the 1990s version of Dickens Great Expectations set?
15 Which King did Leonardo DiCaprio play in The Man in the Iron Mask?
16 Which regular member of the Friends cast starred in Lost in Space?
17 Which role did Rupert Everett play in The Madness of King George?
18 Which animation film was originally a 50s musical set in Siam?
19 What is the name of Kate Winslet's character in Titanic?
20 Who played the title role in Emma?
21 Which character did Julia Roberts play in Steven Spielberg's Hook?
22 Which movie was a biopic about the life of David Helfgott?
23 Which Apollo mission was filmed in 1995 with Tom Hanks?
24 In which film did Susan Sarandon play Sister Helen Prejean?
25 What was Pierce Brosnan's first outing as 007?

## Answers

***20th C The Movies 90s***

**1** Anthony Edwards. **2** Oprah Winfrey. **3** Julia Roberts. **4** Pete Postlethwaite. **5** Scent of a Woman. **6** Jennifer Aniston. **7** Anjelica Houston. **8** Nixon. **9** Junior. **10** Little Voice. **11** Ted Danson. **12** Clint Eastwood. **13** Nicolas Cage. **14** New York. **15** Louis XIV. **16** Matt LeBlanc. **17** The Prince of Wales. **18** The King and I. **19** Rose. **20** Gwyneth Paltrow. **21** Tinkerbell. **22** Shine. **23** 13. **24** Dead Man Walking. **25** Goldeneye.

# Quiz 53 Pot Luck 27

1 What was the name of the boat on which Robert Maxwell was last seen alive?
2 In 90s cricket what did Northamptonshire add to their name?
3 Private detective Albert Campion was played by which ex Dr Who?
4 Who took over the ITV franchise from TVS in 1991?
5 Why were people partyting in Paris the evening before Bastille Day in 1998?
6 Who had an 80s No 1 with Coward Of The County?
7 Who said, "To err is human but it feels divine"?
8 Which widow of a rock star appeared in Dallas?
9 The German terrorist group The Red Army Faction were more usually as which Gang?
10 Which Rugby League team made a fashion statement and became Blue Sox in the 90s?
11 Birds Eye Peas were advertised as being, "Fresh as the moment when the pod went..." what?
12 Which soccer manager's autobiography was An Englishman Abroad?
13 Who created a famous garden at Sissinghurst in Kent?
14 How were Armstrong, Conlon, Hill and Richardson known collectively?
15 At which sport did Ian Black win international success?
16 Who performed He's A Tramp in the Disney movie Lady And The Tramp?
17 Which character first said "bloody" 78 times in a TV comedy show?
18 Jersey Joe Walcott was a world champion in which sport?
19 Igor Sikorsky developed which means of transport?
20 In American Football where do the Chargers come from?
21 Who wrote the novel The Power and The Glory?
22 Vehicles from which place use the international registration letter V?
23 In 1998 which Top of the Pops presenter was voted Britain's best dressed man in 1998?
24 Who was the first New Zealand cricketer to be knighted?
25 Which Bond girl was Honor Blackman?

## Answers

***Pot Luck 27***

**1** Lady Ghislaine. **2** Steelbacks. **3** Peter Davison. **4** Meridian. **5** France had won the World Cup. **6** Kenny Rogers. **7** Mae West. **8** Priscilla Presley. **9** Baader-Meinhof Gang. **10** Halifax. **11** Pop. **12** Bobby Robson. **13** Vita Sackville-West. **14** Guildford Four. **15** Swimming. **16** Peggy Lee. **17** Alf Garnett. **18** Boxing. **19** Helicopter. **20** San Diego. **21** Graham Greene. **22** Vatican City. **23** Jamie Theakston. **24** Richard Hadlee. **25** Pussy Galore.

# Quiz 54 20th C World Tour

1 In which country are the world's tallest buildings, the Petronas Towers?
2 In 1997 which airline replaced the flag on its tail fin with ethnic designs from around the world?
3 Where is there the valley of the Kings, scene of a terrorist attack in 1997?
4 In which decade of the 20th century did the first scheduled passenger air service begin?
5 What was Ethiopia called before it was called Ethiopia?
6 What is California's answer to Scotland's Silicon Glen called?
7 What name was given to the effect which warmed the waters of the Pacific, notably in the 1990s?
8 Andy Elson's world tour by balloon was thwarted in 1998 because he could not cross which country's air space?
9 What was Ho Chi Minh city before it was called Ho Chi Minh city?
10 In which continent is over half of the world's rainforests?
11 What was replaced by Brasilia as Brazil's capital in the 60s?
12 Which country is known as the Land of the Long White Cloud?
13 Which desert expanded by 251,000 sq miles between 1940 and 1990?
14 What was St Petersburg called for most of the 20th century?
15 On which island will you find Bondi Beach?
16 Which Californian resort is famous for its Golden Gate bridge?
17 In which country is the headquarters of the Save the Children Fund?
18 Which country contains the Biblical rivers of the Tigris and the Euphrates?
19 Transamazonica is a roadway across which large South American country?
20 Which German airport has am main after its name?
21 If a car's index mark is GBA, where does it come from?
22 What is the Pacific terminus of the Trans Siberian Railway?
23 In which US state did skateboards originate as an alternative to surfing?
24 Which item essential for world travel, is made in Seattle?
25 To the nearest thousand, how many islands does Indonesia have?

## Answers

***20th C Travel & Leisure World Tour***

**1** Malaysia. **2** British Airways. **3** Egypt. **4** 2nd decade - it was 1914. **5** Abyssinia. **6** Silicon Valley. **7** El Nino. **8** China's. **9** Saigon. **10** America. **11** Rio de Janeiro. **12** New Zealand. **13** Sahara. **14** Leningrad. **15** Australia. **16** San Francisco. **17** England. **18** Iraq. **19** Brazil. **20** Frankfurt. **21** Alderney. **22** Vladivostok. **23** California. **24** Jets. **25** 13.

# Quiz 55 Pot Luck 29

1 Which former Tory MP lost the Derbyshire South seat in 1997?
2 In NYPD Blue who played Bobby Simone?
3 Barbara Castle was a long standing PM for which constituency?
4 Who wrote the Clayhanger series of novels?
5 Who had an 80s No 1 with Making Your Mind Up?
6 In baseball where do the Tigers come from?
7 Who founded Body Shop?
8 Whose secret agent partner was Penfold?
9 In cricket which English team became Bears in the 90s?
10 Which group had a No 1 album in 1986 titled Once Upon A Time?
11 Jonathan Power has been a world champion in which sport?
12 What are the international registration letters of a vehicle from Switzerland?
13 How much in old pence was a tanner worth in predecimal days?
14 In Germany what are strumpfhose?
15 1994 was the Chinese year of which creature?
16 Who were the first landlords of the Rovers Return in Coronation Street?
17 "Adopt, adapt, improve" was adopted as which group's motto?
18 Which actor's real name is Walter Matasschansayasky?
19 Who sailed solo round the world in Gipsy Moth IV in 1966-67?
20 What did Tic-Tac throw in the Bond movies with deadly results?
21 In S Africa what does the I stand for in IFP?
22 In TV ads which drink claimed, "It's what your right arm's for"?
23 Which Rugby League team became Bulldogs in the 90s?
24 What is the motto of the Scout movement?
25 In which decade was Hugh Grant born?

## Answers

***Pot Luck 29***

**1** Edwina Currie. **2** Jimmy Smits. **3** Blackburn. **4** Arnold Bennett. **5** Bucks Fizz. **6** Detroit. **7** Anita Roddick. **8** Dangermouse. **9** Warwickshire. **10** Simple Minds. **11** Squash. **12** CH. **13** Six. **14** Tights. **15** Dog. **16** Jack and Annie Walker. **17** The Round Table. **18** Walter Matthau. **19** Francis Chichester. **20** Bowler hat. **21** Inkatha. **22** Courage. **23** Batley. **24** Be prepared. **25** 60s.

# Quiz 56 Bands

1 The Proclaimers were King of the what in 1990?
2 Chrissie Hynde was the female member of which successful band?
3 Which band had a 90s album titled Our Town - Greatest Hits?
4 Which Irish group has a name which means family?
5 Which groups first hit was titled House of Love?
6 Who rereleased the 1984 No 8 hit Young At Heart in 1993?
7 Which group recorded the track that Welsh soccer fans changed to Bobby Gould Must Go?
8 Which group was founded by Ian Broudie?
9 Which hit making band featured Andy Summers and Stewart Copeland?
10 In which city were Pulp formed?
11 Falco's Rock Me Amadeus was sung in which language?
12 How many songs by the Bee Gees were in the film Saturday Night Fever?
13 Which Status Quo hit opened the 1985 Live Aid concert?
14 Who released an album in 1996 called A Different Beat?
15 Who told us to Keep On Running in a 60s No 1 hit?
16 Who had an insect sounding hit with The Fly in 1991?
17 Siobhan Fahey and Marcella Detroit were in which band in the 90s?
18 How many members are in the group Boyz II Men?
19 Where is the native home country of Bjorn Again?
20 Which 60s group included Pete Quaife and Mick Avory?
21 Which all girl group were first to sell more than a million copies of an album in the UK?
22 Who were Naked In The Rain in a No. 4 hit from July 1990?
23 Who formed a rock band in 1989 called Tin Machine?
24 What was 2 Unlimited's first UK No 1 from 1993?
25 Which company used Queen's I Want To Break Free in TV commercials?

## Answers

***Bands***

**1** Road. **2** Pretenders. **3** Deacon Blue. **4** Clannad. **5** East 17. **6** Bluebells. **7** Manic Street Preachers. **8** The Lightning Seeds. **9** The Police. **10** Sheffield. **11** German. **12** 7. **13** Rockin' All Over The World. **14** Boyzone. **15** Spencer Davis Group. **16** U2. **17** Shakespear's Sister. **18** Four. **19** Australia. **20** The Kinks. **21** Eternal. **22** Blue Pearl. **23** David Bowie. **24** No Limit. **25** Shell.

# Quiz 57 UK Leaders

1 For how long did the UK's first woman Prime Minister hold this office?
2 How old was Tony Blair when he became PM?
3 Who did Paul Gascoigne describe as "nice and cuddly"?
4 What position in government did John Major hold before he became PM?
5 Who won Leon Brittan's parliamentary seat when he became an EC Commissioner?
6 Which Tory Party Chairman and MP for Chingford's wife was paralysed in the Brighton bombing of 1984?
7 Who was Education Secretary, Home Secretary and Chancellor in the 90s?
8 Who was the first Labour Prime Minister?
9 In the 1990 Tory leadership who first stood against Margaret Thatcher?
10 As Prime Minister Andrew Bonar Law represented which party?
11 Former Labour leader Neil Kinnock was a European Commissioner in charge of which department?
12 Who was the last prime minister to be created an earl?
13 Which left wing MP and former council leader wrote If Voting Changed Anything They'd Abolish It?
14 Who was sacked as Deputy Leader of the Tory Party in William Hague's first major reshuffle?
15 Baroness Margaret Jay is the daughter of which ex PM?
16 Who delivered the first Budget speech to be televised - in March 1990?
17 Who did George Carey replace as Archbishop of Canterbury?
18 Which MP shared a beefburger with his young daughter to try and prove British beef was safe to eat?
19 Whose resignation speech in 1990, with allusions to a game of cricket, precipitated the downfall of Margaret Thatcher?
20 Who was Britain's second youngest PM this century?
21 Who was Mrs Thatcher's press secretary during her last years as PM?
22 What was John Major's constituency when he was PM?
23 On leaving No 10 Margaret Thatcher became which Baroness?
24 Which middle name did Winston Churchill share with Charlie Chaplin?
25 Who is the century's longest serving MP for Old Bexley and Sidcup?

## Answers

***UK Leaders***

**1** 11 years. **2** 43. **3** Margaret Thatcher. **4** Chancellor of the Exchequer. **5** William Hague. **6** Norman Tebbit. **7** Kenneth Clarke. **8** Ramsay MacDonald. **9** Michael Heseltine. **10** Conservative. **11** Transport. **12** Harold Macmillan. **13** Ken Livingstone. **14** Peter Lilley. **15** James Callaghan. **16** John Major. **17** Robert Runcie. **18** John Gummer. **19** Geoffrey Howe. **20** John Major. **21** Bernard Ingham. **22** Huntingdon. **23** Kesteven. **24** Spencer. **25** Edward Heath.

# Quiz 58 Pot Luck 31

Level 2

1 Dunfermline East has been the 90s seat of which prominent politician?
2 Who wrote the novel Watership Down?
3 Who played Timothy Lumsden in Sorry!?
4 Which food was not rationed in World War II but was rationed after it?
5 In advertising campaign, which sign meant "happy motoring"?
6 Who had an 80s No 1 with The Tide Is High?
7 Della Street was whose secretary?
8 What is Mick Jagger's middle name?
9 In basketball where do the Suns come from?
10 In TV ads what colour was Arthur the cat?
11 Who was the first chemist to be Britain's Prime Minister?
12 Under which name did the frock wearing Daniel Carroll find fame?
13 Which country lies immediately to the south of Estonia?
14 Which show gave Barbara Dickson a hit with Another Suitcase in Another Hall?
15 Who was Prime Minister of Australia from 1983-1991?
16 On which river was the Kariba dam built?
17 Which Dennis Potter drama was shown in 1987, eleven years after it was banned from TV screens?
18 Who set fire to his guitar at the Monterey Pop Festival in 1967?
19 In which Bond film did Britt Ekland appear?
20 Vehicles from which country use the international registration letter P?
21 Which female presenter interviewed Charles and Diana before their wedding?
22 Other than the title of a movie, what is Airforce One in the USA?
23 In which decade did Spain join the European Union?
24 Which city does writer Beryl Bainbridge come from?
25 A Fistful of Dollars was filmed on location in which country?

## Answers

***Pot Luck 31***

**1** Gordon Brown. **2** Richard Adams. **3** Ronnie Corbett. **4** Bread. **5** Esso. **6** Blondie. **7** Perry Mason. **8** Philip. **9** Phoenix. **10** White. **11** Margaret Thatcher. **12** Danny La Rue. **13** Latvia. **14** Evita. **15** Bob Hawke. **16** Zambezi. **17** Brimstone and Treacle. **18** Jimi Hendrix. **19** The Man With The Golden Gun. **20** Portugal. **21** Angela Rippon. **22** The President's plane. **23** 80s. **24** Liverpool. **25** Italy.

# Quiz 59 20th C Headline Makers

Level 2

1. Fleur Lombard was the first woman to die on duty in which profession?
2. Who took out an injunction against Martin Steenning after he tried to take photographs of her?
3. How many babies did Mandy Allwood expect when she sold her story?
4. What was the occupation of Philip Lawrence who was killed outside his place of work in December 1995?
5. What was the name of the NATO spokesman in the 1999 Kosovo crisis?
6. Which former Tory MP hosted a late night Radio 5 Live phone in show?
7. Which British player moved to Chelsea in July 1999 for a cool £10 million?
8. Nicoletta Mantovani hit the headlines through her relationship with which big figure in the entertainment world?
9. Released on June 22nd 1999, Patrick Magee was known as which Bomber?
10. Timothy McVeigh was convicted for which bombing?
11. Who was dubbed Red Ken?
12. Which First lady had to give evidence over the Whitewater scandal?
13. Which outgoing MP in the 1997 General Election had the initials MDX?
14. What movement for the terminally ill was begun by Cicely Saunders?
15. Which woman space traveller published The Space Place in 1997?
16. Marc Dutroux hit the headlines over a 'house of horrors' in which country?
17. Who penned a ballad from Belmarsh Gaol?
18. What was the surname of the couple who disappeared with their foster daughters after they feared they would be taken away from them?
19. What was Clive Sinclair's personal transport vehicle called?
20. Which party leader once made a pop video with Tracey Ullman?
21. Who defended her nursery children from a machete attack in 1995?
22. Which sports commentator said, "Do my eyes deceive me or is Senna's Lotus sounding a bit rough!"?
23. About which British politician did Francois Mitterand say, "She has the mouth of Marilyn Monroe and the eyes of Caligula"?
24. Who was convicted of murdering her fiance Lee Harvey after she alleged he had been killed in an road rage attack?
25. Who was the last British Wimbledon singles champion of the 20th century?

## Answers

***20th C Headline Makers***

**1** Fire fighter. **2** Princess Diana. **3** Eight. **4** Head teacher. **5** Jamie Shea. **6** Edwina Currie. **7** Chris Sutton. **8** Luciano Pavarotti. **9** Brighton Bomber. **10** Oklahoma. **11** Ken Livingstone. **12** Hillary Clinton. **13** Michael Portillo. **14** Hospice Movement. **15** Helen Sharman. **16** Belgium. **17** Jonathan Aitken. **18** Bramley. **19** C5. **20** Neil Kinnock. **21** Lisa Potts. **22** Murray Walker. **23** Margaret Thatcher. **24** Tracie Andrews. **25** Virginia Wade.

# Quiz 60 Pot Luck 32

1 What was the frequency of Radio Luxembourg?
2 What is the set of fans at the front of a jet engine called?
3 On TV who presented Saturday Night Armistice?
4 In cricket what did Sussex add to their name in the 90s?
5 Who had a national airline called Garuda?
6 Which British PM imposed a10.30pm TV curfew in 1973?
7 Which musical featured the song Rhythm Of Life?
8 Who was the first tennis player to be BBC Sports Personality in the 1990s?
9 In which month of the year is Battle of Britain week?
10 How is Declan McManus better known?
11 Which daughter of feminist writer Vera Brittain became a British MP?
12 Who was the first US golfer to win the US amateur title in three consecutive years?
13 Which British entertainer used the catchphrase, "She knows, you know"?
14 Who made No 1 with Boombastic?
15 In American Football where do the Chiefs come from?
16 Where in Devon is the railway station St. David's?
17 What was advertised by persuading you that your fingers should do the walking?
18 Entebbe international airport is in which country?
19 What is David Frost's middle name?
20 What does the letter C stand for in the media organisation CNN?
21 Who said, "I married beneath me. All women do"?
22 What relation is TV cook Sophie Grigson to late cookery expert Jane?
23 Which American novelist wrote For Whom the Bell Tolls?
24 Andy Linnighan scored a last minute FA Cup winner for which team?
25 Sheryl Crow sang the title song for which Bond film?

## Answers

***Pot Luck 32***

**1** 208. **2** Compressor. **3** Armando Iannucci. **4** Sharks. **5** Indonesia. **6** Heath. **7** Sweet Charity. **8** Greg Rusedski. **9** September. **10** Elvis Costello. **11** Shirley Williams. **12** Tiger Woods. **13** Hylda Baker. **14** Shaggy. **15** Kansas City. **16** Exeter. **17** Yellow pages. **18** Uganda. **19** Paradine. **20** Cable. **21** Nancy Astor. **22** Daughter. **23** Ernest Hemingway. **24** Arsenal. **25** Tomorrow Never Dies.

# Quiz 61 20th C TV Sitcoms

1 Who was Patsy's boss in Absolutely Fabulous, as played by Kathy Burke?
2 Which member of the cast of Friends has a son called Julian in real life?
3 Which star of the sitcom Babes in the Wood represented the UK in the Eurovision Song Contest in 1991?
4 Which premature pensioner played Denise in The Royle Family?
5 Which actor from Only Fools and Horses is the father of Emily Lloyd?
6 What was the surname of the couple who lived next door to the Goods in The Good Life?
7 Which They Think It's All Over regular starred in Holding the Baby?
8 Which sitcom was based in the restaurant Le Chateau Anglais?
9 Where was It Ain't Half Hot Mum set?
10 What was the occupation of Gladys Emmanuel in Open All Hours?
11 In the first series of Yes Minister what was Jim Hacker's department?
12 Which elderly relative did the Trotters live with in the first series of Only Fools and Horses?
13 What was Blackadder called in Blackadder's Christmas Carol?
14 What was Tracey's son called in Birds of a Feather?
15 Who was the brother of Hyacinth Bucket's neighbour Elizabeth?
16 Which two sitcom stars advertised Surf soap powder?
17 In which sitcom did Margaret Thatcher read a scene with its stars at an awards ceremony in 1984?
18 Which series revolved around Diana and Tom in a retirement home?
19 Which ex Bond girl played the mother in Law in The Upper Hand?
20 Which sitcom centred on Bill and Ben and their family?
21 What was Alf Garnett's film star nickname for his son in law?
22 Which series with Rowan Atkinson and James Dreyfus was set in the fictitious town of Gasforth?
23 Miss Jones was the only female lodger in which sitcom with Leonard Rossiter?
24 Who was the shop owner in Open All Hours?
25 Grantleigh, in the village Cricket St Thomas was the setting for which series?

**Answers**

***20th C TV Sitcoms***

**1** Magda. **2** Lisa Kudrow. **3** Samantha Janus. **4** Caroline Aherne. **5** Roger Lloyd Pack. **6** Leadbetter. **7** Nick Hancock. **8** Chef!. **9** India. **10** Nurse. **11** Administrative Affairs. **12** Grandad. **13** Ebenezer Blackadder. **14** Garth. **15** Emmet. **16** Pauline Quirke & Linda Robson. **17** Yes Minister. **18** Waiting For God. **19** Honor Blackman. **20** 2 Point 4 Children. **21** Shirley Temple. **22** The Thin Blue Line. **23** Rising Damp. **24** Arkwright. **25** To The Manor Born.

# Quiz 62 Pot Luck 33

1 Which US city was named after a British Prime Minister?
2 Where is the normal terminus if you travel from Bristol to London?
3 Who had an 80s No 1 with I Want To Know What Love Is?
4 If E=mc2 according to Einstein, what does m stand for?
5 Which Tory MP lost the Edinburgh Pentlands seat in 1997?
6 In baseball where do the Brewers come from?
7 Which insurance company said they wouldn't make a drama out of a crisis?
8 Under what name was Lionel Begleiter better known?
9 Rushcliffe has been the 80s and 90s seat of which prominent politician?
10 The Harry Lime theme was used in which film?
11 Geet Sethi has been a world champion in which sport?
12 What are the international registration letters of a vehicle from Iceland?
13 In early TV ads Consulate cigarettes were described as, "Cool as a.." what?
14 Where in Libya did Australian troops take a seaport occupied by the Italians in 1941?
15 At which sport did Karen Briggs win international success in the 80s and 90s?
16 Under which name did Alfonso D'Abruzzo find fime as an actor?
17 According to the inventor Thomas Edison genius is made up how many per cent of inspiration?
18 In which decade was Emily Lloyd born?
19 Which C S wrote The African Queen?
20 Who was world professional billiards champion between 1968 and 1980?
21 On a US Monopoly board, what are B & O, Reading, Short Line and Pennsylvania?
22 Which ex MP's memoirs were logged in Upwardly Mobile?
23 To the nearest million what is the population of Madrid?
24 In Rugby League what did Oldham add to their name in the 90s?
25 Who had the catchphrase, "By Jove, I needed that"?

## Answers

***Pot Luck 33***

**1** Pittsburgh. **2** Paddington. **3** Foreigner. **4** Mass. **5** Malcolm Rifkind. **6** Milwaukee. **7** Commercial Union. **8** Lionel Bart. **9** Kenneth Clarke. **10** The Third Man. **11** Billiards. **12** IS. **13** Mountain stream. **14** Tobruk. **15** Judo. **16** Alan Alda. **17** One. **18** 70s. **19** Forester. **20** Rex Williams. **21** Stations. **22** Norman Tebbit. **23** 3 million. **24** Bears. **25** Ken Dodd.

# Quiz 63 Motor Sports

1. In which 98 Grand Prix did David Coulthard move aside to let Mika Hakkinen win?
2. In which decade did Frank Williams launch his own racing team?
3. Which British driver got himself in the money stakes with deals with Sauber and Sony Playstation?
4. On which race track was Jim Clark killed?
5. Heinz-Harlad Frentzen moved to Jordan from which team?
6. Which motor race was first held on the old Sarthe circuit?
7. Who was the first Brit to claim the World Rally title?
8. In which US state is the Daytona Beach circuit?
9. Which Grand Prix provided Damon Hill's only victory in 1998?
10. In which decade was the Le Mans 24 hour race first held?
11. Which team did Nigel Mansell drive with when he was Formula 1 champ?
12. Who was the last Fin before Mika Hakkinen to be Formula 1 champion?
13. Which team did Johnny Herbert move to for the 1999 Grand Prix season?
14. Mika Hakkinen ended up with how many points in becoming 1998 world champion?
15. Which Grand Prix has been held at Mosport and Mont Tremblant?
16. In 1998 the Algerian government claimed that which top driver was in fact an Algerian?
17. James Hunt was born in and died in which city?
18. Who was the first person to clock up over 250 Grand Prix starts?
19. Rod Dennis has been managing director of which team?
20. Who was the first Brit to be Formula 1 champion?
21. In the 90s how many points have been awarded for finishing third in a Grand Prix?
22. What was the last Grand Prix outside Britain in which Damon Hill raced?
23. Which team did Jim Clark drive for at Formula 1?
24. In which year was Nigel Mansell Indy Car champion?
25. When Michael Schumacher was first Formula 1 champ he was with which team?

## Answers

***Motor Sports***

**1** Australian. **2** 70s. **3** Johnny Herbert. **4** Hockenheim. **5** Williams. **6** Le Mans 24 Hours. **7** Colin McRae. **8** Florida. **9** Belgian. **10** 20s. **11** Williams. **12** Keke Rosberg. **13** Stewart. **14** 100. **15** Canadian. **16** Michael Schumacher. **17** London. **18** Riccardo Patrese. **19** McLaren. **20** Mike Hawthorn. **21** 4. **22** Hungarian. **23** Lotus. **24** 1993. **25** Benetton.

# Quiz 64 Pot Luck 34

1 Which politician was involved in charges made by male model Norman Scott ?
2 English writer P G Wodehouse took out citizenship in which country?
3 What type of disaster took place in Skopje in 1963?
4 John George Diefenbaker was once PM of where?
5 Under what name did Thomas Hicks become a famous entertainer?
6 What is 50 mph in kilometres per hour?
7 Which musical featured the song My Favourite Things?
8 In WWI according to the Germans, who were the Ladies from Hell?
9 Which drink was advertised with the song I'd Like To Teach The World To Sing?
10 James Braddock was a world champion in which sport?
11 How did Virginia Woolf's life end?
12 What was the surname of underwater film makers Hans and Lotte?
13 What was the title of Dick Francis's first novel set in the horse racing world?
14 In which sport could the Heat take on the Magic?
15 In advertising what type of service was promoted using a giant letter X?
16 Who made No 1 with Killer?
17 Who said, "Talking jaw to jaw is better than going to war"?
18 In which decade did Luxembourg join the European Union?
19 Ian Wright has scored FA Cup Final goals for Arsenal and who else?
20 Who won a Booker Prize for Paddy Clarke Ha Ha Ha?
21 Klagenfurt international airport is in which country?
22 What did the letter A stand for in GATT?
23 Which Red Indian tribe featured in Dances With Wolves?
24 Which golf course includes the Rabbit and the Seal?
25 Father's Day was first celebrated in which country?

## Answers

***Pot Luck 34***

**1** Jeremy Thorpe. **2** US. **3** Earthquake. **4** Canada. **5** Tommy Steele. **6** 80. **7** The Sound Of Music. **8** Highland soldiers in kilts. **9** Coca Cola. **10** Boxing. **11** Drowned herself. **12** Hass. **13** Dead Cert. **14** Basketball. **15** Building Society - The Halifax. **16** Adamski. **17** Winston Churchill. **18** 50s. **19** Crystal Palace. **20** Roddy Doyle. **21** Austria. **22** Agreement. **23** Sioux. **24** Troon. **25** USA.

# Quiz 65 Movie Moguls

1 Which blonde actress made her debut as a producer in Private Benjamin?
2 On which Isle was Anthony Minghella born?
3 Who directed the first three Godfather films?
4 Which Indecent Proposal star made a directorial debut in Ordinary People?
5 Who directed the 1999 movie whose stars included Leonardo DiCaprio?
6 Which director sacked Harvey Keitel from the cast of Apocalypse Now?
7 That Thing You Do was the directorial debut of which double Oscar winner?
8 Who directed Oscar nominated John Travolta in Pulp Fiction?
9 Out of 11 films how many did Grace Kelly make for Hitchcock?
10 Sliding Doors director Peter Howitt starred in which Liverpool sitcom?
11 Which celebrity couple co founded the production company Simian Films?
12 Who directed Tea With Mussolini?
13 Which actor, whose name was linked with Catherine Zeta Jones in 1999, co produced One Flew Over the Cuckoo's Nest?
14 Based on a novel by Nicholas Evans, what was Robert Redford's first film as director and star?
15 Who directed the original Rear Window, remade in the 90s with Christopher Reeve?
16 Which woman starred in and directed The Prince of Tides?
17 Which 'man with no name' directed The Bridges of Madison County?
18 What was Quentin Tarantino's follow up to Reservoir Dogs?
19 Which actor/director founded The Sundance Film Festival?
20 Which director adapted Stephen King's The Shining for the big screen?
21 Which hugely successful director co wrote and produced Poltergeist?
22 Taylor Hackford is the husband of which 50 plus British actress?
23 Who directed Ben Kingsley in his first Oscar winning role as a civil rights hero?
24 Which novel by E M Forster did David Lean make into a film in 1984 with Peggy Ashcroft and Judy Davis?
25 Which director of Titanic gave Arnold Schwarzenegger his big break in The Terminator?

**Answers**

***20th C The Movies Directors and Producers***

**1** Goldie Hawn. **2** Isle of Wight. **3** Francis Ford Coppola. **4** Robert Redford. **5** Woody Allen. **6** Francis Ford Coppola. **7** Tom Hanks. **8** Quentin Tarantino. **9** Three. **10** Bread. **11** Hugh Grant & Liz Hurley. **12** Franco Zeffirelli. **13** Michael Douglas. **14** The Horse Whisperer. **15** Alfred Hitchcock. **16** Barbra Streisand. **17** Clint Eastwood. **18** Pulp Fiction. **19** Robert Redford. **20** Stanley Kubrick. **21** Steve Spielberg. **22** Helen Mirren. **23** Richard Attenborough - for Gandhi. **24** A Passage to India. **25** James Cameron.

# Quiz 66 Pot Luck 35

1 Which Prize was awarded to Desmond Tutu in 1984?
2 In the musical Oliver which character sings As Long As He Needs Me?
3 In 1994 which Grand Prix saw the controversial Schumacher/Hill collision?
4 Valentina Harris cooks up food particularly from which country?
5 Arthur Griffith founded which political group in 1905?
6 In baseball where do the Orioles come from?
7 In advertising which DIY store claimed that it was "the big one"?
8 Who had an 80s No 1 with Desire?
9 With which sport is Anne Marie Moser-Proll associated?
10 What was Buddy Holly's real first name?
11 Who had a horse called Topper?
12 In which decade was Ralph Fiennes born?
13 Who was the first female member of the Ground Force?
14 Vehicles from which country use the international registration letter T?
15 In the 90s which athlete's autobiography was titled How Long's The Course?
16 Which national company was Ringo Starr's first employer?
17 Michelle Martin has been a 90s world champion in which sport?
18 In which country is the deepwater port of Thunder Bay?
19 Who wrote the thriller The Odessa File?
20 In the 90s how many points have been awarded for finishing fifth in a Grand Prix?
21 In which country was Telly Savalas born?
22 On a computer keyboard which letter on the same line is immediately left of the H?
23 Who wrote, "He who can does. He who cannot, teaches"?
24 Which Bond villain did Gert Frobe play?
25 With which sport was Charles Buchan associated?

## Answers

***Pot Luck 35***

**1** Nobel Peace. **2** Nancy. **3** Australian. **4** Italy. **5** Sinn Fein. **6** Baltimore. **7** Texas. **8** U2. **9** Skiing. **10** Charles. **11** Hoppalong Cassidy. **12** 60s. **13** Charlie Dimmock. **14** Thailand. **15** Roger Black. **16** British Railways. **17** Squash. **18** Canada. **19** Frederick Forsyth. **20** 2. **21** USA. **22** G. **23** George Bernard Shaw. **24** Goldfinger. **25** Soccer.

# Quiz 67 Books

1 How did the barrister Rumpole refer to his wife Hilda?
2 Which county did Catherine Cookson come from and write about?
3 Who won a Booker Prize for Midnight's Children?
4 In which decade of the century did H G Wells die?
5 Under which name did American author Samuel Langhorne Clemens write?
6 At the very end of the 19th C who wrote the novel that produced the most filmed horror character of the 20th C?
7 Whose sports based novels of the 90s include Comeback and To The Hilt?
8 Aunt Agatha and Bingo Little feature in the escapades of which man about town?
9 Which writer of horrific happenings was himself involved in a road accident while out walking in 1999?
10 In which decade was The Lord Of The Rings first published?
11 Who is Frank Richards' most famous creation?
12 Who penned the airport lounge best seller titled Airport?
13 Which writer was influenced by their upbringing in Slad, Gloucestershire?
14 In 1917 which Joseph endowed an annual literary prize in America?
15 David John Cornell wrote spy stories under which name?
16 What type of jungle animal was Shere Khan?
17 Georges Simenon created which character known by one name?
18 In book selling what does the N stand for in NBA?
19 Which American novelist with an English place surname wrote White Fang?
20 Who wrote the children's classic Swallows And Amazons?
21 What was the first name of New Zealand novelist Ms Marsh?
22 Which fictional detective refers to using the little grey cells?
23 What was the particular link between Jean Plaidy, Phillipa Carr, Victoria Holt?
24 Which of the Mitfords wrote Love In A Cold Climate?
25 In the books as opposed to the TV series, where did Morse's sidekick Lewis come from?

## Answers

***Books***

**1** She who must be obeyed. **2** Durham. **3** Salman Rusdie. **4** 40s. **5** Mark Twain. **6** Bram Stoker. **7** Dick Francis. **8** Bertie Wooster. **9** Stephen King. **10** 50s. **11** Billy Bunter. **12** Arthur Hailey. **13** Laurie Lee. **14** Pulitzer. **15** John Le Carre. **16** Tiger. **17** Maigret. **18** Net. **19** Jack London. **20** Arthur Rackham. **21** Ngaio. **22** Hercule Poirot. **23** They are the same person. **24** Nancy. **25** Wales.

# Quiz 68 Pot Luck 36

1 Who was the first MP elected for the SDP?
2 Which song says, "The words of the prophet are written On the subway halls"?
3 In which country did General Jaruzelski impose martial law in 1981?
4 On which channel did Nigel Slater cook up Real Food?
5 Which chair was kidnapped by students from the Cranfield Institute of Technology in 1978?
6 Devon Malcolm took nine wickets in a Test innings against which country?
7 Which musical featured the song The Street Where You Live?
8 Henley has been the 80s and 90s seat of which prominent politician?
9 In cricket which English team became Hawks in the 90s?
10 How is John Virgo known on Big Break?
11 Who sang the title sang for the Bond film A View To A Kill?
12 The Cod War of the 70s was between Britain and which country?
13 Which Desmond wrote the 80s book studying fans behaviour called The Soccer Tribe?
14 What's Alvin Stardust's real name?
15 At which sport did Karen Brown win international success?
16 Which family were the subject of Two Point Four Children?
17 Which Disney film had the theme tune A Whole New World?
18 Hellenikon international airport is in which country?
19 In TV ads who has sung the praises of Kenco Coffee and Renault cars?
20 Who was the target of the failed 'Bomb Plot' of 1944?
21 Who made No 1 with Young At Heart?
22 In basketball where do the Celtics come from?
23 In honours what does the G stand for in GC?
24 Who wrote the novel The Go Between?
25 In which Gloucester Street was the West's House of Horrors?

## Answers

***Pot Luck 36***

**1** Shirley Williams. **2** Sound of Silence. **3** Poland. **4** Channel 4. **5** Mastermind chair. **6** South Africa. **7** My Fair Lady. **8** Michael Heseltine. **9** Hampshire. **10** Mr Trick Shot. **11** Duran Duran. **12** Iceland. **13** Morris. **14** Bernard Jewry. **15** Hockey. **16** The Porters. **17** Aladdin. **18** Greece. **19** Lesley Garrett. **20** Hitler. **21** Bluebells. **22** Boston. **23** George. **24** L P Hartley. **25** Cromwell Street.

# Quiz 69 Solo Singers

1 In which decade was singer Bruce Springsteen born?
2 Who had a hit with You're All That Matters to Me in 1992?
3 Stevie Wonder was given the keys to which city in recognition of his talents in 1984?
4 Which costume was worn by David Bowie on his Ashes to Ashes video?
5 Who, in 1994, did a cover of Jennifer Rush's The Power of Love?
6 George Michael was brought up in which city?
7 Who had a hit with Mysterious Girl in 1996?
8 Whose first album was titled Soul Provider?
9 Who was Dancing on the Ceiling in 1986?
10 Which senior star released an album in 1996 called Strong Love Affair?
11 Which American city links songs by Bruce Springsteen and Elton John?
12 What type of creature is Michael Jackson's pet Muscles?
13 Which record label did David Bowie sign to in 1995?
14 How old was Elvis Presley when he died?
15 What was the first UK top ten hit from March 1997 for Sash!?
16 QWhat is in brackets in the title of Cher's The Shoop Shoop Song?
17 Spice Girl Mel C joined which artist on the hit When You're Gone?
18 Which hit got to No 2 for former Neighbours star Natalie Imbruglia in 1997?
19 Who is the oldest female solo singer to top the UK charts?
20 Who was Old Before I Die in a 1997?
21 Who made it big in 1996 with Flava?
22 In which decade was superstar Michael Bolton born?
23 What was Louise's first UK top ten hit?
24 Which American rapper was Loungin' in a UK No 7 from 1996?
25 What was Bjork's first UK top ten hit?

## Answers

***Solo Singers***

**1** 1940s. **2** Curtis Stigers. **3** Detroit. **4** Pierrot. **5** Celine Dion. **6** London. **7** Peter Andre. **8** Michael Bolton. **9** Lionel Richie. **10** Ray Charles. **11** Philadelphia. **12** Snake. **13** Virgin. **14** 42. **15** Encore Une Fois. **16** It's In His Kiss. **17** Bryan Adams. **18** Torn. **19** Cher. **20** Robbie Williams. **21** Peter Andre. **22** 1950s. **23** Light Of My Life. **24** LL Cool J. **25** Army of Me.

# Quiz 70 Pot Luck 37

Level 2 

1 In which decade were LPs first sold in the UK?
2 Peter Mandelson was called in as spin doctor to run whose 1987 campaign?
3 In 1984 who scored the first nine dart 501 finish in a major event?
4 Which new British coin was first issued in the UK in 1983?
5 What is the first name of restaurateur and TV cook Mrs Paul Rankin?
6 Who had an 80s No 1 with You Win Again?
7 In a long running TV series, who had a boss called Dr Gillespie?
8 Which chocolate bar helped you "work, rest and play"?
9 Which musical featured the song Shall We Dance?
10 After 1918 British women were allowed to vote if they were what age?
11 What was Britain's first daily game show for teenagers?
12 What are the international registration letters of a vehicle from Estonia?
13 Which Rugby League team became Rams in the 90s?
14 Who played Whitney Houston's manager in the Bodyguard?
15 In which country did English born US citizen Charlie Chaplin die?
16 In which decade did Finland join the European Union?
17 Who promised that, "You too can have a body like mine"?
18 1993 was the last Chinese year of the Cock, but when will be the next one?
19 Which Boat Race radio commentator said, "I don't know who's ahead - it's either Oxford or Cambridge"?
20 Which famous lady participated in the opening in '92 of Euro Disney Paris?
21 In which decade was Rupert Everett born?
22 On which children's TV show would you visit the Roundabout Stop?
23 In American Football where do the Broncos come from?
24 Who wrote the novel The Cruel Sea?
25 Whose motto is "Per ardua ad astra"?

## Answers

***Pot Luck 37***

**1** 1950s. **2** Neil Kinnock's. **3** John Lowe. **4** £1. **5** Jeanne. **6** Bee Gees. **7** Dr Kildare. **8** Mars. **9** The King And I. **10** 30. **11** Blockbusters. **12** EST. **13** Dewsbury. **14** Gary Kemp. **15** Switzerland. **16** 90s. **17** Charles Atlas. **18** 2005. **19** John Snagge. **20** Cher. **21** 60s. **22** Playdays. **23** Denver. **24** Nicholas Monsarrat. **25** RAF.

# Quiz 71 Scandals & Disasters

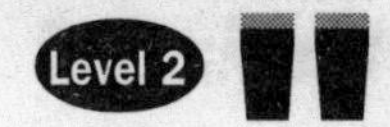

1 Which politician got entangled with Antonia da Sancha?
2 Which Open Tennis tournament was John McEnroe expelled from?
3 Robert Maxwell drowned near which islands?
4 Which disaster took place in Kobe, Japan in 1995?
5 Charles Rolls of Rolls Royce fame was actually in what type of vehicle when he died?
6 In 1996 Stephen Cameron became the first fatality of which increasingly violent trend?
7 Whose downfall and disgrace revolved round a stay at the Paris Ritz in September 1993?
8 Bandleader Glenn Miller was last seen in an aircraft leaving which country?
9 In 1998 the Festina team was banned from what over drug allegations?
10 Where was the USA's worst nuclear accident, in 1979?
11 On which of the Canary Islands did a collision of two jumbo jets take place making it one of the worst air disasters in history?
12 Who was the first US President to resign while in office?
13 Where in Wales was a school engulfed by a slag heap in 1966?
14 Which Olympic Games were the scene of a terrorist attack by Palestinian guerrillas?
15 Onto which road did a British Midlands aeroplane crash in 1990?
16 What was the first name of Dr Crippen's wife?
17 Ernest Saunders and Gerald Ronson were convicted for their roles in the scandal in which company?
18 Who were Liverpool's opposition when the Hillsborough disaster took place?
19 The Herald of Free Enterprise capsized outside which port?
20 How did 40s murderer John Haigh dispose of his victims' bodies?
21 Policewoman Yvonne Fletcher was shot outside which London embassy?
22 What was the nationality of the jet shot down in Russian air space in 1983?
23 Who or what was Sefton, injured in a bomb blast in Hyde Park in 1982?
24 Which year was known as the 'winter of discontent'?
25 Which Brighton hotel was bombed during a Tory Party conference in 1984?

## Answers

***Scandals & Disasters***

**1** David Mellor. **2** Australian. **3** Canary Islands. **4** Earthquake. **5** Aeroplane. **6** Road rage. **7** Jonathan Aitken. **8** England. **9** Tour de France. **10** Three Mile Island. **11** Tenerife. **12** Richard Nixon. **13** Aberfan. **14** Munich. **15** M1. **16** Cora. **17** Guinness. **18** Nottm Forest. **19** Zeebrugge. **20** Acid bath. **21** Libya. **22** Korean. **23** Horse. **24** 1979. **25** Grand.

# Quiz 72 Pot Luck 38

Level 2 

1 Who kept saying that it was time for bed in The Magic Roundabout?
2 The sinking of which ship prompted the Sun's "Gotcha!" headline?
3 Who was Sean Penn married to for 27 months before divorce was filed?
4 From which show does Love Changes Everything come?
5 In EastEnders what were Cindy & Ian Beale's twins called?
6 In baseball where do the Royals come from?
7 What colour is Laa Laa?
8 For what did Georgie O'Keefe become famous?
9 St Albans has been the 90s seat of which prominent Tory politician?
10 In economics what does the letter G stand for in GNP?
11 The Spanish soccer team Real Betis play at home in which city?
12 Which character brought the phrase, "You silly old moo" to TV?
13 To the nearest million what is the population of the USA?
14 Who made No 1 with Spaceman?
15 In which country was Michael J Fox born?
16 How much was the top prize on Cilla Black's The Moment of Truth?
17 Under which name did Leonard Slye ride across the silver screen?
18 On which movies soundtrack from the 90s did Brenda Lee feature?
19 Who did Harry Enfield play in the first series of Men Behaving Badly?
20 Which politician said, "He got on his bike and looked for work..."?
21 A-Ha sang the title song for which Bond film?
22 In advertising who or what was "Your flexible friend"?
23 Which German soccer striker was known as The Bomber?
24 Which writer came up with Catch 22 in the 60s?
25 Bourgas international airport is in which country?

## Answers

***Pot Luck 38***

**1** Zebedee. **2** General Belgrano. **3** Madonna. **4** Aspects of Love. **5** Peter & Lucy. **6** Kansas City. **7** Yellow. **8** Painting. **9** Peter Lilley. **10** Gross. **11** Seville. **12** Alf Garnett. **13** 265 million. **14** Babylon Zoo. **15** Canada. **16** £20,000. **17** Roy Rogers. **18** Dick Tracy. **19** Dermot. **20** Norman Tebbit. **21** The Living Daylights. **22** Access Card. **23** Gerd Muller. **25** Joseph Heller. **25** Bulgaria.

# Quiz 73 20th C Rich & Famous

**1** Which golfer announced he was leaving his wife and three children for Brenna Cepalak in 1996?
**2** Marina Mowatt is the daughter of which British Princess?
**3** Fitness trainer Carlos Leon was the father of which singer/actress's child?
**4** Whose portrait in 1996 was described by Brian Sewell as looking like "a pensioner who is about to lose her bungalow."?
**5** In which North African country was Mohammed Al_Fayed born?
**6** Longleat is the stately home of which Marquess?
**7** What is Madonna's daughter called?
**8** In addition to be Earl of Wessex Prince Edward became Viscount of where on his marriage?
**9** Lady Sarah Chatto is he daughter of which famous lady?
**10** Caroline Conran, one time wife of Sir Terence, is a writer in her own right on which subject?
**11** In 1996 who did The Spice Girls say was their Girl Power role model?
**12** What is Frankie Dettori's real first name?
**13** How did Sir Ranulph Twisleton-Wykeham-Fiennes achieve fame?
**14** Madeleine Gurdon is the third wife of which millionaire?
**15** Who was the first Princess to appear on The Archers?
**16** What is the first name of Charles' brother of Saatchi & Saatchi?
**17** In which country was Earl Spencer's acrimonious divorce settlement heard?
**18** Who did Stella McCartney dedicate her first collection for Chloe to?
**19** In which North African country was Yves St Laurent born as Henri Donat Mathieu?
**20** Which child of Princess Grace of Monaco competed in the 1988 Olympics?
**21** Which former England captain was Viv Richards' best man?
**22** Which member of the Royal Family suffered a mild stroke when in the Caribbean in 1998?
**23** Which multi million pound sport is Bernie Ecclestone associated with?
**24** How many brothers and sisters does Tony Blair have?
**25** Which member of the Royal Family converted to Catholicism in the 1990s?

## Answers

***20th C Rich and Famous***

**1** Nick Faldo. **2** Alexandra. **3** Madonna. **4** The Queen. **5** Egypt. **6** Bath. **7** Lourdes Maria. **8** Severn. **9** Princess Margaret. **10** Cookery. **11** Margaret Thatcher. **12** Lanfranco. **13** Explorer. **14** Andrew Lloyd Webber. **15** Margaret. **16** Maurice. **17** South Africa. **18** Her mother Linda. **19** Algeria. **20** Prince Albert. **21** Ian Botham. **22** Princess Margaret. **23** Motor racing. **24** None. **24** The Duchess of Kent.

# Quiz 74 **Pot Luck 39**

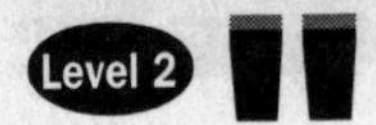


1. Who said 50000 rifles were preferable to 50000 votes?
2. Which fictional hero has been played on TV by Peter Cushing, Alan Badel and Colin Firth?
3. Who is credited with inventing the Tarzan yodel?
4. In cricket what did Middlesex add to their name in the 90s?
5. Which Tory MP lost the Enfield seat in 1997?
6. Who had an 80s No 1 with I Think We're Alone Now?
7. What is Channel 5's quiz without a quizmaster for older contestants called?
8. England soccer captain Billy Wright married one of which singing sisters?
9. Who wrote The Children Of Men?
10. Which British broadcaster talked about an "Up and under!"?
11. Which act banned government employees from disclosing confidential information?
12. What did the S stand for in the name of T S Eliot?
13. Jack Sharkey was a world champion in which sport?
14. The title of an Arnold Wesker play was about what With Everything?
15. Who had a brother in law called Onslow?
16. Who wrote the song MacArthur Park?
17. Which musical featured the song How To Handle A Woman?
18. Which driver gave Jordan their first ever Grand Prix victory?
19. Who was the first man to feature in ads wearing Polly Peck tights?
20. Which gorge is spanned by the Clifton Suspension Bridge?
21. Which British liner was sunk by a German submarine in 1915?
22. Who wrote the novel The Godfather?
23. Vehicles from which country use the international registration letter S?
24. Who was leader of the Liberals from 1967-1976?
25. What was Marilyn Monroe's last film?

## Answers

***Pot Luck 39***

**1** Mussolini. **2** Mr Darcy. **3** Johnny Weismuller. **4** Crusaders. **5** Michael Portillo. **6** Tiffany. **7** 100 Per Cent Gold. **8** Beverley Sisters. **9** P D James. **10** Eddie Waring. **11** Official Secrets Act. **12** Stearns. **13** Boxing. **14** Chips. **15** Hyacinth Bucket. **16** Jim Webb. **17** Camelot. **18** Damon Hill. **19** Paul Grady as Lily Savage. **20** Avon. **21** Lusitania. **22** Mario Puzo. **23** Sweden. **24** Jeremy Thorpe. **25** The Misfits.

# Quiz 75 20th C TV Drama

1 Which TV and Movie actor played Dr Phillip Chandler in St Elsewhere?
2 In which series did Paul Nicholls play Terry Sydenham?
3 How did Assumpta perish in Ballykissangel?
4 Who did Charlie marry in Casualty?
5 In Heartbeat who was Nick's second wife?
6 In which capital city did the action of The Ambassador take place?
7 Which TV detective was obsessed with his little grey cells?
8 What is Sam's profession in Silent Witness?
9 Who co starred with Robson Green in Grafters?
10 Which actor replaced Nigel Le Vaillant in Dangerfield?
11 How many Talking Heads were there in the first series in 1988?
12 What was the name of the doctor played by Simon Shepherd in Peak Practice?
13 Which writer links Soldier, Soldier, Peak Practice and Bramwell?
14 Who played opposite Francesca Annis in Reckless?
15 Which drama series takes place in Skelthwaite in Yorkshire?
16 In which serial did Colin Firth shoot to fame opposite Jennifer Ehle?
17 For which drama did John Thaw win the Best Actor BAFTA in 1999?
18 In Juliet Bravo what was Juliet Bravo?
19 Why Didn't They Ask Evans was the first in a murder mystery series by which famous author?
20 Charlie Hungerford was which detective's ex father in law?
21 Which famous detective did Jeremy Brett play for many years on TV?
22 Lucy Gannon's drama series Hope and Glory was set where?
23 Which 80s drama mini series was based on Paul Scott's Raj Quartet?
24 In which south coast county was Howard's Way set?
25 In which series did Saskia Wickham play Dr Erica Matthews?

## Answers

***20th C TV Drama***

**1** Denzel Washington. **2** City Central. **3** Electrocuted. **4** Baz. **5** Jo. **6** Dublin. **7** Poirot. **8** Pathologist. **9** Stephen Tompkinson. **10** Nigel Havers. **11** Six. **12** Will Preston. **13** Lucy Gannon. **14** Robson Green. **15** Where the Heart Is. **16** Pride & Prejudice. **17** Goodnight Mister Tom. **18** Radio call sign. **19** Agatha Christie. **20** Bergerac's. **21** Sherlock Holmes. **22** School. **23** The Jewel in the Crown. **24** Hampshire. **25** Peak Practice.

# Quiz 76 Pot Luck 40

Level 2

1 Dying in 1972, under which name was Emmanuel Goldberg better known?
2 Dav Whatmore left Lancashire to coach which cricket team?
3 Who played the Rev Tony Blair in Sermon From St Albions?
4 What has been the commonest name for Popes through the millennium?
5 Which great entertainer made his film debut in Pennies From Heaven?
6 Who was David Beckham's best man at his wedding to Posh?
7 Which musical featured the song Ol' Man River?
8 Who wrote The Camomile Lawn, seen on TV starring Felicity Kendal and Tara Fitzgerald?
9 Blackburn has been the 90s seat of which prominent politician?
10 Who sang the theme to One Foot in the Grave?
11 Peter Gilchrist has been a world champion in which sport?
12 Who made No 1 with Return Of The Mack?
13 What was the name of Tom Mix's horse?
14 In which country is the deepwater port of Townsville?
15 Who wrote My Family And Other Animals?
16 Whose one line was "Nice hat" in Friends?
17 In which country was Keanu Reeves born?
18 In which decade did Sweden join the European Union?
19 In which sport could the Knicks take on the Nets?
20 Which politician stated, "Read my lips: no new taxes"?
21 Which famous Michael has promoted Kwik Save in TV ads?
22 The Irish dramatist Samuel Beckett settled in which city?
23 Long Beach airport was built in which US state?
24 Who followed Matt Busby as Man Utd manager?
25 In which decade did Alcatraz close?

## Answers

***Pot Luck 40***

**1** Edward G Robinson. **2** Sri Lanka. **3** Harry Enfield. **4** John. **5** Louis Armstrong. **6** Gary Neville. **7** Showboat. **8** Mary Wesley. **9** Jack Straw. **10** Eric Idle. **11** Billiards. **12** Mark Morrison. **13** Tony. **14** Australia. **15** Gerald Durrell. **16** Sarah, Duchess of York. **17** Lebanon. **18** 90s. **19** Basketball. **20** George Bush. **21** Barrymore. **22** Paris. **23** California. **24** Wilf McGuinness. **25** 60s.

# Quiz 77 Sporting Chance

1 Which city has a team of Bulls and a team of Bears?
2 Which Man Utd player was replaced by Solskjaer in the 1999 European Champions' Cup Final?
3 What is the nickname of record breaking sprinter Maurice Greene?
4 Who was the first boxer to twice regain the world heavyweight title?
5 At which country did Edmonds and Emburey form a lethal spin attack?
6 What was Sue Barker's best placing in the Wimbledon singles?
7 Which sport do Essex Metropolitan play?
8 Ballustrol, Medinah and Oakmont are all types of what?
9 In basketball where do the Rockets come from?
10 Who was the first Scot to captain England at cricket?
11 Which country does tennis player Marcelo Rios come from?
12 What was the sport of Stirling Moss's sister Pat?
13 Which country does marathon man Abel Anton come from?
14 How was Walker Smith Robinson better known?
15 Who captained India in cricket's 1999 World Cup?
16 The Melbourne Cup is run at which ground?
17 Peter Nichol became the first Brit in 25 years to win the British Open in which sport?
18 Who told a Wimbledon umpire, "You are the pits of the world"?
19 Which Robin was the first yachtsman to sail non stop around the world?
20 Which player has played the most league games for Man Utd?
21 Allan Lamb first played in England for which county?
22 Who fought George Foreman in the Rumble In The Jungle?
23 Who had Derby victories riding Troy, Henbit, Nashwan and Erhaab?
24 With which athletics event was Geoff Capes particularly associated?
25 Teddy Sherringham was with club when he was the top league scorer in England?

## Answers

***Sporting Chance***

**1** Chicago. **2** Cole. **3** Kansas Cannonball. **4** Muhammad Ali. **5** Middlesex. **6** Semi finals. **7** Netball. **8** American golf course. **9** Houston. **10** Mike Denness. **11** Chile. **12** Rallying. **13** Spain. **14** Sugar Ray Robinson. **15** Azharuddin. **16** Fleminghton Park. **17** Squash. **18** John McEnroe. **19** Knox-Johnson. **20** Bobby Charlton. **21** Northants. **22** Muhammad Ali. **23** Willie Carson. **24** Shot. **25** Spurs.

# Quiz 78 Pot Luck 41

**1** Who was Hitler's Minister of Propaganda?
**2** In 1998 which Royal appeared on Des O'Connor Tonight?
**3** On which mountain did woman climber Alison Hargreaves perish in 1995?
**4** Which WWII escapade was led by Guy Gibson?
**5** Who had an 80s No 1 with Don't Turn Around?
**6** What have Bobby Robson, Graham Taylor and Terry Venables all advertised on TV?
**7** Who played plumber Frank Carver in Love Hurts?
**8** What does the p in plc stand for?
**9** Until its division in the 1990s, what was the capital of Yugoslavia?
**10** Which national newspaper did not publish for nearly a year in the late 70s?
**11** Which music hall star and radio comic had the catchphrase, "The day that war broke out"?
**12** What are the international registration letters of a vehicle from Poland?
**13** In which decade did the Sex Discrimination Act come into force in Britain?
**14** Where in England was David Hockney born?
**15** Princess Margaret plays which musical instrument?
**16** On which river was the Tarbela dam built?
**17** Which famous sporting figure refused conscription to Vietnam in 1967?
**18** Who wrote Farewell My Lovely and the Lady in The Lake?
**19** Which politician spoke of a "short, sharp shock" for young offenders?
**20** Which country did Idi Amin go to when he fled Uganda?
**21** In American Football where do the Browns come from?
**22** The first students from where graduated in June 1973?
**23** In which decade was Sean Penn born?
**24** In economics what does the letter F stand for in IMF?
**25** In the Army what is the equivalent of Admiral in the Navy?

**Answers**

***Pot Luck 41***

**1** Goebbels. **2** Prince Edward. **3** K2. **4** The Dam Busters. **5** Aswad. **6** Yellow Pages. **7** Adam Faith. **8** Public. **9** Belgrade. **10** The Times. **11** Rob Wilton. **12** PL. **13** 70s. **14** Bradford. **15** Piano. **16** Indus. **17** Muhammad Ali. **18** Raymond Chandler. **19** Willie Whitelaw. **20** Saudi Arabia. **21** Cleveland. **22** The Open University. **23** 60s. **24** Fund. **25** General.

# Quiz 79 20th C Movies Comedies

Level 2

**1** What was dubbed 'an equal, not a sequel' to Four Weddings and a Funeral?
**2** What was the first name of Truman in The Truman Show?
**3** Which 1997 film was the then most successful British movie of all time?
**4** Mike Nichols' The Birdcage was a remake of which musical?
**5** Who played the Nutty Professor in the 1996 remake of Jerry Lewis's film?
**6** Which wife of Laurence Olivier appeared in 101 Dalmatians?
**7** What type of shop does Wendowlene own in A Close Shave?
**8** Who or what is Priscilla in The Adventures of Priscilla, Queen of the Desert?
**9** In the original Pink Panther movie what is the Pink Panther?
**10** Which Monty Python film contains 'Always Look on the Bright Side of Life'?
**11** Who was Elwood's brother in The Blues Brothers?
**12** Which country singer starred in 9 to 5?
**13** Where does Goldie Hawn's husband die in Private Benjamin?
**14** Which member of the Arquette family starred in Desperately Seeking Susan with Madonna?
**15** What is Crocodile Dundee's real first name?
**16** Who was the male star of The Witches of Eastwick who famously said "I'm a horny little devil"?
**17** Of the Three Men and a Baby who had appeared in Cheers?
**18** Who scripted as well as starring in A Fish Called Wanda?
**19** Who was the Working Girl of the title in the film in which Harrison Ford also starred?
**20** Which 1988 film with Michelle Pfeiffer was about Mafia wives?
**21** Who played the private eye hired by Roger Rabbit?
**22** What is Jim Carrey's profession in Liar Liar?
**23** Where does the most infamous scene in When Harry Met Sally take place?
**24** Inside what toy does a love scene in Honey I Shrunk The Kids take place?
**25** In which 80s film did Arnold Schwarzenegger play Danny De Vito's brother?

## Answers

***20th C The Movies Comedies***

**1** Notting Hill. **2** Truman. **3** The Full Monty. **4** La Cage aux Folles. **5** Eddie Murphy. **6** Joan Plowright. **7** Wool. **8** Bus. **9** Diamond. **10** Life of Brian. **11** Jake. **12** Dolly Parton. **13** In bed. **14** Rosanna. **15** Mick. **16** Jack Nicholson. **17** Ted Danson. **18** John Cleese. **19** Melanie Griffith. **20** Married to the Mob. **21** Bob Hoskins. **22** Lawyer. **23** Restaurant. **24** Lego brick. **25** Twins.

# Quiz 80 Pot Luck 42

1 What do Bluebell, Severn Valley and Watercress have in common?
2 Who was Edward VII's Queen?
3 Which country recorded 17 straight wins in Rugby Union in the late 90s?
4 Why were Hope and Crosby 'like Webster's Dictionary'?
5 What is the RAF equivalent to the army rank of Major?
6 In which decade of the 20th century was Jack Nicholson born?
7 Which musical featured the song I Talk To The Trees?
8 What was held for the first time on 11th Nov, 1921?
9 In basketball where do the Kings come from?
10 Who made No 1 with Should I Go Or Should I Stay?
11 What did the second E stand for in Premium Bonds' ERNIE?
12 Which country did tennis playing sisters Katerina and Manuela Maleeva originally come from?
13 In which year did Bill Hayley's Rock Around The Clock top the charts?
14 In advertising which chocolates were said to "Grow on you"?
15 At which sport did Ken Buchanan win international success?
16 Spiro Agnew was vice president to which US President?
17 Who sang the title sang for the Bond film The Spy Who Loved Me?
18 Calgary International airport is in which country?
19 Ansel Adams worked in which field in America?
20 Which politician stated that, "A week is a long time in politics"?
21 Which Liverpool legend was manager of the year six times from 1976 to 1983?
22 Who wrote the novel Doctor Zhivago?
23 In which decade did the Netherlands join the European Union?
24 Who created the, "Ooh, you are awful, but I like you" character Mandy?
25 In which country is the Francorchamps race track?

## Answers

***Pot Luck 42***

**1** (Preserved) railways. **2** Alexandra. **3** South Africa. **4** They were Morocco bound. **5** Squadron Leader. **6** 30s. **7** Paint Your Wagon. **8** Poppy Day. **9** Sacramento. **10** The Clash. **11** Equipment. **12** Bulgaria. **13** 1955. **14** Roses. **15** Boxing. **16** Nixon. **17** Carly Simon. **18** Canada. **19** Photographer. **20** Harold Wilson. **21** Bob Paisley. **22** Boris Pasternak. **23** 50s. **24** Dick Emery. **25** Belgium.

# Quiz 81 Sporting Chance

1 Which city has a team of Bulls and a team of Bears?
2 Which Man Utd player was replaced by Solskjaer in the 1999 European Champions' Cup Final?
3 What is the nickname of record breaking sprinter Maurice Greene?
4 Who was the first boxer to twice regain the world heavyweight title?
5 At which country did Edmonds and Emburey form a lethal spin attack?
6 What was Sue Barker's best placing in the Wimbledon singles?
7 Which sport do Essex Metropolitan play?
8 Ballustrol, Medinah and Oakmont are all types of what?
9 In basketball where do the Rockets come from?
10 Who was the first Scot to captain England at cricket?
11 Which country does tennis player Marcelo Rios come from?
12 What was the sport of Stirling Moss's sister Pat?
13 Which country does marathon man Abel Anton come from?
14 How was Walker Smith Robinson better known?
15 Who captained India in cricket's 1999 World Cup?
16 The Melbourne Cup is run at which ground?
17 Peter Nichol became the first Brit in 25 years to win the British Open in which sport?
18 Who told a Wimbledon umpire, "You are the pits of the world"?
19 Which Robin was the first yachtsman to sail non stop around the world?
20 Which player has played the most league games for Man Utd?
21 Allan Lamb first played in England for which county?
22 Who fought George Foreman in the Rumble In The Jungle?
23 Who had Derby victories riding Troy, Henbit, Nashwan and Erhaab?
24 With which athletics event was Geoff Capes particularly associated?
25 Teddy Sherringham was with club when he was the top league scorer in England?

**Answers**

***Sporting Chance***

**1** Chicago. **2** Cole. **3** Kansas Cannonball. **4** Muhammad Ali. **5** Middlesex. **6** Semi finals. **7** Netball. **8** American golf course. **9** Houston. **10** Mike Denness. **11** Chile. **12** Rallying. **13** Spain. **14** Sugar Ray Robinson. **15** Azharuddin. **16** Fleminghton Park. **17** Squash. **18** John McEnroe. **19** Knox-Johnson. **20** Bobby Charlton. **21** Northants. **22** Muhammad Ali. **23** Willie Carson. **24** Shot. **25** Spurs.

# Quiz 82 Pot Luck 43

1 What has been the century's best attended exhibition at the British Museum?
2 In the advertising campaign, which drink could be taken "Anytime, any place anywhere"?
3 Which of the four major blood groups is the commonest in the UK?
4 Sarah Fitz-Gerald has been a 90s world champion in which sport?
5 Who directed the classic 30s western Stagecoach?
6 Who had an 80s No 1 with Heart?
7 Which London Palace was destroyed in 1936?
8 Which bandleader had the same name as a British Prime Minister?
9 In cricket which English team became Gladiators in the 90s?
10 Lord Nuffield made his name in which industry?
11 Which school did Billy Bunter attend?
12 Which leader did Hitler meet in the Brenner Pass in WWII?
13 In which musical do the sweeps sing Chim Chim Cheree?
14 In Rugby League what did Leigh add to their name in the 90s?
15 On a computer keyboard which letter on the same line is between C and B?
16 Which band features Brian Harvey on lead vocals?
17 In which decade did Gary Player last win the British Open?
18 In which city was the peace treaty signed that brought World War I to an end?
19 Which Chinese year follows the year of the Sheep?
20 What does the letter C stand for in OPEC?
21 To the nearest million what is the population of Bombay?
22 Vehicles from which country use the international registration letter C?
23 Which country was Prince Philip born in?
24 Who presented the first edition of Top Of The Pops?
25 Birkdale golf course is in which resort?

## Answers

***Pot Luck 43***

**1** Treasures of Tutankhamen. **2** Martini. **3** O. **4** Squash. **5** John Ford. **6** Pet Shop Boys. **7** Crystal Palace. **8** Edward Heath. **9** Gloucestershire. **10** Motor. **11** Greyfriars. **12** Mussolini. **13** Mary Poppins. **14** Centurions. **15** V. **16** East 17. **17** 70s. **18** Versailles. **19** Monkey. **20** Countries. **21** 10 million. **22** Cuba. **23** Greece. **24** Jimmy Savile. **25** Southport.

# Quiz 83 TV Selection

Level 2

1. Who played John Wilder in The Power Game?
2. The original presenters of the BBC'S Breakfast Time were Frank Bough, Selena Scott, and one other. Who?
3. Who introduced It'll be Alright on the Night?
4. Which artist played a digeridoo?
5. The Simpsons became the longest-running cartoon family in 1997, replacing whom?
6. Who was the original weatherman on BBC's Breakfast Time?
7. Which character in EastEnders was Mark's wife?
8. In which year did the BBC TV schools service begin?
9. Which actress had to survive on her own on a desert isle?
10. Who was Jennifer Paterson's cooking partner?
11. What was the name of the first space ship used by Blake's 7?
12. Which fictional village was *Heartbeat* set in?
13. Which rodent starred on TVAM?
14. What was an Admag, banned by Parliament in 1963?
15. Who presented The Human Body?
16. What was the profession of the major characters in *This Life*?
17. What did the ARP Warden call Captain Mainwaring?
18. In which decade was *Hi-De-Hi!* first set?
19. Which early evening programme did Mel and Sue introduce?
20. Who is the current host of Going for a Song?
21. Which actress played *The Sculptress*?
22. Who was Lovejoy's original love interest?
23. Which actor was Maxwell Smart?
24. Who played Tom Howard's wife in Howard's Way?
25. In which city was PI Daniel Pike based?

## Answers

***TV Selection***

**1** Patrick Wymark. **2** Nick Ross. **3** Dennis Norden. **4** Rolf Harris. **5** *The Flintstones*. **6** Francis Wilson. **7** Ruth. **8** September 1957. **9** Joanna Lumley. **10** Clarrisa Dickson Wright. **11** The Liberator. **12** Aidensfield. **13** Roland Rat. **14** An advertisement broadcast in the guise of a genuine programme. **15** Sir Robert Winston. **16** Lawyers. **17** Napoleon. **18** 1950s. **19** Late Lunch. **20** Michael Parkinson. **21** Pauline Quirke. **22** Lady Jane Felsham. **23** Don Adams. **24** Jan Harvey. **25** Glasgow.

# Quiz 84 Pot Luck 44

1 In 1954 what was tested at Bikini Atoll?
2 Who wrote Dinnerladies?
3 Which city is snooker player Willie Thorne's home town?
4 Who was the BBC's royal correspondent at the time of Princess Diana's death?
5 Eurostar will take you to which station in Paris?
6 In which decade of the century did a woman first sit in the Commons?
7 Which musical featured the song Food, Glorious Food?
8 According to the advertising campaign Ian Botham couldn't eat three what?
9 Who was US President when America entered World War II?
10 Who became the first black athlete to captain the British team?
11 Who was appointed Vice President of the European Commission in July 1999?
12 Who made No 1 with Dreams?
13 What was being advertised by Lorraine Chase's Luton Airport character?
14 In which country is the deepwater port of Valparaiso?
15 What was the name of Fitz's wife in Cracker?
16 What was the third Bond film for which Shirley Bassey sang the title song?
17 In the 90s how many points have been awarded for finishing sixth in a Grand Prix?
18 In which decade was Kenneth Branagh born?
19 Who had a No 1 in the 60s with Mike Sarne before becoming a TV actress?
20 Which animal appeared on British eggs in 1957?
21 Which instrument is particularly associated with bandleader Buddy Rich?
22 Which English soccer international was known as 'Crazy Horse'?
23 Findel international airport is in which country?
24 Who wrote East Of Eden?
25 Whose motto is, "Let not the deep swallow me up"?

**Answers**

***Pot Luck 44***
**1** Hydrogen bomb. **2** Victoria Wood. **3** Leicester. **4** Jennie Bond. **5** Gare Du Nord. **6** Second decade. **7** Oliver. **8** Shredded Wheat. **9** Franklin Roosevelt. **10** Kriss Akabusi. **11** Neil Kinnock. **12** Gabrielle. **13** Campari. **14** Chile. **15** Judith. **16** Moonraker. **17** 1. **18** 60s. **19** Wendy Richard. **20** Lion. **21** Drums. **22** Emlyn Hughes. **23** Luxembourg. **24** John Steinbeck. **25** RNLI.

# Quiz 85 Media

1 Which former Soviet Communist Party newspaper was relaunched as a tabloid in 1996?
2 In 1997 The Duchess of York was signed up by which US newspaper to write a weekly column?
3 Who bought Virgin Radio from Richard Branson in 1997?
4 What was the original target audience for Sky's UK Living?
5 Where is the HQ of the BBC World Service?
6 In which decade was Cosmopolitan magazine launched in the UK?
7 How frequently is Private Eye published?
8 What did CMTV stand for?
9 Where did The Times offices move to in 1986?
10 What did G stand for in GLR?
11 What did C stand for in the shopping channel QVC?
12 Which national radio station was launched by the BBC in the 1990s?
13 In which decade of the century did radio's Desert Island Discs begin ?
14 What does Q stand for in the magazine title GQ?
15 At the end of the century Test Match Special was broadcast on which national radio network?
16 In which decade could Radio Times and TV Times first publish details of programmes on all channels?
17 How is Sianel Pedwar Cymru - Channel 4 in Wales - abbreviated?
18 In which county were Pinewood Studios?
19 Meridian broadcast to which area of the UK ?
20 What does I stand for in ILR?
21 In which decade was Radio Times first published?
22 Tribune supported which political party?
23 Which magazine paid around £1 million for the exclusive rights to David Beckham and Victoria Adams' wedding photos?
24 Which sitcom characters have guest edited Marie Claire?
25 In which decade was The Sun first published?

## Answers

***Media***

**1** Pravda. **2** New York Times. **3** Chris Evans. **4** Women. **5** Bush House. **6** 70s. **7** Fortnightly. **8** Country Music Television. **9** Wapping. **10** Greater. **11** Convenience. **12** Radio 5 Live. **13** 40s. **14** Quarterly. **15** Radio 4 Long Wave. **16** 1990s. **17** S4C. **18** Buckinghamshire. **19** S & SE England. **20** Independent. **21** 1920s. **22** Labour. **23** O.K. **24** Edina & Patsy. **25** 60s.

# Quiz 86 Pot Luck 45

1 Which Tory MP lost the Putney seat in 1997?
2 In a one-off performance who appeared with Boyzone on Top of the Pops in 1998?
3 Where in America is the Rockefeller University?
4 In which country was Leo McKern born?
5 In American Football where do the Cardinals come from?
6 Who had an 80s No 1 with I Owe You Nothing?
7 Which musical featured the song Tonight?
8 Sheffield Brightside has been the 90s seat of which prominent politician?
9 Which pop singer played Adrian's mother in The Growing Pains of Adrian Mole?
10 In which decade did the Republic of Ireland join the European Union?
11 Which Rugby League team became Tigers in the 90s?
12 What are the international registration letters of a vehicle from Mexico?
13 To the nearest million what is the population of Switzerland?
14 Which character was given The Kabin by Rita in Coronation Street?
15 At which sport did Susan Cheeseborough win international success?
16 Who wrote the novel The French Lieutenant's Woman?
17 Tampa airport was built in which US state?
18 Which football club have a ground with the Matthew Harding stand?
19 Which university is at Uxbridge in Middlesex?
20 In finance what does the letter P stand for in PIN?
21 Which road led Chris Rea to write Road To Hell?
22 What is a young person interested in if they join the YOC?
23 Who announces the results of a parliamentary election?
24 Who had a Morris Minor car named Miriam?
25 What type of animals take part in the Courser's Derby?

## Answers

***Pot Luck 45***

**1** David Mellor. **2** Andrew Lloyd Webber. **3** New York. **4** Australia. **5** Phoenix. **6** Bros. **7** West Side Story. **8** David Blunkett. **9** Lulu. **10** 70s. **11** Castleford. **12** MEX. **13** 7 million. **14** Sharon. **15** Gymnastics. **16** John Fowles. **17** Florida. **18** Chelsea. **19** Brunel. **20** Personal. **21** M25. **22** Birds. **23** Returning officer. **24** Lovejoy. **25** Greyhounds.

# Quiz 87 80s

1 Which Michael had a 1989 hit with Love Changes Everything?
2 Which coloured day of the week was a hit for New Order in 1983 and 1988?
3 Who had a man in 1986 who was So Macho?
4 Which Radio 1 DJ would not play Relax by Frankie Goes to Hollywood on his early morning show?
5 Which actor had a hit with Under The Boardwalk in 1987?
6 Which group had a hit in 1988 with Harvest for the World?
7 Which TV weatherperson was celebrated in a 1988 hit for the Tribe of Toffs?
8 Who gave Lessons in Love in 1986?
9 Which group made Private Investigations in a 1982 hit?
10 According to the 1984 hit by Pat Benatar Love is a what?
11 Which Summer gave Bryan Adams a hit in 1985?
12 Who had a hit with You Take Me Up in 1984?
13 Singers of Heartache, Pepsi and Shirley were backing singers to who?
14 Who did a cover of Everything I Own in the 80s?
15 Who had a hit in 1988 with The Only Way Is Up?
16 Which American lady had a hit in 1989 with The Wind Beneath My Wings?
17 Who had a hit in 1981 with Oh Superman?
18 Which group had a hit in 1989 about The Living Years?
19 Who tool Ride On Time to the UK Top Spot for six weeks in 1989?
20 Which rock band had a UK No 1 in 1986 with The Final Count Down?
21 Which group were Going Back To My Roots in a No 4 hit from 1981?
22 Which group asked Don't Get Me Wrong in 1986?
23 Whose only Top Ten UK hit was Your Love Is King from 1984?
24 Who had a hit in 1987 with Never Can Say Goodbye?
25 In 1980 who were All Out of Love?

## Answers

***80s***

**1** Ball. **2** Blue Monday. **3** Sinitta. **4** Mike Read. **5** Bruce Willis. **6** Christians. **7** John Kettley. **8** Level 42. **9** Dire Straits. **10** Battlefield. **11** 69. **12** The Thompson Twins. **13** Wham!. **14** Boy George. **15** Yazz. **16** Bette Midler. **17** Laurie Anderson. **18** Mike and the Mechanics. **19** Black Box. **20** Europe. **21** Odyssey. **22** Pretenders. **23** Sade. **24** The Communards. **25** Air Supply.

# Quiz 88 Pioneers

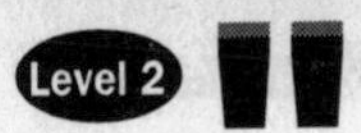


1 What was the first name of the world's first test tube baby?
2 Jane Couch was the first woman to be granted a professional licence to do what?
3 In which city did the original Wallace and Gromit models get lost in 1996?
4 What sort of radio was designed by British inventor Trevor Baylis?
5 The Ishihara Test is a test for what?
6 Which pioneer in men's appearance had the first names King Camp?
7 Air flight pioneer Amy Johnson vanished over which river?
8 What was the name of Clive Sinclair's electric trike?
9 Reaching which place led to the quote, "Great God, this is an awful place"?
10 Who accompanied Dr Michael Stroud on the first unsupported crossing of the Antarctic?
11 In 1993 Barbara Harmer became the first woman pilot of what?
12 Who was the first racing driver to win the world drivers' championship in his own car?
13 Which country was the first in the world to have a woman Prime Minister?
14 What was the first item of non stick cookware marketed by Teflon?
15 Which flags along with that of the UN were planted on the top of Everest by Hillary and Tensing?
16 In the Whitbread Round the World Race who skippered the all women crew of Maiden?
17 David Scott and James Irwin were the first people to drive where?
18 Who introduced the first personal stereo ?
19 In which decade were camcorders introduced?
20 Which items of sports equipment were developed by US ice hockey players Scott and Brennan Olson?
21 Gro Harlem Brundtland was the first woman PM in which country?
22 Who was the USA's first spacewoman?
23 Who was the first black archbishop of Cape Town?
24 What sort of wave was seen for the first time at a sporting fixture in 1986?
25 Which Scandinavian country was the first to ban aerosol sprays because of the potential damage to the environment?

## Answers

***Pioneers***

**1** Louise. **2** Box. **3** New York. **4** Clockwork radio. **5** Colour blindness. **6** Gillette. **7** Thames. **8** C5. **9** The South Pole. **10** Ranulph Fiennes. **11** Concorde. **12** Jack Brabham. **13** Ceylon later Sri Lanka. **14** Frying pan. **15** Britain & Nepal. **16** Tracey Edwards. **17** Moon. **18** Sony. **19** 80s. **20** Rollerblades. **21** Norway. **22** Sally Ride. **23** Desmond Tutu. **24** Mexican wave. **25** Sweden.

# Quiz 89 Glitterati

1 Which famous daughter was made chief designer at Chloe in 1997?
2 Which supermodel was married to Rod Stewart?
3 What is the occupation of Vanessa Feltz's husband?
4 Which Royal sold her autobiography for $1.3 million to Simon & Schuster?
5 Who designed Sophie Rhys-Jones' wedding dress?
6 Which French chef is famed for his Manoir aux Quat'Saisons restaurant?
7 Flamenco dancer Joaquin Cortes hit the headlines in 1996 over his relationship with which supermodel?
8 Which Italian fashion designer was murdered on the orders of his ex wife?
9 Michael Flatley shot to fame during an interval filler on which programme?
10 Which perfume house did Helena Bonham-Carter advertise?
11 Who designed the see through black dress Caprice wore at the 1996 Narional TV Awards which shot her to stardom?
12 Whose 50th birthday party did Prince Charles host at Highgrove in the summer of 1997?
13 Which pop star did model Iman marry in 1992?
14 Which crimper to the famous launched his Hairomatherapy products in the 90s?
15 What type of creature did Anthea Turner pose nude with on the front of Tatler?
16 Who has been the husband of Catherine Deneuve, Marie Helvin and Catherine Dyer?
17 What is the name of Terence and Shirley Conran's dress designer son?
18 Who did Princess Diana's make up before her wedding in 1981?
19 In which country was Ivana Trump born and brought up?
20 Which drink did The Spice Girls promote?
21 Which Royal did The Beatles mention in Penny Lane?
22 Which soap star launched a perfume called Scoundrel?
23 Which blonde model appeared in Batman?
24 Which TV soap did Russell Grant appear in as himself?
25 The 11th Duke of Devonshire married one of which famous family of sisters?

## Answers

***Glitterati***

**1** Stella McCartney. **2** Rachel Hunter. **3** Surgeon. **4** The Duchess of York. **5** Samantha Shaw. **6** Raymond Blanc. **7** Naomi Campbell. **8** Gucci. **9** Eurovision Song Contest. **10** Yardley. **11** Versace. **12** Camilla Parker-Bowles. **13** David Bowie. **14** Nicky Clarke. **15** Snake. **16** David Bailey. **17** Jasper. **18** Barbara Daly. **19** Czechoslovakia. **20** Pepsi. **21** The Queen. **22** Joan Collins. **23** Jerry Hall. **24** Brookside. **25** Mitford.

# Quiz 90 TV Trivia

Level 2 

**1** Who with Greg Dyke was credited with saving TV am?
**2** Which model advertised Pizza Hut with Jonathan Ross?
**3** Who found fame in the docu soap about a driving school?
**4** Which TV personality appeared on The Archers - as himself - for their 10,000th episode?
**5** From which part of her house did Delia Smith present her 90s TV series?
**6** Which comedy duo began as stand up comics called The Menopause Sisters?
**7** Which airline did Jeremy Spake from Airport work for?
**8** In which supermarket ad did Jane Horrocks play Prunella Scales' daughter?
**9** Fred Housego shot to fame as a winner on which TV show?
**10** Who replaced Danny Baker on Pets Win Prizes?
**11** Who provided the music for The Wombles?
**12** Who or what did Barbara Woodhouse train?
**13** Which Ready Steady Cook regular was also a regular presenter on Breakfast Time?
**14** What is the subject of the Quentin Wilson show All the Right Moves?
**15** What was Keith Floyd's TV show based on Far East cooking called?
**16** Who interviewed Prince Edward and Sophie Rhys Jones in a pre wedding programme?
**17** Who wrote and sang the theme music to Spender?
**18** Which early presenter of the Big Breakfast wore glasses?
**19** Who was the original presenter of Gladiators with Ulrika Jonsson?
**20** Which drama series was based on the Constable novels by Nicholas Rhea?
**21** Which series had the tag line "The truth is out there...."?
**22** Who worked together on The Frost Report and went on to have their own successful series together?
**23** Which quiz began with "Your starter for ten.."?
**24** Which work of reference do the celebrity and the expert possess in Countdown?
**25** Which soap powder did Robbie Coltrane advertise?

## Answers

***TV Trivia***

**1** Roland Rat. **2** Caprice. **3** Maureen Rees. **4** Terry Wogan. **5** Conservatory. **6** French & Saunders. **7** Aeroflot. **8** Tesco. **9** Mastermind. **10** Dale Winton. **11** Mike Batt. **12** Dogs. **13** Fern Britton. **14** Property. **15** Far Flung Floyd. **16** Sue Barker. **17** Jimmy Nail. **18** Chris Evans. **19** John Fashanu. **20** Heartbeat. **21** The X Files. **22** The Two Ronnies. **23** University Challenge. **24** Dictionary. **25** Persil.

# Quiz 91 Rugby

1. Who is England's most capped Union player?
2. In which decade did Ireland last win the Five Nations?
3. Who led the British Lions in their all conquering tour of S Africa in the 70s?
4. Which Erica made a clean breast of things at Twickenham in 1982?
5. Apart from Rugby, Rob Andrew captained Cambridge in which other sport?
6. In 1998 against which team did England suffer their worst ever Union defeat?
7. Who led England to their Grand Slam triumph of 1980, the first for nearly a quarter of a century?
8. What injury did Welsh captain Gwyn Jones suffer in Dec 1997 at the Arms Park?
9. Which club thought Wendall Sailor was joining them in 1998?
10. Who did Scotland beat 85-3 to in a 1999 World Cup qualifier?
11. In what year was League's Regal Trophy last contested?
12. Which team played the Welsh in the first game at the Millennium Stadium?
13. Which creature name did Hunslet adopt in the 90s?
14. Who captained the Lions' New Zealand Tour of 1993?
15. At what age did Will Carling first become England skipper?
16. Which country was thrashed 96-13 by South Africa in 1998?
17. What position did Gareth Edwards play?
18. Martin Johnson was at which club when he became England skipper?
19. Jonathan Davies was League's 1994 Man of Steel when playing for which team?
20. In which pool were England drawn for the 1999 World Cup?
21. Which team did Bath beat in 97-98 European Cup?
22. Which country does Wales coach Graham Henry come from?
23. Who was man of the match as Sheffield Eagles sensationally beat Wigan in a Challenge Cup final?
24. Which club did legendary French player Phillippe Sella join?
25. In which year did Lawrence Dallaglio take over as England's captain?

## Answers

***Rugby***

**1** Rory Underwood. **2** 80s. **3** Willie John McBride. **4** Rowe. **5** Cricket. **6** Australia. **7** Bill Beaumont. **8** Broke his neck. **9** Wigan. **10** Spain. **11** 1996. **12** S Africa. **13** Hawks. **14** Gavin Hastings. **15** 22. **16** Wales. **17** Scrum half. **18** Leicester. **19** Warrington. **20** Pool B. **21** Brive. **22** New Zealand. **23** Mark Aston. **24** Saracens. **25** 1997.

# Quiz 92 The Movies The Oscars

Level 2

1 Which not-so-dizzy blonde won an Oscar for Cactus Flower?
2 Who did Loretta Lynn choose to play her in Coal Miner's Daughter?
3 How tall is an Oscar in centimetres?
4 Whose 1989 Oscar for Glory was the first awarded to a black American for 50 years?
5 Following his True Grit Oscar what did John Wayne's fellow actors and his horse wear while filming a new movie?
6 In which decade of the 20th century were The Oscars born?
7 For which film was Judi Dench nominate for her first Oscar?
8 What is the name of the daughter of Oscar winner Joel Gray who starred in Dirty Dancing?
9 Who was up for an Oscar as Sally Field's daughter in Steel Magnolias?
10 Which actress was the second in history to win an Oscar (for Roman Holiday) and a Tony (for Ondine) in the same year?
11 Which French actor was Oscar nominated for Cyrano de Bergerac?
12 For which movie did Barbra Streisand win an Oscar for Evergreen?
13 Which anniversary did The Oscars celebrate in 1998?
14 Which 1996 multi Oscar winner was based on a novel by Michael Ondaatje?
15 For which film did Robert de Niro win his first Oscar?
16 Which Fonda won an honorary award in 1980?
17 Who won an Oscar for the music of Chariots of Fire?
18 What was the nationality of Sophie in the Oscar winning Sophie's Choice?
19 Dr Haing S Ngor was only the second non professional actor to win an Oscar in which film?
20 Which Stevie Wonder song won an Oscar for The Woman in Red?
21 Which was the first family to boast three generations of Oscar winners including middle generation John?
22 Who won a Best Supporting Actor award for Hannah and her Sisters?
23 Which successful song from Top Gun was a hit for Berlin?
24 In which film did Cher win an Oscar playing Loretta Castorini?
25 1987 was a successful year for Michael Douglas but which movie won him an Oscar?

## Answers

***The Movies The Oscars***

**1** Goldie Hawn. **2** Sissy Spacek. **3** 30cm. **4** Denzel Washington. **5** Eye patches. **6** 20s. **7** Mrs Brown. **8** Jennifer. **9** Julia Roberts. **10** Audrey Hepburn. **11** Gerard Depardieu. **12** A Star is Born. **13** 70th. **14** The English Patient. **15** The Godfather II. **16** Henry. **17** Vangelis. **18** Polish. **19** The Killing Fields. **20** I Just Called to Say I Love You. **21** Huston. **22** Michael Caine. **23** Take My Breath Away. **24** Moonstruck. **25** Wall Street.

# Quiz 93 On Line

1 What was BT called before 1991?
2 In which decade of this century were airmail letters first carried?
3 Which Defence Department first set up the messaging system which became the Internet?
4 In telephone terms what was a party line?
5 Which telecommunications company took its name from the Roman messenger of the gods?
6 What was BT's Speaking Clock service called?
7 What is the purpose of a dataglove?
8 BarclaySquare was an early Internet site offering what?
9 What is a message sent to a newsgroup on the Internet called?
10 What was the BBC's introduction to the Internet called?
11 What was set up in 1984 to monitor the telecommunications industry?
12 What colour were special airmail post boxes which used to be seen on city streets?
13 On the Internet what does the first B stand for in BBS?
14 Pong was an early console type game based on which sport?
15 What was the videotext service of BT called?
16 What does V stand for in VR?
17 How many bits are there in a byte?
18 From Earth, where was the destination of the longest long distance telephone call?
19 What does D stand for in ISDN?
20 Which company launched CDi in the early 1990s?
21 On the Internet what is Spam?
22 In the WIMP system of computing what did W stand for?
23 What does D stand for in CAD?
24 What was the name of the first satellite to relay live TV pictures between the USA and Europe?
25 On the Internet what is a firewall?

## Answers

***On Line***

**1** British Telecom. **2** 2nd decade. **3** Pentagon. **4** Shared phone line. **5** Mercury. **6** Timeline. **7** Allows people to touch over long distances. **8** Shopping. **9** Article. **10** Webwise. **11** Oftel. **12** Blue. **13** Bulletin. **14** Tennis. **15** Prestel. **16** Virtual. **17** Eight. **18** Moon. **19** Digital. **20** Phillips. **21** Junkmail. **22** Windows. **23** Design. **24** Telstar. **25** Security barrier.

# Quiz 94 90s

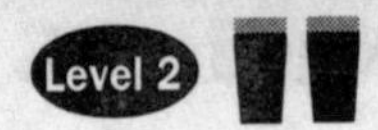

1 Which country is home to Whigfield?
2 What was Loved by Shanice in 1991 and 1992?
3 Who sang about Black Betty in both 1977 and 1990?
4 Which Wimbledon champion sang with John McEnroe?
5 Which liquid product featured the hit Like A Prayer in its advertisement?
6 Danny, Joe, Sonnie, Jon and Jordan were better known as which group?
7 Who asked you to Please Come Home for Christmas in 1994?
8 Which group took a cover of More Than A Woman to No 2 in 1998?
9 What was Blur's first top ten hit?
10 Who said Let's Get Rocked in a 1992 hit?
11 Who released an album in the 90s called Bilingual?
12 Who recorded the original version of Boyzone's Father and Son?
13 Which group were a Sight For Sore Eyes?
14 Who were Ready Or Not from 1996?
15 Who released an album in 1996 called K?
16 Who had a No.1 in 1991 with his debut single The One and Only?
17 Which Sunday paper featured the audition ads for Upside Down?
18 Which song gave The Corrs their first UK Top Ten hit?
19 Which hit by the Spice Girls gave them their 8th UK No. 1?
20 Which hit gave All Saints their 3rd UK No 1 hit in September 1998?
21 What was Boyzone's first UK Top Ten hit ?
22 Who had a UK No 1 with Gym and Tonic in October 1998?
23 What nationality are the vocal and instrumental group Aqua?
24 What was Jamiroquai's first UK Top Ten hit?
25 Which label do Shamen record on?

## Answers

***90s***

**1** Denmark. **2** Your Smile. **3** Ram Jam. **4** Pat Cash. **5** Pepsi. **6** New Kids On The Block. **7** Bon Jovi. **8** 911. **9** There's No Other Way. **10** Def Leppard. **11** Pet Shop Boys. **12** Cat Stevens. **13** M People. **14** The Fugees. **15** Kula Shaker. **16** Chesney Hawkes. **17** People. **18** Dreams. **19** Goodbye. **20** Bootie Call. **21** Love Me For A Reason. **22** Spacedust. **23** Danish. **24** Too Young To Die. **25** One Little Indian.

# Quiz 95 Technology & Industry

1 Which telescope was launched into space on board a space shuttle in 1990?
2 Which UK airport became the first to be connected to a city railway system?
3 In the late 60s Owen Finlay Maclaren pioneered what useful item for parents of small children?
4 What was the OFT?
5 In which decade were windscreen wipers patented in the UK?
6 Who launched the Skytrain air service?
7 Which city was the HQ of the European Space programme?
8 Which Bank of England chief said losses in industry in the north east was a small price to pay for low inflation?
9 What type of aircraft was the Hawker Siddley Harrier?
10 What does the Transalaska Pipeline System transport?
11 What was the name of the world's first nuclear powered submarine?
12 Robin Leigh-Pemberton held the top job at which organisation from 1983 to 1993?
13 Which company linked with Sky Television to form BSkyB?
14 In which decade was the Mersey Tunnel opened?
15 What did the first letter I stand for in ICI?
16 What was Britain's first king size cigarette called?
17 In which country were do Daewoo cars originally produced?
18 Which country was the first in the world to introduce a driving test?
19 What did Guinness adopt as its trademark in the 60s?
20 Which Andrei built the first factory to mass produce rubber tyres?
21 Which underground line runs to Heathrow Airport?
22 Which Trade & Industry Secretary resigned in 1998?
23 What does Volkswagen actually mean?
24 The first cheque guarantee card was produced by which British bank?
25 In which city are the headquarters of the IMF?

## Answers

***Technology & Industry***

**1** Hubble. **2** Heathrow. **3** Baby Buggy. **4** Office of Fair Trading. **5** 20s. **6** Freddie Laker. **7** Paris. **8** Eddie George. **9** Jump jet. **10** Oil. **11** Nautilus. **12** Bank of England. **13** BSB. **14** 30s. **15** Imperial. **16** Rex. **17** Korea. **18** France. **19** Harp. **20** Michelin. **21** Piccadilly. **22** Peter Mandelson. **23** People's car. **24** Midland. **25** Washington.

# Quiz 96 20th C Leaders

Level 2 

1 Sir Christopher Bland replaced Sir Marmaduke Hussey as Chairman of which corporation in 1996?
2 Paul Keating was a controversial Prime Minister of which country?
3 Which Tory Home Secretary refused an application for British citizenship by the Al Fayed brothers in 1996?
4 Who fought the 1997 election, on behalf of the Referendum Party?
5 Aung San Suu Kyi is a controversial leader in which country?
6 Which Russian leader was buried in 1998 in his family's vault?
7 What was the full name of the trades union which Arthur Scargill led?
8 Who in Tony Blair's Cabinet was a racing tipster for the Glasgow Herald?
9 Who became president of the European Commission in 1995?
10 Which spouse of a party leader deputised for Jimmy Young on Radio 2?
11 Which French Prime Minister funeral's was attended by his wife and his mistress in 1996?
12 Who was only the second heir to the throne to marry this century?
13 Which Eurovision winner became an MEP in the 1999 elections?
14 Which political party leader's aunt was a big lottery winner in 1998?
15 Which Press Secretary left Downing Street for Radio 5 Live?
16 Which world leader married Graca Machel in 1998?
17 Which royal autographed a Man Utd football on a tour of Malaysia?
18 Bill Clinton was Governor of which US state he became President?
19 Who did William Hague beat in the final round of the contest for the Tory Party leadership after the 1997 election?
20 Earl Spencer appeared on whose US chat show?
21 Who replaced King Hussein as King of Jordan?
22 Which surname of a British leader was Ronald Reagan's middle name?
23 What was the surname of the British Roman Catholic Cardinal who died in June 1999?
24 Which daughter of a Prime Minister was a former girlfriend of convicted ex MP Jonathan Aitken?
25 Michael Cashman became an MEP in the 1999 elections after starring for three years in which TV soap?

**Answers**

***20th C Leaders***
**1** BBC. **2** Australia. **3** Michael Howard. **4** James Goldsmith. **5** Burma. **6** Tsar Nicholas II. **7** National Union Of Mineworkers. **8** Robin Cook. **9** Jacques Santer. **10** Glenys Kinnock. **11** Francois Mitterand. **12** Prince Charles. **13** Dana. **14** William Hague's. **15** Charlie Whelan. **16** Nelson Mandela. **17** The Queen. **18** Arkansas. **19** Kenneth Clarke. **20** Oprah Winfrey. **21** Abdullah. **22** Wilson. **23** Hume. **24** Carol Thatcher. **25** EastEnders.

# Quiz 97 20th C TV On the Box

1. What was the name of the live weekday programme which Vanessa Feltz fronted in her £2 million deal with the BBC?
2. In which series did Michelle Collins play holiday rep Vicki?
3. What is the first name of the builder in Ground Force?
4. Which broadcaster famously said during the Falklands conflict, "I counted them all out and I counted them all back"?
5. David Wilkinson featured in the docu soap about which West End store?
6. Which song did Robson & Jerome sing on Soldier Soldier which launched their singing career?
7. Sharron Davies aka Gladiator Amazon was an Olympic medallist in which sport?
8. Fred Dibnah found fame on TV as a member of what profession?
9. Which Michael Palin series followed in the steps of Phileas Fogg?
10. In which decade did the BBC's Film review programme with Barry Norman begin?
11. What colour was the chair in the first series of Mastermind?
12. Where are the Pebble Mill studios?
13. At what time of day was Multi Coloured Swap Shop shown?
14. What was the manageress managing in The Manageress?
15. Who played Wooster in the 90s version of Jeeves & Wooster?
16. The action of Sharpe took place during which war?
17. Who was the subject of The Private Man, The Public Role?
18. Who narrated The Wombles?
19. In which drama series were Miles and Egg major characters?
20. Where on a Teletubby is its TV screen?
21. In which US state was Sweet Valley High?
22. Which Coronation Street actress played Jimmy Nail's ex wife in Spender?
23. What was the name of Robson Green's character in Soldier Soldier?
24. Which airline was the subject of the docu soap Airline?
25. In which decade did Newsnight start?

## Answers

***20th C TV On The Box***

**1** The Vanessa Show. **2** Sunburn. **3** Tommy. **4** Brian Hanrahan. **5** Selfridges. **6** Unchained Melody. **7** Swimming. **8** Steeplejack. **9** Around the World in 80 Days. **10** 70s. **11** Black. **12** Birmingham. **13** Morning. **14** Football club. **15** Hugh Laurie. **16** Napoleonic. **17** Prince Charles. **18** Bernard Cribbins. **19** This Life. **20** Tummy. **21** California. **22** Denise Welch - Natalie. **23** Dave Tucker. **24** Britannia Airways. **25** 80s.

# Quiz 98 Sports Bag

Level 2

1 Who said in 1998, "The ball doesn't know how old you are"?
2 Which post war cricketer played his first England game aged 18 and his last aged 45?
3 In which sport was Richard Upton found positive in a drugs test in 1998?
4 In the 1998 play offs, which Sunderland player missed the final penalty?
5 In which sport in 90s Britain did Leopards overcome Sharks in a final?
6 Terry Mancini played soccer for which country?
7 In which decade did Alex Higgins first become snooker world champion?
8 What has been won by Australia II and America 3?
9 In which country and in which sport has a Blackadder played in the 90s?
10 Which Arsenal player scored in the 1998 World Cup Final?
11 Which former England captain added Dylan to his name in honour of Bob Dylan?
12 Where was the Derby held during Word War I and World War II?
13 Who was known as The Manassa Mauler?
14 How many people are there in an official tug of war team?
15 In 1994 who won the US Amateur Championship for the first time?
16 In which sport did Steve Baddeley win 143 caps in the 80s?
17 Who did Damon Hill move to when he was dropped by Williams?
18 Which country does boxer Vitali Klitschko come from?
19 In the 90s in which sport in England did Braves perform at a Craven Park?
20 Who won golf's US Open in 1994 and 1997?
21 Which English club did Daniel Amokachi join after 1994 World Cup success with Nigeria?
22 What is the surname of the first father and son cricket captains of England?
23 In 1998 which British boxer took on Shannon Briggs and Zeljko Mavrovic?
24 Golf star Vijay Singh comes from where?
25 The early days of which sport featured the Renshaw twins, the Baddeley twins and the Doherty brothers?

## Answers

***Sports Bag***

**1** Mark O'Meara. **2** Brian Close. **3** Swimming. **4** Michael Gray. **5** Basketball. **6** Republic of Ireland. **7** 70s. **8** America's Cup. **9** New Zealand - Rugby Union. **10** Petit. **11** Bob Willis. **12** Newmarket. **13** Jack Dempsey. **14** Eight. **15** Tiger Woods. **16** Badminton. **17** Arrows. **18** Ukraine. **19** Rugby League. **20** Ernie Els. **21** Everton. **22** Cowdrey. **23** Lennox Lewis. **24** Fiji. **25** Tennis.

# Quiz 99 20th C Screen Legends

1 Which swashbuckling hero's autobiography was My Wicked Wicked Ways?
2 What is Sean Connery's profession in The Name of the Rose?
3 Who did Ali McGraw marry after they had made The Getaway together?
4 Who spoke for the first time in Anna Christie?
5 Whose voice did Marni Nixon dub in the classic My Fair Lady?
6 In which film did David Niven play James Bond?
7 I Could Go on Singing was the last film of which screen legend?
8 Who was the first actress to receive four Oscars?
9 John Hinckley's obsession with Jodie Foster led him to attempt to kill who?
10 Who got her first big break in Grease 2?
11 Who played Charlie Chaplin in Richard Attenborough's1992 film?
12 Which star of Gypsy and West Side Story married Robert Wagner twice ?
13 Which legendary dancer was Oscar nominated for The Towering Inferno?
14 Which British born comedian completed a record 60th year of a contract with NBC in 1996?
15 Bogart's trademark sneer was due to an injury sustained in which conflict?
16 Which Swedish actress won the Best Supporting Actress Oscar for Murder on the Orient Express?
17 Who uttered the famous lines "Frankly my dear I don't give a damn"?
18 Who was jailed for her 'obscene' stage play Sex?
19 Omar Sharif is a worldwide expert in which game?
20 Which British actor's autobiography was called 'What's It All About?'?
21 Which screen legend's daughter shot JR in Dallas?
22 Which Joan's career revived in Whatever Happened to Baby Jane??
23 Which much loved US actor won the Best Actor Oscar for The Philadelphia Story?
24 Which red haired actress had the Margarita cocktail named after her as her real name was Margarita Cansino?
25 What colour are Elizabeth Taylor's eyes?

## Answers

***20th C The Movies Screen Legends***

**1** Errol Flynn. **2** Friar. **3** Steve McQueen. **4** Greta Garbo. **5** Audrey Hepburn. **6** Casino Royale. **7** Judy Garland. **8** Katharine Hepburn. **9** Ronald Reagan. **10** Michelle Pfeiffer. **11** Robert Downey Junior. **12** Natalie Wood. **13** Fred Astaire. **14** Bob Hope. **15** WWI. **16** Ingrid Bergman. **17** Clark Gable. **18** Mae West. **19** Bridge. **20** Michael Caine. **21** Bing Crosby. **22** Crawford. **23** James Stewart. **24** Rita Hayworth. **25** Violet.

# Quiz 100 Entertainment

1 Whose work for orchestra and chorus, Standing Stone was premiered at the Albert Hall in 1997?
2 In which decade of the 20th century did the Gang Show cease to be staged annually in London?
3 Who was made principal conductor of the Birmingham Symphony orchestra in 1980?
4 In which part of London is The Round House?
5 The Sealed Knot Society re enacts battles of which war?
6 Followers of raga music call themselves what?
7 Marie Rambert founded a company in what branch of entertainment?
8 Which J A owned over half British cinemas by the mid 1940s?
9 Which ethnic group popularised salsa dancing in New York in the 1980s?
10 Which home town of Robin Hood has an 'experience' centre in his honour?
11 What and where is the Mathser?
12 How many piers does Blackpool have?
13 What type of tennis is usually played by children on a smaller court?
14 What was the first Web browser called?
15 Which dancer founded the company Dash?
16 Which seaside resort has Britain's largest theatre - and largest stage?
17 Which Russian city was famous for its State Circus?
18 The company whose full name was Radio Keith Orpheum produced what?
19 Who were Michael 'Rage' Hardy and James 'Smarty' Cools' female partner in Virtua Cop 2?
20 In which English county is the longest pleasure pier?
21 In which Austrian city, home of Mozart, has an annual music festival been held since 1920?
22 Who is the Princess in the Super Mario Gang?
23 Where in Japan is the Nintendo company based?
24 In which country did rap music begin?
25 What is BT's online gaming service called?

**Answers**

***Entertainment***
**1** Paul McCartney. **2** 70s. **3** Simon Rattle. **4** Hampstead. **5** English Civil War. **6** Ragamuffins. **7** Ballet. **8** Rank. **9** Puerto Ricans. **10** Nottingham. **11** Beer selling establishment, Munich. **12** Three. **13** Short tennis. **14** Mosaic. **15** Wayne Sleep. **16** Blackpool. **17** Moscow. **18** Films - RKO. **19** Janet. **20** Essex. **21** Salzburg. **22** Daisy. **23** Kyoto. **24** USA. **25** Wireplay.

# The Hard Questions

If you thought that this section of this book would prove to be little or no problem, or that the majority of the questions could be answered and a scant few would test you then you are sorely mistaken. These questions are the *hardest* questions *ever*! So difficult are they that any attempt to answer them all in one sitting will addle your mind and mess with your senses. You'll end up leaving the pub via the window while ordering a pint from the horse brasses on the wall. Don't do it! For a kick off there are 3,000 of them, so at 20 seconds a question it will take you over 16 hours and that's just the time it takes to read them. What you should do instead is set them for others – befuddle your friends' minds.

Note the dangerous nature of these questions though. These are you secret weapons use them accordingly unless, of course, someone or some team is getting your back up. In which case you should hit them hard and only let up when you have them cowering under the bench whimpering "uncle".

These questions work best against league teams, they are genuinely tough and should be used against those people who take their pub quizzes seriously. NEVER use these questions against your inlaws.

# Quiz 1 80s Music

1. Somewhere In My Heart was the only Top Ten hit for which group?
2. Who asked you to Kiss Me in 1985?
3. What was Amazulu's only UK Top Ten hit?
4. Whose Harbour was taken to No 10 in 1988 by All About Eve?
5. Who were on the Road to Nowhere in 1985?
6. Whose first UK Top Ten hit was The Look?
7. Who had a No 4 hit with (Something Inside) So Strong?
8. What was the first Top Ten UK hit for Heart?
9. What was the Pretenders first Top Ten hit of the 80s?
10. Which Soft Cell No 1 from 1981 got to No. 5 in 1991?
11. Who did some Wishful Thinking in their only UK Top Ten hit?
12. Which successful 80s band was fronted by Graham McPherson?
13. Which duo had a Top 20 hit from 1983 with First Picture Of You?
14. Who was Right Here Waiting on their first UK Top Ten hit from 1989?
15. Who was the only US act to achieve three successive UK No 1s in the 80s?
16. Which vocalist had a No 8 hit in 1987 with the Moonlighting theme?
17. Who had a US No1 and a UK No 2 with Funkytown in 1980?
18. Which group had a No 5 in 1987 with It Doesn't Have To Be This Way?
19. Which female vocalist expressed Self Control in 1984?
20. Which artist spent the most number of weeks in the UK chart in 1989?
21. Which Pet Shop Boys video featured Sir Ian McKellen as Dracula?
22. Which song gave Steve Winwood his highest UK chart position?
23. What was the Oscar-winning song from Working Girl?
24. Who had a hit with Captain Beaky and Wilfred the Weasel in 1980?
25. Who requested "If you'll be my bodyguard" in his No. 4 from 1986?

## Answers

**80s Music**

**1** Aztec Camera. **2** Stephen Tin Tin Duffy. **3** Too Good To Be Forgotten. **4** Martha's. **5** Talking Heads. **6** Roxette. **7** Labi Siffre. **8** Alone. **9** Talk of The Town. **10** Tainted Love. **11** China Crisis. **12** Madness. **13** Lotus Eaters. **14** Richard Marx. **15** Blondie. **16** Al Jarreau. **17** Lipps Inc.. **18** Blow Monkeys. **19** Laura Branigan. **20** Bobby Brown. **21** Heart. **22** Higher Love. **23** Let The River Run. **24** Keith Michell. **25** Paul Simon

# Quiz 2 Pot Luck 1

1 What was Abba's last UK No 1 of the 70s?
2 Who was Pope at the beginning of the 20th C?
3 In which unusual place were Nick Anderson and Julie Boone married?
4 What star sign is David Bellamy?
5 How many storeys are there in the circular tower of Strasbourg's new Euro parliament building?
6 Where in England was Jenny Agutter born?
7 What was awarded Best Film at the Motion Picture Academy Awards in '96?
8 Which coin ceased to be legal tender at midnight on 31st December 1969?
9 Which actor played the Mock Turtle in a 1966 BBC screened version of Alice In Wonderland?
10 In which country is the Alex Fraser bridge?
11 Who is attributed to have described a starlet as "the original good time that was had by all"?
12 What are the international registration letters of a vehicle from the Yemen?
13 Who became LWT's Deputy Controller of Programmes after a career in football management?
14 Wichita international airport is in which US state?
15 What is Ryan O'Neal's real first name?
16 Whose autobiography was called The Day Gone By?
17 What star sign is shared by Robert De Niro and Sean Penn?
18 Who was the defending champion when Jimmy Connors first won Wimbledon singles?
19 Abadan International airport is in which country?
20 How many Grand Prix had Eddie Jordan's team entered before they won?
21 In which soap did Demi Moore find fame?
22 Which country does the airline Island Air come from?
23 Which liner launched in 1907 was called the Grand Old Lady of the Atlantic?
24 Who directed The Dirty Dozen?
25 What is Axl Rose's real name?

**Answers**

***Pot Luck 1***

**1** Take A Chance On Me. **2** Leo XIII. **3** Shark Tank. **4** Capricorn. **5** 17. **6** Taunton. **7** The English Patient. **8** Half Crown. **9** Sir John Gielgud. **10** Canada. **11** Bette Davis. **12** AND. **13** Jimmy Hill. **14** Kansas. **15** Patrick. **16** Richard Adams. **17** Leo. **18** Jan Kodes. **19** Iran. **20** 127. **21** General Hospital. **22** Belize. **23** The Mauritania. **24** Robert Aldrich. **25** William Bailey.

# Quiz 3 The Royals

1 Which monarch said, "The thing that impresses me most about America is the way parents obey their children"?
2 Who said that pregnancy was, "an occupational hazard of being a wife"?
3 Who wrote the words to "I Vow to Thee My Country" which was sung at Princess Diana's wedding and at her funeral?
4 Who had the Queen for tea in her Glasgow council house in July 1999?
5 What is Princess Margaret's eldest grandson called?
6 Who was the first fund raising manager of the Diana Memorial Fund?
7 How old was Elizabeth Taylor when she first danced in front of George V?
8 In which year was the TV film Royal Family made?
9 Who was George V's doctor who announced in 1936 "The King's life is moving peacefully to its close"?
10 Which Earl owned a restaurant called Deals with Viscount Linley?
11 What was the name of the intruder found in the Queen's bedroom in 1982?
12 Where did the Queen, as Princess Elizabeth, spend her 21st birthday?
13 Which monarch asked a party leader to form the first Labour government?
14 Which Royal said "I should like to be a horse" when asked her ambition?
15 Where was Princess Anne when she famous told journalists to "Naff off!"?
16 What did Queen Mary reputedly describe to Stanley Baldwin as "a pretty kettle of fish"?
17 Which Olympic athlete was born on the same day as Princess Diana?
18 What was Princess Michael of Kent's maiden name?
19 Which hospital was Princess Diana taken to after her tragic car accident?
20 In which city did the Queen say, "I sometimes sense that the world is changing almost too fast for its inhabitants"?
21 Which lawyer presided over the divorce of Charles and Diana?
22 How old will the Queen be if she becomes the longest reigning monarch in British history?
23 Who was described by the Queen as, "more royal than the rest of us"?
24 Who said, "I don't feel relaxed at Buckingham Palace.... I don't expect anyone does when they visit their mother in law"?
25 For how long were Charles and Diana divorced?

## Answers

***The Royals***

**1** Edward VIII. **2** Princess Anne. **3** Cecil Spring-Rice. **4** Susan McCarron. **5** Samuel. **6** Paul Burrel. **7** Three. **8** 1969. **9** Viscount Dawson. **10** Lichfield. **11** Michael Fagin. **12** South Africa. **13** George V. **14** The Queen. **15** Badminton. **16** The abdication. **17** Carl Lewis. **18** Von Reibnitz. **19** La Pitie Salpetriere. **20** Islamabad. **21** Anthony Julius. **22** 89. **23** Princess Michael of Kent. **24** Mark Phillips. **25** One year.

# Quiz 4 Pot Luck 2

1 Which character opened the New York Stock Exchange on June 8th 99?
2 What is the population of Austria to the nearest million?
3 What star sign is shared by Steve Bruce and Alex Ferguson?
4 Who had a UK No 3 hit with 7 Seconds in 1994?
5 Where are the 2004 Summer Olympic Games being held?
6 In which country was Yul Brynner born?
7 Which British character actor made his film debut in The Maltese Falcon?
8 According to the modern Olympics founder Baron de Coubertin, "The essential thing is not conquering but..." what?
9 Who were England playing when David Gower did his Biggles impression?
10 In which decade was the Sydney Harbour bridge opened?
11 Which comedian has four initials, J P M S?
12 Vehicles from which country use the international registration letter RI?
13 In which movie did Garbo say, "I want to be alone"?
14 Truax Field international airport is in which US state?
15 In the cartoon characters Pip, Squeak and Wilfred, what kind of creature was Pip?
16 What was ORAC?
17 When she died how old was Karen Carpenter?
18 Which TV personality married hairdresser Stephen Way in 1998?
19 Who wrote, "What is this life if full of care, We have no time to stand and stare?"?
20 Which paper's 17 June 1977 headline was (Prince) 'Charles To Marry Astrid - Official!'?
21 Which writer said, "An atheist is a man who has no invisible means of support."?
22 Which country does the airline Ansett come from?
23 How many goals did Gary Lineker score for his country?
24 Which singer/actress began her career in the film Here Come the Huggetts?
25 What is Alexander McQueen's real first name?

## Answers

***Pot Luck 2***

**1** Noddy. **2** 8 million. **3** Capricorn. **4** Youssou N'Dour. **5** Athens. **6** Siberia. **7** Sydney Greenstreet. **8** Fighting well. **9** Queensland. **10** 1930s. **11** Julian Clary. **12** Indonesia. **13** Grand Hotel. **14** Wisconsin. **15** Dog. **16** A computer (in the Sci-Fi Tv show Blake's Seven). **17** 32. **18** Gloria Hunniford. **19** W H Davies. **20** Daily Express. **21** John Buchan. **22** Australia. **23** 48. **24** Petula Clark. **25** Lee.

# Quiz 5 20th C Who's Who

1. Who was Jeremy Thorpe talking about when he said, "Greater love hath no man than this than he lay down his friends for his life"?
2. Which major event was covered by war correspondent, Martha Gellhorn?
3. Who said, "When you marry your mistress you create a job vacancy"?
4. Who was Tony Blair's first President of the Board of Trade?
5. Which title did Tony Benn relinquish to sit in the House of Commons?
6. What did Jorge Luis Borges refer to as "a fight between two bald men over a comb"?
7. Who said, "How can you rule a country which produces 246 different kinds of cheese?"?
8. To whom was Nancy Astor speaking when she said, "You'll never get on in politics my dear, with that hair"?
9. Who wrote a book on disarmament called In Place of Fear?
10. Who planned to be the Gromyko of the Labour Party for the next 30 years?
11. Whose last words were, "Now it's on to Chicago and let's win there"?
12. Which woman was President of the Oxford Union in 1977?
13. Who put forward the industrial relations legislation In Place of Strife?
14. Who was the last emperor of Vietnam?
15. Who did Neil Kinnock say was "a ditherer, a dodger, a ducker and a weaver"?
16. Who was the first freely elected Marxist president in Latin America?
17. Paddy Ashdown was in which military unit before entering politics?
18. Who was the official British observer of the atomic bomb at Nagasaki?
19. Who said, "History is littered with wars which everybody 'knew' would never happen"?
20. Which US committee won the Nobel Peace Prize in 1997?
21. Who was First Secretary of State in John Major's last government?
22. Whose help in an election "was like being measured by an undertaker"?
23. Who held the post of Minister of Technology from 1966-1970?
24. Who was runner up to John Major in the Personality of the Year award for 1996 organised by the Today programme?
25. Who said, "There cannot be a crisis next week, my schedule is already full"?

## Answers

***20th C Who's Who***

**1** Harold Macmillan. **2** D Day landings. **3** James Goldsmith. **4** Margaret Beckett. **5** Viscount Stansgate. **6** Falklands conflict. **7** Charles de Gaulle. **8** Shirley Williams. **9** Aneurin Bevan. **10** Denis Healey. **11** Bobby Kennedy. **12** Benazir Bhutto. **13** Barbara Castle. **14** Bao Dai. **15** John Major. **16** Allende. **17** Royal Marines **18** Sir Leonard Cheshire. **19** Enoch Powell. **20** Land Mines. **21** Michael Heseltine. **22** Edward Heath. **23** Tony Benn. **24** Lisa Potts. **25** Henry Kissinger.

# Quiz 6 Pot Luck 3

1. What is Rupert Murdoch's real first name?
2. Who was the first Britain to become World Fly Fishing Champion?
3. Who wrote the novel Mostly Harmless?
4. Who did Jimmy White lose to in his first World Championship snooker final?
5. Who followed Calvin Coolidge as US President?
6. Where in England was Rowan Atkinson born?
7. Which sports event had the most viewers in 1994?
8. Theodore Francis international airport is in which US state?
9. What is Billy Idol's real name?
10. What was Adam Ant's last UK No 1 of the 80s?
11. In 1999 super athlete Carl Lewis revealed that he was suffering from what?
12. What are the international registration letters of a vehicle from Afghanistan?
13. Which actor wrote a book called Vet Behind the Ears?
14. What sport did Lawrence Dallaglio play in June 99 while England played in Australia?
15. What star sign is Patsy Kensit?
16. Who replaced John Masefield as Poet Laureate ?
17. Who did Boris Becker beat when he won his first Wimbledon men's singles?
18. What was the largest passenger ship ever built who made her last voyage in 1968?
19. Ain el Bay International airport is in which country?
20. Which British battleship sank the German battlecruiser The Scharnhorst in 1943?
21. What was the first surname of Jane Rossington in Crossroads?
22. Which country does the airline Avianca come from?
23. Who directed M*A*S*H?
24. What is Mark Knopfler's middle name?
25. Who was the last group to have a Xmas No 1 in the 80s?

## Answers

***Pot Luck 3***

**1** Keith. **2** Tony Pawson. **3** Douglas Adams. **4** Steve Davis. **5** Herbert Hoover. **6** Newcastle Upon Tyne. **7** Torvill & Dean's Olympic Dance. **8** Rhode Island. **9** William Broad. **10** Goody Two Shoes. **11** Arthritis. **12** AFG. **13** Christopher Timothy. **14** Beach rugby. **15** Pisces. **16** C Day Lewis. **17** Kevin Curren. **18** Queen Elizabeth. **19** Algeria. **20** Duke of York. **21** Richardson. **22** Colombia. **23** Robert Altman. **24** Freuder. **25** Band Aid II.

# Quiz 7 Soccer

1 Denis Irwin joined Man Utd from which club?
2 What was the first London club that David Seaman played for?
3 Who was the first England player born after the World Cup triumph to become a full international?
4 In how many games did Mick Channon captain England?
5 Which country was the first to lose in two World Cup finals?
6 When did Scotland make their first appearance in the World Cup?
7 Who said, "You're not a real manager until you've been sacked"?
8 In Germany in which decade was the Bundesliga formed?
9 Against which country was England's Ray Wilkins sent off?
10 What would Ryan Giggs' surname have been if he had used his father's name instead of his mother's?
11 Which club did Peter Beardsley join when he left Liverpool in 1991?
12 Steve Davis became a director of which soccer club in 1997?
13 Emmanuel Petit joined Arsenal from which soccer club?
14 When did Arsenal move to Highbury?
15 How many minutes of extra time were played in the Euro 96 final before Germany's Golden Goal winner?
16 Which team did Aberdeen beat in the 1983 European Cup Winners' Cup final?
17 Who did Billie Hampson play for in an FA Cup Final when aged nearly 42?
18 How many goals did Brian Kidd score for England?
19 In what decade was Scotland's first abandoned international match?
20 Who was the first Englishman to play for A C Milan?
21 How many of Gordon Banks's 73 England games ended in clean sheets?
22 Which Arsenal manager signed Dennis Bergkamp?
23 In which year did Wales make it to the World Cup final stages for the only time in the century?
24 Which team has played at home at Pound Park, Selhurst Park and Upton Park during the century?
25 Turek played in goal for which World Cup winning country?

**Answers**

***Soccer***

**1** Oldham. **2** QPR. **3** Tony Adams. **4** Two. **5** Hungary. **6** 1954. **7** Malcolm Allison. **8** 60s. **9** Morocco. **10** Wilson. **11** Everton. **12** Leyton Orient. **13** Monaco. **14** 1913. **15** Five. **16** Real Madrid. **17** Aston Villa. **18** One. **19** 60s. **20** Jimmy Greaves. **21** 35. **22** Bruce Rioch. **23** 1958. **24** Charlton. **25** W Germany.

# Quiz 8 Pot Luck 4

1 In which country was Cyril Cusack born?
2 What star sign is shared by Maureen Lipman and Glenda Jackson?
3 Who or what are Pharos, Kelpe, Swift and Emma?
4 In which decade was the London Philharmonic Orchestra founded?
5 TV's Yes Minister took its title from the real-life writings of which Labour politician?
6 What is the population of Belgium to the nearest million?
7 Who had a UK No 1 hit with Hey Girl Don't Bother Me?
8 Who wrote the first theme music used in The Sky at Night?
9 Susan Ballion is better known by which name?
10 In which country is the Gladesville bridge?
11 Who directed The Big Sleep and Gentlemen Prefer Blondes?
12 Vehicles from which country use the international registration letter WG?
13 Who sang the theme song for Trainer?
14 What's the link between a certain Peter Scott and Lauren Bacall, Liz Taylor and Sophia Loren?
15 In which year was the talkie The Jazz Singer released?
16 In which city is the Burrows Toy Museum?
17 Who said, "The great thing about the Spice Girls is that you can listen to them with the sound off"?
18 What was CBS TV news broadcaster Walter Cronkite's stock closing phrase?
19 Alborg Roedslet International airport is in which country?
20 What was Oliver Reed's real first name?
21 Tacoma international airport is in which US state?
22 Which country does the airline Sansa come from?
23 Who was England skipper in Terry Venables' first game in charge?
24 Who is the first composer to appear on a British banknote?
25 Which Dad's Army actor said he had conked out in the Times in 1983?

**Answers**

***Pot Luck 4***

**1** South Africa. **2** Taurus. **3** Queen's corgis. **4** 40s. **5** Richard Crossman - in his diaries. **6** 10 million. **7** Tams. **8** Sibelius. **9** Siouxsie Sioux. **10** Australia. **11** Howard Hawks. **12** Grenada. **13** Cliff Richard. **14** He robbed them. **15** 1927. **16** Bath. **17** George Harrison. **18** And that's the way it is. **19** Denmark. **20** Robert. **21** Seattle. **22** Costa Rica. **23** David Platt. **24** Edward Elgar. **25** John Le Mesurier.

# Quiz 9 Film Classics

**1** Which film classic took its name from Ernest Dowson's Cynara?
**2** In Casablanca who played Sam, who was asked to "play it again"?
**3** What was the first word in Citizen Kane?
**4** Which 60s film told of the exploits of Robert Gold and Diana Scott?
**5** In which film did Groucho Marx say, "Either this man is dead or my watch has stopped"?
**6** What was the motto of MGM?
**7** What was Melissa Mathison's contribution to E.T.?
**8** What are the final words of The Face of Fu Manchu?
**9** The title of the movie In Which We Serve comes from which book?
**10** "It was beauty killed the beast" was the last line of which film?
**11** In which film did Bacall say to Bogart, "If you want me just whistle"?
**12** "Mean, moody, magnificent." was the slogan used to advertise which film?
**13** In which film does the heroine say, "I am big, It's the pictures that got small"?
**14** Which character said, "Love means never having to say you're sorry"?
**15** What was the name of the very first sci fi movie made in 1902?
**16** Who directed The Day of the Jackal in 1973?
**17** About which film did Victor Fleming say, "This picture is going to be one of the biggest white elephants of all time"?
**18** In which film did Mae West say, "Why don't you come up some time and see me."?
**19** In Bringing Up Baby, what is Baby?
**20** Whose recording of a Bond theme reached highest in the UK's charts?
**21** Which film finishes with Joe E. Brown saying "Nobody's perfect" to Jack Lemmon?
**22** What is the name of Katharine Hepburn's character in The African Queen?
**23** About which film did Bob Hope say, "I thought it was about a giraffe."?
**24** Which company used the slogan A Diamond is Forever which Ian Fleming used for the book turned film Diamonds Are Forever?
**25** In which film did Bette Davis say, "fasten your seatbelts it's going to be a bumpy night"?

## Answers

***Film Classics***

**1** Gone With the Wind. **2** Dooley Wilson. **3** Rosebud. **4** Darling. **5** A Day at the Races. **6** Ars Gratia Artis. **7** Scriptwriter. **8** The world shall hear from me again. **9** Book of Common Prayer. **10** King Kong. **11** To Have and Have Not. **12** The Outlaw. **13** Sunset Boulevard. **14** Oliver. **15** Voyage to the Moon. **16** Fred Zimmerman. **17** Gone With the Wind. **18** She Done Him Wrong. **19** Leopard. **25** Duran Duran. **21** Some Like It Hot. **22** Rose Sayer. **23** Deep Throat. **24** De Beers. **25** All About Eve.

# Quiz 10 Pot Luck 5

1 What was Burt Lancaster's profession when he worked in the circus?
2 Which politician said, "You let a bully come into your front yard, and the next day he'll be on your porch"?
3 What was the Bee Gees' last UK No 1 of the 70s?
4 What is Anthony Quayle's real first name?
5 Who wrote the novel The Detached Retina?
6 Stapleton International airport is in which US state?
7 Which character did James Cagney play in White Heat?
8 In housemaster Eric Anderson's words who was "maddening, pretty full of himself and very argumentative"?
9 Where in England was David Bowie born?
10 Which poet has "Under Ben Bulben" carved on his gravestone?
11 Actor Gary Webster was a county player in which sport?
12 What are the international registration letters of a vehicle from Andorra?
13 What colour were the horses for Edward and Sophie's wedding carriage ride?
14 What is David Seaman's middle name?
15 Alfonso Bonilla Aragon International airport is in which country?
16 Rowan Atkinson attended which university?
17 Junior Braithwaite was the original lead singer with which group?
18 Who said "There's only one difference between a madman and me. I am not mad."?
19 How old was Charlie Watts when he took part in the Rolling Stones 1999 tour?
20 Where was the Stone of Scone stolen from on 25th December 1950?
21 Under which name does Sheila Holland write romantic fiction?
22 Which country does the airline Augusta come from?
23 What star sign is Sir David Attenborough?
24 Who directed the movie Heaven Can Wait?
25 What is Adam Faith's real name?

## Answers

***Pot Luck 5***

**1** Acrobat. **2** Lyndon Johnson. **3** Tragedy. **4** John. **5** Brian Aldiss. **6** Colorado. **7** Cody Jarrett. **8** Tony Blair. **9** Brixton. **10** W B Yeats. **11** Badminton. **12** AND. **13** White. **14** Andrew. **15** Colombia. **16** Newcastle. **17** The Wailers. **18** Salvador Dali. **19** 58. **20** Westminster Abbey. **21** Charlotte Lamb. **22** Australia. **23** Taurus. **24** Warren Beatty. **25** Terry Nelhams.

# Quiz 11 TV Soaps

1. Which 60s pop star played a hairdresser in Albion Market?
2. Which ex soap star used to host The Saturday Banana?
3. Which EastEnders actress recorded the song Little Donkey?
4. Who was the head of the sect which Zoe joined in Coronation Street?
5. Which soap actress switched on the Oxford Street Christmas lights in 1983?
6. Who played Mrs Eckersley in Emmerdale before becoming more famous in EastEnders?
7. As well as Liz McDonald which other character has Beverley Callard played in Coronation Street?
8. Who played Malcolm Nuttall in Coronation Street?
9. Rosa di Marco in EastEnders was which assistant of Dr Who in a previous life?
10. Who did Angie leave Albert Square with as she headed for Majorca?
11. In which soap did Chris Lowe of The Pet Shop Boys appear as himself?
12. Which EastEnders character was played by David Scarboro until the actor's early death?
13. Which soap actress played Marsha Stubbs in Soldier Soldier?
14. What were the second surname Valene had in Knot's Landing?
15. Which actor who found fame as a soap star played DI Monk in the first series of Birds of a Feather?
16. Who left EastEnders and appeared in the drama Real Women?
17. What did Bill Roache alias Ken Barlow study at university?
18. The scorer Charles of Telly Addicts has been a regular in which soap for many years?
19. What was the name of the EastEnders video about the Mitchell brothers released in 1998?
20. In EastEnders what football team did Simon Wicks support?
21. What was Kylie Minogue's character's profession in Neighbours?
22. In what type of vehicle did Fallon leave at the end of The Colbys?
23. Which Coronation Street actor conducted the Halle Orchestra in 1989?
24. What is Sinbad's real name in Brookside?
25. In which soap was soap's first test tube baby born?

## Answers

***TV Soaps***

**1** Helen Shapiro. **2** Susan Tully. **3** June Brown. **4** Nirab. **5** Pat Phoenix. **6** Pam St Clement. **7** June Dewhurst. **8** Michael Ball. **9** Leela. **10** Sonny. **11** Neighbours. **12** Mark Fowler. **13** Denise Welch. **14** Gibson. **15** Ross Kemp. **16** Michelle Collins. **17** Medicine. **18** The Archers. **19** Naked Truths. **20** West Ham. **21** Car mechanic. **22** Flying saucer. **23** William Tarmey. **24** Thomas. **25** Crossroads.

# Quiz 12 Pot Luck 6

1 What is Ben Hollioake's middle name?
2 What is the name of the Westminster building near Big Ben designed to provide extra accommodation for MPS?
3 In which film did Mae West say, "Beulah, peel me a grape"?
4 Sky Harbour international airport is in which US state?
5 Under what name did Karol Wojtyla become known to millions?
6 Who said, "People who meet me for the first time leave thinking 'What a miserable git'"?
7 What's the first word of Stand By Your Man?
8 What name did Amy Johnson's De Haviland Gipsy Moth have?
9 Star Trek actor DeForest Kelley wanted to train as what?
10 Actress Lucy Davis is the daughter of which comedian?
11 Michael Lubowitz is better known by which name?
12 Vehicles from which country use the international registration letter YV?
13 What star sign is shared by Dennis Taylor and Brendan Foster?
14 Amborovy International airport is in which country?
15 What is the most popular creation of Terry Nation's?
16 What is the population of Brazil to the nearest million?
17 Who co presented Nice Time with Kenny Everett and Jonathan Routh?
18 What was Harold Wilson's real first name?
19 Who had a UK No 1 hit with Seasons In The Sun?
20 Which element symbol Bk was discovered in 1950?
21 Sky Harbour international airport is in which US state?
22 In which city did Rudolf Nureyev seek asylum and defect to the West?
23 How many years were between Sir Harold Macmillan's maiden speeches in the Houses of Lords and Commons?
24 Who wrote the story The Country Of The Blind?
25 When did the Queen present her first Christmas Day TV broadcast?

## Answers

***Pot Luck 6***

**1** Caine. **2** Portcullis House. **3** I'm No Angel. **4** Arizona. **5** Pope John Paul II. **6** Rowan Atkinson. **7** Sometimes. **8** Jason 1. **9** Doctor. **10** Jasper Carrott. **11** Manfred Mann. **12** Venezuela. **13** Capricorn. **14** Madagascar. **15** The Daleks. **16** 158 million. **17** Germaine Greer. **18** James. **19** Terry Jacks. **20** Berkelium. **21** Arizona. **22** Paris. **23** 60. **24** H G Wells. **25** 1957.

# Quiz 13 Around The UK

Level 3 

1 Which UK holiday resort had the motto "It's so bracing" from 1909?
2 Who created the Angel of the North?
3 What did the National Trust ban on its land in 1997?
4 Who designed Liverpool's Roman Catholic Cathedral?
5 Which London building designed by Alfred Waterhouse in the 19th century remains one of the most visited today?
6 In which city is the Bate Collection of Historical Instruments?
7 In which year was the first Mersey tunnel completed?
8 Where is the English end of the English Channel where it reaches its widest point?
9 Lots of people visit Alton Towers, but which county is it in?
10 Which architect was responsible for London's National Theatre?
11 In which county is the longest cave system in the UK?
12 Which London borough has the most blue plaques?
13 Who designed the eastern facade of Buckingham Palace early this century?
14 Edward Maddrell was the last Briton this century to have which language as his native tongue?
15 In which city is the world's oldest surviving passenger station?
16 In which Park are the Yorkshire based gardens of Tropical World?
17 Which city are you in if you visit the East Midlands Gas Museum?
18 To the nearest quarter of a million, how many people visited London Zoo in 1990?
19 In which city was the International Garden Festival held in 1984?
20 Which was the first of the UK cathedrals to charge admission?
21 How often does the Leeds International Pianoforte Competition take place?
22 Ben Nevis is the highest mountain in the UK, but which mountain comes next in height?
23 In which English county did Sir Robert Baden Powell hold his first Scout camp in 1907?
24 Which city has the oldest public library in England?
25 In which country was Coventry Cathedral architect Basil Spence born?

## Answers

***Around the UK***

**1** Skegness. **2** Antony Gormley. **3** Deer Hunting. **4** Edwin Lutyens. **5** Natural History Museum. **6** Oxford. **7** 1934. **8** Lyme Bay. **9** Staffordshire. **10** Denys Lasdun. **11** West Yorkshire. **12** Westminster. **13** Aston Webb. **14** Manx. **15** Manchester. **16** Roundhay Park. **17** Leicester. **18** 1,250,000. **19** Liverpool. **20** St Paul's. **21** Every three years. **22** Ben Macdhui. **23** Dorset. **24** Manchester. **25** India.

# Quiz 14 Pot Luck 7

1 What have Americans Bobby Riggs, Bob Falkenberg and Ted Schroeder all done?
2 What star sign is Freddie Starr?
3 What is Dionne Warwick's real first name?
4 When was the Daily Mirror founded?
5 Who described a Hollywood studio set as, "The biggest train set a boy ever had"?
6 In Mork and Mindy, what was the Orkan phrase for 'Goodbye'?
7 San Antonio international airport is in which US state?
8 Who wrote the novel The Story So Far?
9 How old was Dodi Fayed at the time of his death in 1997?
10 In which country is the Angostura bridge?
11 Where in England was John Cleese born?
12 What are the international registration letters of a vehicle from Bangladesh?
13 Which union leader said in the 70s, "Come on (lads) get your snouts in the trough"?
14 In which country did Basil Hume study theology?
15 Which cartoons are associated with Kim Casalli?
16 Where was William Kellogg working when he decided to sell cornflakes?
17 In Robin's Nest what was Robin's Nest?
18 On which special day did Charlie Chaplin die in 1977?
19 Amilcar Cabral International airport is in which country?
20 Which national newspaper reappeared in 1979 following a year-long strike?
21 Who was Sgt Fletcher in the Miss Marple series with Joan Hickson before becoming another detective's assistant?
22 What was Blondie's last UK No 1 of the 80s?
23 What is Elle Macpherson's real name?
24 Who directed Apocalypse Now?
25 Which country does the airline Braathens SAFE come from?

## Answers

***Pot Luck 7***

**1** Won Wimbledon men's singles. **2** Capricorn. **3** Marie. **4** 1903. **5** Orson Welles. **6** Nanu Nanu. **7** Texas. **8** Eric Ambler. **9** 42. **10** Venezuela. **11** Weston Super Mare. **12** BD. **13** Sidney Weighell. **14** Switzerland. **15** Love is. **16** Hospital. **17** Fulham restaurant. **18** Christmas Day. **19** Cape Verde. **20** The Times. **21** Kevin Whately. **22** The Tide Is High. **23** Eleanor Gow. **24** Francis Ford Coppola. **25** Norway.

# Quiz 15 90s

1. What finally knocked (Everything I Do) I Do It For You off the No 1 position?
2. How many singles had the Manic Street Preachers put out before releasing a single that made the top three?
3. Before B*Witched who last made the top twenty with a song called Rollercoaster?
4. Which UK male vocalist had a Peacock Suit at No 5 in 1996?
5. What was the first UK No 1 in the 1990s by Wet Wet Wet?
6. The theme from Friends was a No 3 hit for which group in 1995?
7. Who partnered Whitney Houston on When You Believe?
8. Which hit for D:Ream gave them their first Top Ten hit?
9. Which country was Rozalla from?
10. What was Snaps' first UK Top Ten hit?
11. What was the first record of the 90s to enter the charts at No 1?
12. Who was featured on Puff Daddy's Come with Me?
13. What was the second successive No 1 for Aqua?
14. Who covered You Might Need Somebody to No 4 in 1997?.
15. Who had a UK No 1 hit with Please Don't Go in 1992?
16. Who joined Cher, Chrissie Hynde and Neneh Cherry on Love Can Build A Bridge?
17. What was the follow up to Saturday Night for Whigfield?
18. What nationality is Tina Arena?
19. Which Ace of Base hit was first to get into the Top Ten after All That She Wants?
20. Who sang with Elton John on his only Top Ten of 1996?
21. Who was the featured vocalist on the No 1 Killer by Adamski?
22. Whose first UK No 1 was Ice Ice Baby?
23. Who joined Debbie Gibson on You're The One That I Want?
24. What was Gina G's follow up to her Eurovision entry?
25. Which airline banned Liam Gallagher for life?

## Answers

***90s***

**1** The Fly. **2** 14. **3** Grid. **4** Paul Weller. **5** Goodnight Girl. **6** Rembrandts. **7** Mariah Carey. **8** Things Can Only Get Better. **9** Zimbabwe. **10** The Power. **11** Bring Your Daughter To The Slaughter. **12** Jimmy Page. **13** Doctor Jones. **14** Shola Ama. **15** KWS. **16** Eric Clapton. **17** Another Day. **18** Australian. **19** The Sign. **20** Luciano Pavarotti. **21** Seal. **22** Vanilla Ice. **23** Craig McLachlan. **24** I Belong To You. **25** Cathay Pacific.

# Quiz 16 Pot Luck 8

Level 3 

1 What first did Bobbie Knox achieve on Aug 21st 1965?
2 Which US politican said, "Always forgive your enemies, but never forget their names."?
3 Declan McManus is better known by which name?
4 Where in Spain is the Dali Museum?
5 Who starred in the films Our Hospitality and The Navigator?
6 In which country was Timothy Dalton born?
7 What was Stephen Potter's word for letting someone know things weren't quite right?
8 Who wrote an autobiography called Stare Back and Smile?
9 Alan Hope was the first person to win an election for which British political party?
10 In which decade was the Greater New Orleans bridge opened?
11 What star sign is shared by Sandy Lyle and Colin Jackson?
12 Vehicles from which country use the international registration letter WAN?
13 Which TV presenter was lead singer with Kenny?
14 Who was the first female to have a UK No 1 hit?
15 How many times did Valenina Tereshkova orbit the Earth in her 1963 space flight?
16 What is actress Debra Winger's real first name?
17 Which of the US state did Arnold Palmer come from?
18 Which continuing TV programme made its debut on 11th November 1953?
19 Aminu International airport is in which country?
20 In which year were the twin Gibb brothers, Maurice and Robin, born?
21 For what was Georgia O'Keefe noted?
22 Who created Dan Dare?
23 What is the population of Chile to the nearest million?
24 Which country does the airline COPA come from?
25 Which Puccini opera was first performed in 1926?

## Answers

***Pot Luck 8***

**1** First scoring sub in an English soccer game. **2** Bobby Kennedy. **3** Elvis Costello. **4** Figueres. **5** Buster Keaton. **6** Wales. **7** One-Upmanship. **8** Joanna Lumley. **9** Monster Raving Loony Party. **10** 1950s. **11** Aquarius. **12** Nigeria. **13** Keith Chegwin. **14** Jo Stafford. **15** 48 times. **16** Marie. **17** Pennsylvania. **18** Panorama. **19** Nigeria. **20** 1949. **21** Painting. **22** Frank Hampson. **23** 14 million. **24** Panama. **25** Turandot.

# Quiz 17 Famous Names

1 Who said, "An alcoholic is someone you don't like who drinks as much as you do"?
2 Who created the Mars bar?
3 What would Diane Keaton's surname have been if she had used her father's name instead of her mother's?
4 Who had the catchphrase "nicky nokky, noo!"?
5 Who is the wife of Brian Blosil and father of their seven children?
6 Arnold Bax said one should try everything once except incest and what?
7 Who was dubbed the Brazilian Bombshell?
8 In 1998 who did Vanity Fair describe as "simply the world's biggest heart throb"?
9 Whose business motto was 'Pile it high, sell it cheap'?
10 Who said "I became one of the stately homos of England"?
11 Journalist Dawn Alford was responsible for 'trapping' which famous in name in the late 90s?
12 How many days after Princess Diana's death was the death of Mother Teresa announced?
13 Which fellow politician was Kenneth Clarke's best man?
14 Which actor owned the restaurant Langan's Brasserie?
15 In which High Street store did Glenda Jackson work?
16 Which ex MP and broadcaster has a daughter called Aphra Kendal?
17 Which playwright went to the same school as Adrian Edmondson?
18 Michael Grade became a director of which soccer club in 1997?
19 Which American said, "Boy George is all England needs; another Queen who can't dress"?
20 What do kd lang's initials stand for?
21 Whose portrait was removed form an exhibition called Sensation at the Royal Academy in 1997?
22 Which singer wrote the novel Amy The Dancing Bear?
23 Jeffrey Archer became Lord Archer of where on elevation to the peerage?
24 Who was John Major's last heritage Secretary?
25 What part of his body did Keith Richards insure for £1 million?

## Answers

***Famous Names***

**1** Dylan Thomas. **2** Forrest Mars. **3** Hall. **4** Ken Dodd. **5** Marie Osmond. **6** Folk dancing. **7** Carmen Miranda. **8** Leonardo DiCaprio. **9** Jack Cohen. **10** Quentin Crisp. **11** William Straw. **12** Five. **13** John Selwyn Gummer. **14** Michael Caine. **15** Boots. **16** Gyles Brandreth. **17** Tom Stoppard. **18** Charlton Athletic. **19** Joan Rivers. **20** Kathryn Dawn. **21** Myra Hindley. **22** Carly Simon. **23** Weston Super Mare. **24** Virginia Bottomley. **25** Third finger, left hand.

# Quiz 18 Pot Luck 9

Level 3 

1 Which US First Lady said, "No one can make you feel inferior unless you consent."?
2 Who brought to an end Jahangir Khan's long unbeaten run of success in squash in the 80s?
3 Which luxury did Esther Rantzen choose on Desert Island Discs?
4 According to Rudyard Kipling what were the "two impostors" to meet and treat the same?
5 Peninsula international airport is in which US state?
6 Who was British Prime Minister when independence was granted to India, Pakistan and Ceylon?
7 When was the Scrabble world championshiop first held?
8 Who wrote the novel The Information?
9 What did Abraham Saperstein start in January 1927?
10 What is Geoffrey Howe's real first name?
11 Who duetted with Barbra Streisand on Till I Loved You in 1988?
12 What are the international registration letters of a vehicle from Barbados?
13 What was David Bowie's last UK No. 1 of the 80s?
14 Where in England was Tom Courtenay born?
15 Jomo Kenyatta was born into which tribe?
16 What star sign is Prince Andrew?
17 Which European country was the first to allow women the vote?
18 Who was the defending champion when Bjorn Borg first won Wimbledon singles?
19 Arlanda International airport is in which country?
20 In which year was Grace Kelly born?
21 Which group recorded the first record played on Radio 1?
22 Which country does the airline TAAG come from?
23 What was first published on 21st December 1913 in the New York World?
24 Who directed The Silence of the Lambs?
25 What is Bob Wilson's middle name?

## Answers

***Pot Luck 9***

**1** Eleanor Roosevelt. **2** Ross Norman. **3** Bath salts. **4** Triumph and Disaster. **5** California. **6** Clement Attlee. **7** 1991. **8** Martin Amis. **9** Harlem Globetrotters. **10** Richard. **11** Don Johnson. **12** BDS. **13** Dancing In The Street. **14** Hull. **15** Kikuyu. **16** Pisces. **17** Finland. **18** Arthur Ashe. **19** Sweden. **20** 1929. **21** The Move. **22** Angola. **23** A crossword. **24** Jonathan Demme. **25** Primrose.

# Quiz 19 US Presidents

1 Which US President did Guiseppe Zangara attempt to assassinate?
2 Who was vice president directly before Spiro Agnew?
3 Who used the line "Randy, where's the rest of me?" as the title of an early autobiography?
4 Which US President had the middle name Wilson?
5 What day of the week was Kennedy assassinated?
6 Dean Acheson was US Secretary of State under which President?
7 Which US President was the heaviest?
8 Which President is credited with the quote, "If you can't stand the heat get out of the kitchen"?
9 Who was the first assassin of a US President this century?
10 Who was the first US President to have been born in a hospital?
11 Which President conferred honorary US citizenship on Winston Churchill?
12 What did Ronald Reagan describe as a shining city on a hill?
13 Who said, "A radical is a man with both feet planted firmly in the air"?
14 In 1996 who was Bob Dole's Vice Presidential candidate?
15 Which US President was described as looking like "the guy in a science fiction movie who is first to see the Creature"?
16 Who described Ronald Reagan's policies as "Voodoo economics"?
17 What type of car was Kennedy travelling in when he was shot?
18 Which aristocratic title is one of Jimmy Carter's Christian names?
19 Al Gore was Senator of which state before becoming Bill Clinton's Vice President in 1992?
20 How old was John F Kennedy's assassin?
21 Who was the Democrat before Clinton to be elected for a second term?
22 Who was Richard Nixon named after?
23 What was the name of the report into J F Kennedy's assassination?
24 What was the name of Kitty Kelley's biography of Jackie Kennedy Onassis?
25 Which president's campaign slogan was "Why not the best"?

## Answers

***US Presidents***

**1** Roosevelt. **2** Hubert Humphrey. **3** Ronald Reagan. **4** Reagan. **5** Friday. **6** Truman. **7** William Taft. **8** Harry S Truman. **9** Leon Czolgosz. **10** Jimmy Carter. **11** Kennedy. **12** USA. **13** Roosevelt. **14** Jack Kemp. **15** Gerald Ford. **16** George Bush. **17** Lincoln. **18** Earl. **19** Tennessee. **20** 24. **21** FD Roosevelt. **22** Richard the Lionheart. **23** Warren Report. **24** Jackie Oh!. **25** Jimmy Carter.

# Quiz 20 Pot Luck 10

1 Which popular actor's last words were, "It's all been rather lovely"?
2 What is the population of Egypt to the nearest million?
3 What is Jane Russell's real first name?
4 Who did Ray Reardon beat in the final in his last snooker World Championship triumph?
5 Who followed Woodrow Wilson as US President?
6 Peterson Field international airport is in which US state?
7 Who had a UK No 1 hit with Kung Fu Fighting?
8 What star sign is shared by Vanessa Redgrave and Bobby Robson?
9 Which sporting world championship has been held at the Kuusinski and Kitka Rivers in Finland?
10 In which country is the Bendorf bridge?
11 Who did Anthea Turner work for before she began her TV career?
12 Vehicles from which country use the international registration letter WAL?
13 Who was the last man to win Wimbledon and the French Open singles in the same year?
14 In which decade was insulin first used to treat a diabetic sufferer?
15 Who wrote the words to Thank Heaven For Little Girls?
16 The fabulous Cullinan diamond was cut into how many separate gems?
17 Who wrote the theme song for Hearts of Gold?
18 Simon Mayo and Timmy Mallet studied at which university?
19 Arturo Marino Benitez International airport is in which country?
20 In which year was the first two-minute silence commemorating the Great War held?
21 Gun toting Wyatt Earp survived to what age?
22 Which country does the airline Tower Air come from?
23 Which song by a solo singer stopped T Rex's classic Ride A White Swan from getting to No 1?
24 What was Bob Hoskins' profession when he worked in the circus?
25 Who resigned in December 1990 as Soviet Foreign Minister?

## Answers

***Pot Luck 10***

**1** John Le Mesurier. **2** 61 million. **3** Ernestine. **4** Perrie Mans. **5** Warren Harding. **6** Colorado. **7** Carl Douglas. **8** Aquarius. **9** Fly fishing. **10** Germany. **11** AA. **12** Sierra Leone. **13** Bjorn Borg. **14** 20s. **15** Alan Jay Lerner. **16** 105. **17** Lynsey de Paul. **18** Warwick. **19** Chile. **20** 1919. **21** 80. **22** USA. **23** Grandad. **24** Fire-eater. **25** Edvard Shevardnadze.

# Quiz 21 Sport 90s Action Replay

1 Who was the first driver in the 90s to win the first F1 race and not end the season as champion?
2 How many century breaks did John Higgins make in the 1998 World Championship?
3 At which ground did Brian Lara make his record innings of 375?
4 What was the score when England met Uruguay at Wembley in 1990?
5 Who won the first all American French Open Men's Singles final for almost 40 years?
6 How many points did Damon Hill score in his season for Arrows?
7 In which sport did Eric Navet of France become a 1990 world champion?
8 Where did Jonathan Edwards set his 1995 triple jump world record?
9 Which jockey went flat out on the flat set a record with 1068 rides in the 1992 season?
10 Who was Jeremy Bates' partner in winning the Australian mixed doubles?
11 After six consecutive finals, how many frames did Stephen Hendry win in the 1998 World Championship?
12 Up to his departure in Nov 98, how many years had Roy Evans been with Liverpool?
13 Who finally beat Bob Beaman's 20 plus year long jump record?
14 Who hit a century in some 22 minutes in a county game in July, 1993?
15 Jim Leighton retired after winning how many Scottish soccer caps?
16 Which horse was Henry Cecil's first Oaks winner of the 90s?
17 Alec Stewart was captain for how many Tests?
18 Which horse finished second when Oath won the 1999 Derby?
19 Against which country did Ryan Giggs make his international debut?
20 Who were the first team in the 90s to bat first in a Nat West Final and win?
21 What is Linford Christie's best time for 100m?
22 In which sport have Uhlenhorst Mullheim dominated 90s Europe?
23 Which snooker star made a witnessed practice break of 149 in 1995?
24 Which American state renewed Mike Tyson's boxing licence in 1998?
25 Sanath Jayasuriya set belted a limited overs century v Pakistan in 1996 off how many balls?

## Answers

***Sport 90s Action Replay***

**1** David Coulthard - in 1997. **2** 14. **3** Recreation Ground. **4** 2-1 to Uruguay. **5** Jim Courier. **6** 7. **7** Show jumping. **8** Sweden. **9** Michael Roberts. **10** Jo Durie. **11** 4. **12** 35. **13** Mike Powell. **14** Glen Chapple - of Lancashire. **15** 91. **16** Lady Carla. **17** 11. **18** Daliapour. **19** Germany. **20** Lancashire. **21** 9.87. **22** Hockey. **23** Tony Drago. **24** Nevada. **25** 48.

# Quiz 22 Pot Luck 11

1 Who was the next British Prime Minister after Arthur Balfour?
2 Who narrated Stoppit and Tidyup?
3 What was Brotherhood Of Man's last UK No 1 of the 70s?
4 What is Russ Abbot's real name?
5 From which country did Angola achieve independence in 1975?
6 Which novel written in 1813 was adapted into one of TV's hits of the 90s?
7 What first appeared in Ohio in 1914 to affect transport?
8 Who said, "Anybody wishing to banish theft from the world must cut off the thief's hands"?
9 What star sign is Michael Caine?
10 Who wrote the novel Evening Class?
11 Which TV presenter was once in a group called Jet Bronx and the Forbidden?
12 What are the international registration letters of a vehicle from Belize?
13 Banting and Best pioneered the use of what?
14 What did Emma Forbes present on Going Live!?
15 Where in England was Dame Judi Dench born?
16 In which decade did Billboard magazine first publish an American hit chart?
17 Asmara International airport is in which country?
18 In which year did Andy Capp first appear in the Daily Mirror?
19 Which was the first European country to abolish capital punishmnent?
20 How many soccer World Cup campaigns was Walter Winterbottom involved with for England?
21 What was Enoch Powell's real first name?
22 Which country does the airline Air Pacific come from?
23 Which Irish TV celebrity received a Papal knighthood for charitable works?
24 On which lake was Donald Campbell killed?
25 Who directed the movie La Dolce Vita?

## Answers

***Pot Luck 11***

**1** Campbell-Bannerman. **2** Terry Wogan. **3** Figaro. **4** Russell Roberts. **5** Portugal. **6** Pride and Prejudice. **7** First traffic lights. **8** Ayatollah Khomeini. **9** Pisces. **10** Maeve Binchy. **11** Loyd Grossman. **12** BH. **13** Insulin. **14** Cooking. **15** York. **16** 30s. **17** Eritrea. **18** 1957. **19** Norway. **20** Four. **21** John. **22** Fiji. **23** Eamonn Andrews. **24** Coniston. **25** Federico Fellini.

# Quiz 23 Who's Who?

1. Who described his acting range as "left eyebrow raised, right eyebrow raised"?
2. Which actor became playwright Arthur Miller's son in law in 1997?
3. Who played the King of Messina in the 90s Much Ado About Nothing?
4. Who said, "I squint because I can't take too much light"?
5. Who was Geena Davis's husband when they made the loss maker Cutthroat Island?
6. In 1993 who tried to buy the rights of his first movie Sizzle Beach USA?
7. Which star of The Krays wrote a prose and poetry book called America?
8. Who owned the LA nightclub The Viper Room at the time of River Phoenix's death there in 1993?
9. Which future First Lady had walk on parts in Becky Sharp and Small Town Girl in the 30s?
10. Who was described by co star Nick Nolte as, "... a ball buster. Protect me from her"?
11. Which sportsman appeared as himself in the 1964 film The Beauty Jungle?
12. Which actress was Roger Moore's first Bond girl?
13. Who was the star of the film based on the record Harper Valley PTA by Jeannie C Riley?
14. Which actress is ex beauty queen Miss Orange County 1976?
15. Which actress perished in the shower in the remake of Psycho?
16. Which film director was Anthony Quinn's father in law?
17. Who wrote the screenplay for The Crying Game?
18. Which novelist appeared in the film Day For Night?
19. What is Barbra Streisand's middle name?
20. How many films had Christopher Reeve made before Superman in 1978?
21. Who starred in Roger Vadim's remake of And God Created Woman?
22. Which actress wrote the novel The Last of the Really Great Whangdoodles?
23. Which film maker's first film was Pather Panchali?
24. Who did Winona Ryder replace on the set of Mermaids?
25. How is Paul Reubens also known in the film and TV world?

## Answers

***Who's Who?***

**1** Roger Moore. **2** Daniel Day-Lewis. **3** Richard Briers. **4** Clint Eastwood. **5** Renny Harlin. **6** Kevin Costner. **7** Steven Berkoff. **8** Johnny Depp. **9** Patricia Nixon. **10** Barbra Streisand. **11** Stirling Moss. **12** Jane Seymour. **13** Barbara Eden. **14** Michelle Pfeiffer. **15** Anne Heche. **16** Cecil B de Mille. **17** Neil Jordan. **18** Graham Greene. **19** Joan. **20** One. **21** Rebecca de Mornay. **22** Julie Andrews. **23** Satyajit Ray. **24** Emily Lloyd. **25** Pee Wee Herman.

# Quiz 24 Pot Luck 12

1 What is Lily Savage's 'daughter' called?
2 Who came on when Gary Lineker was controversially pulled off in his last international?
3 Stewart Goddard is better known by which name?
4 What star sign is shared by Prince Andrew and Princess Michael of Kent?
5 Who was the US President during World War I?
6 What is Neil Simon's real first name?
7 Which theatre was home to the final edition of TV's The Good Old Days?
8 Who had a UK No 1 hit with Ms. Grace?
9 What is the population of France to the nearest million?
10 In which country is the Great Belt East bridge?
11 In which country was Emilio Estevez born?
12 Vehicles from which country use the international registration letter ROU?
13 Which Corrie wedding took place the same year as Meg & Hugh Mortimer?
14 Which comedian said of his wild image, "... really I am Mr Mortgage"?
15 Where in Britain were the first deaths caused by an air raid?
16 Who was the last undisputed boxing world heavyweight champion before Mike Tyson?
17 Which country's invasion of Ethiopia in 1935 forced Haile Selassie to flee?
18 What is John Cleese's middle name?
19 Augusto C Sandino International airport is in which country?
20 Which star duetted with David Essex on True Love Ways in 1994?
21 Raleigh international airport is in which US state?
22 Which country does the airline Air Littoral come from?
23 Which brand had to apologise for a logo said to be like the Arabic for Allah?
24 King George VI conferred an Order of Merit on which former PM in 1951?
25 What was Hudson's first name in the TV series Upstairs Downstairs?

**Answers**

***Pot Luck 12***

**1** Bunty. **2** Alan Smith. **3** Adam Ant. **4** Pisces. **5** Woodrow Wilson. **6** Marvin. **7** The City Varieties Theatre, Leeds. **8** Tymes. **9** 58 million. **10** Denmark. **11** USA. **12** Uruguay. **13** Ray and Deirdre Langton's. **14** Rik Mayall. **15** Great Yarmouth. **16** Leon Spinks. **17** Italy. **18** Marwood. **19** Nicaragua. **20** Catherine Zeta Jones. **21** North Carolina. **22** France. **23** Nike. **24** Clement Attlee. **25** Angus.

# Quiz 25 Famous Faces

Level 3 

1 Which former Gladiator presented Finders Keepers?
2 What is Rowan Atkinson's middle name?
3 Which part of Dave Allen's body is partly missing?
4 Which TV interviewer was South of England show jumping champion in 1964?
5 Who designed the original Blue Peter badge?
6 Which Brit won the American Sportscasters' Association International Award in 1989?
7 Who played Pte Mick Hopper in Lipstick on Your Collar before shooting to film superstardom?
8 How old was Twiggy when she appeared on This Is Your Life?
9 Who was the first sports presenter on Newsnight?
10 What luxury did Bob Monkhouse choose on Desert Island Discs?
11 Whose TV debut was presenting Hippo on Sky's Superchannel?
12 Where does Roseanne have a tattoo of a pink rose?
13 Which star of EastEnders appeared on a Sammy Davis Jr Special along with Mandy Rice-Davies?
14 What was the Earl of Wessex's TV programme about his great uncle called?
15 What was Jo Brand's profession before being a successful comic?
16 For which series did Emma Thompson win her second successive best actress BAFTA?
17 Which TV detective had received the George Cross?
18 Des O'Connor had a football trial with which club?
19 What was Zoe Ball's first children's show on terrestrial TV?
20 What relation is Jon to Peter Snow?
21 Which famous TV face was part of the girl band Faith, Hope and Charity?
22 Jim Davidson became a director of which soccer club in 1981?
23 Who presented the first edition of News At Ten?
24 Which character did Anthony Andrews play in The Pallisers before finding fame in Brideshead Revisited?
25 What was Trevor McDonald's codename for This Is Your Life?

**Answers**

***Famous Faces***

**1** Diane Youdale. **2** Sebastian. **3** Finger. **4** Jonathan Dimbleby. **5** Tony Hart. **6** Harry Carpenter. **7** Ewan McGregor. **8** 20. **9** David Davies. **10** Picture of Marilyn Monroe. **11** Gaby Roslin. **12** Foot. **13** Wendy Richard. **14** Edward on Edward. **15** Psychiatric nurse. **16** The Fortunes of War. **17** Frost. **18** Northampton Town. **19** The O Zone. **20** Cousin. **21** Dani Behr. **22** Bournemouth. **23** Alastair Burnet. **24** Lord Stockbridge. **25** Burger.

# Quiz 26 Pot Luck 13

1. What was Bette Davis' real first name?
2. In which decade was Alzheimer's disease first clinically described?
3. What star sign is Glenda Jackson?
4. Who was the first British Prime Minister to be born overseas?
5. Robert Mueller Municipal Airport is in which US state?
6. Which sitcom star was married to script writer Jeremy Lloyd for only four months?
7. What was the first name of the original food manufacturer Mr Heinz?
8. How old was Ronald Reagan when he became US President?
9. Which country does the airline Garuda come from?
10. Which Brit broke the land speed record in 1990 in Thrust 2?
11. Who wrote The Ghost Road?
12. What are the international registration letters of a vehicle from Bahrain?
13. In which sport did Hollywood star Sonja Henie win Olympic Gold?
14. Which soccer side does Tim Vincent support?
15. In which brothers pop group was Craig Logan not a brother?
16. What was David Cassidy's last UK No 1 of the 70s?
17. Where in England was Albert Finney born?
18. In soccer, who holds Liverpool's league appearance record?
19. Balice International airport is in which country?
20. Panama proclaimed independence in 1903 from which country?
21. How old was Jimi Hendrix when he died?
22. Which sculptor died in a fire in a studio in the 70s?
23. Who directed How The West Was Won?
24. What is Christian Slater's real name?
25. Which song by a solo singer stopped Penny Lane from getting to No 1?

## Answers

***Pot Luck 13***

**1** Ruth. **2** First decade. **3** Taurus. **4** Bonar Law. **5** Texas. **6** Joanna Lumley. **7** Henry. **8** 69. **9** Indonesia. **10** Richard Noble. **11** Pat Barker. **12** BRN. **13** Ice skating. **14** Wrexham. **15** Bros. **16** Daydreamer. **17** Salford. **18** Ian Callaghan. **19** Poland. **20** Colombia. **21** 27. **22** Barbara Hepworth. **23** John Ford. **24** Christian Hawkins. **25** Release Me.

# Quiz 27 Euro Tour

1 In which city is the Glynn Vivian Art Gallery and Museum?
2 Which city did Truman Capote describe as "eating an entire box of chocolate liqueurs in one go"?
3 Where in Europe is the Sikkens Museum of Signs?
4 Which monarch popularised the Homburg which came from the German town of the same name?
5 What is Switzerland's largest city?
6 Which city was the cultural capital of Europe in 1990?
7 Which architect designed the Pompidou Centre in Paris?
8 In which European city would you go to the Bardini Museum and the Bargello Museum?
9 What is the name of the lake which remained when the Zuider Zee was closed and reclaimed in 1932?
10 Which country was the first to break away from Yugoslavia after Tito's death?
11 Where is the Optimisticeskaja cave, the second longest in the world?
12 How many countries does the Danube pass through?
13 Which European country saw one of the major avalanches of the 20th century in December 1916?
14 What is the second largest of the Ionian Islands?
15 Where is Tingwall airport?
16 Where would you be if the Parliament was called The Althing?
17 Down which valley does the Mistral blow?
18 Inishmor is part of which island group?
19 Syracuse is part of New York, but where does it exist in Europe?
20 Which European country was first this century to give women the vote?
21 What is Europe's second largest city in terms of population?
22 Where would you spend stotinki?
23 Which French phrase described an innovative movement in the cinema?
24 Which was the first European city this century to open an underground railway system?
25 What is the longest river in Portugal, and the fifth longest in Europe?

**Answers**

***Euro Tour***

**1** Swansea. **2** Venice. **3** The Hague. **4** Edward VII. **5** Zurich. **6** Glasgow. **7** Richard Rodgers. **8** Florence. **9** Ijsselmeer. **10** Slovenia. **11** Ukraine. **12** Seven. **13** Italy. **14** Corfu. **15** Lerwick. **16** Iceland. **17** Rhone. **18** Aran. **19** Sicily. **20** Finland. **21** London. **22** Bulgaria. **23** Nouvelle vague. **24** Paris. **25** Tagus.

# Quiz 28 Pot Luck 14

1 Who said "A man is only as old as the woman he feels."?
2 Donna Gaines is better known by which name?
3 Which team were at home when Matthew Fox died in an after match street brawl?
4 In which decade was the Academy of Ancient Music orchestra founded?
5 What is the population of Germany to the nearest million?
6 What had Edmund Hillary worked at before taking up mountain climbing?
7 In which American state is the Isabella Stewart Gardner Museum?
8 Which group was Martine McCutcheon in before finding fame in EastEnders?
9 Who first read the football results on Grandstand?
10 In which decade was the Kincardine bridge opened?
11 How old was Bjorn Borg when he decide to retire?
12 Vehicles from which country use the international registration letter RM?
13 Who was resident chef on Good Morning With Anne & Nick?
14 Which country did Thor Heyerdahl's Kon-Tiki set sail from on its journey to Eastern Polynesia?
15 Which element is named after Pierre and Marie Curie?
16 What star sign is shared by Leslie Ash and Lynn Redgrave?
17 What was Mr Magoo's first name?
18 In 1912 Albert Berry made the first successful what?
19 Benina International airport is in which country?
20 Which rectory burned down in 1939 was said to be the most haunted place in Britain?
21 Who was runner up when Jody Scheckter won the F1 championship?
22 Which country does the airline Gulf Air come from?
23 What is Alistair Cooke's real first name?
24 How old was Laurel and Hardy producer Hal Roach when he died in 1992?
25 Who was West German Chancellor from 1969 to 1974?

## Answers

***Pot Luck 14***

**1** Groucho Marx. **2** Donna Summer. **3** Gillingham. **4** 70s. **5** 82 million. **6** Bee keeping. **7** Massachusetts. **8** Milan. **9** Leonard Martin. **10** 1930s. **11** 26. **12** Madagascar. **13** Ainsley Harriott. **14** Peru. **15** Curium. **16** Pisces. **17** Quincy. **18** Parachute jump. **19** Libya. **20** Borley. **21** Giles Villeneuve. **22** Bahrain. **23** Alfred. **24** 100. **25** Willy Brandt.

# Quiz 29 Charts

1 Who was the first female with two UK million-selling singles?
2 Which was the first Spice Girls hit which did not reach No 1?
3 Whose debut album Ten Good Reasons was the UK's top seller in '89?
4 Which female artist was the first to achieve 32 consecutive UK Top 10 hits?
5 Who was the first act to put his first eleven hits into the UK Top Ten?
6 Who topped the US chart in 1976 with the triple-platinum album Breezin'?
7 Who sang on at least one hit every year for 33 years?
8 Which band released the chart topping album Steeltown in 1984?
9 Which hit reached No 1 in the UK and US for Phil Collins?
10 Who was the first UK male to score two US Top Ten hits?
11 Whose debut single was How Do I Live?
12 Who had a UK No 1 in 1998 with You Make Me Wanna?
13 Who was the first act to release eight singles which entered at No 1?
14 Which group achieved the UK's biggest selling album of 1994?
15 What was on the original double A side of Prince's No 1 hit 1999?
16 What was the title of U2's third UK No 1?
17 Who was the first UK group to top the US chart after The Beatles?
18 Who was the first female to score twelve hits in the American Top Five?
19 Who, after Gerry and the Pacemakers, were first to reach No 1 with their first three releases?
20 Who had a UK No 10 hit in 1987 with Walk The Dinosaur?
21 What was the Monkees' first Top Ten UK hit after their first No 1?
22 What was the top selling single of 1998?
23 What was the Manic Street Preachers' second UK Top Ten hit?
24 Whose first UK Top Ten hit was You're Still The One?
25 What was the first Top Ten hit of the 90s for Michael Jackson?

## Answers

***Charts***

**1** Celine Dion. **2** Stop. **3** Jason Donovan. **4** Madonna. **5** Gary Glitter. **6** George Benson. **7** Diana Ross. **8** Big Country. **9** A Groovy Kind of Love. **10** Lonnie Donegan. **11** LeAnn Rimes. **12** Usher. **13** Take That. **14** Bon Jovi. **15** Little Red Corvette. **16** Discotheque. **17** Animals. **18** Olivia Newton-John. **19** Frankie Goes to Hollywood. **20** Was (Not Was). **21** A Little Bit of Me A Little Bit of You. **22** Never Ever. **23** A Design For Life. **24** Shania Twain. **25** Black or White.

# Quiz 30 Pot Luck 15

Level 3 

1 What was Phil Collins' last UK No 1 of the 80s?
2 What are Paul Ince's middle names?
3 Who discovered the layer of electrically charged particles in the upper atmosphere which now bears his name?
4 Since the first to 18 frames began in snooker's World Championship who recorded the lowest losing score in a final?
5 What was replaced by Teletext Ltd in 1993?
6 In which year did Alcock and Brown make their Atlantic crossing?
7 Which singer wrote the musical Someone Like You?
8 In Coronation Street how did Ken Barlow's first wife die?
9 Who created the St Trinians schoolgirls?
10 In which country is the Howrah bridge?
11 Who was the first person to fly at over 100 miles an hour?
12 What are the international registration letters of a vehicle from Brunei?
13 What was Oliver Hardy's real first name?
14 Who wrote Babel Tower?
15 Benito Juarez International airport is in which country?
16 Otis Barton was a pioneer in exploring where?
17 Where in England was Nigel Hawthorne born?
18 What would the Kelvin Scale have been called if it had adopted the originator's first name?
19 What is Sigourney Weaver's real name?
20 In which principal language did TV station S4C begin transmitting in 1982?
21 In which year were the first Winter Olympics?
22 Which country does the airline Gronlandsfly come from?
23 What star sign is Bob Carolgees?
24 Who directed The Exorcist?
25 What was Jeremy Beadle's profession when he worked in the circus?

## Answers

***Pot Luck 15***

**1** A Groovy Kind of Love. **2** Emerson Carlyle. **3** Edward Appleton. **4** John Parrot. **5** Oracle. **6** 1919. **7** Petula Clark. **8** Electrocuted with a hair dryer. **9** Ronald Searle. **10** India. **11** Lionel Twiss. **12** BRU. **13** Norvell. **14** A.S. Byatt. **15** Mexico. **16** Underwater. **17** Coventry. **18** William Scale. **19** Susan Weaver. **20** Welsh. **21** 1924. **22** Greenland. **23** Taurus. **24** William Friedkin. **25** Ringmaster.

# Quiz 31 20th C Celebs

1. Who said, "Some women get excited about nothing - and then they marry him"?
2. What was the occupation of Roger Moore's father?
3. Which newspaper did Lord Linley sue in 1990?
4. What breed of dog was Barry Manilow's Bagel?
5. Who was fashion designer of the year in 1990?
6. Which White House resident's book was a bestseller in the late 80s?
7. Who was the fourth successive PM this century to go to a state school?
8. Who became Paul Mowatt's mother in law when he joined the Royal Family in the 90s?
9. Pamela Stephenson stood for Parliament for which party?
10. Which TV presenter owned a restaurant called Midsummer House?
11. Who was Jeremy Irons' best man?
12. What is the name of Dave Stewart and Siobhan Fahey's son?
13. Who said, "I'd rather have a cup of tea than go to bed with someone – any day"?
14. Who is the famous mother of Elijah Blue?
15. Who designed Victoria Adams' wedding dress?
16. Which rock star did Cindy Crawford name her first son after?
17. What did Michael Jackson say instead of "I do" when he married Lisa Marie Presley?
18. Who said, "The only place a man wants depth in a woman is in her decolletage"?
19. In which Sydney cathedral did Michael Hutchence's funeral take place?
20. Who became chief designer at Givenchy in 1996?
21. Whose first West End club was the Hanover Grand?
22. Who was Axl Rose's famous singer father in law?
23. Who was Joaquim Cortes' girlfriend, who was rushed to hospital after a suspected overdose in 1997?
24. Who designed the dress which made the most at Diana's dress auction?
25. Richard Gere won a scholarship to the University of Massachusetts in which sport?

## Answers

***20th C Celebs***

**1** Cher. **2** Policeman. **3** Today. **4** Beagle. **5** Vivienne Westwood. **6** Millie the dog. **7** Thatcher. **8** Princess Alexandra. **9** Blancmange Thrower. **10** Chris Kelly. **11** Christopher Biggins. **12** Django. **13** Boy George. **14** Cher. **15** Vera Wang. **16** Presley. **17** Why not?. **18** Zsa Zsa Gabor. **19** St Andrew's. **20** Alexander McQueen. **21** Piers Adam. **22** Don Everly. **23** Naomi Campbell. **24** Victor Edelstein. **25** Gymnastics.

# Quiz 32 Pot Luck 16

1 Florence Nightingale was the first and chemist Dorothy Hodgkin was the second woman to be awarded what?
2 Who was the only British PM to die at No 10 Downing Street?
3 What is Richard Gere's real name?
4 How is J Murray Spangler's invention known today?
5 South Pole explorer Roald Amundsen vanished flying over where?
6 What is the name of Sophie Rhys-Jones' elder brother?
7 In which US state was Buddy Holly born?
8 In On the Up how did Mrs Wembley respond when offered a drink?
9 Pioneering doctor Elizabeth Garrett Anderson took her medical exams in which language?
10 Oakland international airport is in which US state?
11 In what year were passport photos first required in Britain?
12 Vehicles from which country use the international registration letter RL?
13 Who was General Manager of the Saturday Superstore?
14 John Landy became the first Australian to do what?
15 In which country was Michael Gambon born?
16 What is the population of Greece to the nearest million?
17 Who was the first person to win the BBC Sports Personality of the Year twice?
18 In his day job which paper does Spiderman work for?
19 Beira International airport is in which country?
20 Who presented the first Gang Show for Scouts in 1932?
21 In which decade did Honda start to manufacture cars?
22 Which country does the airline Transavia Airlines come from?
23 What was West Indian fast bowler Joel Garner's nickname?
24 What star sign is shared by Roger Daltrey and Quincy Jones?
25 Who had a UK No 1 hit with Forever and Ever?

**Answers**

***Pot Luck 16***
**1** Order Of Merit. **2** Campbell-Bannerman. **3** Richard Gere. **4** Hoover. **5** North Pole. **6** David. **7** Texas. **8** Just the one!. **9** French. **10** California. **11** 1915. **12** Lebanon. **13** Mike Read. **14** Sub four minute mile. **15** Ireland. **16** 10 million. **17** Henry Cooper. **18** Daily Bugle. **19** Mozambique. **20** Ralph Reader. **21** 60s. **22** Netherlands. **23** Big Bird. **24** Pisces. **25** Slik.

# Quiz 33 First 50 Years

1 The British police adopted fingerprinting after it had been used where?
2 In what month was the attack on Pearl Harbor?
3 Which magazine ran the "Your country needs you!" ad which was then used widely for recruitment?
4 What did the Labour Party change its name from after the 1906 Election?
5 Who was British PM when independence was granted to India and Pakistan?
6 In 1939 who described the actions of Russia as "a riddle wrapped in a mystery inside an enigma"?
7 Whose epitaph reads "Hereabouts died a very gallant gentleman"?
8 In which month did the 1951 election take place?
9 Who became mayor of Cologne in 1945?
10 At which Embassy did Kim Philby work with Guy Burgess after WWII?
11 In 1910 Paul Ehrlich developed a cure for which disease?
12 Who was Churchill referring to when he said "never was so much owed by so many to so few"?
13 In Nazi Germany what was Endl slung?
14 Who founded the American Institution of Public Opinion in 1935?
15 Who was the first President of the National Union of Women's Suffrage Societies?
16 Who did L S Amery say "In the name of God go!" to in 1940?
17 Which writer and politician became Lord Tweedsmuir?
18 At which British airport did Neville Chamberlain wave the Munich agreement in 1938 believing he had averted war?
19 "A bridge too far" referred to airborne landings in which country?
20 Which future MP was president of the Oxford Union in 1947?
21 On whose tomb are the words "They buried him among Kings because he had done good toward God and toward his house"?
22 Tora tora tora was the signal to attack Pearl Harbor but what does it mean?
23 Who said Chamberlain was "a good mayor of Birmingham in an off year"?
24 The Rotary Club was founded in 1905 in which American city?
25 Who was Hitler's Prime Minister in Prussia?

## Answers

***First 50 Years***

**1** India. **2** December. **3** London Opinion. **4** Labour Representative Committee. **5** Attlee. **6** Churchill. **7** Captain Oates. **8** October. **9** Konrad Adenauer. **10** Washington. **11** Syphilis. **12** RAF pilots in the Battle of Britain. **13** The Final Solution. **14** Gallup. **15** Millicent Fawcett. **16** Neville Chamberlain. **17** John Buchan. **18** Heston. **19** Netherlands. **20** Tony Benn. **21** Unknown Soldier. **22** Tiger. **23** Lloyd George. **24** Chicago. **25** Goering.

# Quiz 34 Pot Luck 17

1 Who said, "It is better to die on your feet than live on your knees"?
2 In which decade did motor car pioneer Henry Ford die?
3 What is Viv Richard's real first name?
4 On what date in 1969 did Neil Armstrong first set foot on the moon?
5 What star sign is Barry Norman?
6 What was the day job that Boris Yeltsin started out with?
7 Where did Tessa Sanderson finish in the 1992 Olympics?
8 Which supermodel said. "I look very scary in the mornings"?
9 What position did Alfred Austin hold from 1896 to 1913?
10 Which Spice Girl appeared in Emmerdale as an extra?
11 What nationality were Mother Teresa's parents?
12 What are the international registration letters of a vehicle from The Bahamas?
13 What was Jason Donovan's last UK No 1 of the 80s?
14 In which year did Tanganyika and Zanzibar merge to form Tanzania?
15 Who wrote the novel Love Solves The Problem?
16 Bandar Seri Begawan International airport is in which country?
17 Who presented sport on Saturday Superstore?
18 Where in England was Bob Hoskins born?
19 What was special about Fred Balasare's 1962 Channel swim?
20 What is Diane Keaton's real name?
21 Lincoln international airport is in which US state?
22 Which country hosted the very first Eurovision Song Contest?
23 How many teams contested the first World Cup held in 1930?
24 Who was Richard Nixon's Vice President from 1973 to 1974?
25 Who directed The Sting?

## Answers

***Pot Luck 17***

**1** Emiliano Zapata. **2** 40s. **3** Isaac. **4** July 20th. **5** Leo. **6** Builder. **7** 4th. **8** Linda Evangelista. **9** Poet Laureate. **10** Mel B. **11** Albanian. **12** BS. **13** Sealed With A Kiss. **14** 1964. **15** Barbara Cartland. **16** Brunei. **17** David Icke. **18** Bury St Edmunds. **19** Swam underwater. **20** Diane Hall. **21** Nebraska. **22** Switzerland. **23** 13. **24** Gerald Ford. **25** George Roy Hill.

# Quiz 35 Sport Who's Who

1 Who was the last person to score for both teams in an FA Cup Final?
2 Which England cricket captain has played hockey for London University?
3 Who was the oldest British Open winner of the century?
4 Which sportswoman wrote the novel Total Zone?
5 Who was the first winner of the first to18 frames format in snooker's World Championship?
6 Who was the only American Wimbledon men's singles champion of the 60s?
7 Who said, "The atmosphere is so tense you could cut it with a cricket stump"?
8 Who was the first National Hunt jockey to reach 1000 wins?
9 Who was the winner of the last Open at Carnoustie before Paul Lawrie?
10 Bill Beaumont established the then record for captaining England _ how many times?
11 Who is the youngest ever Wightman Cup player?
12 Who was hacked down when Scholes got his second England booking v Sweden?
13 Roberto Rempi was the doctor of which sportsperson in a 90s drugs row?
14 Who won the Oaks on Dunfermline, Sun Princess and Unite?
15 Which record breaker became Master of Pembroke College, Oxford in the 80s?
16 Arnaud Massey is the only Frenchman to have won what?
17 Which snooker champion was a torch-bearer at the 1956 Melbourne Olympics?
18 John Potter has been England's most capped player in which sport?
19 Who was the British soccer manager sacked by Real Madrid in 1990?
20 Who was champion jockey on the flat five times in the 50s?
21 Who was Ole Gunnar Solskjaer playing for before he joined Man Utd?
22 Who scored England's winner in Italia 90 v Egypt?
23 Who was runner up when Niki Lauda won his last F1 championship?
24 What is Brian Lara's middle name?
25 Who rode Arkle to a hat trick of Cheltenham Gold Cup triumphs?

**Answers**

***Sport Who's Who***

**1** Gary Mabbutt. **2** David Gower. **3** Robert de Vincenzo - 44 years 93 days. **4** Martina Navratilova. **5** Cliff Thorburn. **6** Chuck McKinley. **7** Murray Walker. **8** Stan Mellor. **9** Tom Watson. **10** 21. **11** Jennifer Capriati. **12** Schwarz. **13** Marco Pantani. **14** Willie Carson. **15** Roger Bannister. **16** Golf's British Open. **17** Eddie Charlton. **18** Hockey. **19** John Toshack. **20** Doug Smith. **21** Molde. **22** Mark Wright. **23** Alain Prost. **24** Charles. **25** Pat Taffe.

# Quiz 36 Pot Luck 18

1 What star sign is shared by John Major and Sir David Frost?
2 Which character was on the first cover of the Beano?
3 What is the population of India to the nearest million?
4 What is Fidel Castro's real first name?
5 At which hospital did the first heart transplant take place?
6 Who had a UK No 1 hit with Free?
7 Which British news reader interviewed Saddam Hussein just before the Gulf War?
8 What did Anne Robinson's report on on Breakfast Time?
9 Who was the next British Prime Minister after Ramsay Macdonald?
10 In which country is the Humen bridge?
11 Who has been Pope longest in the 20th C?
12 Vehicles from which country use the international registration letter RCB?
13 What did the M stand for in J M Barrie's name?
14 Who was in charge at Blackburn after Roy Hodgson's sacking and before Brian Kidd's arrival?
15 Who wrote an autobiography called I Was Ena Sharples' Father?
16 Bill Skate and Julius Chan had been 90s Prime Ministers of which country?
17 Which veteran rock musician said, "If I had my time again I would like to take up archaeology"?
18 Which future film star played Angela Reid in Emmerdale?
19 Bole International airport is in which country?
20 How many caps did Bobby Robson gain as an England player?
21 Which British fashion designer received her OBE on 15th December 1992?
22 Hubert Humphrey was Vice President to which US President?
23 What is Robson Green's middle name?
24 Which country does the airline Kiwi International Airlines come from?
25 In which year was the State Opening of Parliament televised for the first time?

## Answers

***Pot Luck 18***

**1** Aries. **2** Big Eggo - an ostrich. **3** 953 million. **4** Ruz. **5** Groote Schuur. **6** Deniece Williams. **7** Trevor McDonald. **8** TV. **9** Baldwin. **10** China. **11** John Paul II. **12** Congo. **13** Matthew. **14** Tony Parkes. **15** Tony Warren. **16** Papua New Guinea. **17** Bill Wyman. **18** Joanne Whalley. **19** Ethiopia. **20** 20. **21** Vivienne Westwood. **22** Lyndon Johnson. **23** Golightly. **24** USA. **25** 1958.

# Quiz 37 Musical Movies

Level 3 

1 Who directed Finian's Rainbow, his first film for a major studio?
2 Who played a character based on Bob Fosse in a 1979 Oscar winning film?
3 Where in Europe was much of Evita filmed?
4 Who directed the film version of Hair?
5 Which musical was Victor Fleming making the same time as he was making Gone With the Wind?
6 What was Xanadu in the title of the film?
7 Who was the voice of O'Malley in The Aristocats?
8 In which 70s musical did Paul Michael Glaser star?
9 How many different hats does Madonna wear in Evita?
10 Who played the title role in the film version of Jesus Christ Superstar?
11 In Cabaret, what was the profession of Sally Bowles' father?
12 In which film was chorus girl Peggy Sawyer told to "come back a star!"?
13 What are the last lines of My Fair Lady?
14 What was the name of the brothel in The Best Little Whorehouse in Texas?
15 Which musical includes the lines "Got no cheque books, got no banks. Still I'd like to express my thanks"?
16 What was the name of the butler in The Rocky Horror Picture Show?
17 Which Club featured in cabaret?
18 "The corn is as high as an elephant's eye" is in which musical?
19 Who was the male star of the movie The Man of La Mancha?
20 What was the name of Bob Fosse's character in All That Jazz?
21 In Saturday Night Fever where does Tony work by day?
22 A Little Night Music was based on which non musical film?
23 What was the name of the sax player in New York New York who fell for Francine?
24 Who was the father in law of the male star of Grease 2?
25 In The Muppet Movie what was the name of the restaurant Doc Hopper wanted to open?

## Answers

***20th C Musical Movies***

**1** Francis Ford Coppola. **2** Roy Scheider. **3** Hungary. **4** Milos Forman. **5** The Wizard of Oz. **6** Roller disco. **7** Phil Harris. **8** Fiddler on the Roof. **9** 39. **10** Ted Neeley. **11** US diplomat. **12** 42nd Street. **13** Where the devil are my slippers. **14** Chicken Ranch. **15** Annie Get Your Gun. **16** Riff Raff. **17** Kit Kat. **18** Oklahoma. **19** Peter O'Toole. **20** Joe Gideon. **21** DIY store. **22** Smiles of a Summer Night. **23** Jimmy. **24** John Mills - star was Maxwell Caulfield. **25** Frogs' Legs.

# Quiz 38 Pot Luck 19

1 What is Billy Ocean's real name?
2 What was The Zaire River called before 27th October 1971?
3 In which London street was Jill Dando murdered?
4 Who is credited with the discovery of galaxies outside of our own?
5 Tom Dennis was the first runner up in a world ranking final in which sport?
6 Logan international airport is in which US state?
7 Alan Freed is usually credited for popularising which expression?
8 What was Duran Duran's last UK No 1 of the 80s?
9 In the 80s, what did AD&D stand for?
10 Which satellite channel was originally called CBN Satellite Service in the US?
11 In which month of the year did Bing Crosby record White Christmas?
12 What are the international registration letters of a vehicle from Canada?
13 What star sign is Suzanne Dando?
14 When was the Daily Star founded?
15 In the early days of Grange Hill what was Tucker Jenkins real first name?
16 Who wrote the novel Fairy Tale?
17 Who was the defending champion when Andre Agassi first won Wimbledon singles?
18 How many people was Howard Hughes' Spruce Goose meant to carry?
19 Boukhalef International airport is in which country?
20 Who beat Ilie Nastase in the 1972 Men's Singles Final at Wimbledon?
21 In which European city is the Belvederen Gallery?
22 Which country does the airline Transkei Airways come from?
23 Where in England was John Hurt born?
24 Who directed the movie The African Queen?
25 What is Sir Norman Fowler's real first name?

## Answers

***Pot Luck 19***

**1** Leslie Charles. **2** Congo. **3** Gowan Avenue. **4** Edwin Hubble. **5** Snooker. **6** Massachusetts. **7** Rock'n'roll. **8** The Reflex. **9** Advanced Dungeons and Dragons. **10** Family Channel. **11** May. **12** CDN. **13** Cancer. **14** 1978. **15** Peter. **16** Alice Thomas Ellis. **17** Michael Stich. **18** 750. **19** Morocco. **20** Stan Smith. **21** Vienna. **22** South Africa. **23** Chesterfield. **24** John Huston. **25** Peter.

# Quiz 39 Quiz & Game Shows

1 What were Neil and Christine Hamilton presented with when they appeared on Have I Got News For You?
2 What was the name of the quiz show on Crackerjack?
3 Which record was broken on the first Record Breakers?
4 Who presented the first edition of The Golden Shot?
5 Mastermind champion Christopher Hughes followed which profession?
6 Which quiz of the 80s was hosted by Angela Rippon?
7 Which US show was University Challenge based on?
8 Which show was based on a Dutch programme called One From Eight?
9 In the very first University Challenge Reading played who?
10 Which Radio 5 Live presenter was the first UK host of Wheel of Fortune?
11 Who is acknowledged as the Creator of Countdown?
12 For how many years were there female winners of Mastermind before the programme had its first male winner?
13 On which part of Double Your Money could you win the £1,000?
14 Who hosted ITV's early rival to Telly Addicts, We Love TV?
15 Which female joined Jeremy Beadle on Game For A Laugh after Sarah Kennedy?
16 Which show offered losers a Dusty Bin?
17 What was the junior version of Big Break called?
18 Who presented Ice Warriors?
19 What surname did Malandra Burrows, later of Emmerdale, use when she appeared on New Faces aged nine?
20 Who replaced Terry Wogan on Blankety Blank?
21 Who first presented The Price is Right in the UK?
22 Which celebrity chef produced the first recipe book spin off from Ready Steady Cook with Brian Turner?
23 Who was the very first woman to be a Call My Bluff team captain, albeit for a one off special?
24 Who hosted What's My Line? when it was revived yet again in 1994?
25 Who did Carol Smillie replace on Wheel of Fortune?

**Answers**

***20th C Quiz and Game Shows***

**1** Brown envelopes. **2** Double or Drop. **3** Biggest one man band. **4** Jackie Rae. **5** Train driver. **6** Masterteam. **7** College Bowl. **8** The Generation Game. **9** Leeds. **10** Nicky Campbell. **11** Armand Jammot. **12** Three. **13** Treasure Trail. **14** Gloria Hunniford. **15** Rustie Lee. **16** 3-2-1. **17** Big Break - Stars of the Future. **18** Dani Behr. **19** Newman. **20** Les Dawson. **21** Leslie Crowther. **22** Anthony Worrall Thompson. **23** Joanna Lumley. **24** Emma Forbes. **25** Angela Ekaette.

# Quiz 40 Pot Luck 20

1 What was John Major's father's profession in the circus?
2 How old was George Gershwin when he died?
3 Who won the 90s European Cup Final staged at Wembley?
4 In which country did Paris born Paul Gaugin spend his childhood?
5 Who was US President at the start of the 20th C?
6 Here we ask what was the year, when Rupert Bear did first appear?
7 Which actress's real name is Ilynea Lydia Mironoff?
8 Which ex Prime Minister became the first Earl of Bewdley?
9 Eugene Wiedmann was the last person to meet his death how in 1939?
10 Which country does the airline Linjeflyg come from?
11 Which knight has appeared on Baywatch?
12 Vehicles from which country use the international registration letter RCH?
13 What is John Humphry's real first name?
14 Who had a UK No 1 hit with Ring My Bell?
15 Whose alter ego was Gayle Tuesday?
16 What star sign is shared by William Shatner and Marlon Brando?
17 What is the population of Iran to the nearest million?
18 Which game show did Annabel Croft star in after Treasure Hunt?
19 Bromma International airport is in which country?
20 On 26th October in which year did the Beatles receive their MBEs?
21 In the classic sitcom Mr Ed, what did Mr Ed call Wilbur?
22 In which decade was the Tay road bridge opened?
23 What was patented in 1903 by Italian merchant Italio Marcione?
24 In which country was Audrey Hepburn born?
25 What is Keanu Reeves' real name?

## Answers

***Pot Luck 20***

**1** Trapeze artist. **2** 38. **3** Barcelona - in 1992. **4** Peru. **5** William McKinley. **6** 1920. **7** Helen Mirren. **8** Stanley Baldwin. **9** Guillotined. **10** Sweden. **11** Sir Paul McCartney. **12** Chile. **13** Desmond. **14** Anita Ward. **15** Brenda Gilhooly. **16** Aries. **17** 62 million. **18** Interceptor. **19** Sweden. **20** 1965. **21** Buddy Boy. **22** 1960s. **23** Ice Cream Cone. **24** Belgium. **25** Keanu Reeves.

# Quiz 41 On the Road

1 Which tree features most frequently in London street names?
2 In which year was the National Parks and Access to the Countryside Act passed?
3 In 1983 which car company ran an April Fool's day ad for an open top car that kept out the rain?
4 The fastest man on land at the beginning of this century came from which country?
5 Which town did Britain's first motorway bypass?
6 Which was the last country in mainland Europe to switch to driving on the left?
7 In what year did the millionth Volkswagen roll of the assembly line?
8 In which country were motorised ambulances first used?
9 By the end of the 80s, what percentage of British households had two cars?
10 When did the first Morris car appear?
11 Which work designed by Aston Webb do people drive under in London?
12 Which Asian country has the longest road network?
13 Where was the world's first production line producing Model T Fords?
14 According to a 50s ad what was the loudest noise in the new Rolls Royce?
15 Where was Stenson Cooke's signature seen by motorists in the early years of the century?
16 What was the starting price for a Morris Cowley when it came of the production line in 1920?
17 Who was the President of the AA at the beginning of the 1990s?
18 When were yellow lines used as parking restrictions on Britain's roads?
19 How old must you be to accompany a learner driver?
20 In which city was the first Model T produced outside the USA?
21 Which celebrity chose a motorway service station as a luxury when he appeared on Desert Island Discs?
22 In which city is the Blackfriars Museum of Antiquities?
23 What animal appears on a road sign to show there are wild animals?
24 Where were London's first traffic lights installed in 1926?
25 Which company manufactured the first car to run on diesel?

## Answers

***On the Road***

**1** Elm. **2** 1949. **3** BMW. **4** Belgium. **5** Preston. **6** Sweden. **7** 1955. **8** France. **9** 20%. **10** 1913. **11** Admiralty Arch. **12** India. **13** Detroit. **14** Electric clock. **15** First AA badge - he was its secretary. **16** £165. **17** Duke of Kent. **18** 1958. **19** 21. **20** Manchester. **21** Noel Edmonds. **22** Newcastle. **23** Stag. **24** Piccadilly Circus. **25** Mercedes Benz.

# Quiz 42 Pot Luck 21

1 Which golfer said, "Grey hair is great. Ask anyone who's bald."?
2 What was Rambo's first name?
3 What is Anthea Turner's middle name?
4 Which Coronation Street actress is patron of the Manchester Taxi Drivers Association?
5 In which decade did Oor Wullie appear in the Sunday Post?
6 Bill Cosby had a professional trial in which sport?
7 What is the most common street name in the UK?
8 What star sign is Michael Jackson?
9 What was Frankie Goes To Hollywood's last UK No. 1 of the 80s?
10 In which country is the Lake Pontchartrain Causeway bridge?
11 How long had Perez Prado been out of the pop charts before his 90s return?
12 What are the international registration letters of a vehicle from Sri Lanka?
13 Which former Coronation Street actor was a skilled stuntman?
14 What did Kent Walton commentate on on World of Sport?
15 What is Tessa Sanderson's middle name?
16 Which actress made her film debut in The Shop at Sly Corner?
17 Who wrote Ash on an Old Man's Sleeve?
18 What is Davina Murphy's real first name?
19 Bujumbura International airport is in which country?
20 Where was the painting The Scream stolen from on 12th December 1994?
21 What is Mica Paris' real name?
22 Who were the first soccer club to have a royal spectator?
23 Who directed the movie East of Eden?
24 Where in England was Glenda Jackson born?
25 Lubbock international airport is in which US state?

**Answers**

***Pot Luck 21***

**1** Lee Trevino. **2** John. **3** Millicent. **4** Liz Dawn - Vera Duckworth. **5** 30s. **6** American football. **7** High Street. **8** Virgo. **9** The Power of Love. **10** USA. **11** 36 years. **12** CL. **13** Bryan Mosley. **14** Wrestling. **15** Ione. **16** Diana Dors. **17** Francis King. **18** Georgina. **19** Burundi. **20** Oslo. **21** Michelle Wallen. **22** Burnley. **23** Elia Kazan. **24** Liverpool. **25** Texas.

# Quiz 43 Legends

1 Who has accumulated the most UK and US Top 10 albums and grossed most income from foreign touring?
2 Who was Elton John's early idol?
3 Which superstar fronted The Nomads and Blackjack before going solo?
4 Who was posthumously awarded a Lifetime Achievement Grammy in 1996?
5 Who compered Buddy Holly's only UK tour?
6 Which artist has spent most weeks in the UK Top Ten?
7 Who married Julianne Phillips in May 1985 in Oregon?
8 Who issued bonds in his name for people to invest in in 1997?
9 Who was the first group to hold the top two US and UK album places on the week of release?
10 Which duo were joined by Tammy Wynette on their No 2 in 1991?
11 Who won the BRIT award for Outstanding Contribution to British Music in 1996?
12 Who had a record eight albums simultaneously in the UK chart three months after his death?
13 Which name links Whitney Houston's childhood nickname with her TV Production company?
14 Who made his stage debut in a 1960 production of The Pyjama Game?
15 What honour was awarded to Eric Clapton in January 1995?
16 Who duetted on the 1992 version of Crying with Roy Orbison?
17 How many UK Top Ten hits has Marvin Gaye had since his death?
18 Who jumped off the top of a moving bus during a Swedish tour and broke a foot?
19 Who was awarded a Lifetime Achievement Award at the 1993 Brit Awards?
20 Who collaborated with Michael Bolton on Bolton's Steel Bars hit?
21 Who did Celine Dion support in his Canadian tour in 1991?
22 Who is the sister of the drummer of the Dakotas during their 60s heyday?
23 Whose autobiography was titled Laughter in the Rain?
24 Which group sponsored Clydebank Football Club in 1993?
25 Who had a rabies jab after biting a rat on stage?

## Answers

***Legends***

**1** Rolling Stones. **2** Winifred Atwell. **3** Michael Bolton. **4** Marvin Gaye. **5** Des O'Connor. **6** Elvis Presley. **7** Bruce Springsteen. **8** David Bowie. **9** Guns 'N'Roses. **10** KLF. **11** David Bowie. **12** Jim Reeves. **13** Nippy. **14** David Cassidy. **15** OBE. **16** k.d.lang. **17** One. **18** Liam Gallagher. **19** Rod Stewart. **20** Bob Dylan. **21** Michael Bolton. **22** Elkie Brooks. **23** Neil Sedaka. **24** Wet Wet Wet. **25** Ozzy Osbourne.

# Quiz 44 Pot Luck 22

1 Which TV series intro said, "Return with us now to those thrilling days of yesteryear..."?
2 What star sign is shared by Peter Gabriel and Stevie Wonder?
3 Who had a UK No 1 hit with Together We Are Beautiful?
4 What is the population of Italy to the nearest million?
5 What is Marie Osmond's real first name?
6 Which boxer is quoted as saying, "He can run, but he can't hide"?
7 Who was Prime Minister at the beginning of the century?
8 Albert Giacometti found fame as what?
9 Which actress's autobiography was called Hold on to the Messy Times?
10 Who first flew in Friendship 7?
11 Who or what was Dale Winton named after?
12 Vehicles from which country use the international registration letter RB?
13 Who wrote the novel Gentlemen Prefer Blondes?
14 Whose barrel organ played the music for The Magic Roundabout?
15 Where did Brad Pitt, Darcey Bussell and William Hague appear together?
16 In which German city was the original Volkswagen factory?
17 What were mortgage rates in Feb 1990 - an all time high?
18 Who sang a solo at Prince Charles and Lady Di's wedding?
19 Calabar International airport is in which country?
20 Who wrote the Channel 4 sitcom Blue Heaven?
21 McCarran international airport is in which US state?
22 Which country does the airline LOT come from?
23 What was W.G. Grace's profession other than a cricketer?
24 Which British gold medallist had the middle name Wipper?
25 In which year did Wimbledon's famous commentator Dan Maskell die?

**Answers**

***Pot Luck 22***

**1** The Lone Ranger. **2** Taurus. **3** Fern Kinney. **4** 58 million. **5** Olive. **6** Joe Louis. **7** Marquis of Salisbury. **8** Sculptor. **9** Sue Johnston. **10** John Glenn. **11** Dale Robertson the actor. **12** Botswana. **13** Anita Loos. **14** Mr Rusty. **15** Madame Tussaud's. **16** Wolfsburg. **17** 15.4%. **18** Kiri Te Kanawa. **19** Nigeria. **20** Frank Skinner. **21** Nevada. **22** Poland. **23** Doctor. **24** Allan Wells. **25** 1992.

# Quiz 45 Heroes & Villains

Level 3 

1 Which prison did Jonathan Aitken go to after he was convicted in 1999?
2 What was the official occupation of Sir Anthony Blunt who was unmasked as a Soviet spy in 1979?
3 Which fictional character was based on Scottish soldier William Ironside?
4 Who said, "Being a thief is a terrific life, but the trouble is they do put you in the nick for it"?
5 Under who did Joseph McCarthy carry out his 'witch hunts'?
6 Where did Ferdinand Marcos live in exile?
7 Which MP wrote The Young Meteors?
8 Which medal did Robert Maxwell win in WWII?
9 Which terrorist group murdered Italian PM Aldo Moro?
10 Which was the first party Oswald Mosley was in Parliament with?
11 Which American was nicknamed Old Blood and Guts?
12 Who was Jeremy Thorpe accused of attempting to murder in 1976?
13 Which Conservative MP was killed by an IRA bomb in 1990?
14 Which organisation handed over Brian Keenan in Beirut after 1600 days?
15 Which stockbroker was given an 18 month prison sentence for his role in the Guinness scandal?
16 According to Neil Kinnock whose principles "produce martyrdom for the followers and never sacrifice the leaders"?
17 Which company headed by Asil Nadir collapsed in 1990?
18 In 1985 Terry Waite returned to Beirut after securing the release of four British hostages where?
19 Which little boy who appeared on TV screens with Saddam Hussein as one of his 'guests' during the Gulf crisis?
20 Where did the Pope land on his arrival in Britain in 1982?
21 General Boris Gromov was the last Soviet soldier to leave where in 1989?
22 In the Profumo scandal which Russian had an affair with Christine Keeler?
23 Who referred to drawing "a line in the sand" about the Gulf War?
24 What was Ronald Biggs official occupation when he was convicted of the Great Train Robbery?
25 What was Mother Teresa's real first name?

**Answers**

***20th C Heroes & Villains***

**1** Standford Hill. **2** Art historian. **3** Richard Hannay. **4** John McVicar. **5** Truman. **6** Hawaii. **7** Jonathan Aitken. **8** Military Cross. **9** Red Brigades. **10** Conservative. **11** Patton. **12** Norman Scott. **13** Ian Gow. **14** Islamic Dawn. **15** Tony Parnes. **16** Arthur Scargill. **17** Polly Peck. **18** Libya. **19** Stuart Lockwood. **20** Cardiff. **21** Afghanistan. **22** Ivanov. **23** George Bush. **24** Carpenter. **25** Agnes.

# Quiz 46 Pot Luck 23

1 What star sign is Jamie Lee Curtis?
2 Where in England was Derek Jacobi born?
3 What was Gary Glitter's last UK No. 1 of the 70s?
4 To become PM Alec Douglas-Home renounced his peerage as what number Earl of Home?
5 What is Kiki Dee's real name?
6 Who played Johnny McKenna in The Detectives?
7 At which university did Joseph Goebbels become a doctor of philosophy?
8 How old was Damon Hill when he started Formula 1 racing?
9 What was the profession of Sir David Frost's father?
10 Who was the only Spice Girl not to have a middle name?
11 How did Jock die in Dallas?
12 Which country does the airline LACSA come from?
13 What did Janet Street Porter sell at auction in 1997?
14 Which songwriter sang backing lyrics on Lily the Pink by Scaffold?
15 What is Bruce Willis' real first name?
16 Which innovation for the car was developed by Prince Henry of Prussia in 1911?
17 How is Joan Molinsky better known?
18 Which British writer won the Nobel Prize for Literature in 1983?
19 The VS-300 was a type of what?
20 Who wrote the novel The Statement?
21 McCoy international airport is in which US state?
22 What are the international registration letters of a vehicle from Algeria?
23 Which Lloyd Webber musical premiered in the US on 10th December 1993?
24 Who directed 2001 : A Space Odyssey?
25 Which TV presenter shares a birth date with Bobby Hatfield of The Righteous Brothers?

## Answers

***Pot Luck 23***

**1** Scorpio. **2** Leytonstone. **3** Always Yours. **4** 14th. **5** Pauline Matthews. **6** Jimmy Tarbuck. **7** Heidelberg. **8** 32. **9** Clergyman. **10** Posh Spice. **11** Helicopter accident. **12** Costa Rica. **13** Dresses. **14** Tim Rice. **15** Walter. **16** Windscreen wipers. **17** Joan Rivers. **18** William Golding. **19** Helicopter. **20** Brian Moore. **21** Florida. **22** DZ. **23** Sunset Boulevard. **24** Stanley Kubrick. **25** Gloria Hunniford.

# Quiz 47 90s News

1 Which David headed the Cult which staged a 1993 mass suicide in
2 Waco?
3 How many Northern Ireland MP's were there at the 1997 General
4 Election?
5 Who won Miss World the first time it was held in India?
6 Who won Taiwan's first democratic Presidential election?
7 Where was the UN Earth summit held in 1992?
8 What number TWA flight exploded shortly after take off in July 1996?
9 What was the name of the mother of the Iowa septuplets born in 1997?
10 Who did Grant Ferrie marry in prison in 1997?
11 Where in the USA was there a total eclipse in 1991?
What was O J Simpson driving in the famous police chase?
12 Britain's worst rail disaster involved a train travelling from where to
London in 1997?
13 Who went on trial for the Oklahoma bombing after Timothy McVeigh
was sentenced to death for the crime?
14 Who was the brother of the nurse Deborah Parry was accused of
15 murdering in Saudi Arabia?
16 What was the name of the judge in the Louise Woodward trial?
17 Who was investigated with Neil Hamilton in the cash for questions affair?
18 Which prominent Nigerian writer was executed in 1996?
19 Name the car in which Andy Green broke the land speed record in
20 1997?
21 Whose sacking caused an attack on Michael Howard by Ann Widdecombe?
Which company won a libel action against Dave Morris and Helen Street?
22 In which city did Princess Diana have her last meeting with Mother Teresa?
Which charity along with the Aids Crisis Trust chiefly benefited from
23 the sale of Diana's dresses at Christie's in 1997 ?
Which Kennedy was due to marry when John F Kennedy's plane
24 crashed on its way to the wedding?
25 In September 1996 who pledged a £1 million making it the then largest
donation to the Labour Party by any individual?

## Answers

***90s News***

**1** Koresh. **2** 17. **3** Irene Skliva. **4** Lee Teng-Hui. **5** Rio. **6** 800. **7** Bobbi McCaughey. **8** Lucille McLauchlan. **9** Hawaii. **10** Ford Bronco. **11** Swansea. **12** Terry Nichols. **13** Frank Gilford. **14** Hiller Zobel. **15** Tim Smith. **16** Ken Saro Wiwa. **17** Thrust. **18** Derek Lewis. **19** McDonalds. **20** New York. **21** Royal Marsden Cancer Fund. **22** Rory. **23** Matthew Harding. **24** Cigarettes. **25** Man Utd football.

# Quiz 48 Pot Luck 24

1. In which US state was Tennessee Williams born?
2. Which Hi De Hi star was a member of a group called Midnight News?
3. Who won soccer's World Cup with his last international goal?
4. What is Robert Redford's real first name?
5. Which country does the airline LTU International Airways come from?
6. In music, in which decade was the Academy of St Martin-in-the-Fields founded?
7. Who was the son of Jor-El and Lara Lor-Van?
8. What star sign is shared by Sir David Attenborough and Paula Yates?
9. Where in Canada is the Lion's Gate bridge?
10. Who had a UK No. 1 hit with Use It Up and Wear It Out?
11. What is the population of Japan to the nearest million?
12. Vehicles from which country use the international registration letter RA?
13. Who was pictured for the first time on new £10 notes isssued in 1975?
14. What is Julian Clary's real name?
15. Which writer was married to actor Clive Swift aka Richard Bucket?
16. In which American state is the Harrah's Auto Collection situated?
17. Who did Eamonn Holmes nickname Miss Tippy Toes?
18. Which musical star played Caroline Winthrop in Crossroads?
19. Carrasco International airport is in which country?
20. What did Richard Branson once pour over Clive Anderson?
21. What was the first single to sell over 2 million copies in the UK?
22. In which country was Anjelica Huston born?
23. What was the name of Rigsby's cat in TV's Rising Damp?
24. Who was Israeli Prime Minister from 1969 to 1974?
25. What are Lawrence Dallaglio's middle names?

## Answers

***Pot Luck 24***

**1** Mississippi. **2** Su Pollard. **3** Gerd Muller. **4** Charles. **5** Germany. **6** 50s. **7** Superman. **8** Taurus. **9** Vancouver. **10** Odyssey. **11** 126 million. **12** Argentina. **13** Florence Nightingale. **14** Julian Clary. **15** Margaret Drabble. **16** Nevada. **17** Anthea Turner. **18** Elaine Paige. **19** Uruguay. **20** Glass of water. **21** Mull Of Kintyre. **22** Ireland. **23** Vienna. **24** Golda Meir. **25** Bruno Nero.

# Quiz 49 20th C Summer Sports

Level 3 

1 How many times was Wes Hall named as Wisden Cricketer of the Year?
2 At which venue did Tony Jacklin win the US Open?
3 Who was the defending champion when Stefan Edberg first won the Wimbledon singles?
4 Who ended Graham Gooch's mammoth 333 England innings at Lord's?
5 Which horse landed the Derby and the Irish Derby in 1993?
6 Who was the last man out in England's 1999 World Cup campiagn?
7 What were the initials of W G Grace's brother who played for England?
8 What was the total prize money for the British Open in 1945?
9 Which country does sprinter David Ezinwa come from?
10 By the end of the 20th century which country has had the most Men's Singles winners at Wimbledon?
11 How many members joined the original International Amateur Athletic Federation?
12 Which assistant manager of England's cricket team sadly died of a heart attack on the 1981 tour of W Indies?
13 At which venue did Greg Norman first win the British Open?
14 In the summer of 98 Jap Stam joined Man Utd from which club?
15 Which golden girl athlete married comedian Bobby Knut?
16 Which Brit won the doubles at Wimbledon in 1987 and in Australia in 1991?
17 Who was the first lady golfer to land the British and US Open in the same year?
18 Which country did 70s French Open women's singles winner Virginia Rusici come from?
19 What is the nickname of cycling's Marco Pantani?
20 What was Sue Barker's highest world ranking?
21 Why was Kiernon Fallon fined £1000 at the 1999 Derby?
22 Gary Sobers' then record Test score of 365 was made against which team?
23 Who was Britian's first Singles winner at Wimbledon in the second half of the 20th century?
24 What is the lowset total for the British Open in the century?
25 In which country was Ted Dexter born?

**Answers**

***20th C Summer Sports***

**1** Never. **2** Hazeltine. **3** Pat Cash. **4** Prabhakar. **5** Commander In Chief. **6** Alan Mullally. **7** E C. **8** £1,000. **9** Nigeria. **10** UK. **11** 17. **12** Ken Barrington. **13** Turnberry. **14** PSV. **15** Donna Hartley. **16** Jeremy Bates. **17** Patty Sheehan. **18** Romania. **19** The Pirate. **20** 6th. **21** Breaking early from the parade. **22** Pakistan. **23** Angela Mortimer. **24** 267. **25** Italy.

# Quiz 50 Pot Luck 25

1 Where in England was Dudley Moore born?
2 What is James Callaghan's real first name?
3 How old was Pope John XXIII when he took office in 1958?
4 What star sign is Annie Lennox?
5 Who co presented Notes and Queries with Clive Anderson?
6 What was Whitney Houston's last UK No 1 of the 80s?
7 Willie Smith was left standing as which sporting first happened in 1955?
8 What was Sophie Rhys-Jones' first car?
9 In 1999 Reg Bailey became chief executive of which Union?
10 What was W.C.Fields' profession when he worked in the circus?
11 Which news journalist has written a book called The Loch Ness Story?
12 What are the international registration letters of a vehicle from Kenya?
13 What links Anna Ford, Geoff Boycott and Paul McCartney?
14 Power to the People was originally a slogan for which movement?
15 Which Heartbeat star played Mickey Malone in Coronation Street?
16 Cebu International airport is in which country?
17 Which British monarch ruled the last time a non Italian pope was in office before John Paul II in Elizabeth II's reign?
18 What is Bo Derek's real name?
19 Who opened the Sydney Opera House in 1973?
20 Who was runner up when Mario Andretti won the F1 championship?
21 Which form of pest control was developed by James Atkinson in 1910?
22 Which country does the airline Theron Airways come from?
23 Who wrote the novel Children of Darkness And Light?
24 Who directed The Seven Samurai?
25 Which person with three names is on the cover of Sgt Pepper's Lonely Hearts Club Band?

**Answers**

***Pot Luck 25***

**1** Dagenham. **2** Leonard. **3** 76. **4** Capricorn. **5** Carol Vorderman. **6** One Moment In Time. **7** First official 147 snooker break. **8** Morris Minor. **9** Mother's Union. **10** Elephant attendant. **11** Nicholas Witchell. **12** EAK. **13** All had roses named after them. **14** Black Panthers. **15** Bill Maynard. **16** Philippines. **17** Henry VIII. **18** Cathleen Collins. **19** The Queen. **20** Ronnie Peterson. **21** Mouse trap. **22** South Africa. **23** Nicholas Mosley. **24** Akira Kurosawa. **25** George Bernard Shaw.

# Quiz 51 20th C 90s Movies

1 On whose life was the film Reversal of Fortune based?
2 Which sitcom did the director of Sliding Doors appear in in the 80s?
3 In which US state is The Horse Whisperer with Redford & Scott Thomas largely set?
4 Which writer directed Sleepless in Seattle?
5 What was the name of the Miss Haversham figure played by Anne Bancroft in the 90s Great Expectations?
6 Which 90s film was a remake of the 1987 German film Wings of Desire?
7 Who had a No 1 hit with the theme from Buddy's Song?
8 What was the name of Bruce Willis's character in Armageddon?
9 Where in Florida was Wild Things set?
10 What year was it in The Fifth Element?
11 Which 1997 film held the record at the time for the biggest opening for a British film, taking £2.5 million in three days?
12 In which film is Elliot Carver the villain?
13 Ten Things I Hate About You is based on which Shakespeare play?
14 Which original Picasso picture was used in Titanic, as one of Rose's possessions?
15 In the 'human' version of 101 Dalmatians what is Roger's occupation?
16 Who played the delicate daughter in Little Women?
17 What is the name of the Sikh bomb disposal expert in The English Patient?
18 What was the eighth Star Trek film called?
19 What is the name of the President in Independence Day?
20 In which film did Morgan Freeman play cop William Somerset?
21 Which studio worked with Disney on Toy Story?
22 What was the first film to have a budget of over $100 million?
23 Which Derek Jarman film was based on a Christopher Marlowe play?
24 What was the name of the weather girl played by Nicole Kidman in To Die For?
25 Which Pennsylvania town is the setting for Groundhog Day?

## Answers

***20th C Movies***

**1** Claus Von Bulow. **2** Bread. **3** Montana. **4** Nora Ephron. **5** Ms Dinsmoor. **6** City of Angels. **7** Chesney Hawkes. **8** Harry Stamper. **9** Blue Bay. **10** 2259. **11** Bean: The Ultimate Disaster Movie. **12** Tomorrow Never Dies. **13** The Taming of the Shrew. **14** The Guitar Player. **15** Computer games programmer. **16** Claire Danes. **17** Kip. **18** The First Contact. **19** Whitmore. **20** Se7en. **21** Pixar. **22** True Lies. **23** Edward II. **24** Suzanne Stone. **25** Punxsutawney.

# Quiz 52 Pot Luck 26

1 What is Joni Mitchell's real first name?
2 Which England soccer boss saved his last game for his biggest victory?
3 "We want eight and we won't wait" was a call for more what?
4 In which comic did Captain Marvel first appear?
5 Who hosted the Searchline spot on Surprise Surprise for five years?
6 The Titanic sank in 1912 but when was the wreck of the ship discovered?
7 What was the first animated series of Lassie called?
8 James M Cox international airport is in which US state?
9 Who was the next British Prime Minister after Asquith?
10 In which decade was the Transbay bridge in San Francisco opened?
11 Which fictional place did Howard's Way take place in?
12 Vehicles from which country use the international registration letter NIC?
13 The electric shaver was invented by a soldier stationed where?
14 What star sign is shared by Liz McColgan and Zola Budd?
15 Where did Reg Holdsworth head for when he left Coronation Street?
16 Who had a UK No 1 hit with Feels Like I'm In Love?
17 What is the population of Mexico to the nearest million?
18 What did Mick Jagger's father do for a living?
19 Congonhas International airport is in which country?
20 Who was Poet Laureate from 1968-1972?
21 In what year did a crossword appear in a British newspaper for the first time?
22 In 1934 a Test match involved who for the first time?
23 Which cigarette company ran the ad "You've come a long way baby"?
24 Which TV detective series made its debut on 18th October 1981?
25 How many years had 10 Downing Street been an official home on 4th December 1985?

## Answers

***Pot Luck 26***

**1** Roberta. **2** Graham Taylor. **3** Battleships. **4** Whiz. **5** Gordon Burns. **6** 1985. **7** Lassie's Rescue Rangers. **8** Ohio. **9** Lloyd George. **10** 1930s. **11** Tarrant. **12** Nicaragua. **13** Alaska. **14** Gemini. **15** Lowestoft. **16** Kelly Marie. **17** 93 million. **18** PE instructor. **19** Brazil. **20** C Day Lewis. **21** 1924. **22** Women. **23** Virginia Slims. **24** Bergerac. **25** 250.

# Quiz 53 20th C TV Classics

Level 3 

1 In what year was the famous Spaghetti Harvest April Fool's Day prank shown on BBC TV?
2 What was the first name of the person The Fugitive was accused of killing?
3 Whose song provided the music for In Sickness and In Health?
4 Who famously announced "Heeeere's Johnny" on the Johnny Carson show from the early 60s?
5 From whose diaries did Jonathan Lynn and Anthony Jay come up with the title Yes Minister?
6 Who presented the first edition of Come Dancing?
7 Which series produced the catchphrase, "Excuse me sir, do you think that's wise?"?
8 Which classic TV series had the catchphrase "Kookie, Kookie lend me your comb"?
9 Who wrote the original scripts of Dr Who?
10 Stuebenville was a US pilot based on which UK classic?
11 In Friday Night Live what football team did Stavros support?
12 Which of Kenny Everett's characters said, "It's all done in the best possible taste"?
13 Which comedy programme won The Golden Rose of Montreux in 1967?
14 On which show was the catchphrase "I'm in charge" first used?
15 Which show had the Flying Fickle Finger of Fate?
16 Who created the drama series Minder?
17 On which TV show did Janice Nicholls regularly appear?
18 Which show had the slogan "The weekend starts here"?
19 What is the longest running children's programme?
20 Who played The Siren in the original Batman TV series?
21 In Upstairs Downstairs where did Lady Marjorie die?
22 What name did Reginald Perrin use when he went his own funeral?
23 Who was the sixth Dr Who?
24 Which role did Colin Welland play in Z Cars many years?
25 Who played Dixon's daughter in the early years of Dixon of Dock Green?

## Answers

***20th C TV Classics***

**1** 1957. **2** Helen. **3** Chas & Dave. **4** Ed McMahon. **5** Richard Crossman. **6** Sylvia Peters. **7** Dad's Army. **8** 77 Sunset Strip. **9** Terry Nation. **10** The Likely Lads. **11** Arsenal. **12** Cupid Stunt. **13** The Frost Report. **14** Sunday Night at the London Palladium. **15** Rowan & Martin's Laugh In. **16** Leon Griffiths. **17** Thank Your Lucky Stars. **18** Ready Steady Go. **19** Sooty. **20** Joan Collins. **21** On the Titanic. **22** Martin Wellbourne. **23** Peter Davison. **24** David Graham. **25** Billie Whitelaw.

# Quiz 54 Pot Luck 27

1 Who directed the movie The Blues Brothers?
2 How many years after the end of the Great War was the first 'Poppy Day' held?
3 What is Don Johnson's real name?
4 Where in England was Michael Palin born?
5 Which US soap actress's real name is Patsy McClenny?
6 Kent County international airport is in which US state?
7 Which long time star of The Bill is a qualified scuba diving instructor?
8 What is Brad Pitt's real first name?
9 You Bet! was based on a game show from which country?
10 Which two countries are joined by the Rainbow bridge?
11 Who is the most famous creation of Mary Tourtel?
12 What are the international registration letters of a vehicle from Tanzania?
13 Who became the first European Player Of The Year?
14 In which city was the peace treaty ending the Vietnam war signed?
15 Who hosted Trick or Treat with Julian Clary?
16 What was the name of the island off Iceland which appeared in 1963 as a result of an underwater volcano?
17 Who is dad to Betty Kitten and Honey Kinny?
18 Why was Al Capone sent to prison in 1931?
19 Costa Smeralda International airport is in which country?
20 Which playwright said, "I think age is a very high price to pay for maturity."?
21 What star sign is Chris Tarrant?
22 Which country does the airline Norontair come from?
23 What was Michael Jackson's last UK No 1 of the 80s?
24 What is Jeremy Paxman's middle name?
25 Who wrote the novel Tycoon in 1996?

## Answers

***Pot Luck 27***

**1** John Landis. **2** Three. **3** Donald Wayne. **4** Sheffield. **5** Morgan Fairchild. **6** Michigan. **7** Mark Wingett. **8** William. **9** Holland. **10** Canada/USA. **11** Rupert Bear. **12** EAT. **13** Stanley Matthews. **14** Paris. **15** Mike Smith. **16** Surtsey. **17** Jonathan Ross. **18** Tax evasion. **19** Sardinia. **20** Tom Stoppard. **21** Libra. **22** Canada. **23** I Just Can't Stop Loving You. **24** Dickson. **25** Harold Robbins.

# Quiz 55 20th C World Tour

Level 3 

1 In what year did the first McDonald's open in Moscow?
2 In which city was the Olympic stadium designed by Pier Luigi Nervi?
3 What was the name by which Lesotho used to be known?
4 Who designed New York's Gugenheim Museum?
5 Which US mountains gave their name to a fever discovered in that area in the early 20th century?
6 Where was Ian Botham talking about when he said everyone should send his mother in law there all expenses paid?
7 In which American state is the Rockefeller Folk Art Collection?
8 In which US state is the only major military academy founded this century?
9 Who designed the Mile High Centre, Boston, and The Glass Pyramids at the Louvre?
10 What would an American be talking about if he mentioned a scallion?
11 Lassa fever is so called as it was first reported in 1970 in Lassa in which country?
12 In which American city would you go to see the Frick Collection?
13 Who designed the Hiroshima Peace Centre?
14 Who said, "Concorde is great. It gives you three extra hours to find your luggage"?
15 In the 50s who designed The Museum of Modern Art in Tokyo?
16 Where did the Pope consecrate the world's biggest church in 1990?
17 In which city was the Olympic stadium designed by Felix Candela?
18 How is Tenochtitlan now known?
19 During which marathon do runners cross the Verrazano Bridge?
20 Whose tomb was opened to the public in Egypt for the first time in 1996?
21 The architect who designed the Sydney Opera House came from which country?
22 In California Suite which city is described as "not Mecca. It just smells like it"?
23 Which airport was opened in 1994 on a specially made island?
24 What is the English title of the new South African National Anthem?
25 Where did the largest rollercoaster in the world open in 1994?

## Answers

***20th C World Tour***

**1** 1990. **2** Rome. **3** Basutoland. **4** Frank Lloyd Wright. **5** Rocky Mountains. **6** Pakistan. **7** Virginia. **8** Colorado USAF. **9** Leah Meng Pei. **10** Spring onion. **11** Nigeria. **12** New York. **13** Kenzo Tange. **14** Bob Hope. **15** Le Corbusier. **16** Ivory Coast. **17** Mexico. **18** Mexico City. **19** New York. **20** Queen Nefertiti. **21** Denmark - It was Jorn Utzon. **22** New York. **23** Kansai. **24** God Bless Africa. **25** Blackpool.

# Quiz 56 Pot Luck 28

Level 3 

1. Alben Barkley was Vice President to which US President?
2. What is the population of Morocco to the nearest million?
3. What star sign is shared by Jackie Stewart and Mike Gatting?
4. Who had a UK No 1 hit with Japanese Boy?
5. What is Van Morrison's real first name?
6. Who said, "Include me out"?
7. Who played Rhett Butler in the TV film sequel to Gone With the Wind?
8. In which country was Nastassja Kinski born?
9. Which city did the first Songs of Praise come from?
10. What does the Chinese expression Gung ho mean, which was adopted by US Marines in WWII?
11. Which country does writer Nadine Gordimer come from?
12. Vehicles from which country use the international registration letter MK?
13. In Ivor the Engine, what was the name of the station?
14. Which British John has held the land speed record?
15. In which calendar month was Prince Charles and Lady Di's engagement announced?
16. What is Clint Eastwood's real name?
17. Who scored Man Utd's FA Cup Final winner v Crystal Palace in 1990?
18. What was dubbed "the eyes and ears of the world"?
19. Crown Point International airport is in which country?
20. Which luxury did Leslie Grantham, aka Dirty Den, choose on Desert Island Discs?
21. La Guardia international airport is in which US state?
22. Which country does the airline MAIT come from?
23. Where in London did The Wind In the Willows writer Kenneth Grahame carry out his day job ?
24. Khatchaturians's Spartacus introduced the first episode of which TV drama in 1971?
25. In which year did Dr Christian Barnard perform the first heart transplant?

## Answers

***Pot Luck 28***

**1** Harry S Truman. **2** 27 million. **3** Gemini. **4** Aneka. **5** George. **6** Samuel Goldwyn. **7** Timothy Dalton. **8** Germany. **9** Cardiff. **10** Work together. **11** South Africa. **12** Macedonia. **13** Llaniog. **14** Cobb. **15** February. **16** Clint Eastwood. **17** Lee Martin. **18** Paramount News. **19** Tobago. **20** Metal detector. **21** New York. **22** Mongolia. **23** Bank Of England. **24** The Onedin Line. **25** 1967.

# Quiz 57 Sounds of the 60s & 70s

1. Who said I was Made For Dancing in a 70s No 4 hit?
2. Who released an album in 1961 called 21 Today?
3. What was the follow up to Fleetwood Mac's first No 1?
4. What was the first UK No 1 by KC and The Sunshine Band?
5. What was the first Top Ten Hit for The Kinks in the 70s?
6. Where was yodeller Frank Ifield born?
7. What was the second 70s No 1 by Mud?
8. Who was the UK's biggest-selling artist in 1967?
9. What UK chart position was achieved by the original release of Je t'aime?
10. Which group did Steve Marriott form after leaving the Small Faces?
11. Which No 1 group from 1974 were recognised by their white berets?
12. Who was On The Rebound in 1961?
13. Which group were fronted by Dennis Locorriere and Ray Sawyer?
14. Which female vocalist said Yes My Darling Daughter in '62 ?
15. How many Top Ten hits had Lindisfarne had before Run For Home?
16. What was the only UK No 1 for the Dave Clark Five?
17. Which group achieved their 4th successive Top Ten hit with Belfast?
18. Which rock group was voted World's Top Band in 1972?
19. Which band consisted of the Cluskeys and John Stokes?
20. What was Brotherhood of Man's first Top Ten hit after Save Your Kisses?
21. Who got to No 10 with Sunshine After The Rain in Jubilee Year?
22. Which Top Ten hit followed Mr Tambourine Man for the Byrds?
23. Who released an album in the 60s called Please Get My Name Right?
24. Who had most weeks in the charts in 1974?
25. Who danced a Morning Dance in 1979?

## Answers

***Sounds of the 60s and 70s***

**1** Leif Garrett. **2** Cliff Richard. **3** Man Of The World. **4** Give It Up. **5** Lola. **6** Coventry. **7** Lonely This Christmas. **8** Engelbert Humperdinck. **9** 2. **10** Humble Pie. **11** The Rubettes. **12** Floyd Cramer. **13** Dr Hook. **14** Eydie Gorme. **15** Two. **16** Glad All Over. **17** Boney M. **18** Alice Cooper. **19** Bachelors. **20** Oh Boy - The Mood I'm In. **21** Elkie Brooks. **22** All I Really Want To Do. **23** Twiggy. **24** The Wombles. **25** Spyro Gyra.

# Quiz 58 Pot Luck 29

1 Who wrote the novel Delta Connection?
2 What is Sid Owen's real name?
3 Who preceeded Hosni Mubarak as President of Egypt?
4 What was the Jam's last UK No. 1 of the 80s?
5 "Even your best friends won't tell you" was part of an ad to promote what?
6 Where in England was Emma Thompson born?
7 Who was the defending champion when Martina Navratilova first won Wimbledon singles?
8 In The Rockford Files what was Jim Rockford's daily fee?
9 How is Lady Nicholas Lloyd better known?
10 What name was given to followers of cartoon characters Pip, Squeak and Wilfred?
11 Who first sang the Neighbours theme song?
12 What are the international registration letters of a vehicle from Uganda?
13 What was the first organisation to have its charter mark withdrawn?
14 In the 70s George Lee was a world champion in which sport?
15 Which river is spanned by the world's longest cantilever bridge?
16 Toothpaste was the first ever TV ad in the UK but what was the first TV ad in colour for?
17 What type of aid was developed by Miller Hutchinson in the early years of the 20th century?
18 In the cartoon characters Pip, Squeak and Wilfred what kind of creature was Squeak?
19 Cuscatlan International airport is in which country?
20 Who was Pope for the shortest length of time in the 20th C?
21 General Mitchell international airport is in which US state?
22 Which country does the airline Pluna come from?
23 Who directed A Passage to India?
24 What star sign is Pauline Quirke?
25 What is Gregory Peck's real first name?

## Answers

***Pot Luck 29***

**1** Hammond Innes. **2** David Sutton. **3** Anwar El-Sadat. **4** Beat Surrender. **5** Listerine mouthwash. **6** Cambridge. **7** Virginia Wade. **8** $200 plus expenses. **9** Eve Pollard. **10** Gugnuncs. **11** Barry Crocker. **12** EAU. **13** Passport Agency. **14** Gliding. **15** St Lawrence. **16** Frozen peas. **17** Hearing aid. **18** Penguin. **19** El Salvador. **20** John Paul I. **21** Wisconsin. **22** Uruguay. **23** David Lean. **24** Cancer. **25** Eldred.

# Quiz 59 Headline Makers

Level 3 

1 How much did Vivian Nicholson win on the pools in 1961?
2 Which boat capsized in the 1997 Vendee Globe round the world race?
3 Who was Mandy Rice-Davies referring to when she said, "Well he would wouldn't he?"?
4 How old was the man who was granted the first divorce in Irish history?
5 How old was Ruth Lawrence when she passed A level maths?
6 Who investigated the cash for questions affair involving Neil Hamilton?
7 In the painting by Michael Browne featuring Eric Cantona who was Alex Ferguson depicted as?
8 What description did Dr Desmond Morris give of a city as opposed to a concrete jungle?
9 Princess Diana made a public apology after underage William and Harry saw which 15 certificate film?
10 Sue Ryder became Baroness Ryder of where along with Cavendish?
11 Which university did Andrew Morton represent on University Challenge?
12 Who founded Gordonstoun school in 1934?
13 What were Bomber Harris's real first names?
14 How many years elapsed between DH Lawrence's writing of Lady Chatterley's Lover and the book's publication?
15 In which city were the 'Chariots Of Fire' Olympic Games?
16 Lindbergh wrote about his New York to Paris flight in which book?
17 Maria Montessori was the first woman in Italy to be awarded a degree in which subject?
18 Rudolf Nureyev took citizenship of which country in 1982?
19 In which country was Pasternak's Dr Zhivago first published?
20 Which Peter co founded the Aldeburgh Festival?
21 Which seat did Cherie Booth unsuccessfully contend in 1983?
22 Child expert Dr Spock won an Olympic gold medal in what event?
23 In 1990 a cinema owner was fined for refusing to remove what from the roof of his house?
24 Which British nurse was imprisoned in Iraq in 1990 for spying?
25 Which athlete sued Mirror Newspapers for libel?

## Answers

***20th C Headline Makers***

**1** £152,000. **2** Exide Challenger. **3** Lord Astor. **4** 68. **5** Nine. **6** Gordon Downey. **7** Julius Caesar. **8** Human zoo. **9** The Devil's Own. **10** Warsaw. **11** Sussex. **12** Kurt Hahn. **13** Arthur Travers. **14** 32. **15** Paris. **16** Spirit of St Louis. **17** Medicine. **18** Austria. **19** Italy. **20** Pears. **21** Thanet East. **22** Rowing. **23** A fibreglass shark. **24** Daphne Parish. **25** Tessa Sanderson.

# Quiz 60 Pot Luck 30

1 Who was the first South African to win snooker's Benson & Hedges Masters?
2 How much did the Dandy cost by the time issue 2000 came out in 1980?
3 Who beat England in their first home defeat in soccer?
4 What is Patrick Macnee's real first name?
5 The rationing of which non food product ended in 1950?
6 Who played Inspector Tsientsin in Reilly Ace of Spies?
7 When did the Chinese TV service begin broadcasting?
8 Doha International airport is in which country?
9 Who was the last Frenchwoman to win a Grand Slam event before Mary Pierce?
10 In which country is the Rio-Niteroi bridge?
11 What was the Bellamy's address in the first episode of Upstairs, Downstairs?
12 Vehicles from which country use the international registration letter MC?
13 Ex PM Anthony Eden became the first Earl of where?
14 In which year was the Independent first published?
15 Enosis was a slogan calling for the unfication of which island with the mainland?
16 In which series was there the Cafe Nervosa?
17 Which Dallas star sang with the Seattle Opera?
18 Gough Whitlam became Prime Minister of which country in 1972?
19 Which TV star wrote a book called Rock Stars in their Underpants?
20 Who had a UK No 1 hit with The Model?
21 In 1954 girls names were first applied to identify what?
22 Which country does the airline LAP come from?
23 What are Damon Hill's middle names?
24 What star sign is shared by Meryl Streep and Lindsay Wagner?
25 What is the population of the Netherlands to the nearest million?

## Answers

***Pot Luck 30***

**1** Perrie Mans. **2** 7p. **3** Ireland. **4** Daniel. **5** Soap. **6** David Suchet. **7** 1958. **8** Qatar. **9** Francoise Durr. **10** Brazil. **11** 165 Eaton Square. **12** Monaco. **13** Avon. **14** 1986. **15** Cyprus. **16** Frasier. **17** Patrick Duffy. **18** Australia. **19** Paula Yates. **20** Kraftwerk. **21** Hurricanes. **22** Paraguay. **23** Ernest Deveraux. **24** Cancer. **25** 16 million.

# Quiz 61 World Leaders

1 Who was described by his foreign minister as having "a nice smile, but he has got iron teeth"?
2 Who became president of Zambia in 1991?
3 Who succeeded Brezhnev as President of the USSR?
4 Who was Nigeria's first president and has been described as the father of modern Nigeria?
5 Who was born Karl Herbert Frahm?
6 Who was chairman of the Organisation of African Unity from 1975-76?
7 Errol Flynn's last film was a documentary tribute to which world leader?
8 Gorbachev introduced the expression perestroika but what does it mean?
9 Who was the first PM of South Africa?
10 Who said of Margaret Thatcher, "She adds the diplomacy of Alf Garnett to the economics of Arthur Daley"?
11 In what year did Hussein become King of Jordan?
12 How was Papa Doc also known?
13 Which leader did Churchill say was like a "female llama surprised in her bath"?
14 Who was the last leader of Communist East Germany?
15 Who did Lionel Jospin replace as French PM?
16 What name was given to the period of rule of Emperor Hirohito?
17 Which part of Lenin was preserved after his death?
18 Who said, "We are not at war with Egypt. We are in armed conflict"?
19 In what year was the world's first woman Prime Minister elected?
20 Who was the leader of ZAPU?
21 Which British Prime Minister was Rudyard Kipling's cousin?
22 Who said, "We have the happiest Africans in the world"?
23 What did Mao Tse Tung call the 'great leap forward'?
24 Which newspaper originally coined the term Iron Lady about Margaret Thatcher?
25 Which role did Harold Macmillan say was, "forever poised between a cliche and an indiscretion"?

## Answers

***World Leaders***

**1** Mikhail Gorbachev. **2** Chiluba. **3** Andropov. **4** Nnamdi Azikiwe. **5** Willy Brandt. **6** Idi Amin. **7** Castro. **8** Reconstruction. **9** Louis Botha. **10** Denis Healey. **11** 1952. **12** Francois Duvalier. **13** Charles de Gaulle. **14** Egon Krenz. **15** Alain Juppe. **16** Showa. **17** Brain. **18** Anthony Eden. **19** 1960. **20** Joshua Nkomo. **21** Stanley Baldwin. **22** Ian Smith. **23** Enforced industrialisation. **24** Red Star. **25** Foreign Secretary.

# Quiz 62 Pot Luck 31

1 According to hippy guru Dr Timothy Leary what did you do before you "drop out"?
2 Who was the first Welshman to become angling's World Freshwater Champion?
3 Who wrote the novel The Rector's Wife?
4 In which year were breathalyser tests introduced in Britain?
5 What is Angus Deayton's real first name?
6 Hancock Field international airport is in which US state?
7 What did Franz Kafka do for a day job?
8 What was the name of the TV profile of Elton John made by his partner David Furnish?
9 Where in England was Julie Walters born?
10 What star sign is Harrison Ford?
11 Which profession did Janet Street-Porter study for before her media career?
12 What are the international registration letters of a vehicle from Ethiopia?
13 Which entertainer said, "He was into animal husbandry - until they caught him at it"?
14 How many policewomen went on duty when women first went on the beat?
15 What was Jive Bunny and the Mastermixers' last UK No 1 of the 80s?
16 How did Guenter Parche leave his mark on sport in the 90s?
17 What is Iggy Pop's real name?
18 Dorval International airport is in which country?
19 Which soap star recorded When I Need You in 1998?
20 What could be bought at the Post Office in late 1966 which had not been available before?
21 In which year were both sides of the Channel Tunnel linked by the service tunnel?
22 Harry Weinstein became a world champion under which name?
23 Whose face appeared for the first time on a bank note in June 1999?
24 Who directed Good Morning Vietnam?
25 Where did the Shining Path terrorists operate?

## Answers

***Pot Luck 31***

**1** Turn on, tune in. **2** Clive Branson. **3** Joanna Trollope. **4** 1967. **5** Gordon. **6** New York. **7** Worked in insurance. **8** Tantrums and Tiaras. **9** Birmingham. **10** Cancer. **11** Architect. **12** ETH. **13** Tom Lehrer. **14** Two. **15** Let's Party. **16** Stabbed Monica Seles. **17** James Osterberg. **18** Canada. **19** Will Mellor. **20** Special Christmas stamps. **21** 1990. **22** Gary Kasparov. **23** Edward Elgar. **24** Barry Levinson. **25** Peru.

# Quiz 63 20th C Olympics

1 Which country broke the India/Pakistan 50 year monopoly of men's hockey tournaments?
2 Who won Great Britain's first medal of the Atlanta Games?
3 Who last won the100m gold for Canada before Donovan Bailey?
4 In which sport did Mike Agassi, father of Andre, compete in the 1948 and 1952 Olympics?
5 In which event did Great Britain's Henry Taylor land eight Golds?
6 Ralph Craig ran the 100 metres for the US in 1912; when did he next compete in the Olympics?
7 Who won Silver when Tessa Sanderson won Gold in the javelin?
8 Which was the first city to host the Summer Olympics twice?
9 In which event did Michelle Smith win bronze in 1996?
10 What did Paavo Nurmi always carry with him during his gold medal winning races?
11 Who won the 400m hurdles in the games sandwiched between Ed Moses' two triumphs?
12 Which country did 70s star Lassie Virren come from?
13 Who wore a T shirt saying "Thank You America For A Wonderful Games"?
14 Why was Finn Volmari Iso-Hollo's 1932 steeplechase win exceptional?
15 In 1956 Australia hosted the Games except for equestrian events which were held in which country?
16 Charles Bennett and Arnold Jackson have both taken gold for Britain in which athletic event?
17 Who came second when Donovan Bailey won 100m Gold?
18 How many Gold medals did Great Britain win in 1996?
19 In which event did an individual first won four successive Golds?
20 At which venue did Steve Redgrave first win Gold?
21 Britain and which other country have won Gold in every Summer Games?
22 In what year did baseball become a medal sport?
23 In which sporting event did John Huish claim 1996 Olympic Gold?
24 Tessa Sanderson first competed in the Olympics in which country?
25 Which country had its only Gold in men's basketball in 1980?

**Answers**

***20th C Olympics***

**1** Germany. **2** Paul Palmer. **3** Percy Williams. **4** Boxing. **5** Swimming. **6** 1948 - yachting team. **7** Tiina Lillak. **8** Paris. **9** 200m butterfly. **10** Stopwatch. **11** Volker Beck. **12** Finland. **13** Daley Thompson. **14** He ran an extra lap by mistake. **15** Sweden. **16** 1500m. **17** Frankie Fredericks. **18** One. **19** Discus. **20** Los Angeles. **21** France. **22** 1992. **23** Archery. **24** Canada. **25** Yugoslavia.

# Quiz 64 Pot Luck 32

1 What is Oprah Winfrey's real name?
2 In which country was Joanna Lumley born?
3 Who wrote the lyrics to "Je ne regrette rien"?
4 Which capital city has the fewest cinemas in relation to its population?
5 Which star of Whose Line Is It Anyway? is a black belt at judo?
6 Dwight Filley were the first names of the presenter of which sporting cup?
7 What was the name of the UK's Lovejoy in US soap Dallas?
8 Which Daily Paper ran the strip cartoon Pop?
9 Which country does the airline Horizon Air come from?
10 What is the population of New Zealand to the nearest million?
11 What star sign is shared by Virginia Wade and Glenys Kinnock?
12 Vehicles from which country use the international registration letter MAL?
13 Who had a UK No. 1 hit with Seven Tears?
14 What is Gordon Brown's real first name?
15 In which European city is the Calouste Gulbenkian Museum?
16 Who narrated The Magic Roundabout when it resumed in the 90s?
17 Capt Webb was a pioneer swimming the Channel but how did Jonathan Webb cross the Channel in 1977?
18 What is Yorkshireman Timothy West's middle name?
19 Douala International airport is in which country?
20 Which ex editor of the Daily Express and News of the World went into broadcasting?
21 What were the Queen and Prince Philip given as a present for baby Prince Andrew while on a visit to the Gambia?
22 In which decade was the New River George bridge West Virginia opened?
23 Which Transport Minister introduced breathalyser tests in the UK?
24 Who said, "You're not drunk if you can lie on the floor without holding on."?
25 In which craft did Valentina Tereshkova make her historic space flight?

## Answers

***Pot Luck 32***

**1** Oprah Winfrey. **2** Kashmir. **3** Michel Vaucaire. **4** Cairo. **5** Tony Slattery. **6** Davis Cup. **7** Don Lockwood. **8** Daily Sketch. **9** USA. **10** 4 million. **11** Cancer. **12** Malaysia. **13** Goombay Dance Band. **14** James. **15** Lisbon. **16** Nigel Planer. **17** Windsurfing. **18** Lancaster. **19** Cameroon. **20** Derek Jameson. **21** Baby crocodile. **22** 1970s. **23** Barbara Castle. **24** Dean Martin. **25** Vostok 6.

# Quiz 65 20th C Hollywood

1 In how many countries did A Few Good Men open simultaneously making it the largest premiere on record?
2 In which film is Vince LaRocca the gangster boyfriend of Deloris?
3 What was the third sequel to Child's Play?
4 The documentary Hearts of Darkness told of the making of which film?
5 Who said, "I knew that with a mouth like mine I just had to be a star or something"?
6 How many years after Terminator was Terminator 2 released?
7 Which director of Madonna's Vogue video directed Alien 3?
8 Which Clint Eastwood film had the highest stuntman ratio?
9 In Reversal of Fortune what is the name of Claus's wife whom he is found guilty of attempting to murder?
10 Which Hollywood couple called one of their children Dakota Mayi?
11 Whose slogan was 'More stars than there are in heaven'?
12 In which 1990 Robert de Niro film did the director's parents both appear?
13 Who played Judy, Doralee and Violet's boss in 9 to 5?
14 What was the name of the first sci fi movie to cost more than $1 million?
15 During the making of which film did Grace Kelly meet Prince Rainier of Monaco thus ending her Hollywood career?
16 Which actor said of Hollywood, "If you say what you mean in this town, you're an outlaw"?
17 What was included inside the wooden horse for Helen of Troy to make the actors more comfortable?
18 Which 50s film held the record for the most number of animals in a film?
19 Who said, "I'm old. I'm young. I'm intelligent. I'm stupid"?
20 What was John Cazale's last film?
21 Who was Tatum O'Neal's equestrian coach in International Velvet?
22 Who directed Eyes Wide Shut?
23 Who won the Best Actress Oscar the year Princess Diana died?
24 How old was Richard Gere when starred in An Officer and a Gentleman?
25 Although Anthony Hopkins starred in the film of Shadowlands who had played it on Broadway and the West End?

**Answers**

***20th C Hollywood***

**1** 51. **2** Sister Act. **3** Bride of Chucky. **4** Apocalypse Now. **5** Barbra Streisand. **6** Seven. **7** David Fincher. **8** The Rookie. **9** Sunny. **10** Don Johnson & Melanie Griffith. **11** MGM. **12** Goodfellas. **13** Dabney Coleman. **14** Forbidden Planet. **15** To Catch a Thief. **16** Kevin Costner. **17** Air conditioning. **18** Around the World in 80 Days. **19** Warren Beatty. **20** The Deer Hunter. **21** Marcia Williams. **22** Stanley Kubrick. **23** Helen Hunt. **24** 30. **25** Nigel Hawthorne.

# Quiz 66 Pot Luck 33

1 Lake Echternach was the first venue for which world championship?
2 In which decade did Dennis the Menace start his menacing?
3 What are Hugh Grant's middle names?
4 Which senior post did Nigel Havers' father hold in Margaret Thatcher's government?
5 How many games did England lose in soccer's 1982 World Cup in Spain?
6 Who wrote the best seller Shogun?
7 How old was Stacey Hillyard when she first became snooker's World Amateur Champion?
8 Hartsfield international airport is in which US state?
9 What star sign is George Best?
10 Where in England was Sir Richard Attenborough born?
11 What was John Lennon's last UK No 1 of the 80s?
12 What are the international registration letters of a vehicle from Fiji?
13 Who was the first Wimbledon men's singles champion after World War II?
14 In 1957 an air service was set up between London and which city?
15 What is Brigitte Bardot's real name?
16 In what year was the ambulance service introduced in London?
17 In all how many England managers did Kevin Keegan play for?
18 In which country is the Salazar bridge?
19 "Dull it isn't" was part of an ad to promote which profession?
20 In which year was the then tallest building the Post Office Tower opened?
21 Greg Lake's I Believe in Father Christmas was based an a suite by which composer?
22 Which country does the airline Varig come from?
23 What was Anthony Newley's real first name?
24 Who directed American Graffiti?
25 Who played Monsieur Alfonse in the TV comedy 'Allo 'Allo?

## Answers

***Pot Luck 33***

**1** Fly fishing. **2** 50s. **3** John Mungo. **4** Attorney General. **5** None. **6** James Clavell. **7** 15. **8** Georgia. **9** Gemini. **10** Cambridge. **11** Woman. **12** FJI. **13** Yvon Petra. **14** Moscow. **15** Camille Javal. **16** 1905. **17** Four. **18** Portugal. **19** Police. **20** 1965. **21** Prokofiev. **22** Brazil. **23** George. **24** George Lucas. **25** Kenneth Connor.

# Quiz 67 20th C Sit Coms

1 Which Deputy Party leader appeared in an episode of Chef!?
2 What was the provisional title of Last of the Summer Wine?
3 Empty Nest was a spin off from which sitcom?
4 Which Seinfeld star was the voice of Hugo in The Hunchback of Notre Dame?
5 Whose song provided the music for Girls On Top?
6 In Man About the House what football team did Robin Tripp support?
7 What was the business owned by Ted Simcock called in A Bit of a Do?
8 What was Jean Boht's codename for This Is Your Life?
9 What was the name of the singles club in Dear John by John Sullivan?
10 In May to December Miss Flood became Mrs Who?
11 What was Polly's surname in Fawlty Towers?
12 On which UK sitcom special did Fergie make a guest appearance?
13 In what type of hospital was Get Well Soon set?
14 In 1979, which sitcom netted the highest audience of the year of 24 million viewers?
15 What was the surname of Rhoda in the sitcom spin off from the Mary Tyler Moore show?
16 When Fawlty Towers was shown in Spain, Manuel became what nationality in order to avoid offence to the Spaniards?
17 Which star of a popular sitcom made a fitness video called Let's Dance?
18 In which state was Roseanne set?
19 Which sitcom star released a solo album called What Is Going to Become of Us All in 1976?
20 Which star of Barbara was mayoress of her home town Blackburn?
21 Which show was originally called These Friends of Mine?
22 What was the name of the house Hester and William rented in French Fields?
23 What was the name of the housekeeper in Father Ted?
24 Who sang the theme music for You Rang M'Lord along with one its stars Paul Shane?
25 Alf Garnett was originally to have had what name?

## Answers

***20th C Sit Coms***

**1** Roy Hattersley. **2** Last of the Summer Wine. **3** The Golden Girls. **4** Jason Alexander. **5** Squeeze. **6** Southampton. **7** Jupiter Foundry. **8** Yeast. **9** 1-2-1. **10** Tipple. **11** Sherman. **12** The Vicar of Dibley. **13** TB sanatorium. **14** To The Manor Born. **15** Morgenstern. **16** Italian. **17** Richard Wilson. **18** Illinois. **19** John LeMesurier. **20** Madge Hindle - Doreen. **21** Ellen. **22** Les Hirondelles. **23** Mrs Doyle. **24** Bob Monkhouse. **25** Alf Ramsey.

# Quiz 68 Pot Luck 34

1. Whose second husband was Max Mallowan?
2. Who was the next British Prime Minister after Lloyd George?
3. Hopkins international airport is in which US state?
4. In which decade was the London Symphony Orchestra founded?
5. On Spitting Image who was seen as a slug?
6. Which pioneering aviator had a plane called Percival Gull?
7. Which Earl has presented Miss World?
8. Who had a UK No 1 hit with A Little Peace?
9. What was Charlotte Brew's famous first?
10. What star sign is shared by Danny La Rue and Roy Walker?
11. Which magician's wife wrote songs on That's Life?
12. Vehicles from which country use the international registration letter MA?
13. How old was Elizabeth Taylor when she appeared in National Velvet?
14. Educationalist Maria Montessori was Italy's first ever female what?
15. What is the population of South Africa to the nearest million?
16. When was the Daily Express founded?
17. Who was the first person in the 90s to have a solo Christmas No 1 hit?
18. Who was Poet Laureate from 1913-1930?
19. Elmas International airport is in which country?
20. Whose autobiography was called Arias and Raspberries?
21. Henri Becquerel shared a Nobel prize for his work in discovering what?
22. Who took the assumed name Sebastian Melmoth when living in Paris?
23. At which ground did Muralitharan take nine wickets v England?
24. Established in 1919 which is the world's oldest surviving airline?
25. Which personality had her shoe replaced by an army boot in a classic Morecambe and Wise sketch?

## Answers

***Pot Luck 34***

**1** Agatha Christie. **2** Bonar Law. **3** Ohio. **4** First of the century. **5** Kenneth Baker. **6** Jean Batten. **7** Lichfield. **8** Nicole. **9** Female Grand National rider. ç0 Leo. **11** Victoria Wood. **12** Morocco. **13** 10. **14** Medical student. **15** 42 million. **16** 1900. **17** Cliff Richard. **18** Robert Bridges. **19** Italy. **20** Harry Secombe. **21** Radioactivity. **22** Oscar Wilde. **23** The Oval. **24** KLM. **25** Shirley Bassey.

# Quiz 69 Books

1 In which Ian Fleming novel did the dog Edison appear?
2 Which MP wrote The Smile on the Face of the Tiger?
3 Which country's national anthem was used by John Steinbeck for his book The Grapes of Wrath?
4 Which British novelist said, "Fame is a powerful aphrodisiac"?
5 Which writer did Sean O'Casey describe as English Literature's performing flea?
6 Which novelist was the cousin of actor Christopher Lee?
7 Ten Days That Shook the World is about what?
8 How was H H Munro better known?
9 Who completed his novel Omerta shortly before his death?
10 What was DH Lawrence's Lady Chatterley's Lover originally to have been called?
11 in Peter Pan, what are Hook's last words?
12 Which novelist wrote The ABC of French Food?
13 What was Ian Fleming's first novel?
14 Which sit com actress was a judge for the Booker Prize in 1985?
15 What was Robert Graves autobiography called?
16 Which opera singer's memoirs were called Full Circle?
17 John Betjeman's book Ghastly Good Taste was on the subject of what?
18 Which country banned Black Beauty for its supposed to racist title?
19 Which novelist is the mother of actress Rudi Davies?
20 What was the first volume of Dirk Bogarde's autobiography called?
21 Which actress wrote the children's book Nibbles & Me?
22 Which children's author's autobiography was called Boy?
23 What was William Golding's follow up to The Lord of the Flies?
24 What is the first name of P G Wodehouse's character Cheesewright?
25 Which French novelist played in goal for Algeria?

## Answers

***Books***

**1** Chitty Chitty Bang Bang. **2** Douglas Hurd. **3** USA. **4** Graham Greene. **5** P.G.Wodehouse. **6** Ian Fleming. **7** Russian Revolution. **8** Saki. **9** Mario Puzo. **10** Tenderness. **11** Floreat Etona. **12** Len Deighton. **13** Casino Royale. **14** Joanna Lumley. **15** Goodbye to All That. **16** Janet Baker. **17** Architecture. **18** Namibia. **19** Beryl Bainbridge. **20** A Postilion Struck By Lightning. **21** Elizabeth Taylor. **22** Roald Dahl. **23** The Inheritors. **24** Stilton. **25** Albert Camus.

# Quiz 70 Pot Luck 35

1 What is Michael Crawford's real name?
2 Which company sponsored snooker's British Gold Cup from 1981-1984?
3 Who directed the three hour silent movie epic The Birth Of A Nation?
4 Who designed the Westminster building to provided MPs with more office space from 2000 onwards?
5 What did Dennis Connor win three times in the 80s?
6 In which European city is the Goulandis Natural History Museum?
7 Who wrote the book The Hammer of God?
8 Wayne Gretzky first played league ice hockey with which team?
9 What was the date of the October 1987 gales that hit Britain?
10 What was launched on Tuesday 30 July, 1938 and kept going to the end of the century?
11 Where in England was actor Tom Baker born?
12 What are the international registration letters of a vehicle from Liechtenstein?
13 Ex PM James Callaghan became Baron Callaghan of where?
14 Esenboga International airport is in which country?
15 Which female was in the coffee shop in Saturday Superstore?
16 What star sign is Mikhail Gorbachev?
17 Who made her TV debut in Dennis Potter's Christabel?
18 What was the last UK No 1 of the 80s featuring Paul McCartney?
19 Who was runner up when James Hunt was F1 champion?
20 What did Che Guevara train to be?
21 What single word did boxer Joe Louis want on his tombstone?
22 Which country does the airline Sahsa come from?
23 In which year was TV personality Ernie Wise born?
24 Who directed the movie Tess?
25 Which TV presenter wrote the novel A Time To Dance?

**Answers**

***Pot Luck 35***
**1** Michael Dumble-Smith. **2** Yamaha. **3** D W Griffith. **4** Sir Michael Hopkins. **5** America's Cup. **6** Athens. **7** Arthur C Clarke . **8** Edmonton Oilers. **9** 15th. **10** The Beano Comic. **11** Liverpool. **12** FL. **13** Cardiff. **14** Turkey. **15** Vicky Licorish. **16** Pisces. **17** Liz Hurley. **18** Ferry 'Cross The Mersey. **19** Niki Lauda. **20** Doctor. **21** Even. **22** Honduras. **23** 1925. **24** Roman Polanski. **25** Melvyn Bragg.

# Quiz 71 Who's Who

Level 3 

1. Who partnered Patti Austin on Baby Come To Me?
2. Which artist was the biggest-selling singles artist in the UK in 1991?
3. Which male singer fronted the group Change before his solo career took off?
4. Which London based group featured two Davies brothers?
5. What nationality is Peter Andre?
6. Who sang with R Kelly on I'm Your Angel?
7. Who featured on You Got The Love with Source?
8. How many members were in the Mancunian band The Smiths?
9. Who partnered Michael McDonald with On My Own?
10. Which act were voted Best British Dance Act at the 1994 BRIT awards?
11. Who was born Gloria Fajarda?
12. Which member of Def Leppard died in 1991?
13. Vince Clarke and Andy Bell achieved chart success as who?
14. Who won a record four BRIT awards in 1995?
15. Who was the lead vocalist for The Go-Gos?
16. How is Douglas Trendle better known?
17. Who was the first British female to win a Grammy award?
18. Who featured on If You Ever by East 17?
19. Who was the oldest solo female singer to have a No 1 by the final year of the century?
20. Which artist has had the most UK Top Ten hits in the 1990s?
21. What relationship was Brian Connolly of Sweet to Mark McManus aka Taggart?
22. Who played the heavy metal guitar on Michael Jackson's Beat It?
23. Which Manic Street Preacher has been missing presumed dead since '95?
24. Which artist has achieved the most consecutive UK Top Ten hits?
25. What nationality were Rednex?

## Answers

***Who's Who***

**1** James Ingram. **2** Bryan Adams. **3** Luther Vandross. **4** Kinks. **5** English. **6** Celine Dion. **7** Candi Staton. **8** 4. **9** Patti Labelle. **10** M People. **11** Gloria Estefan. **12** Steve Clark. **13** Erasure. **14** Blur. **15** Belinda Carlisle. **16** Buster Bloodvessel. **17** Petula Clark. **18** Gabrielle. **19** Cher. **20** Madonna. **21** Brother. **22** Eddie Van Halen. **23** Richey Edwards. **24** Madonna. **25** Swedish.

# Quiz 72 Pot Luck 36

1 Who had a UK No. 1 hit with I've Never Been To Me?
2 Eppley Airfield international airport is in which US state?
3 What is Hardy Amies' real first name?
4 Which role did John McEnroe's ex father in law play in Peyton Place?
5 What is the population of Spain to the nearest million?
6 Who first coined the phrase apartheid?
7 Richard Nixon was Vice President to which US President?
8 Which country of islands was declared a republic in 1987?
9 Who is the youngest female tennis player to win the US Open?
10 In which country is the Sky Train Rail bridge?
11 Who played Scott Robinson before Jason Donovan in Neighbours?
12 Vehicles from which country use the international registration letter LT?
13 In which country was Sam Neill born?
14 What is Gene Hackman's real name?
15 What was the world's first atomic powered ship called?
16 Which soap boasted a cafe called the Hot Biscuit?
17 Veteran presenter Frank Bough won an Oxbridge blue for which sport?
18 In which year did Dennis the Menace push Biffo off the Beano's front cover?
19 Ferihegy International airport is in which country?
20 Who was the defending champion when Virginia Wade won the Wimbledon singles?
21 What star sign is shared by Kate Bush and Daley Thompson?
22 How many 'victories' did The Red Baron claim in aerial dogfights?
23 "Desperation, Pacification, Expectation, Acclamation, Realization" was part of an ad to promote what?
24 Which by-election was won by Shirley Williams in November 1981 to become the first SDP MP?
25 What is Michael Barrymore's middle name?

## Answers

***Pot Luck 36***

**1** Charlene. **2** Nebraska. **3** Edwin. **4** Rodney Harrington. **5** 39 million. **6** Rev J C du Plessis. **7** Dwight Eisenhower. **8** Fiji. **9** Tracey Austin. **10** Canada. **11** Darius Perkins. **12** Lithuania. **13** N. Ireland. **14** Gene Hackman. **15** Lenin. **16** Dallas. **17** Soccer. **18** 1974. **19** Hungary. **20** Chris Evert. **21** Leo. **22** 80. **23** Chocolate. **24** Crosby. **25** Ciaran.

# Quiz 73 20th C Rich & Famous Level 3

1. Whose marriage was headlined in Variety as "Egghead weds Hourglass"?
2. At whose castle did Elizabeth Taylor spend her 60th birthday?
3. Who launched her own perfume called White Diamonds?
4. Josie Borain was the partner of which rich and famous person during his difficult divorce settlement?
5. What is Jose Carreras middle name?
6. Marion and Tito were two members of which famous family group?
7. What breed of dog was Madonna's Chiquita?
8. Whose funeral caused Sam Goldwyn say, "The only reason people showed up was to make sure he was dead"?
9. From which year did Martina Navratilova compete officially as an American rather than a Czech player?
10. Lady Elizabeth Anson is the sister of which Lord?
11. Chevy Chase was a professional in which sport?
12. Which woman was head of Sock Shop?
13. What was the name of John Gummer's daughter photographed burger munching in the early days of the BSE scare?
14. Who was the first British royal to visit the Soviet Union after 1917?
15. Who said, "I'd rather go mad than see a psychiatrist"?
16. Where was the wedding of David Beckham and Victoria Adams held?
17. Prince Charles said, "Diana only married me so that she could . . ." what?
18. Who said, "I never really hated a man enough to give him his diamonds back"?
19. What did Elvis's widow Priscilla call her child by a different partner?
20. Which disease did Lord Snowdon suffer from as a child?
21. Which ex MP had the car registration plate ANY 1 on his Rolls Royce?
22. Which name is shared by the daughters of Tony Curtis and Vanessa Feltz?
23. What type of car was Isadora Duncan test driving when her scarf caught in the wheel spokes and strangled her?
24. Who said, "I'm into pop because I want to get rich, famous and laid"?
25. Which sportsman said of his autobiography, "I can honestly say I have written one more book than I have read"?

## Answers

***20th C Rich & Famous***

**1** Arthur Miller & Marilyn Monroe. **2** Sleeping Beauty's. **3** Elizabeth Taylor. **4** Earl Spencer. **5** Maria. **6** Jackson Five. **7** Chihuahua. **8** Louis B Mayer. **9** 1981. **10** Lichfield. **11** Tennis. **12** Sophie Mirman. **13** Cordelia. **14** Princess Anne. **15** Michael Caine. **16** Luttrellstown Castle. **17** Go through red lights. **18** Zsa Zsa Gabor. **19** Navarone. **20** Polio. **21** Jeffrey Archer. **22** Allegra. **23** Bugatti. **24** Bob Geldof. **25** Merv Hughes.

# Quiz 74 Pot Luck 37

1. What was Madonna's last UK No 1 of the 80s?
2. Who was the famous wife of pilot Jim Mollison?
3. What is Dame Barbara Cartland's real first name?
4. In which year did Carry On star Hattie Jacques die?
5. Who was the first US President to be re-elected for a fourth term of office?
6. What does the P stand for in BUPA?
7. Who did John Spencer defeat in snooker's first knockout World Championship final?
8. Who wrote The Lady Who Liked Clean Rest Rooms?
9. Who was the first woman weather presenter on BBC TV?
10. Which university did Michael Jordan play basketball for?
11. Which were the first country to win soccer's World Cup on foreign soil?
12. What are the international registration letters of a vehicle from Guatemala?
13. Where was Kenneth Branagh born?
14. In what year did the first woman qualify as a barrister in the UK?
15. How many years after her death were Garbo's ashes returned to her Swedish homeland?
16. What is Cheryl Baker's real name?
17. In what year was Australia reached by air from England?
18. Cricketer Anil Humble has qualified as what?
19. Fornebu International airport is in which country?
20. Which company first advertised "Is it true blondes have more fun?"?
21. Which writer described newspaper reports of his own death as being "greatly exaggerated"?
22. What star sign is Omar Sharif?
23. In which year did the world's longest-running stage play The Mousetrap open?
24. Who directed Out Of Africa?
25. Which country does the airline LAM come from?

## Answers

***Pot Luck 37***

**1** Like A Prayer. **2** Amy Johnson. **3** Mary. **4** 1980. **5** Franklin D Roosevelt. **6** Provident. **7** Gary Owen. **8** J P Donleavy. **9** Barbara Edwards. **10** North Carolina. **11** Italy. **12** GCA. **13** Belfast. **14** 1921. **15** Nine. **16** Rita Crudgington. **17** 1919. **18** Engineer. **19** Norway. **20** Clairol. **21** Mark Twain. **22** Aries. **23** 1952. **24** Sydney Pollack. **25** Mozambique.

# Quiz 75 Murder Most Foul

1 Who was murdered along with O J Simpson's estranged wife Nicole?
2 Who was nicknamed the Vampire of Dusseldorf?
3 Who was the first woman to be executed for murder in Texas after 1863?
4 The Sicilian Specialist by Norman Lewis is a thinly disguised fictional account of which assassination plot?
5 Where was Martin Luther King assassinated?
6 What was the real name of Butch Cassidy?
7 Who was convicted with Jon Venables of the murder of Jamie Bulger?
8 Which famous name was killed by Kenneth Halliwell?
9 Under what name did Dr Crippen leave the country after the murder of his wife?
10 In which Lake did Peter Hogg dump the body of his wife in 1976 although it was 11 years before he was jailed?
11 Keith Blakelock was killed in riots where?
12 Where did Michael Ryan carry out an horrific massacre?
13 How many men did Dennis Nilsen admit to killing between 1978 and 1983?
14 Where did John Christie live?
15 Who did Gaetano Bresci assassinate?
16 What was gangster Lucky Luciano's real first name?
17 What was the name of Ruth Ellis's lover whom she murdered?
18 How was murderer Pedro Alonzo Lopez nicknamed?
19 How old was the Yorkshire Ripper when he was captured?
20 What was the name of the Captain who sent the first wireless telegraphy message which brought about the capture of Dr Crippen?
21 Who was convicted of the murderof aviator Charles Lindbergh's son?
22 On which island did Martin Bryant massacre 34 people in 1996?
23 What was the name of the rally which Yitzhak Rabin had attended just before his assassination?
24 What was the name of the man killed in the A6 Murder, for which James Hanratty was hanged?
25 Who did the Boston Strangler say he worked for in order to gain his victims' confidence?

## Answers

***Murder Most Foul***

**1** Ronald Goldman. **2** Peter Kurten. **3** Karla Faye Tucker. **4** JF Kennedy. **5** Memphis. **6** Robert LeRoy Parker. **7** Robert Thompson. **8** Joe Orton. **9** Robinson. **10** Wast Water. **11** Tottenham. **12** Hungerford. **13** 15. **14** 10 Rillington Place. **15** King Umberto I of Italy. **16** Salvatore. **17** David Blakely. **18** The Monster of the Andes. **19** 34. **20** Kendall. **21** Bruno Hauptmann. **22** Tasmania. **23** Peace Yes Violence No. **24** Michael Gregsten. **25** Model agency.

# Quiz 76 Pot Luck 38

1 What is Rob Lowe's middle name?
2 Where were the 1996 Summer Olympic Games held?
3 What sort of toys does Peter Baldwin, the former Derek Wilton of Coronation St, collect?
4 What is the population of Sweden to the nearest million?
5 Which newsreader wrote Cats in the News, and Dogs in the News?
6 What was the name of the Italian cruise ship hijacked by Palestinian terrorists in October 1985?
7 In which US state is John F Kennedy buried?
8 What was Dudley Moore chasing in France in Tesco ads?
9 Who had a UK No 1 hit with Pass The Dutchie?
10 In which decade was London Southwark bridge opened?
11 What did Big Bertha shell in 1918?
12 Vehicles from which country use the international registration letter LS?
13 Which Prime Minister was quoted as saying, "I must follow them; I am their leader"?
14 How is the Council for Encouragement for Music and the Arts now known?
15 Which controversial book contained the line, "You can't ravish a tin of sardines"?
16 Whose 1991 autobiography was called Still On My Way to Hollywood?
17 John F Kennedy was one of how many children?
18 In which English city was Cary Grant born?
19 Freeport International airport is in which country?
20 In comic strip what was the name of Black Bob's owner?
21 What was blonde bombshell Jayne Mansfield's IQ measured at?
22 Which country does the airline TAP come from?
23 What did George Bernard Shaw describe as "a perpendicular expression of a horizontal desire"?
24 What was the title of the first Carry On film - Carry On?
25 What star sign is shared by Elvis Costello and Julio Iglesias?

## Answers

***Pot Luck 38***

**1** Hepler. **2** Atlanta. **3** Toy theatres. **4** 9 million. **5** Martyn Lewis. **6** Achille Lauro. **7** Virginia. **8** Chickens. **9** Musical Youth. **10** 1970s. **11** Paris. **12** Lesotho. **13** Andrew Bonar Law. **14** Arts Council of Great Britain. **15** Lady Chatterley's Lover. **16** Ernie Wise. **17** 9. **18** Bristol. **19** The Bahamas. **20** Andrew Glenn. **21** 163. **22** Portugal. **23** Dancing. **24** Sergeant. **25** Virgo.

# Quiz 77 Sporting Chance

1 Why does the leader of the Tour de France wear a yellow jersey?
2 Where did golfer Mark Calcavecchia win his only British Open?
3 In the season Damon Hill was F1 champion how many races did he win?
4 Who was Czechoslovakia's only Wimbledon Men's Singles winner of the 20th century, playing as a Czech?
5 As well as Red Rum which other Red did Brian Fletcher ride to a Grand National victory?
6 How many games had Steve Davis won before Denis Taylor opened his account in the classic 1985 World Snooker final?
7 How many times did Terry Venables play for England?
8 In which country did Lynn Davies set the British long jump record that has stood for 30 years?
9 What was the first sport shown on ITV?
10 What was Jack Dempsey's nickname?
11 Brian Barnes played golf for Scotland in the 70s but where was he born?
12 What do JPR Williams initials stand for?
13 Who went airborne during a cricket match with David Gower in the Gooch led Australia tour?
14 How old was Stephen Hendry when he appeared on This Is Your Life?
15 Who has won the Badminton Horse Trials on Priceless and Master Craftsman?
16 Which boxer appeared in the film Spirit of Youth?
17 In which year did none of the four golf majors go to an American?
18 Who was team leader of Williams when Damon Hill was promoted to No 2?
19 What was the name of the horse on which Pat Eddery first won the Derby?
20 Who were the first winners of hockey's English National Cup?
21 What breed of dog was Steffi Graf's Ben?
22 In what year was snooker's World Championship first contested?
23 What is the middle name of golfer Mark James?
24 In how many games did Ray Wilkins captain England?
25 At which race circuit did Ayrton Senna lose his life?

## Answers

***Sporting Chance***

**1** Its sponsor printed its newspaper on yellow paper. **2** Troon. **3** 8. **4** Jan Kodes. **5** Red Alligator. **6** 8. **7** Twice. **8** Switzerland. **9** Boxing. **10** Manassa Mauler. **11** London. **12** John Peter Rhys. **13** John Morris. **14** 21. **15** Virginia Leng - nee Holgate. **16** Joe Louis. **17** 1993. **18** Alain Prost. **19** Grundy. **20** Hounslow. **21** Boxer. **22** 1927. **23** Hugh. **24** Ten. **25** Imola.

# Quiz 78 Pot Luck 39

1 Who or what were Alderney, Aukland, Hillsborough, Twilight?
2 Which convenience food did Joel Cheek develop?
3 How many Royal Variety shows did Morecambe and Wise both appear in?
4 Who was the first non English speaking winner of Wimbledon women's singles?
5 Who was on stage with Wogan in 1990 when George Best appeared to be drunk?
6 Discovered in the 30s Jonker and President Vargas were types of what?
7 Hamilton Kindley Field International airport is in which country?
8 Who did Cliff Thorburn beat in the final in his only snooker World Championship triumph?
9 Who wrote The Stone Dairies?
10 What is Nigel Davenport's real first name?
11 In which country is the Trois-Rivieres bridge?
12 What are the international registration letters of a vehicle from Guyana?
13 What appeared in the destination display on Man Utd's double decker bus after the 1999 European triumph?
14 What star sign is Gloria Hunniford?
15 Which Pope died in 1978 after a mere 33 days in office?
16 Where in the UK was Robert Carlyle born?
17 What was Kylie Minogue's last UK No. 1 of the 80s?
18 Who was Poet Laureate at the time of the Queen's Coronation?
19 What is Bono's real name?
20 What is Sir Terence Conran's middle name?
21 Bradley International airport is in which US state?
22 Jeffrey Hunter was the lead in the original pilot for which successful series?
23 Who scored England's last goal under Graham Taylor?
24 Who directed the blockbusting movie Alien?
25 Freddie Mercury died in which year?

## Answers

***Pot Luck 39***

**1** 1999 royal wedding horses. **2** Instant coffee. **3** Five. **4** Suzanne Lenglen. **5** Omar Sharif. **6** Diamond. **7** Bermuda. **8** Alex Higgins. **9** Carol Shields. **10** Arthur. **11** Canada. **12** GUY. **13** Excursion 2-1 Match. **14** Aries. **15** John Paul I. **16** Glasgow. **17** Hand On My Heart. **18** John Masefield. **19** Paul Hewson. **20** Orby. **21** Connecticut. **22** Star Trek. **23** Ian Wright. **24** Ridley Scott. **25** 1991.

# Quiz 79 20th C Comedies

Level 3 

1 Who wrote the lyrics for the song from Notting Hill sung by Elvis Costello?
2 What was Michael Palin's occupation in A Private Function?
3 Which boxer appeared in the film Carry On Constable?
4 Which film tells of the exploits of singer Deco Duffe?
5 What was the name of the orphanage where The Blues brothers were brought up?
6 Airplane! was triggered off by which movie?
7 How old was Macaulay Culkin when he was cast for his role in Home Alone?
8 In Private Benjamin what is the name of Benjamin's captain?
9 What was the name of the High School in Porky's?
10 What was Tootsie's name before he turned into Tootsie?
11 Who was the leader of the band that appeared in The Brady Bunch Movie?
12 Who directed The Cable Guy?
13 What type of drug is Sherman Klump trying to perfect in The Nutty Professor?
14 In what year does Demolition Man take place?
15 Which comedy contained the son A Wink and a Smile?
16 What was Steve Martin's first film?
17 In which category was Mrs Doubtfire Oscar nominated?
18 On which film was Three Men and a Baby based?
19 Which canine caper had the song The Day I Fall in Love?
20 Whose poems returned to the best sellers list after Four Weddings and a Funeral?
21 Who was both Oscar and BAFTA nominated for When Harry Met Sally?
22 What was the third Road movie?
23 What was the signal for an angel getting its wings in It's A Wonderful Life?
24 Who was Louise Lasser's husband when she starred with him in What's Up Tiger Lily?
25 What was the first sequel to The Pink Panther called?

**Answers**

***20th C Comedies***

**1** Herbert Kretzmer. **2** Chiropodist. **3** Freddie Mills. **4** The Commitments. **5** Saint Helen of the Blessed Shroud. **6** Zero Hour!. **7** Nine. **8** Lewis. **9** Angel Beach. **10** Michael Dorsey. **11** Davy Jones. **12** Ben Stiller. **13** Weight loss. **14** 2032. **15** Sleepless in Seattle. **16** The Jerk. **17** Best Make up. **18** Trois Hommes et un Couffin. **19** Beethoven's 2nd. **20** W H Auden. **21** Nora Ephron - writer. **22** Road to Morocco. **23** Bell ringing. **24** Woody Allen. **25** A Shot in the Dark.

# Quiz 80 Pot Luck 40

1 On which date in 1945 did Hitler take cyanide then shoot himself?
2 What is Val Kilmer's real name?
3 Who devised Monopoly?
4 Who did Neville Chamberlain follow as British Prime Minister?
5 Who was Anne Sullivan's most famous pupil?
6 Who wrote the words to Land of Hope and Glory?
7 Which state was particularly threatened by the leak on Three Mile Island in 1979?
8 What does dyb dyb dyb mean?
9 Which wartime classic was the title of a 1980 film with Hanna Schygulla & Mel Ferrer?
10 Who composed the music played by the Royal Philarmonic to launch the Rover 75?
11 Where was the UN Atomic Energy Agency based when it was set up in 1957?
12 Oran International airport is in which country?
13 Which Esholt inn was originally used as The Woolpack?
14 What star sign is shared by Tommy Lee Jones and Oliver Stone?
15 Which retailing operation was started by Sam Walton?
16 In the 90s Babrak Karmal and Sultan Ali Keshtmond have been Prime Minister in which country?
17 Which Pet Shop Boys video did Sir Ian McKellen appear in ?
18 Which Commission reported on the death of John F Kennedy in 1964?
19 Vehicles from which country use the international registration letter LB?
20 In what year was the Kellogg Company set up to manufacture cornflakes?
21 In which river is the Boulder Dam?
22 Which country does the airline Ladeco come from?
23 What is the population of Thailand to the nearest million?
24 What is Gene Hackman's middle name?
25 Who had a UK No 1 hit with Candy Girl?

## Answers

***Pot Luck 40***

**1** April 30th. **2** Val Kilmer. **3** Charles Darrow. **4** Baldwin. **5** Helen Keller. **6** A.C.Benson. **7** Pennsylvania. **8** Do your best. **9** Lili Marlene. **10** Dave Stewart. **11** Vienna. **12** Algeria. **13** The Commercial. **14** Virgo. **15** Wal-Mart. **16** Afghanistan. **17** Heart. **18** Warren. **19** Liberia. **20** 1906. **21** Colorado. **22** Chile. **23** 60 million. **24** Alden. **25** New Edition.

# Quiz 81 20th C TV Ads

Level 3 

**1** Which actor famous for a series of TV ads writes poetry under the pseudonym Robert Williams?
**2** Toothpaste was famously the first ad on ITV. What was the second?
**3** "Nice one Cyril" was the slogan to advertise what?
**4** What did the Hoddles advertise when they performed in a TV ad?
**5** Which drink suitable for children was advertised by Sharron Davies?
**6** Who famously threw away her ring and fur coat but kept her VW Golf?
**7** Which Dynasty character is 'worth it' in the hair ads?
**8** Who played Prunella Scales daughter in the Tesco ads?
**9** Who wrote Adiemus which was used by BA to advertise their services?
**10** Characters from which soap were used to advertise BT?
**11** Which company said, "Never forget you have a choice"?
**12** Which supermarket chain sacked John Cleese because customers found his ads very unfunny?
**13** Which personality famous for voiceovers described this way of earning money as the late 20th century equivalent of taking in washing?
**14** Which wine store used Pachelbel's Canon as an advertising theme?
**15** Which lager was advertised to the accompaniment of Verdi's La forza del destino?
**16** Which female writer is credited with coming up with the slogan "Go to work on an egg"?
**17** Which theme music did BT use to promote their Internet services?
**18** When did Guinness first say their drink was "good for you"?
**19** "Does she or doesn't she..?" was a slogan used to advertise what?
**20** Which make of car had the slogan Vorsprung durch Technik?
**21** When did the word pinta enter the English language via an ad for milk?
**22** What was advertised as the chocolate bar you could eat "without ruining your appetite"?
**23** Who made over 50 ads for Schh you know who in nine years?
**24** According to the ad, what put the T in Britain?
**25** When did the first anti drink driving campaign start?

## Answers

***20th C TV Ads***

**1** Bob Hoskins. **2** Drinking chocolate. **3** Wonderloaf bread. **4** Breakfast cereal. **5** Ribena Toothkind. **6** Paula Hamilton. **7** Sammy Jo. **8** Jane Horrocks. **9** Carl Jenkins. **10** EastEnders. **11** British Caledonian Airways. **12** Sainsbury's. **13** John Peel. **14** Thresher. **15** Stella Artois. **16** Fay Weldon. **17** E.T. **18** 1930. **19** Hair colour. **20** Audi. **21** 1958. **22** Milky Way. **23** William Franklin. **24** Typhoo. 25 1964.

# Quiz 82 Pot Luck 41

1. In which American state is the Merril Collection and the Burke Museum of Fine Arts?
2. From 1903 to 1958 all the Popes bar one had which name?
3. What star sign is Pauline Collins?
4. What is Whoopi Goldberg's real name?
5. What was Mud's last UK No 1 of the 70s?
6. Which political party had the Golden Lion in Ashburton, Devon as its meeting place?
7. Who hosted the quiz show Home Truths?
8. What was the first oldies pop song used in a Levi's TV ad?
9. Which actress played a hotel manager in The Duchess of Duke Street?
10. What was the name of William Shatner's Doberman Pinscher dog?
11. Which nation was the first to ratify the United Nations charter in 1945?
12. What are the international registration letters of a vehicle from Jordan?
13. Who wrote the novel Time and Tide?
14. What is the Alaskan terminus of the Alaskan Highway?
15. Put a tiger in your tank was originally an advertising slogan for what?
16. In which year did David Bedford set a new 10,000m record?
17. What is Mel Gibson's middle name?
18. In which country was Julie Christie born?
19. In the 60s the last London trolleybus journey started where?
20. What was Buster Keaton's actual first name?
21. Cannon international airport is in which US state?
22. Which country does the airline VIASA come from?
23. To the nearest 30 minutes how long was the longest speech ever made at the United Nations?
24. Who directed Back To The Future?
25. Richard Daley was mayor of which city for 21 years?

## Answers

***Pot Luck 41***

**1** Texas. **2** Pius. **3** Virgo. **4** Caryn Johnson. **5** Oh Boy. **6** Monster Raving Loony Party. **7** Steve Wright. **8** I Heard It Through The Grapevine. **9** Gemma Jones. **10** Kirk. **11** Nicaragua. **12** HKJ. **13** Edna O'Brien. **14** Fairbanks. **15** Esso petrol. **16** 1973. **17** Columcille. **18** India. **19** Wimbledon. **20** Joseph. **21** Nevada. **22** Venezuela. **23** 4.5 hours. **24** Robert Zemeckis. **25** Chicago.

# Quiz 83 Media

**1** All human life is there was a slogan used to advertise which newspaper?
**2** Which newspaper published detailed photographs of Diana's car crash?
**3** In 1980 which radio station ran an April Fool's day prank saying Big Ben's clockface would be replaced by a digital one?
**4** Who founded the Pergamon Press?
**5** Who drew Felix the Cat?
**6** In what profession did Bruce Bairnsfather find fame?
**7** In radio's Beyond Our Ken which Kenneth Williams character's catchphrase was, "The answer lies in the soil"?
**8** Which newspaper was launched in January 1990?
**9** When he was on Desert Island Discs, which newspaper did Des O'Connor ask to have delivered regularly as his luxury?
**10** Tessa Sanderson won libel damages in 1990 against which newspapers?
**11** Who was DC Thomson's first cartoonist allowed to sign his name?
**12** Who found fame on radio as Lady Beatrice Counterblast?
**13** Who created the line from a cartoon, "Happiness is a warm puppy"?
**14** Whose poem For the Fallen was printed in The Times in 1914?
**15** When did the Popeye cartoon begin?
**16** For which magazine did a pregnant Cindy Crawford pose naked?
**17** Which group of people did radio producer D G Bridson describe as "The wriggling ponces of the spoken word"?
**18** Who said, "When a journalist enters the room, your privacy ends and his begins"?
**19** Which radio DJ said, "And don't forget on Sunday you can hear the two minute silence on Radio One"?
**20** Who was Little Jim in The Goons?
**21** "Good girls go to heaven, bad girls go everywhere" was the slogan used to launch which magazine?
**22** Which journalist took the name Cassandra?
**23** Who scripted The Navy Lark?
**24** Who launched the news magazine Now! around 1980?
**25** Which classic radio show had the line, "Can I do you now sir"?

## Answers

***Media***
**1** The News of the World. **2** Bild. **3** BBC World Service. **4** Robert Maxwell. **5** Otto Messmer. **6** Cartoonist. **7** Arthur Fallowfield. **8** The Independent on Sunday. **9** The Sporting Life. **10** Sunday Mirror/People. **11** Dudley Watkins. **12** Betty Marsden. **13** Charles Schultz. **14** Laurence Binyon. **15** 1933. **16** W. **17** Disc jockeys. **18** Warren Beatty. **19** Steve Wright. **20** Spike Milligan. **21** Cosmopolitan. **22** William Connor. **23** Lawrie Wyman. **24** James Goldsmith. **25** ITMA.

# Quiz 84 Pot Luck 42

1 In which country was the Zoo Bridge constructed?
2 The Windmill Theatre which "never closed" in World War II shut down in which year?
3 What star sign is shared by Meatloaf and Luciano Pavarotti?
4 In what context was Julia Lang's voice often heard from the 50s onwards?
5 Which Adam and the Ants video did Diana Dors appear in?
6 Which school featured in Press Gang?
7 Thomas Marshal was Vice President to which US President?
8 What did the French artist Henri Matisse begin a career in?
9 What is the population of Turkey to the nearest million?
10 Which country does the airline Avensa come from?
11 Who was the German soldier in Rowan and Martin's Laugh In?
12 Vehicles from which country use the international registration letter LAR?
13 What is Paul Boateng's middle name?
14 Spear of the Nation was an armed wing of which group?
15 Who had a UK No. 1 hit with The Final Countdown?
16 What is Osbert Lancaster best known for producing?
17 According to Dateline figures, the highest percentage of male clients are in which profession?
18 Who co-wrote Stand by Your Man with Tammy Wynette?
19 Santander International airport is in which country?
20 Who created Desperate Dan?
21 Ellen Church is recognised as being the first female what?
22 Actress Dulcie Gray played Kate in which TV drama series?
23 How many nations took part in the 1996 Olympics?
24 What is Brian Walden's real first name?
25 Which liner launched in 1934 was the largest of her time?

## Answers

***Pot Luck 42***

**1** Germany. **2** 1964. **3** Libra. **4** Radio's Listen with Mother. **5** Prince Charming. **6** Norbridge High. **7** Woodrow Wilson. **8** Law. **9** 63 million. **10** Venezuela. **11** Arte Johnson. **12** Libya. **13** Yaw. **14** ANC. **15** Europe. **16** Cartoons. **17** Accountancy. **18** Billy Sherrill. **19** Spain. **20** Dudley Watkins. **21** Air hostess. **22** Howards' Way. **23** 197. **24** Alastair. **25** Queen Mary.

# Quiz 85 Words & Music

1 Who was the first female to top the singles chart with a self-composed song?
2 Whose album Fat of the Land debuted at No 1 in more than 20 countries?
3 What was the first UK No 1 written by Shakin' Stevens himself?
4 What was the first TV theme to top the UK charts?
5 Who used and wrote under the pseudonym Bernard Webb?
6 Whose book of poems was called Songs for While I'm Away?
7 Who won Grammys for Best Album, Male Vocalist and Producer in 1986?
8 Lennon and McCartney wrote Goodbye for which vocalist?
9 Who was described as "a woman who pulled herself up by her bra straps"?
10 How many times was "Walk On By" sung by Gabrielle in the first chorus?
11 What type of vehicle were Reo Speedwagon named after?
12 What was Barry Manilow's Mandy originally titled in the US?
13 What was Sir Cliff Richard's first self produced UK No 1?
14 What was the first UK No 1 with "rock and roll" in the title?
15 Which song by Paul Simon begins "Wish I Was a Kellogg's Corn Flake"?
16 In the film Grease, who sang Beauty School Dropout?
17 On what date did Elton John first sing his biggest selling single in public?
18 What was the average age of a soldier in World War II in the UK No 1 hit 19?
19 Which artist was the subject of a 1991 biography by Randy Taraborelli?
20 Which Kenny Rogers song was written by Lionel Richie?
21 Which song by Lisa Stansfield featured in Indecent Proposal?
22 Who co-wrote Fame with David Bowie?
23 Who was Michael Jackson's massive hit Ben originally intended for?
24 Whose 1991 autobiography was called And The Beat Goes On?
25 Who was Willy Russell's co-writer on the musical Tallulah Who?

## Answers

***Words & Music***

**1** Kate Bush. **2** Prodigy. **3** Oh Julie!. **4** Eye Level. **5** Paul McCartney. **6** Phil Lynott. **7** Phil Collins. **8** Mary Hopkin. **9** Madonna. **10** 3. **11** A fire engine. **12** Brandy. **13** Mistletoe and Wine. **14** Rock and Roll Waltz. **15** Punky's Dilemma. **13** Frankie Avalon. **17** 6th Sept 1997. **18** 26. **19** Michael Jackson. **20** Lady. **21** In All The Right Places. **22** John Lennon. **23** Donny Osmond. **24** Sonny Bono. **25** Suzy Quatro.

# Quiz 86 Pot Luck 43

1 Cardinal Basil Hume's father was Scottish but which country was his mother from?
2 In which year was the Sun first published?
3 Who wrote that the female of the species is more deadly than the male?
4 Which soccer side does Robert Lindsay support?
5 In which country did Frank and Tessa finally marry in Love Hurts?
6 Who painted The Art of the Game which depicted Eric Cantona as Christ?
7 How many times was Stirling Moss runner up in the F1 championship?
8 What is Nicholas Parsons' real first name?
9 Which Police Constable was taken prisoner in the 1980 London Iranian embassy siege?
10 What star sign is Gladys Knight?
11 Charlotte international airport is in which US state?
12 Which celebrity was born in Craighton Road, Eltham in 1903?
13 Who said ,"Money is like an arm or a leg, use it or lose it."?
14 What colour were the covers of the crime novels published in the 1930s by Victor Gollancz?
15 What was Olivia Newton-John's last UK No 1 of the 70s?
16 Who wrote the novel Honours Even?
17 Rosemary Brown is better known by which name?
18 The 'girl in the polka dot dress' was a key witness in whose assassination?
19 Who said, "Brevity is the soul of lingerie.."?
20 In which country was Olivia De Havilland born?
21 Which writer said, "Where large sums of money are involved, it is advisable to trust nobody."?
22 Who directed the classic movie High Noon?
23 Which country does the airline VASP come from?
24 In which year was Indira Gandhi assassinated by Sikh extremists?
25 What is Meg Ryan's real name?

## Answers

***Pot Luck 43***

**1** France. **2** 1964. **3** Rudyard Kipling. **4** Derby County. **5** Russia. **6** Michael Browne. **7** Four. **8** Christopher. **9** Trevor Lock. **10** Gemini. **11** North Carolina. **12** Bob Hope. **13** Henry Ford. **14** Yellow. **15** Summer Nights. **16** Nigel Godwin Tranter. **17** Dana. **18** Bobby Kennedy. **19** Dorothy Parker. **20** Japan. **21** Agatha Christie. **22** Fred Zinnemann. **23** Brazil. **24** 1984. **25** Margaret Hyra.

# Quiz 87 Unforgettables

1 What would Pablo Picasso's surname have been if he had used his father's name instead of his mother's?
2 In what country was British choreographer Sir Frederick Ashton born?
3 Who made the film Renaldo and Clara with Bob Dylan?
4 Who said, "The hardest thing to understand in the world is income tax"?
5 Four minute miler Dr Roger Bannister has published papers on what?
6 Which orchestral conductor was married to one of the subjects of the film Hilary and Jackie?
7 Groucho Marx resigned from where as he didn't care to belong to any club that would have him as a member?
8 Which of the Barrymores wrote the memoir We Barrymores?
9 Which British composer wrote the theme music for the film Murder on the Orient Express?
10 Who said, "Middle age is when your age starts to show around your middle"?
11 What was Humphrey Bogart's middle name?
12 Which director's autobiography was called The Name Above the Title?
13 About whom did Kenneth Tynan say, "What one sees in other women drunk, one sees in... sober"?
14 Who designed the WRAC uniform?
15 The expression Great White Hope was used to describe which black boxer's opponents?
16 Where did Anne Frank die?
17 Who created Bugs Bunny?
18 What as Buster Keaton's real first name?
19 Whose famous teacher was Anne Sullivan?
20 In which craft did Bernard Leach find fame?
21 Where was blues singer Leadbelly when he was 'discovered' musically?
22 In which film did Harold Lloyd hang from a clockface?
23 Which Marx brother was not in Duck Soup?
24 How many England caps did Stanley Matthews win in 22 years?
25 Which political party did Emmeline Pankhurst join in 1926?

**Answers**

***Unforgettables***
**1** Ruiz. **2** Ecuador. **3** Joan Baez. **4** Albert Einstein. **5** Neurology. **6** Daniel Barenboim. **7** Friars Club. **8** Lionel. **9** Richard Rodney Bennett. **10** Bob Hope. **11** De Forrest. **12** Frank Capra. **13** Greta Garbo. **14** Norman Hartnell. **15** Jack Johnson. **16** Belsen. **17** Chuck Jones. **18** Joseph. **19** Helen Keller. **20** Pottery. **21** Prison. **22** Safety Last. **23** Gummo. **24** 54. **25** Conservative.

# Quiz 88 Pot Luck 44

1 What is the population of Zimbabwe to the nearest million?
2 What is Rowan Atkinson's middle name?
3 What star sign is shared by Ian Botham and Billy Idol?
4 In which decade was the BBC Scottish Symphony Orchestra founded?
5 What did Elizabeth Andrews find in the 80s that posed important security questions?
6 Who had a UK No 1 hit with Rhythm Is A Dancer?
7 Which hairdresser said "The only place where success comes before work is in the dictionary"?
8 Sir Richard Greenbury resigned in June 99 as chairman of which big company?
9 Which international team was captained by Alistair Campbell in 1999?
10 In which decade was the Benjamin Franklin suspension bridge opened?
11 Who wrote the karaoke classic line, "And now the end is near.."?
12 Vehicles from which country use the international registration letter KWT?
13 What was Gillian Taylforth's autobiography called?
14 Which ex Prime Minister went on a cruise to improve his health, and died?
15 Which song by a solo singer stopped T Rex's Jeepster from getting to No 1?
16 How many years did Petra the dog appear on Blue Peter?
17 Pollock's Toy Museum is in which city?
18 What was the name of the female version of Biggles created by EW Johns?
19 Satolas International airport is in which country?
20 As a player what was Alf Ramsay's first club?
21 Who said "Discretion is a polite word for hypocrisy."?
22 Which country does the airline Rottnest Airbus come from?
23 Which TV and radio star set a world record for kissing in 1978?
24 What is Harrison Ford's real name?
25 At what weight did Chris Eubank win the WBO title in 1990?

## Answers

***Pot Luck 44***

**1** 12 million. **2** Sebastian. **3** Sagittarius. **4** 30s. **5** Intruder in the Queen's bedroom. **6** Snap. **7** Vidal Sassoon. **8** Marks & Spencer. **9** Zimbabwe cricket team. **10** 1920s. **11** Paul Anka - in My Way. **12** Kuwait. **13** Kathy and Me. **14** Ramsay MacDonald. **15** Ernie The Fastest Milkman in the West. **16** 15. **17** London. **18** Worrals of the WAAF. **19** France. **20** Southampton. **21** Christine Keeler. **22** Australia. **23** James Whale. **24** Harrison Ford. **25** Middleweight.

# Quiz 89 Famous Firsts

Level 3 

1 Who was the first person to make a solo trek to the South Pole on foot?
2 In what year was the first external heart pacemaker fitted?
3 Who was the first woman to sail around the world?
4 SRN1 was the first what?
5 The first Miss World came from which country?
6 What did Carlton Magee devise in the US for motorists?
7 What was first revealed at Lord's in 1975?
8 What was the name of the first long lasting perfume, launched in Japan in 1993?
9 Which two national teams made the first flight over Everest in a hot air balloon?
10 In which country was the first kidney transplant carried out?
11 What was Lester Piggott's first Derby winner back in 1954?
12 Which British bank was the first to issue cash dispenser cards?
13 Which orchestra was the first in London to be conducted by a woman?
14 Which support group was founded in Ohio in 1935?
15 Who founded the Cubism movement with Picasso?
16 Joseph Mornier patented which building material?
17 Who was the first black American to win the Nobel Peace prize?
18 In what year did Plaid Cymru win its first seat in the House of Commons?
19 Jacqui Mofokeng was the first black woman to win what?
20 At what mph did Malcolm Campbell set the land speed record in 1931?
21 In which category did Marie Curie win her second Nobel Prize, becoming the first person to win a Nobel Prize twice?
22 Where was the first nuclear reactor built, by Enrico Fermi?
23 Who led the team which made the first successful overland crossing of Antarctica?
24 Who was the first Governor General of Pakistan?
25 After record breaking flights to Australia and Cape Town where was Amy Johnson's plane lost?

## Answers

***Famous Firsts***

**1** Erling Kagge. **2** 1952. **3** Naomi James. **4** Cross channel Hovercraft. **5** Sweden. **6** Parking meter. **7** A streaker. **8** Shiseido. **9** Australia/UK. **10** USA. **11** Never Say Die. **12** Barclays. **13** Royal Philharmonic. **14** Alcoholics Anonymous. **15** Braque. **16** Reinforced concrete. **17** Ralph Bunche. **18** 1966. **19** Miss South Africa. **20** 246. **21** Chemistry. **22** Chicago. **23** Fuchs. **24** Jinnah. **25** Thames Estuary.

# Quiz 90 Pot Luck 45

1 Where are the 2002 Winter Olympic Games being held?
2 What is Jennifer Jason Leigh's real name?
3 Chris Collins took a show biz name from someone in a local pub dominoes team; what was it?
4 Who was the defending champion when Billie Jean King first won Wimbledon singles?
5 What star sign is actress Kathy Staff?
6 How much were the first Penguin books?
7 What was the Pet Shop Boys' last UK No 1 of the 80s?
8 Stop me a buy one was originally an advertising slogan for what?
9 What is Richard Dunwoody's real first name?
10 In which country was the Verrazano Narrows bridge built?
11 What is the name of the Doctor played by Harrison Ford in The Fugitive?
12 What are the international registration letters of a vehicle from Cambodia?
13 Who replaced Damon Hill at Williams?
14 Who wrote the line, "Do not go gentle into that good night"?
15 Which ex tennis player has run a foundation for terminally ill children through the 90s?
16 What was the first product made by Heinz?
17 In which country did Argentina first win soccer's World Cup?
18 What is Joan Collins' middle name?
19 Queen Alia International airport is in which country?
20 Which part was played by Burgess Meredith in the '60s Batman TV series?
21 Albuquerque international airport is in which US state?
22 Which country does the airline Aero Lloyd come from?
23 Who directed the movie Trading Places?
24 Where in Australia was swashbuckling Errol Flynn born?
25 Who wrote the novel The Tailor of Panama?

## Answers

***Pot Luck 45***

**1** Salt Lake City. **2** Jennifer Morrow. **3** Frank Skinner. **4** Margaret Smith. **5** Cancer. **6** 6d. **7** Heart. **8** Ice cream. **9** Thomas. **10** USA. **11** Richard Kimble. **12** K. **13** Heinz-Harald Frentzen. **14** Dylan Thomas. **15** Andrea Jaeger. **16** Horseradish sauce. **17** Argentina. **18** Henrietta. **19** Jordan. **20** The Penguin. **21** New Mexico. **22** Germany. **23** John Landis. **24** Hobart. **25** John Le Carre.

# Quiz 91 Horse Racing

1 Which horse gave Lester Piggott his 30th victory in an English Classic?
2 On the flat what is the most number of winners achieved by a jockey in a season in the 20th century?
3 Which horse finished first in the abandoned 1993 Grand National?
4 The Coronation Cup celebrates which coronation?
5 In the 1989 Oaks which 'winning' horse was later disqualified after a post-race test?
6 Who rode Red Rum for the third Grand National triumph?
7 Who was the first National Hunt jockey to employ an agent?
8 How many winners did Frankie Dettori ride in his 1994 super season?
9 Which of the English Classics has Lester Piggott won least times?
10 At the beginning of the century what did Sceptre achieve in 1902?
11 Which horse gave Richard Dunwoody his first Grand National success?
12 What's the only Derby winner of the century to have a date as its name?
13 In which year did the Grand National witness Devon Loch's sensational fall 50 yards from home?
14 Which was the first English Classic to be raced in Scotland?
15 Which horse was the first on which Lester Piggott won two Classics?
16 Who sponsored the 1000 Guineas from 1984 to 1992?
17 What was the last Grand National winner ridden by an amateur before Mr Fisk?
18 Who trained the prolific winner Brigadier Gerard?
19 What was the name of the horse on which Geoff Lewis won his only Derby?
20 To the nearest 1,000, how many rides did the legendary Willie Shoemaker make?
21 Which horse gave Mick Kinane his first 2000 Guineas success?
22 Who was the youngest jockey to win the Grand National in the 20th century?
23 What did Golden Miller win five years in a row back in the 30s?
24 Who won the Oaks on Oh So Sharp and on Diminuendo?
25 How many times has Lester Piggott ridden over 200 winners in a season?

## Answers

***Horse Racing***

**1** Rodrigo de Triano. **2** 269. **3** Esha Ness. **4** Edward VII. **5** Aliyssa. **6** Tommy Stack. **7** Jonjo O'Neill. **8** 233. **9** 1000 Guineas. **10** Won four Classics. **11** West Tip. **12** April the Fifth. **13** 1956. **14** St Leger - in 1989. **15** Crepello. **16** General Accident. **17** Grittar. **18** John Hislop. **19** Mill Reef. **20** 40,000. **21** Tirol. **22** Bruce Hobbs. **23** Cheltenham Gold Cup. **24** Steve Cauthen. **25** Never.

# Quiz 92 The Oscars

1 Who was the only British actor to win the best Actor Oscar in the 80s?
2 Whose Oscar was sold in 1994 for over half a million dollars?
3 Which film won the Best Film Oscar on the 60th anniversary of the awards?
4 For which film did Katharine Hepburn win the first of her four 20th century Oscars?
5 Robert de Niro was Oscar nominated for his portrayal of which ex con in Cape Fear?
6 Who eventually played the part Kate Winslet went for in Sense & Sensibility?
7 For which film did Barbra Streisand win her second Oscar?
8 Who was the first actress to win an Oscar for playing the role of an Oscar nominee?
9 Who was the first woman to receive an Oscar for acting and scripting?
10 Who was the oldest winner of the Best Actress Oscar in the 20th century?
11 Which 1994 film won the Oscar for best costume design?
12 Who failed to win an Oscar after six nominations but received an honorary award in 1993?
13 How many times was Richard Burton nominated for an Oscar, though he never won?
14 For which 1990 film did Bruce Joel Rubin win Best Screenplay Oscar?
15 In 1982 who won a special award for 50 years of film making?
16 What was the first film to have its whole cast Oscar nominated?
17 In 1990 which short cartoon won Nick Park an Oscar?
18 Which movie won Best Film the year Charles and Diana were married?
19 Who was Oscar nominated in the same year as her daughter?
20 What was Best Picture the year of the Los Angeles Olympics?
21 Who was the first British actor in the 90s to win the Best Actor Oscar?
22 In 1986 which film had 11 nominations and won nothing?
23 Who were the first father and son to win acting Oscars for the same film?
24 In 1990 who won an achievement Oscar with Myrna Loy?
25 For which film did Callie Khouri win an Oscar in 1991 for screenplay?

## Answers

***The Oscars***

**1** Ben Kingsley. **2** Vivienne Leigh. **3** Rain Man. **4** Morning Glory. **5** Max Cady. **6** Imogen Stubbs. **7** A Star is Born - the song. **8** Maggie Smith. **9** Emma Thompson. **10** Jessica Tandy. **11** The Adventures of Priscilla Queen of the Desert. **12** Deborah Kerr. **13** Seven. **14** Ghost. **15** Mickey Rooney. **16** Who's Afraid of Virginia Woolf?. **17** Creature Comforts. **18** Chariots of Fire. **19** Diane Ladd. **20** Amadeus. **21** Daniel Day Lewis. **22** The Color Purple. **23** Walter & John Huston. **24** Sophia Loren. **25** Thelma and Louise.

# Quiz 93 TV Times

1. Which celebrity couple had the number plate 8 DEB?
2. Which TV cook went to the same school as Jeffrey Archer?
3. What was William Shatner's codename for This Is Your Life?
4. Which TV detective wrote A Cook For All Seasons under his own name?
5. Which British programme won The Golden Rose of Montreux in 1995?
6. Who wrote the song which launched Channel 5?
7. Which former Breakfast Time presenter is a former Miss Great Britain?
8. Who was the first woman on This is Your Life when it transferred to ITV in 1969?
9. Who was the first BBC Sports Personality of the Year of the 1990s?
10. Which actor wrote the show Mac and Beth?
11. Who was described by an interviewee as "the thinking woman's crumpet gone stale"?
12. Who hosted the BBC version of You've Been Framed, Caught In the Act?
13. Which 80s medical drama had the same production company as Hill Street Blues?
14. Which West End show starring ex EastEnder Anita Dobson closed after just three weeks in 1993?
15. Which TV writer was born Romana Barrack?
16. Eileen Downey shot to fame in a docu soap about what?
17. Whose song provided the music for In The Seven Faces of Woman?
18. What is the name of cafe owned by Hayley's husband in Coronation Street?
19. How much was Seinfeld offered for each episode of his comedy show when he announced in 1998 he wanted to quit?
20. What was Michael Barrymore's occupation before becoming a TV star?
21. Who was the third soccer player to win BBC Sports Personality of the year?
22. Which Gilbert & Sullivan opera was playing on Derek Wilton's car radio as he suffered his fatal heart attack in Coronation Street?
23. Which character opened the first ever episode of Crossroads and closed the last ever one?
24. What was Tosh Lines' real first name in The Bill?
25. Wilma's vacuum cleaner in The Flintstones was which animal?

**Answers**

***TV Times***

**1** Paul Daniels & Debbie McGee. **2** Keith Floyd. **3** Beam. **4** George Baker. **5** Don't Forget Your Toothbrush. **6** The Spice Girls. **7** Debbie Greenwood. **8** Twiggy. **9** Paul Gascoigne. **10** Michael Praed. **11** Melvyn Bragg. **12** Shane Richie. **13** St Elsewhere. **14** Eurovision. **15** Carla Lane. **16** Hotel. **17** Charles Aznavour. **18** Roy's Rolls. **19** $5 million. **20** Hairdresser. **21** Michael Owen. **22** The Mikado. **23** Jill. **24** Alfred. **25** Elephant.

# Quiz 94 Technology

**1** What was the name of the first home computer to be manufactured?
**2** What was France's on line telecom service called?
**3** Who developed the Gaia Theory?
**4** How was Trevor Baylis's revolutionary radio powered?
**5** Alan Roberts' special super glue was used to join what?
**6** What does O stand for in the equipment NOSE which imitates he human nose?
**7** What was the occupation of Bruce Rushin who designed the £2 coin to symbolize the progress of technology in British history?
**8** Sir Jagadis Chandra Bose's invention the crescograph measures what?
**9** Which play by Capek introduced the word robot?
**10** What type of camera did Edwin Land develop?
**11** Edward Salk developed a vaccine against what?
**12** Which hospital performed the first heart surgery on a baby in its mother's womb?
**13** Adolf Loos was a designer of what?
**14** In which islands is Bikini Atoll where the first atomic bombs were tested?
**15** Who was the first Nobel Prize winner to come from Pakistan?
**16** What was the first shopping mall on the Internet called?
**17** Leslie Rogge was the first person to be arrested due to what?
**18** Who led the team which invented transistors in the 1940s?
**19** What was the codename of the first atomic bomb dropped on Hiroshima?
**20** In 1908 Wilbur Wright travelled what record breaking number of miles in 2 hours 20 minutes?
**21** William Henry Hoover started making vacuum cleaners because his original trade was dying out; what was it?
**22** Which company manufactured the first electric razor?
**23** How long did Bleriot's first cross channel flight last?
**24** What nationality of plane first broke the 100mph sound barrier?
**25** The first air collision took place over which country?

## Answers

***Inventiona and Technology***
**1** Altair. **2** Minitel. **3** Sanford. **4** Clockwork. **5** Wounds. **6** Olfactory. **7** Art teacher. **8** Plant movements. **9** R.U.R.. **10** Polaroid. **11** Polio. **12** Guy's. **13** Buildings. **14** Marshall Islands. **15** Abdus Salam. **16** The Branch Mall. **17** The Internet. **18** Shockley. **19** Little Boy. **20** 77. **21** Harness maker. **22** Schick. **23** 43 minutes. **24** French. **25** Austria.

# Quiz 95 20th C Leaders

Level 3 

1 Paddy Ashdown is fluent in which oriental language?
2 How is Tenzin Gyatso better known?
3 Roy Jenkins became Lord Jenkins of where?
4 Which politician was a judge for the Booker Prize in 1988?
5 Neil Kinnock became MP for which constituency when he entered Parliament in 1970?
6 Who was the first leader of the Belgian Congo?
7 Who replaced Geoffrey Howe as Foreign Secretary in Thatcher's government?
8 Who was Greece's first socialist Prime Minister?
9 Canadian leader Lester Pearson won the Nobel Peace prize for his mediation role in which conflict?
10 Who was Pope during WWII?
11 Which former Tory Party Chairman wrote I Have No Gun But I Can Spit?
12 What was Ronald Reagan's last film?
13 Who formulated his Sinatra Doctrine - foreign policy to be constructed on a My Way basis?
14 Vaclav Havel and George VI both lost what part of their bodies?
15 Which former leader wrote the novel The Cardinal's Hat?
16 Which 'stalking horse' stood for the Tory leadership against Margaret Thatcher in 1989?
17 Where was Nelson Mandela's first foreign trip to after his release from prison?
18 Who did Jonathan Sacks replace as Chief Rabbi in 1990?
19 In 1990 Transport Minister Cecil Parkinson called for a new inquiry into the sinking of what ship?
20 Which leader has played in goal for Polish soccer side Wotsyla?
21 Who became first President of Israel?
22 In 1990 who faced banners saying Goodbye Pineapple Face?
23 Who took over as President of Romania after Ceaucescu was executed?
24 Who did Lord McNally describe as the Kevin Keegan of politics?
25 Who did Thatcher describe as "a man we can do business with"?

**Answers**

***20th C Leaders***

**1** Mandarin. **2** The Dalai Lama. **3** Hillhead. **4** Michael Foot. **5** Bedwelty. **6** Lumumba. **7** John Major. **8** Papandreou. **9** Suez. **10** Pius XII. **11** Kenneth Baker. **12** The Killers. **13** Eduard Shevardnadze . **14** Lung. **15** Mussolini. **16** Sir Anthony Meyer. **17** Zambia. **18** Lord Jakobovits. **19** Titanic. **20** The Pope. **21** Chaim Weizmann. **22** Manuel Noriega. **23** Ion Iliescu. **24** Paddy Ashdown. **25** Gorbachev.

# Quiz 96 Space - The Final Frontier Level 3

1 What was the name of the first chimpanzee the Americans sent in space?
2 How long did the record breaking space walk from space shuttle Endeavour last in 1993?
3 Where did the European space probe Ulysses set off for in 1991?
4 What did Neil Armstrong say immediately before "the eagle has landed"?
5 Which space first was achieved by Toyohiro Akiyama in 1991?
6 On what date in 1997 did Pathfinder land on Mars right on schedule?
7 Who was the next American in space after Shephard?
8 In which year were all three astronauts on the first moon landing expedition born?
9 Which probe sent back the first major pictures of Jupiter in 1995?
10 Who made the first untethered space walk of the 1990s?
11 On which ship did President Nixon welcome the astronauts back form the Moon?
12 On which island is the Kennedy Space centre?
13 Which scientist located Pluto?
14 In what year was Hale Bopp first seen?
15 Which astronaut said, "Houston we have a problem"?
16 What is Neil Armstrong's middle name?
17 What was the name of the Japanese Moon orbiter launched in 1990?
18 Which cosmonaut returned to Earth in 1996 after spending a record breaking 438 days in space?
19 Who was the second Soviet cosmonaut?
20 What was the nationality of the journalist who accompanied a docking mission to MIR in 1990?
21 What was the name of the first probe to send back pictures from Mars?
22 How long did Sergei Krikalyev spend on Mir in the early 90s?
23 What was the role of Rocco Petrone in the Apollo XI project?
24 Who was the first woman to captain a space shuttle crew?
25 How many orbits of the moon were there on the first manned orbit?

## Answers

***Space – The Final Frontier***

**1** Ham. **2** Five hours. **3** The Sun. **4** Tranquillity base here. **5** First fare paying passenger. **6** 4th July. **7** Virgil Grissom. **8** 1930. **9** Galileo. **10** Mark Lee. **11** Hornet. **12** Merritt. **13** Clyde Tombaugh. **14** 1995. **15** James Lovell. **16** Alden. **17** Muses-A. **18** Polyakov. **19** Titov. **20** Japanese. **21** Viking. **22** Ten months. **23** Launch director. **24** Eileen Collins. **25** 10.

# Quiz 97 Sports Bag

Level 3 

1 At which venue did Sandy Lyle win the British Open?
2 In women's hockey which country has won the World Cup most times?
3 In which sport did actor Noel Harrison compete in the 1952 Olympics?
4 In which year did Graham Hill win the Le Mans 24 hour race?
5 Who did Terry Griffiths beat in the final in his only snooker World Championship triumph?
6 Great Britain's Rugby League side toured where for the first time in 1984?
7 The Stoke Poges golf club was used for location shots for which film?
8 In Red Rum's first Grand National triumph which 9 -1 favourite had led the field until the final dash?
9 In how many games did Bobby Charlton captain England?
10 Anton Geesink was the first person out of Japan to win a judo world championship, but which country did he come from?
11 Who played Harlequins in the first Rugby Union game at Twickenham?
12 How many of his 45 races did Mike Hawthorn, F1 world champion , win?
13 In which decade were the Badminton Horse Trials first held?
14 In how many of his 39 Tests was Mike Brearley not the captain?
15 Name France's last Wimbledon Men's Singles winner of this century.
16 Who did Spurs meet in the first all British European final?
17 In which soap did Fred Trueman appear as himself?
18 Which was the last horse before Nijinsky to win the triple of Derby, 2000 Guineas and St Leger?
19 In which UK event did Tony Jacklin make the first live TV hole in one?
20 When Wimbledon became Open in 1968 what was the men's singles prize money?
21 Britain's William Lane became a world champion in which sport?
22 In which events did Gert Frederiksson win six Olympic Golds?
23 Who was the defending champion when Chris Evert first won Wimbledon singles?
24 Which first is held by the New Zealander E J 'Murt' O'Donoghue?
25 Which British Open winner's dad was a professional at Hawkstone Park, Shropshire?

## Answers

***Sports Bag***

**1** Sandwich. **2** Netherlands. **3** Alpine skiing. **4** 1972. **5** Dennis Taylor. **6** Papua New Guinea. **7** Goldfinger. **8** Crisp. **9** Three. **10** Holland. **11** Richmond. **12** 3. **13** 40s. **14** 8. **15** Yvon Petra. **16** Wolves. **17** Emmerdale. **18** Bahram. **19** Dunlop Masters. **20** £2,000. **21** Angling. **22** Canoeing. **23** Billie Jean King. **24** 147 snooker break. **25** Sandy Lyle.

# Quiz 98 20th C Film Legends

Level 3 

1 What was Katharine Hepburn and Spencer Tracy's first film together?
2 Which actress said, "I'm as pure as driven slush"?
3 In which film did James Cagney say "You dirty double crossing rat" which led to his catchphrase?
4 In which sport did John Kelly compete in the 1920 Olympics?
5 Who said, "All I need to make a comedy is a park, a policeman and a pretty girl"?
6 Which actor was Tony Hancock impersonating with his "Ha harr Jim lad" routine?
7 Who was "the man you love to hate"?
8 Which famous character was played by Butterfly McQueen in Gone With the Wind?
9 Why was Buddy Ebsen forced to quit his role as the Tin Man in The Wizard of Oz?
10 In what year did David Lean die?
11 In which country did Steve McQueen die?
12 Whose autobiography was called The Ragman's Son?
13 In which state did Robert Redford found the Sundance Institute?
14 How old was Shirley Temple when she received an honorary?
15 What would Rita Hayworth's surname have been if she had used her father's name instead of her mother's?
16 On which 30s screen legend was Catwoman in Batman based?
17 Which Marilyn Monroe co star said, "Kissing her is like kissing Hitler"?
18 About who or what did Elizabeth Taylor say, "It was like an illness one had a very difficult time recuperating from"?
19 Which musical star was a cousin of Rita Hayworth?
20 For which film did Elizabeth Taylor win her second Oscar?
21 Which character did Frank Sinatra play in From Here to Eternity?
22 How old was Mae West when she starred in the film Sextet?
23 Which lingerie company did Jane Russell work for in the 1970s?
24 Who has the nickname 'The Stick' as a child?
25 Who said, "I never forget a face, but in your case I'll make an exception"?

## Answers

***20th C Film Legends***

**1** Woman of the Year. **2** Tallulah Bankhead. **3** Blonde Crazy. **4** Rowing. **5** Charlie Chaplin. **6** Robert Newton - in Treasure Island. **7** Erich Von Stroheim. **8** Prissy. **9** He was allergic to the make up. **10** 1991. **11** Mexico. **12** Kirk Douglas. **13** Utah. **14** Six. **15** Cansino. **16** Jean Harlow. **17** Tony Curtis. **18** Making Cleopatra. **19** Ginger Rogers. **20** Who's Afraid of Virginia Woolf?. **21** Angelo Maggio. **22** 85. **23** Playtex. **24** Sophia Loren. **25** Groucho Marx.

# Quiz 99 20th C TV Trivia

Level 3 

1 Who was the first sportsman to appear on This Is Your Life?
2 What was the first feature film shown on BBC2?
3 In Tutti Frutti, who was bass player with The Majestics?
4 Which TV presenter once held the title Miss Parallel Bars?
5 Which newsreader was a judge for the Booker Prize in 1987?
6 Margo Turner's life was researched for This Is Your Life and then became the basis for which drama series?
7 Which Coronation Street star played Christine Keeler's mother in Scandal?
8 Which TV presenter produced a fitness video called Fit For Life?
9 In which real life store did Wendy Richard used to work?
10 What was Winston Churchill referring to when he said, "Why do we need this peep show?"?
11 In which event did Bill Nankeville, father of Bobby Davro, compete in the 1948 Olympics?
12 What was the first Dr Who series called in which The Daleks appeared?
13 In Minder what football team did Terry McCann support?
14 Which show of the 50s used the catchphrase 'Goody goody gumdrops'?
15 Where was Brian Hanrahan when he "counted them all out, and counted them all back"?
16 Which TV presenter wrote The Hired Man with Howard Goodall?
17 Which building designed by Norman Shaw in the 19th C appeared on TV screens throughout the 20th C?
18 What was Nigel Kennedy's codename for This Is Your Life?
19 What did Harry Enfield study at university?
20 Which music was used for the BBC's last World Cup coverage of the century?
21 Who was the only woman in the 1980s to win the BBC Sports Personality of the Year single handed?
22 Which newsreader advertised Cow & Gate baby food as a child?
23 What was the occupation of Noel Edmonds' father?
24 Who was the first soap star to receive an honour from the Queen?
25 Who presented Channel 4's religious series Canterbury Tales?

## Answers

***20th C TV Trivia***

**1** Stanley Matthews. **2** Kiss Me Kate. **3** Fud O'Donnell. **4** Carol Smillie. **5** Trevor McDonald. **6** Tenko. **7** Jean Alexander. **8** Gloria Hunniford. **9** Fortnum & Mason. **10** Commercial TV. **11** 1500 metres. **12** The Dead Planet. **13** Fulham. **14** Whirligig. **15** Port Stanley. **16** Melvyn Bragg. **17** New Scotland Yard. **18** Bow. **19** Politics. **20** Faure's Pavane. **21** Fatima Whitbread. **22** Martyn Lewis. **23** Headmaster. **24** Violet Carson. **25** Ian Hislop.

# Quiz 100 Entertainment

1 Which London theatre saw the premiere of Look Back in Anger?
2 Which show made critic Robert Helpmann say, "The trouble with nude dancing is that not everything stops when the music does"?
3 According to bishop Mervyn Stockwood who would "go to the Folies Bergere and look at the audience"?
4 Who wrote the music for the show Betjeman with words by the poet himself?
5 What is the name of the theatre in Scarborough linked with Alan Ayckbourn?
6 The slogan "The Big One" was originally used to advertise what?
7 Which brothers bought Shepperton studios in 1994?
8 Who founded the New York City ballet in 1928?
9 To which conductor did Vaughan Williams dedicate his 8th Symphony to?
10 Who was known as big hearted Arthur?
11 What food has sexual overtones in Bertolucci's Last Tango in Paris?
12 Which stage play was the last to be banned by the Lord Chamberlain in the UK?
13 What did critic John Mason Brown describe as "chewing gum for the eyes"?
14 In what year did Elstree studios open?
15 Where is the location of the Glastonbury Festival?
16 On whose life was the short lived musical Winnie based?
17 Which singer had the first names Harry Lillis?
18 Which studios did the Rank Organisation open in 1936?
19 How many Gilbert & Sullivan operas are there?
20 Which show made critic Clive Barnes say, "It gives pornography a bad name"?
21 Who wrote the book on which the musical Whistle Down the Wind was based?
22 The first great rock charity show was in aid of the people of which country?
23 What was the name of Hylda Baker's silent friend?
24 In what year did the first Edinburgh Festival take place?
25 Which London theatre is home to the ENO?

## Answers

***Entertainment***

**1** Royal Court. **2** Oh Calcutta. **3** A psychiatrist. **4** Mike Read. **5** Stephen Joseph Theatre. **6** Circus. **7** Scott. **8** Balanchine. **9** Barbirolli. **10** Arthur Askey. **11** Butter. **12** Early Morning. **13** TV. **14** 1926. **15** Pilton. **16** Winston Churchill. **17** Bing Crosby. **18** Pinewood. **19** 13. **20** Oh Calcutta. **21** Mary Hayley Bell. **22** Bangladesh. **23** Cynthia. **24** 1947. **25** Coliseum.

## HOW TO SET UP YOUR OWN

# PUB QUIZ

It isn't easy, get that right from the start. This isn't going to be easy. Think instead of words like; 'difficult', 'taxing', 'infuriating' consider yourself with damp palms and a dry throat and then, when you have concentrated on that, put it out of your mind and think of the recognition you will receive down the local, imagine all the regulars lifting you high upon their shoulders dancing and weaving their way around the pub. It won't help but it's good to dream every once in a while.

## What you will need:

- A good selection of biros (never be tempted to give your own pen up, not even to family members)
- A copy of The Best TV Pub Quiz Book Ever
- A set of answer sheets photocopied from the back of the book
- A good speaking voice and possibly a microphone and an amp
- A pub
- At least one pint inside you
- At least one more on your table
- A table

## What to do:

Choose your local to start with, there is no need to get halfway through your first quiz and decide you weren't cut out for all this and then find yourself in the roughest pub in Christendom 30 miles and a long run from home.

Chat it through with the landlord and agree on whether you will be charging or not, if you don't then there is little chance of a prize for the winners other than a free pint each and this is obviously at the landlord's discretion – if you pack his pub to bursting then five free pints won't worry him, but if it's only you and a two others then he may be less than unwilling, as publicans tend to be.

If you decide on a payment entry keep it reasonable, you don't want to take the fun out of the quiz; some people will be well aware that they have very little hope of winning and will be reluctant to celebrate the fact by mortgaging their house.

Once location and prize are all sorted then advertising the event is paramount, get people's attention, sell sell, sell or, alternatively, stick up a gaudy looking poster on the door of the bogs. Be sure to specify all the details, time, prize and so on – remember you are selling to people whose tiny attention span is being whittled down to nothing by alcohol.

After this it is time for the big night, if you are holding the event in the 'snug' which seats ten or so you can rely on your voice, if not you should get hold of a good microphone and an amplifier so that you can boom out your questions and enunciate the length and breadth of the pub (once again, clear this with the landlord and don't let liquid anywhere near the electrical equipment). Make sure to practice, and get comfortable with the sound of your own voice and relax as much as possible, try not to rely on alcohol too much or "round one" will be followed by "rown' too" which will eventually give way to "runfree". Relax with your voice so that you can handle any queries from the teams, and any venomous abuse from the 'lively' bar area.

When you enter the pub make sure you take everything listed above. Also, make sure you have a set of tie-break questions and that you instruct everybody who is taking part of the rules – and be firm. It will only upset people if you start handing out impromptu solutions and let's face it the wisdom of Solomon is not needed when you are talking pub quiz rules; 'no cheating' is a perfectly healthy stance to start with.

Finally, keep the teams to a maximum of five members, hand out your answer papers and pens and, when everybody is good and settled, start the quiz. It might not be easy and it might not propel you to international stardom or pay for a life of luxury but you will enjoy yourself. No, really.

## ANSWERS Part One

| | |
|---|---|
| 1 ____ | 16 ____ |
| 2 ____ | 17 ____ |
| 3 ____ | 18 ____ |
| 4 ____ | 19 ____ |
| 5 ____ | 20 ____ |
| 6 ____ | 21 ____ |
| 7 ____ | 22 ____ |
| 8 ____ | 23 ____ |
| 9 ____ | 24 ____ |
| 10 ____ | 25 ____ |
| 11 ____ | 26 ____ |
| 12 ____ | 27 ____ |
| 13 ____ | 28 ____ |
| 14 ____ | 29 ____ |
| 15 ____ | 30 ____ |

# ANSWERS Part Two

1 ____________________

2 ____________________

3 ____________________

4 ____________________

5 ____________________

6 ____________________

7 ____________________

8 ____________________

9 ____________________

10 ____________________

11 ____________________

12 ____________________

13 ____________________

14 ____________________

15 ____________________

16 ____________________

17 ____________________

18 ____________________

19 ____________________

20 ____________________

21 ____________________

22 ____________________

23 ____________________

24 ____________________

25 ____________________

26 ____________________

27 ____________________

28 ____________________

29 ____________________

30 ____________________

## ANSWERS Part Three

1 __________

2 __________

3 __________

4 __________

5 __________

6 __________

7 __________

8 __________

9 __________

10 __________

11 __________

12 __________

13 __________

14 __________

15 __________

16 __________

17 __________

18 __________

19 __________

20 __________

21 __________

22 __________

23 __________

24 __________

25 __________

26 __________

27 __________

28 __________

29 __________

30 __________